# Cheese
## FOR
# DUMMIES®

# Cheese FOR DUMMIES®

by *culture: the word on cheese*,
**Laurel Miller, Thalassa Skinner**

**Foreword by Chef Ming Tsai**
Chef/owner of Blue Ginger and host of *Simply Ming*

John Wiley & Sons Canada, Ltd.

**Cheese For Dummies®**

Published by
John Wiley & Sons Canada, Ltd.
6045 Freemont Blvd.
Mississauga, ON L5R 4J3
www.wiley.com

For general information on John Wiley & Sons Canada, Ltd., including all books published by Wiley Publishing, Inc., please call our distribution centre at 1-800-567-4797. For reseller information, including discounts and premium sales, please call our sales department at 416-646-7992. For press review copies, author interviews, or other publicity information, please contact our publicity department, Tel. 416-646-4582, Fax 416-236-4448.

For technical support, please visit www.wiley.com/techsupport.

Wiley publishes in a variety of print and electronic formats and by print-on-demand. Some material included with standard print versions of this book may not be included in e-books or in print-on-demand. If this book refers to media such as a CD or DVD that is not included in the version you purchased, you may download this material at http://booksupport.wiley.com. For more information about Wiley products, visit www.wiley.com.

Library and Archives Canada Cataloguing in Publication Data
    Cheese for dummies / Culture Magazine : The Word on Cheese, Laurel Miller, Thalassa Skinner.
Includes index.
    1. Cheese. 2. Cheesemaking. I. Miller, Laurel, 1969– II. Skinner, Thalassa III. Title: Culture magazine.

SF271.C44 2012      641.3'73      C2011-907378-1

ISBN 978-1-118-09939-1 (pbk); 978-1-118-14551-7 (ebk); 978-1-118-14552-4 (ebk); 978-1-118-14553-1 (ebk)

Printed in the United States

1 2 3 4 5 RRD 16 15 14 13 12

WILEY

# About the Authors

**Laurel Miller** is a Western U.S.-based food and travel writer, contributing editor at *culture: the word on cheese,* and culinary educator and owner of The Sustainable Kitchen. She grew up on a small California ranch raising dairy goats and a menagerie of other animals, which is what inspired her to teach people about sustainable agriculture and seasonal eating. When not writing or working part-time in a cheese shop, Laurel can be found indulging her street food obsession in the back alleys of the world. She is lactose intolerant.

**Thalassa (Lassa) Skinner** works as a cheesemonger in Napa, California, where she spends much of her time pairing local wines and beers with cheeses and infusing everyone she meets with the glories of cheese. She is a founder/owner of *culture: the word on cheese* and teaches classes at the San Francisco Cheese School and other venues throughout the Napa Valley and beyond. A dual citizen of both the United States and Australia, Lassa also has a home in South Australia's Barossa Valley and may be the only person on earth who has managed, promoted, and helped grow farmers' markets on two continents. Her dog Samantha (who is, in fact, an Aussie) has a distinctly cheese-centric palate and, though partial to camembert, has learned to accept that even she will have to wait until kidding season is complete before she can savor local goat milk cheeses again.

*culture: the word on cheese,* the first consumer magazine about cheese, and its website, www.culturecheesemag.com, was founded in 2008. Cheese embodies comfort yet oozes mystery. It conjures a better place and time, green swaths, happy cows, and ancient know-how. New cheesemakers appear each year. Shoppers seek wider selections of cheeses from specialty stores to supermarkets. The dizzying range of offerings comes from cow, goat, sheep, buffalo, or rarer animals' milks, aged and fresh. Yet while we love it, we barely know it. That's why *culture* magazine serves up the notable and obscure, with pairings and recipes, gorgeous photography, and introductions to dedicated farmers, makers, and mongers around the world. It's why *culture* is the word on cheese!

# Authors' Acknowledgments

The authors wish to thank the following people, without whom this book would not have been possible:

To Tracy Barr, *editor extraordinaire,* for turning this into something we can be proud of, as well as for your patience, good humor, and talking us off the ledge more than once. To everyone at ***culture*** magazine for supporting this project (even when dubious) and helping us see it through to the very end: Kate Arding, Stephanie Skinner, Elaine Khosrova, Eilis Maynard, and Will Fertman. A special shout-out to a group of women who went the extra mile: Michele Buster, Cecile Delannes, Ursula Heinzelmann, Sheri LaVigne, Tami Parr, and Daphne Zepos. Thank you for putting up with us and our hundreds of e-mails! And an extra special thanks to Kate Arding, who willingly shared her considerable expertise and feedback when we most needed her, and provided the photography.

At Wiley: Anam Ahmed, Erika Zupko, and Lindsay Humphreys. And Robert Hickey—without whom this book would never have happened.

And to everyone else who provided expert advice, translation, support, contacts, recipes, or book contributions: Martin and Sarah Aspinwall, Barbara Backus, Joshua Bernstein, Josepha Bertolini, Giana Ciancio, Kathleen Cotter, Olivier Charbonneau, Bryan Dayton, Laure Dobouloz, Gordon Edgar, Jody Farnham, Will Fertman, Janet Fletcher, Camilla Ferenczi, Natalie Fryar, Jennifer Giambroni, Bryce Gilmore, Lionel Giraud, Malcolm Griffiths, Laurie Gutteridge, Ryan Hardy, Caroline Hostettler, Konrad Huesser, Ricardo Huijon, Christine Hyatt, Steve Jenkins, Mary Karlin, Paul Kinstedt, Betty Kloster, Jen Kruch, Andy Lax, Leah Mayor, Eilis Maynard, Max McCalman, Rebekah McCaul, Neville McNaughton, Drew Neiman, Patricia Michelson, Hilary Miller, Dr. Robert M. Miller, Lora Lea Misterly, Jeanne Rodier, Mark Roeland, Rebecca Sherman-Orozco, Fons Smits, Adam Spannaus, Cathy Strange, Bobby and Danette Stuckey, Will Studd, Ellen Sutton, Suzanne Swan, Ming Tsai, Juliana Uruburu, Bart van Kessel, Nancy Vineyard, Laura Werlin, Sarah Zaborowski, and Red Herring Design.

Laurel Miller wishes to thank: My family, for believing in my writing (P.S. Mom, the book is finished!); ***culture*** magazine for bringing me aboard this project; Sheri LaVigne of The Calf & Kid, for her mentorship, knowledge, and time. Grant Martin for tolerating my low output during the completion of this book; Charles Thoeming for his always sage advice; Juliana Uruburu, who told me about culture from the very beginning; and Sean, for everything else.

Lassa Skinner wishes to thank: My cheesemongering best man, Ricardo Huijon; my ***culture***-d partners, who make everything happen; Michael Blum, for making that crucial decision that led to the book's contract; Tony Bogar, whose support and sage words helped at crucial times; my ever-eager and forward-driving family; John Skovgaard, for listening and providing calm amidst the storm; Ellen Sutton, who had beer, wine, and grilled lamb ready when most necessary; and my wise, wonderful cheese industry mates who always listen, lend hands, and are there when needed most.

## Publisher's Acknowledgments

We're proud of this book; please send us your comments at `http://dummies.custhelp.com`. For other comments, please contact our Customer Care Department within the U.S. at 877-762-2974, outside the U.S. at 317-572-3993, or fax 317-572-4002.

Some of the people who helped bring this book to market include the following:

**Acquisitions, Editorial, and Vertical Websites**

**Editors:** Robert Hickey, Anam Ahmed

**Project Editor:** Tracy L. Barr

**Production Editor:** Lindsay Humphreys

**Editorial Assistant:** Kathy Deady

**Technical Editors:** Kate Arding, Daphne Zepos

**Recipe Tester:** Emily Nolan

**Nutrition Analyst:** Patricia Santelli

**Cover photo:** © iStock/ rolfbodmer

**Cartoons:** Rich Tennant
(`www.the5thwave.com`)

**Composition Services**

**Project Coordinator:** Kristie Rees

**Layout and Graphics:**
Joyce Haughey, Sennett Vaughan Johnson, Corrie Niehaus, Lavonne Roberts

**Proofreaders:** Bryan Coyle, Susan Moritz, Lisa Stiers

**Indexer:** Rebecca R. Plunkett

**Photos:** Kate Arding,
*culture: the word on cheese*

---

**John Wiley & Sons Canada, Ltd.**

Deborah Barton, Vice President and Director of Operations

Jennifer Smith, Publisher, Professional & Trade Division

Alison Maclean, Managing Editor, Professional & Trade Division

**Publishing and Editorial for Consumer Dummies**

Kathleen Nebenhaus, Vice President and Executive Publisher

Kristin Ferguson-Wagstaffe, Product Development Director

Ensley Eikenburg, Associate Publisher, Travel

Kelly Regan, Editorial Director, Travel

**Publishing for Technology Dummies**

Andy Cummings, Vice President and Publisher

**Composition Services**

Debbie Stailey, Director of Composition Services

# Contents at a Glance

*Foreword* ........................................................ *xxi*

*Introduction* ..................................................... 1

## Part I: Getting to Know Cheese ..................... 7
Chapter 1: A Crash Course in Cheese ................................ 9
Chapter 2: Tracing Cheese from Farm to Table ...................... 17
Chapter 3: A Hard Look at Soft Cheeses ............................ 39
Chapter 4: Grate Tastes: Hard Cheeses ............................. 59

## Part II: Choosing and Serving Cheese ............ 73
Chapter 5: Using the Senses to Taste and Learn about Cheese ....... 75
Chapter 6: Purchasing Pointers .................................... 85
Chapter 7: Serving and Storing Cheese ............................. 95

## Part III: Cheese Around the World ................ 109
Chapter 8: The Americas ........................................... 111
Chapter 9: The British Isles and Ireland .......................... 135
Chapter 10: France ................................................ 147
Chapter 11: Italy ................................................. 165
Chapter 12: Spain, Portugal, and Other Mediterranean Countries .... 179
Chapter 13: The Rest of Europe .................................... 197
Chapter 14: Off-the-Map Cheesemaking .............................. 213

## Part IV: Eating, Drinking, and Cooking with Cheese ... 229
Chapter 15: Making Cheese the Life of the Party ................... 231
Chapter 16: Having a Drink with Your Cheese ....................... 245
Chapter 17: Cooking with Cheese, Pt. 1: Appetizers, Salads, and Sides ................. 263
Chapter 18: Cooking with Cheese, Pt. 2: Main Dishes and Desserts ....... 289
Chapter 19: Making Cheese at Home ................................. 317

## Part V: The Part of Tens ............................................. 331

Chapter 20: Ten of the World's Most Bizarre Cheeses ............................... 333
Chapter 21: Ten of America's Most Influential Artisanal Cheesemakers ............... 339
Chapter 22: Ten Cheese Festivals You Shouldn't Miss ............................... 345
Chapter 23: Ten Cheese Festivals You Shouldn't Miss ............................... 351

## Appendix: Metric Conversion Guide ......................... 357

## Index ......................................................... 361

# Recipes at a Glance

## Condiments

Buttermilk-Oat Crackers ...................................................................... 241

Caramelized Shallots in Port Wine ...................................................... 244

Cherry Preserves .................................................................................. 242

Chile-Citrus Olives ............................................................................... 240

## Beverages

Blueberry Cobbler ................................................................................ 262

The SweetWater ................................................................................... 261

The Widow's Kiss .................................................................................. 260

## Appetizers

Comté Wafers ...................................................................................... 267

Crispy Cheese Croquettes ................................................................... 268

Gougères ............................................................................................. 270

Queso Fundido con Pollo ..................................................................... 269

## Salads and Soup

Bistro Salad with Poached Egg and Parmigiano-Reggiano .................... 276

Fennel, Tangerine, and Hazelnut Salad with Crottin ............................. 278

Nectarine, Prosciutto, and Arugula Salad with Crescenza Toasts ......... 272

Salad Greens with Roasted Pears, Cornbread Croutons,
 and Camembert Dressing ................................................................... 274

Sopa de Quinoa ................................................................................... 280

## Side Dishes

Grilled Asparagus with Chèvre and Orange Zest .................................. 281

Haricot Verts and Miniature Tomatoes with Bocconcini ........................ 284

Israeli Couscous with Preserved Lemon, Sugar Snap Peas, Feta, and Mint .......... 282

Pan-Roasted Wild Mushrooms over Cheddar Polenta with Pumpkinseed Oil ....... 286

Wood-Roasted New Potatoes with Délice du Jura and Black Truffle Oil ............... 285

## Main Dishes

Blue Cheese and Potato Tartlets ............................................................................. 302

Broiled Gruyère Sandwiches with Maple-Caramelized Apples .............................. 298

Chicken Cacciatore with Ricotta Salata ................................................................. 293

Farmstead's Cheesemonger Mac 'n' Cheese .......................................................... 294

Grilled Peaches with Mascarpone, Pistachios, and Raspberries ........................... 307

Grilled Sausages with Grapes, Wilted Greens, and Pecorino Romano .................. 296

New Classic Cheese Souffle ................................................................................... 304

Peppered Pear and Goat Cheese Scones ............................................................... 299

Sheep Milk Ricotta Gnocchi with Fresh Peas, Spring Onions, and Bacon ............. 290

Stinky Cheese Omelet with Herb Topping .............................................................. 300

## Desserts

Aged Gouda and Walnut Biscotti ........................................................................... 308

Dried Apricot-Goat Cheese Tart ............................................................................ 312

Ginger-Poached Pears with Roquefort-Honey Ice Cream ...................................... 314

Rhubarb-Brown Sugar Cake with Strawberry-Rhubarb Compote
  and Crème Fraiche ............................................................................................. 310

## Cheese

Chèvre .................................................................................................................... 326

Crème Fraiche ........................................................................................................ 325

Mozzarella .............................................................................................................. 328

Ricotta .................................................................................................................... 324

# Table of Contents

*Foreword*..................................................................*xxi*

*Introduction* .................................................. 1
   About This Book ...................................................1
   Conventions Used in This Book...............................2
   What You're Not to Read..........................................2
   Foolish Assumptions................................................2
   How This Book Is Organized ..................................3
      Part I: Getting to Know Cheese .......................3
      Part II: Choosing and Serving Cheese...............4
      Part III: Cheese Around the World ...................4
      Part IV: Eating, Drinking, and Cooking with Cheese.......4
      Part V: The Part of Tens ...................................4
   Icons Used in This Book ..........................................5
   Where to Go from Here.............................................5

*Part 1: Getting to Know Cheese*............................ 7

## Chapter 1: A Crash Course in Cheese ...........................9
   Accidents Happen: How Cheese Came to Be ...............9
      From oops!. ...............................................10
      . . . To ahhh! ...........................................10
      Hankering for a hunk of cheese: The cheese industry today.........10
   Key Things to Know about Cheese.............................12
      It's alive! ..................................................12
      Styled out .................................................12
      It has its own language: Speaking cheese geek ..........13
      You can enjoy it in a variety of ways..................14
   Cheese! To Your Health ..........................................15
   Budget Travel: Exploring the World through Cheese.............16

## Chapter 2: Tracing Cheese from Farm to Table ..................17
   Got Milk — And What Kind? Understanding Cheese's Key Ingredient...17
      White gold: A quick look at milk's composition ...........18
      Examining the three main milks used in cheesemaking ...........19
   Making Cheese ......................................................23
      Smart starter: Heating the milk and adding the starter culture ....25
      Curd is the word: Letting the fluid milk coagulate .............26

Placing the curds in forms and draining the whey.........................27
Worth its salt: Applying or adding salt .............................................28
Ripe for the picking ...........................................................................29
Exploring Cheese Styles.................................................................................31
Getting cultured: Bacteria and mold ..............................................31
Rinding your business........................................................................32
Where in the World? ......................................................................................34
Digging into the importance of terroir ...........................................34
Demystifying designations................................................................35

**Chapter 3: A Hard Look at Soft Cheeses** . . . . . . . . . . . . . . . . . . . . . . **39**
Soften Up: Understanding the Soft Cheese Basics ....................................40
Getting Fresh...................................................................................................41
Whey to go! Fresh cheese from leftovers .......................................43
Pasta filata: Stringy, stretchy, fresh cheeses................................43
Surface-Ripened Soft Cheeses......................................................................44
Bloomy-rind soft cheeses: Fluffy, furry, velvety rinds .................45
Washed-rind soft cheeses: An odiferous array .............................47
Mold-ripened: Wrinkly soft cheeses ...............................................49
A Semi-Softie at Heart....................................................................................50
Pressed, brined, and dry-salted fresh semi-soft cheeses .............50
I'm (not) melting! Fresh semi-soft cheeses that stay in shape.......51
Semi-soft rindless cheeses full of buttery flavors.........................52
Down to earth: Mushroomy, grassy-tasting semi-softs.................53
Semi-soft washed rinds ......................................................................53
Feeling Blue .....................................................................................................55
Mellow blues........................................................................................55
Blues with attitude.............................................................................56
High octane blues ...............................................................................57

**Chapter 4: Grate Tastes: Hard Cheeses** . . . . . . . . . . . . . . . . . . . . . . . **59**
Hard to Beat: Understanding the Basics......................................................59
Going Topless: A Rundown of Rindless Hard Cheeses .............................61
It's better buttery and mild ..............................................................61
Going mild for rindless cheeses........................................................62
Looking at Natural-Rind Hard Cheeses.......................................................63
Buttery cheeses with natural rinds .................................................63
Earthy natural rind delights .............................................................64
Natural-rind nutty cheeses ...............................................................65
Bursting with flavor: Sharp natural-rind cheeses .........................65
Washed-rind and Wonderful Cheeses..........................................................66
Nice and nutty.....................................................................................67
Slightly stinky cheeses ......................................................................68
Trying Out Coated-rind and Clothbound Hard Cheeses ...........................68
Coated-rind cheeses with a nutty flavor.........................................69
Sharp to earthy coated-rind cheeses ..............................................70
Sweet, butterscotchy coated-rind cheeses .....................................71

## Part II: Choosing and Serving Cheese ............................ 73

### Chapter 5: Using the Senses to Taste and Learn about Cheese ..... 75
Discovering What You Like and Don't Like .................................................... 76
Evaluating the Characteristics of Cheese ...................................................... 77
    Using your common sense(s) ............................................................ 77
    Ten "technical" (if sometimes odd) terms used
      to describe cheese ........................................................................ 78
Finding the Cheese You Like, with or without
  a Cheesemonger's Help ............................................................................ 80
    Going local ........................................................................................ 80
    Browsing the cheese section at your grocery store ................... 81
Taking the Cheese Challenge ......................................................................... 81

### Chapter 6: Purchasing Pointers ................................. 85
Where to Buy: Exploring Your Options ......................................................... 85
    What's in store ................................................................................. 85
    Online offerings ................................................................................ 87
    To market, to market: Buying direct ........................................... 89
When to Buy: The Best Time to Buy Certain Cheeses ................................. 91
What to Buy: Making Your Dairy Dollars Count .......................................... 93
    Counter proposal: Having a dialogue with your cheesemonger .... 93
    Telling the difference between a cheese
      that's ripe and past its prime ..................................................... 94

### Chapter 7: Serving and Storing Cheese ........................ 95
Cheesy Accessories: All about Knives and Boards ...................................... 95
    Knifestyles of the rich and famous ............................................... 96
    Chairman of the board .................................................................... 97
Serving Basics ................................................................................................. 99
    Cutting to the chase ........................................................................ 99
    Serving it at the ideal temperature ............................................ 101
    Putting together a cheese plate ................................................... 101
    Arranging your items: General principles .................................. 102
On the Road or in the Cupboard: Storing and
  Traveling with Cheese ............................................................................ 105
    Putting your cheese to bed: Successful storage ....................... 105
    Tips for traveling with cheese ..................................................... 107

## Part III: Cheese Around the World ............................ 109

### Chapter 8: The Americas ...................................... 111
American Cheese, Please ............................................................................... 111
    The West Coast ............................................................................... 113
    The Pacific Northwest .................................................................... 115
    The Southwest and the Rockies ................................................... 119

The Midwest .................................................................. 120
The South ...................................................................... 122
The Northeast and New England ................................. 123
Oh, Canada! ........................................................................... 125
British Columbia .......................................................... 127
Alberta and Ontario ..................................................... 128
Quebec and the Maritimes ......................................... 129
Mexican Cheeses: Taste and Tradition ............................ 130
Getting Fresh in Central and South America .................. 132

## Chapter 9: The British Isles and Ireland ...................... 135

Oh, Britannia! Cheeses of the United Kingdom ............. 135
Key characteristics of British cheeses ...................... 136
The Southwest and West ............................................. 139
The Southeast and East ............................................... 140
The Midlands ................................................................ 141
The North of England and the Borders ..................... 142
Cheeses from Scotland and Wales ............................. 143
Cheeses from the Emerald Isle ......................................... 144

## Chapter 10: France ......................................................... 147

Fancying France .................................................................. 147
Becoming the King of Cheese ..................................... 148
Shopping for French cheeses in the States .............. 148
Cheeses from the North ...................................................... 150
Île-de-France and its fabulous cheeses ..................... 150
Normandy's cheeses .................................................... 153
Cheeses from Western France ........................................... 154
Loire Valley .................................................................. 155
Pays Basque .................................................................. 156
Cheeses from the South and Southeast ............................ 157
Midi-Pyrenees ............................................................... 158
Auvergne ........................................................................ 158
Rhône-Alpes and Haute-Savoie ................................. 159
The cheeses of Corsica ................................................ 160
Cheeses from Eastern France ............................................ 161
Burgundy ....................................................................... 161
Champagne ..................................................................... 162
Alsace-Lorraine ............................................................ 163
Franche-Comté .............................................................. 164

## Chapter 11: Italy ............................................................. 165

Cheeses from the North ...................................................... 166
Valle d'Aosta and Piedmont ....................................... 167
Lombardy ....................................................................... 168
Friuli-Venezia Giulia and Veneto .............................. 169

Cheeses from Central Italy .................................................. 172
    Emilia-Romagna.................................................. 172
    Tuscany.................................................................. 174
Cheeses from Southern Italy .............................................. 175
    Campania .............................................................. 175
    Puglia/Sardinia and Sicily ................................. 176

**Chapter 12: Spain, Portugal, and Other Mediterranean Countries ...................................................... 179**

Simply Spain............................................................................ 179
    Cheese regions in the north ............................... 181
    Cheeses of the Basque Country ........................ 184
    Cheese from central and southern Spain ....... 185
    Spain's island cheeses........................................ 187
Portugal................................................................................... 188
    A thorny situation: Thistle rennet ................... 190
    North and central Portuguese cheeses............ 190
    Cheeses from southern Portugal ...................... 191
The Magnificent Mediterranean ....................................... 192
    Turkish cheese, please....................................... 192
    Greece .................................................................... 194
    Hello, halloumi: A famous Cypriot cheese...... 195

**Chapter 13: The Rest of Europe ...................................... 197**

The Hills Are Alive: A Brief Primer on Alpine Cheeses ........... 197
Holey Cheese! Styles from Switzerland............................. 198
    Good eats from Berner Oberland and Emmental ...... 199
    Fondue cheeses from Fribourg-Vaud .............. 200
    Raclette from Valais............................................ 201
    Specialties of the Jura Mountains.................... 201
    Cheeses from the "bread basket": Nordost-Schweiz...... 202
Looking at Cheeses from Germany .................................... 203
    Cheeses from the North...................................... 203
    Cheeses from Bavaria and Allgäu .................... 205
Exploring Cheeses from the Netherlands.......................... 207
    Gouda ..................................................................... 207
    Boerenkaas ........................................................... 209
    Edam........................................................................ 209
    Graskaas................................................................. 210
Cheeses from the Nordic Countries ................................. 210

**Chapter 14: Off-the-Map Cheesemaking ...................... 213**

Antipodean Artisans: Australia and New Zealand................ 213
    Aussie ingenuity.................................................. 214
    New Zealand: A new era for Kiwi cheesemakers ...... 220

Subsistence and Barter: Cheese in Central Asia.................................223
More than a luxury item.................................................224
Cheese that transcends borders: Part 1 .............................225
Nomad's Land: The Middle East .......................................226
The lifestyle and terrain of the pastoralists .....................226
Cheese that transcends borders: Part 2 .............................228

## Part IV: Eating, Drinking, and Cooking with Cheese .... 229

### Chapter 15: Making Cheese the Life of the Party . . . . . . . . . . . . . 231

Creating Great Plates .........................................................231
How much is enough? Deciding on serving size......................231
Selecting cheeses for a plate ..........................................232
Arranging your plate .......................................................234
Picking Sides ....................................................................234
Savory..............................................................................235
Sweet ...............................................................................235
Composing the Components...............................................238
Keeping it simple and other tips.....................................238
Complimentary condiments you can make yourself..............239

### Chapter 16: Having a Drink with Your Cheese. . . . . . . . . . . . . . . . . 245

The Noble Grape................................................................245
A few rules and tips to get the best matches .....................246
A quick primer on wine and a few pairings to win you over........247
Bad relationships .............................................................250
A quick list of time-tested pairings .................................250
Hop to It: Pairings for Beer Nuts.......................................251
Sorting through styles of beer..........................................252
Finding a perfect pairing .................................................252
If the Spirit Moves You........................................................255
White spirits .....................................................................255
Brown spirits ....................................................................257
The Teetotaling Table...........................................................258
Mixing Things Up: DIY Cocktails..........................................259

### Chapter 17: Cooking with Cheese, Pt. 1: Appetizers, Salads, and Sides . . . . . . . . . . . . . . . . . . . . . . . . . . . . . . . . . . . . . . . . . . 263

Cheese in the Kitchen .......................................................264
Measure by measure: Cheese conversion chart......................264
Which cheese do I choose? .............................................265
How Appetizing! Cheesy Starters Your Guests Will Love.............266
Soup, Salad, and Side Days..................................................271

**Chapter 18: Cooking with Cheese, Pt. 2: Main Dishes and Desserts . . . 289**

The Main Event .......................................................................289

Cheese for Breakfast and Brunch.............................................297

The Sweet Hereafter.................................................................305

**Chapter 19: Making Cheese at Home............................. 317**

Sourcing Your Equipment and Supplies....................................318

    Equip yourself ...................................................................318

    Getting the (rest of the) goods for cheesemaking.................321

    Where to get your milk........................................................321

A Quick Review of the Basic Cheesemaking Steps.....................322

Four Cheeses to Make on Your Own.........................................323

**Part V: The Part of Tens ................................. 331**

**Chapter 20: Ten of the World's Most Bizarre Cheeses........... 333**

Casu Marzu.............................................................................333

Airaq......................................................................................334

Pule........................................................................................334

Chhurpi...................................................................................335

Moose Cheese .........................................................................335

Leipäjuusto..............................................................................336

Caravane ("Camelbert").........................................................336

Milbenkäse (Spinnenkäse).......................................................337

Stinking Bishop .......................................................................338

Cougar Gold............................................................................338

**Chapter 21: Ten of America's Most Influential Artisanal Cheesemakers . . . . . . . . . . . . . . . . . . . . . . . . . . . . . . . . 339**

Alison Hooper and Bob Reese, Vermont Butter & Cheese Creamery...339

Tom and Nancy Clark, Old Chatham Sheepherding Company ..............340

Mary Keehn, Cypress Grove Chevre .......................................340

Judy Schad, Capriole Farmstead Goat Cheeses.......................341

Cary Bryant and David Gremmels, Rogue Creamery ...............341

Cindy and Liam Callahan, Bellwether Farms ...........................342

Jennifer Bice, Redwood Hill Farm............................................343

Mike and Carol Gingrich, Uplands Cheese Company................343

Sue Conley and Peggy Smith, Cowgirl Creamery....................344

Mateo and Andy Kehler, Jasper Hill Farm ...............................344

**Chapter 22: Ten Cheese Festivals You Shouldn't Miss ........... 345**

The Festival of Cheese, American Cheese Society.....................345

California Artisan Cheese Festival.............................................346

Cheese School of San Francisco ..............................................346

Vermont Cheesemaker's Festival.............................................346

Oregon Cheese Festival ...................................................347
Great British Cheese Festival...........................................347
Bra Cheese Festival .........................................................347
Great Wisconsin Cheese Festival......................................348
The Great Canadian Cheese Festival.................................348
Seattle Cheese Festival ...................................................348
Amish Country Cheese Festival........................................349

**Chapter 23: Ten Cheese Festivals You Shouldn't Miss** . . . . . . . . . . **351**
Banon (Surface-ripened, Goat Milk).................................351
Barely Buzzed (Coated-Rind, Cow Milk)...........................351
Stracchino di Crescenza (Fresh, Cow Milk) ......................352
Epoisses (Washed-Rind, Cow Milk)..................................352
Clisson (Washed-Rind, Goat Milk)....................................353
Pleasant Ridge Reserve (Firm, Cow Milk).........................353
Pondhopper (Firm, Goat Milk).........................................354
Comté (Firm, Cow Milk)..................................................354
Rogue River Blue (Blue, Cow Milk)...................................355
Abbaye de Belloc (Semi-Firm, Sheep Milk) .......................355

*Appendix: Metric Conversion Guide*............................. *357*

*Index*......................................................................... *361*

# Foreword

*I* have always loved cheese, and my travels throughout Europe over the years have fed this passion of mine. During my last stint in France, where I spent 2 ½ years living and cooking in Paris, I developed a greater appreciation for the craft of cheesemaking and the role that cheese plays in French cuisine. Curiously enough, cheese is never served at the beginning of the meal. This is a purely American custom. Cheese is enjoyed at the end, before dessert, giving diners the opportunity to finish off their bottle of wine.

Cheese can also make it into your cooking repertoire. Personally, aged cheese is an ingredient I like to cook with because it is a great source of *umami,* the fifth taste of savoriness, which adds depth of flavor in a way similar to soy sauce. That's why you will find Parmigiano Reggiano and Gorgonzola on the East-West menu of my restaurant Blue Ginger in Wellesley, Mass. I am fortunate to have the Wasik family, one of the country's best cheesemongers, as neighbors. They have a stellar reputation for procuring the best cheeses and nurturing them in their cellar. I am proud to feature a Wasik's Cheese Plate in the Lounge at Blue Ginger and at monthly wine dinners.

Cheese may be a familiar food, but it is a vast subject. This book provides the essential information you need in an easy-to-digest format and incorporates delicious serving suggestions. The material is extremely current, with content you won't find in other resources. The folks at **culture** magazine bring years of experience and an educated palate to the table. They provide infallible guidance on how to assemble a cheese plate, and their wine pairing advice is spot on.

*Cheese For Dummies* is a title that should not be overlooked by foodies or self-professed cheese connoisseurs. This book will make you fall in love with cheese if you haven't already. Now that great cheese is easy to find in local cheese shops and even grocery stores, you don't have to travel the world to enjoy it.

Peace and Good Eating,

Ming Tsai
Chef/owner of Blue Ginger restaurant and host of Simply Ming

# Introduction

∙∙∙∙∙∙∙∙∙∙∙∙∙∙∙∙∙∙∙∙∙∙∙∙∙∙∙∙∙∙∙∙∙∙∙∙∙∙∙∙∙∙∙∙∙∙∙∙∙∙∙∙∙∙∙∙∙∙∙∙∙∙∙∙∙∙

*W*e may be cheese geeks, but we understand that, like wine, learning about cheese can be confusing, overwhelming, and (in the wrong hands) pretentious. Our goal is to demystify cheese — which is, after all, mostly milk — and help you feel comfortable with buying, tasting, and serving it. The best advice we can give you is, there are no "wrongs" when it comes to cheese, so have fun with it.

## About This Book

Our goal throughout this book is to turn you on to cheese so that you can appreciate and enjoy it in all of its fresh, creamy, buttery, squeaky, hard, aged, crumbly, nutty, stinky glory. We also provide you with some inspired seasonal recipes featuring cheese and tempt you with descriptions of interesting styles and varieties (donkey milk or cheese mites, anyone?).

Each chapter is divided into sections, and each section contains information about a particular cheese-related topic, such as

✔ How cheese is made and aged, and an overview of cheesemaking terms

✔ The different styles of cheese and rind types and how to identify what you like

✔ How to buy, serve, and store cheese economically and safely

✔ How to pair cheese with different alcoholic and non-alcoholic beverages, make cheese-friendly cocktails, and create a cheese plate to remember

✔ How to cook with cheese (we include simple, elegant, seasonal recipes for inspiration), how to make your own cheese plate condiments, and how to make ricotta, mozzarella, and other fresh cheeses

Whatever aspects of cheese interest you, this book is designed for dog-earring and flipping, so have at it!

# Conventions Used in This Book

To help you navigate through this book, we've set up a few conventions:

- ✔ Unless otherwise noted, cheeses that are named for the regions in which they originated (like Brie, which originated in the Brie region in France) are capitalized; others, like chèvre, the French word for "goat," are lowercased.

- ✔ *Italic* is used for emphasis and to highlight new words or terms that are defined.

- ✔ **Boldfaced** text is used to indicate the action part of numbered steps.

- ✔ `Monofont` is used for Web addresses.

In addition, the recipes in this book include preparation, cooking and processing times, and the yield you can expect from your efforts. All temperatures are Fahrenheit.

# What You're Not to Read

To help you navigate through the content in this book, we make it easy to identify what material you can safely skip. Sidebars and text preceded by the "Technical Stuff" or "Ask the Expert" icons aren't required reading for you to gain a solid working knowledge of cheese, but they're interesting tidbits that we think you'll enjoy. We've also ensured that they're educational, so if you like trivia — especially of the cheesy kind — we recommend giving them a look.

# Foolish Assumptions

In writing this book, we made some assumptions about you:

- ✔ You like, but don't know anything about, cheese.

- ✔ You know the basics about cheese but want more technical information and trivia.

- ✔ You know a fair amount about cheese but want to delve more deeply into the technical, cultural, and historic aspects; learn more about pairing and tasting; or discover the professional facets of the cheese industry such as affinage, cheesemongering, or cheesemaking.

> ✔ You're knowledgable about wine, beer, or spirits, and want to know how to pair cheese accordingly (FYI: *Wine For Dummies*, *Beer For Dummies*, and *Whiskey and Spirits For Dummies*, all published by John Wiley & Sons, are excellent reference guides for pairing novices).
>
> ✔ You're into food and want to know how to put together a cheese plate, or you're looking for delicious, cheese-centric, and home cheesemaking recipes.

# How This Book Is Organized

One of our main goals while writing this book was to make the information easy to read, understand, and find. To that end, we organized this very broad subject into several sections, each containing chapters devoted to a particular cheese-related topic. Following is a quick run-down of the parts and the kinds of info you'll find in each.

## Part 1: Getting to Know Cheese

This part is designed to give you fundamental knowledge about cheese. Here, we explore the history of cheese, its nutritional benefits, the basics of cheesemaking, the different styles of cheese and types of rinds, and how and why cheese is aged. We also take a look at *terroir* (the geography and climate of a place of origin) and discuss *designation* (the country- or European Union-specific terms for certain regional foods, beer, and wine), how those terms apply to cheeses of note, and why it's important to designate these products.

You may be wondering why the information in these chapters is significant. Can't you like a cheese without knowing any of this stuff? Sure. But by learning these things, you can begin to understand *what* you like about a cheese and increase your appreciation of it as a handmade product. This knowledge can also help you choose other cheeses, opening up a whole world that you may not have known existed. You'll also gain an understanding of why artisan cheese is such an important cultural and subsistence food throughout much of the world, and why supporting domestic cheesemakers and small-scale agriculture is so crucial.

## Part II: Choosing and Serving Cheese

This part shows you how to put the cheesemaking terminology and other information from Part I to good (tasting) use. In these three chapters, we explain how to use all of your senses to assess and flavor-profile cheeses so that you can discover what you like and don't like. Once you know that, the rest is easy: We show you how to purchase cheese (including tips on how to talk to a cheesemonger like a pro), serve, and store cheese.

## Part III: Cheese around the World

Pay a visit to this part for an armchair tour of cheese history, cheese culture, and types of cheeses from around the world. Here, you can find out how geography and climate play a major role in the style, production, and flavor of a cheese. Whether it inspires you to look for new varieties at your local shop or grocery store or to buy a plane ticket, you'll learn that cheese has no language barrier.

## Part IV: Eating, Drinking, and Cooking with Cheese

If you love cheese straight-up, chances are you enjoy cooking with it or pairing it with wine, beer, spirits, or non-alcoholic drinks, as well. In this part, we expand your cheese repertoire by explaining the basics of cooking with cheese; providing you with a variety of easy, seasonal recipes; and explaining the fundamentals of beverage pairing.

We also show you how to create an impressive cheese plate (and what to serve alongside) and provide you with essential information and recipes for home cheesemaking.

## Part V: The Part of Tens

Whether you're looking for unusual trivia (how about maggot cheese or milking a moose?), the most influential cheesemakers in the United States, or what cheese festivals are worth checking out, this part is where to find it.

# Icons Used in This Book

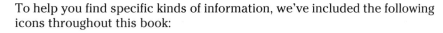

To help you find specific kinds of information, we've included the following icons throughout this book:

This icon highlights any wisdom we have to offer about how to buy, serve, or store cheese, or suggested reading for the topic at hand.

When you see this icon, you know that we're telling you essential cheese information. This is the stuff that you need to know.

This icon appears beside answers to common questions or insider info gleaned from cheese industry folks in all capacities.

We use this icon to point out technical information that we find fascinating, but that you don't really need to know (our feelings won't be *too* hurt if you skip it). Just think of these bits as fun trivia or ways to impress and educate your friends over a plate of (what else?) cheese.

This icon indicates how to best serve or pair a cheese with other foods or beverages, or what applications (cooking, melting, snacking, and so on) the cheese is best used for.

# Where to Go from Here

Think of this book as a reference manual. It's structured so that each chapter or section stands on its own. If you just want to know how to make a stand-out cheese plate or beverage pairing for your next party, head to Chapter 16. Chapters 3 and 4 break down the different styles of soft and hard cheeses and provide you with serving suggestions for each. If you want to know how cheese is made — from the animal to the plate — Chapter 2 takes you there. Bottom line: Where you go from here depends entirely on where your interest, or palate, takes you.

# Part I
# Getting to Know Cheese

The 5th Wave    By Rich Tennant

"This is where we make our goat cheese. We add a starter culture, plenty of salt, and lastly, the goat."

## In this part . . .

Although this book is intended for cheese neophytes, it's got plenty of material for those of you in possession of more than just basic information. It doesn't matter whether you can't tell a camembert from a cheddar, or whether you're a dedicated caseophile: The chapters in this part provide you with what you need to know to increase your cheese IQ.

Here, you discover the history of cheese, the various types of milk and how they affect the outcome of the final product; the basic steps of cheesemaking; the different styles of cheese and types of rinds; how and why cheese is aged; and the meaning of terroir and designations.

With this information in hand, you're ready to launch into the rest of the book. But feel free to refer back to this part as your appetite and vocabulary for cheese grows.

# Chapter 1

# A Crash Course in Cheese

*In This Chapter*

▶ Discovering the origins of cheese

▶ Getting a background on cheese basics

▶ Learning the health benefits of daily dairy consumption

▶ Recognizing cheese as a global food

*1*t's hard to believe that something as complex, delicious, and diverse as cheese is made from just a few key ingredients. Thousands of different varieties of cheese are produced around the world from the milk of cows, goats, sheep, water buffalo, yaks, camels — even reindeer and horses. Depending upon the country, this ancient food can hold significant cultural, nutritive, and economic value.

In this chapter, we give you a brief overview of cheese: its history, why it's good for you, where it comes from, and a few other basic nuggets. Consider the info here just enough to whet your appetite; you can find more detailed information on each of these topics and a slew of others in the upcoming chapters.

# Accidents Happen: How Cheese Came to Be

We'd love to be the ones to provide a definitive answer to the much-debated question of how cheese was discovered. But the truth is, historians and archaeologists don't have any conclusive evidence on who first made cheese, or where. The origin of cheese is believed to have occurred during the Neolithic period (beginning some 12,000 years ago), although some experts suggest it predates recorded history. Things are equally murky as to where said cheese was produced: Europe, Central Asia, North Africa, or the Middle East.

## From oops!. . .

The most commonly held theory on the origin of cheese suggests that an Arab nomad unwittingly created the first batch of cheese after discovering the milk he'd stored in an animal-stomach bag (most likely that of a sheep) had curdled.

The idea certainly makes sense. After all, cured animal skins and organs were frequently used as vessels or containers for food and water, and the stomach lining of young *ruminants* (cud-chewing mammals) such as sheep, goats, and cows naturally contain *rennet*, the enzyme used to make cheese.

Thus, milk stored in an animal stomach, jostled around during a long day or days of traveling, and subject to a hot climate could very well result in the formation of cheese. But let's face it: Folks have been letting milk ferment for thousands of years, so it's very possible that cheese was "discovered" multiple times throughout history, in different parts of the world.

## . . . To ahhh!

While there's little doubt that cheese was first made or (more likely) discovered when milk, carried in a bag made from an animal stomach, curdled into cheese, intentional cheesemaking is believed to have originated with the domestication of sheep and goats, between 8,000 and 3,000 BCE. Some research shows the ancient Sumerians were the first to intentionally and systematically make cheese. Egyptian and Mesopotamian hieroglyphics also include cheese (we'd hate to depart for the Underworld without it, too).

However it came to be, cheesemaking today runs the gamut from humble subsistence food to culinary art form (with all due respect to Da Vinci!).

Crafting a high-quality cheese requires more than just good milk. Also needed is an understanding of microbiology, chemistry, and *affinage* (aging), as well as a well-trained palate. Even with these skills, a controlled environment is still an essential part of the cheesemaking process: you need to be able to create a consistent product (which may or may not have seasonal variations depending upon what the animals are eating; see Chapter 2) that is largely based upon stable and hygienic conditions.

## Hankering for a hunk of cheese: The cheese industry today

Until the early 1980s, cooking for a living wasn't necessarily deemed a particularly impressive occupation in the United States. In the early and mid-part of the 20th century, line cooks were traditionally former convicts, societal misfits, the uneducated, or down-on-their-luck loners. Hard to believe, right?

Today, culinary schools are filled to capacity, and kitchen work — one of the more stressful, unglamorous jobs imaginable — has a high-profile status attached to it. Since the era of the celebrity chef began, other food-and-drink-related occupations have joined the ranks of coolness: winemakers, farmers, craft brewers, coffee roasters, distillers, mixologists, *charcuterers* (makers of cured meat products), butchers, and cheesemakers. Skillfully growing or crafting a beautiful, delicious product from the most humble of ingredients is now recognized and celebrated as a viable career — something we find really exciting.

Cheesemongers are also having their moment. Walk into a cheese shop in Brooklyn, Seattle, San Francisco, or Chicago, and you'll see that slinging dairy products is currently the hipster career of choice. We're poking fun, but it's really true that the cheese industry has, in the last five years, attracted the kind of alternative, Gen X/Y following currently saturating the restaurant, small farm, and artisan food industries.

What does this mean for the future of cheese, besides greater demand for mongers? Well, it means cheese has finally achieved a level of recognition and appreciation heretofore unseen in the United States. There's even a Certification Exam for Cheese Professionals established to set standards of accreditation within the country (to find out more about this, go to www. cheesesociety.org/events-education/certification-2).

In addition, consumers are growing increasingly savvy about artisan cheeses, and it doesn't appear their appetite will be sated anytime soon. Cheese shops are springing up across the nation, and with them, greater demand for cheese-related occupations such as buying, distributing, and cheesemaking. You'd be surprised how many mid-life career changers out there have ditched an urban, corporate existence for a herd of goats and a cheesemaking vat. While not all of these folks are successful, their intentions prove that there's just something about cheese that nourishes both the body and soul.

Americans aren't just curious about cheese; they're crazy for it. The total cheese consumption per capita in the U.S. increased from 23.81 pounds in 1989 to 32.9 pounds in 2009 — and it's still rising.

Those hipsters behind the cheese counter? Don't dismiss them as a pop culture cliché. Here's why:

> ✔ If they're working at a serious cheese shop or counter, odds are they're highly trained and very knowledgeable about not just cheese, but food in general. They can likely tell you the best cheeses to use for specific recipes and what techniques work best, or how to pair that $40 per pound, 5-year aged domestic Gouda with a wine, craft beer, or whisky that will do it justice.

✔ Unlike the wine industry, which until fairly recently had a reputation for pretense, the incoming generation of cheesemakers and cheesemongers are more interested in making good cheese accessible to everyone — not just those who can afford it. These younger industry employees are likely on a tight budget, and they're just as happy to steer you toward a great, affordable snacking cheese or give you some wallet-friendly advice for your next dinner party. Likewise, cheese shops and counters that cut-to-order offer consumers a chance to taste a range of different varieties without spending a lot of money.

In Part II, we tell you everything you need to know about purchasing cheese, from where and how to buy it to what to tell the cheesemonger to ensure that you get something that suits your taste.

# Key Things to Know about Cheese

The cheesemaking process has changed little over the centuries, despite increased knowledge about microbiology and chemistry. Cheesemakers are, in essence, like chefs, with a multitude of recipes at their fingertips. Their most important decisions, however, are what type of milk to use (cow, sheep, and goat milk are the most common) and how to ensure that milk is of the highest quality. In this section, we highlight some important general points about cheese. Head to Chapter 2 to find out about cheesemaking, from milk to mold (which, in this industry, is usually a good thing).

## It's alive!

Cheese is a living product, because of the cultures, mold, and bacteria it contains. This is why it continues to ripen as it ages (and why storing it properly is important). A sheep's stomach may have worked well for storage back in the day (refer to the earlier section "From oops!..."), but for your health (as well as the best-tasting product), keep your cheese refrigerated and wrapped up. Chapter 7 has more information on storing cheese.

## Styled out

Every style of cheese — fresh, semi-soft, washed rind, blue, semi-firm, or hard — has its special characteristics and properties, which are developed by making specific adjustments during the cheesemaking process. In Chapters 2, 3, and 4, we discuss what makes one cheese different from another.

The *rind* of a cheese is its skin. It's an important part of the cheese that's the result of bacteria and molds used during the cheesemaking process; these same microorganisms also work to create a specific style of cheese as dictated by the cheesemaker. The rind also protects the cheese so that it can age. With certain styles, such as surface-ripened cheeses, the rind is the actual mold that ripens and flavors the entire wheel, making it crucial to the end product.

The Internet is home to some great cheese resources. Check out the following:

- ✔ *culture: the word on cheese:* Yes, that's us, but we're not shy! The *culture* online library profiles an extensive compendium of cheese varieties, compiled by our team of experts (www.culturecheesemag.com).
- ✔ **American Cheese Society:** The American Cheese Society (ACS) is a professional industry organization that's also open to consumers (www.cheesesociety.org).

## *It has its own language: Speaking cheese geek*

Cheese is a complex subject, without a doubt. But the really difficult, technical stuff comes with its production. We provide you with the basics of cheese-making in Chapter 2 so that you're able to develop a working knowledge of how it's made and the vocabulary that goes along with it. After all, you never know when you'll need to say, "I think this surface-ripened could have used a bit more *Geotrichum*." We kid.

What's more important for you, as a cheese lover, to know is the terminology associated with the different styles of cheese and types of rinds. We break all of that information down for you in Chapters 2, 3, and 4. Even if you don't commit these things to memory, as long as you know what qualities you like in a cheese — buttery, sharp, stinky — your cheesemonger can help you select something that you'll enjoy.

What if you don't *have* a cheesemonger? We understand that's most often the case. After reading Chapter 5, in which we explain how to use your senses to evaluate cheeses, you'll not only know what flavors and textures you like, but what types of milk and styles you prefer (to help you along, we also offer you suggestions on what to try the next time you're shopping for cheese). Even without a cheesemonger present, as long as you know you want a stinky cheese or a strong blue, you'll know what styles or key words to look for.

The point is, *don't be intimidated by cheese.* As cheesemongers, we get a lot of customers who feel uncomfortable selecting a cheese for various reasons, and there's no reason for you to feel that way.

If you don't know how to pronounce the name of a foreign cheese, don't sweat it. Most cheesemongers aren't fluent in French/Italian/Spanish/German either, and we've all had to learn the correct way to say the names of certain cheeses. If you don't want to make a stab at it, all you have to do is point to the cheese in question and ask something along the lines of, "Could I please try some of the French cow milk cheese in the lower right corner? How do I pronounce that, anyway?" Your cheesemonger will be more than happy to comply. We do provide pronunciation tips on some of the more esoteric cheeses in this book, but there are cheese books written with language skills in mind. One we recommend is *The Cheese Lover's Companion* (HarperCollins), by Ron and the late Sharon Tyler Herbst.

## *You can enjoy it in a variety of ways*

As we note earlier, one of the many truly great things about cheese is its diversity: in style, type of milk, flavor, recipe, and production method. Another great thing about cheese is its accessibility. You don't need to spend a lot of money, own a passport, or be a certain age to enjoy a great cheese, nor do you require any prior knowledge or cooking ability whatsoever.

Anyone can slice off a hunk or put together an impressive cheese plate. (Don't believe us? Turn to Chapters 7 and 15.) Cheese is an equal opportunity food, as well as an ingredient that can enliven everything from bread or salad to soups and dessert, as we show you in Chapters 17 and 18. You can also make fresh cheese yourself, even if the closest you've ever been to a cow is the milk in your latte (look at Chapter 19 for instructions and encouragement).

---

## Ten reasons to eat some cheese, right now

As if you *need* a reason (especially after reading about the nutritional benefits that follow)! But we understand that cheese can be both a financially and calorically detrimental habit. So in case you need that extra nudge, here are some of our favorite reasons to buy a hunka:

✔ Your cholesterol test results were fine.

✔ It's finally tomato season.

✔ It's Monday.

✔ It's Wednesday.

✔ A friend has a bottle of 1982 Dom Perignon and doesn't want to drink alone.

✔ The dentist said, "No cavities."

✔ You met your deadline.

✔ Housewarming gift — to yourself.

✔ It's spring (kidding season!), and your favorite cheese shop just received the first local chèvre of the year.

✔ You need to increase your calcium intake — doctor's orders!

# Cheese! To Your Health

Cheese gets a bad rap for its high saturated fat content, and as a result, calorie counters often shun it — or substitute its plasticky, bland, low- or non-fat equivalent. Guess what? The health benefits of cheese and other dairy products far outweigh the drawbacks, and studies show that a moderate amount of dairy in your diet helps contribute to the prevention of tooth decay, as well as lowers cholesterol and promotes weight loss. Here are the details:

✔ **It inhibits tooth decay.** Studies from the beginning of the 1990s show that the casein and whey proteins in cheese actually inhibit tooth decay, as well as strengthen teeth and help to restore enamel. Cheese also increases the flow of saliva, which washes away acids and sugars that contribute to tooth decay. Don't ditch your toothpaste, but eating a small portion of semi-firm cheese after a meal is beneficial to your teeth and gums.

✔ **It's loaded with good stuff.** Cheese is an excellent source of calcium, phosphorous, vitamin A, and protein. High protein foods take more energy to metabolize, which assists with weight loss.

In general, goat milk contains more vitamins A and D than that of cow or sheep, but cow milk is higher in folic acid and zinc. Sheep milk has significantly more vitamins B2 and B12 and more conjugated linoleic acid (CLA) than goat or cow milk. In other words…eat 'em all!

✔ **It helps prevent certain diseases.** Many cheeses are high in *conjugated linoleic acid* (CLA), which lowers cholesterol and helps prevent hypertension and diabetes. CLA and Omega-3 fatty acids are higher in cheese made from animals that have grazed exclusively on fresh grass. CLA levels are also more significant in certain types of cheese such as fresh, surface-ripened, and alpine styles. The nutritional value also varies depending upon the type of cheese and animal species it comes from.

✔ **What about its salt content?** Salt is a necessary ingredient in cheese production, as we explain in Chapter 2, so if you're really trying to cut sodium out of your diet, you might want to skip the cheese (remember, too, that salt adds flavor, so a cheese devoid of any would be pretty bland).

Parmigiano Reggiano is a lower sodium variety that's very versatile and full-flavored, so it's a win-win. It's also lower in fat because it's made with partially skimmed milk.

A food writer and registered dietician friend of Laurel's once said, over a plate of Parmigiano Reggiano, "Everything in moderation. Including moderation." We agree. Immoderately.

# Budget Travel: Exploring the World through Cheese

Cheese is one of the most universal foods. It's made and/or eaten on every continent except Antarctica, and most cultures eat dairy products in some form. We take you on a tour of the cheesemaking areas of the world in Part III.

Because cheese is so ubiquitous throughout the world, it makes for both an excellent armchair travel companion, as well as a fun way to explore other cultures when you're on the road. With the proliferation of more specialized cheese distributors, esoteric imports (such as Paski sir, a delicious, hard sheep milk cheese from Croatia, or sheep milk feta from Australia) are available here in the United States, as are excellent pasteurized versions of "benchmark" cheeses such as Brie or camembert. Also available are incredible domestic cheeses coming from dairies with just 50 goats or 5 cows, and fine, clothbound cheddars produced in volume.

Flip through Part III to take a brief tour of the global cheese scene. You'll be inspired to try cheeses from all over the world or, if you're already a traveler, to discover cheese-centric destinations that may inspire your next jaunt (***culture: the word on cheese** highlights cheese-centric destinations in every issue*).

At the risk of sounding redundant, cheese is one of the few foods that's able, through a bit of organic and human-assisted alchemy, to truly provide a sense of place (much like wine). As you discover more about how cheese is made and as you try more cheeses, you'll discover seasonal variations and subtle flavors that hint at the cheese's origin (think of cows grazing on wild onion; goats browsing wild herbs; pasture grass growing from soil rich in minerals; wheels of cheese aging for months or even years in a natural limestone cave).

Or if that's more geeked out than you care to get, just grab a glass of wine, a cold beer, or a dram of Scotch (see Chapter 16), and enjoy it with a nice wedge of cheese and some fresh bread — using our pairing tips. The cheese — and the choice — is up to you.

# Chapter 2

# Tracing Cheese from Farm to Table

**In This Chapter**

▶ Exploring the different types of milk and how cheese is made

▶ Examining what determines a cheese's style

*I*t's hard to believe that something as complex, delicious, and downright diverse as cheese is made of just a few key ingredients. Hundreds of types of cheeses are made around the world — from the milk of cows, goats, sheep, water buffalo, yak, camels, reindeer, donkeys, and horses. Depending on the country, this ancient food can hold significant nutritive and cultural value.

In this chapter, we explore the basics of cheesemaking, starting with its key component, milk, and then move on to what makes one cheese's *style* (the various categories of cheese, depending upon age, moisture content, texture, and rind) different from another.

## Got Milk — and What Kind? Understanding Cheese's Key Ingredient

The cheesemaking process has changed little over the centuries, despite increased knowledge about microbiology and chemistry. Cheesemakers are, in essence, like chefs, with a multitude of recipes or cheesemaking processes at their fingertips. However, cheesemakers' most important decision is what type of milk to use, and then they have to ensure that that milk is of the highest quality.

Milk is such a commonplace food, most folks don't give it much thought, unless they're concerned about its fat content. Yet it's an incredibly complex liquid, with seasonal and chemical variations, depending on the species it comes from. Milk is the key ingredient in cheese, and both the type of milk (cow, sheep, goat, and so on) and its composition (amount of water, milk fat, lactose, minerals, and so on) play essential roles in the kind of cheese produced and its quality.

## White gold: A quick look at milk's composition

Milk is composed of water and solids. Here, we break those down into the components most critical in cheesemaking:

- ✔ **Water:** All milk is composed of at least 82 percent water; cow milk is over 87 percent water.

- ✔ **Butterfat:** Also known as *milk fat*, butterfat is the natural fatty constituent of milk and the chief component of butter. (*Clarified* butter is milk fat without water or liquid.)

- ✔ **Protein:** Casein (pronounced "cay-seen") is the main protein in milk and is, together with butterfat, what becomes the solids (*curds*) when milk is coagulated to make cheese.

- ✔ **Lactose:** The main sugar in milk.

- ✔ **Minerals:** Calcium and phosphorous are the main mineral components of milk.

Different animal breeds have different chemical compositions to their milk. The best example is a Jersey cow versus a Holstein cow. The Jersey, which is significantly smaller than a Holstein, produces milk with higher butterfat, which is a great trait for making creamy, oozy cheeses, but not for longer-aged, drier cheeses. Generally, Holsteins produce more milk, but it's lower in butterfat. Table 2-1 lists the average percentages of fat, protein, and lactose in the milk of different animals.

| Table 2-1 | Milk Averages by Butterfat | | |
|-----------|------|---------|---------|
| *Animal* | *Fat* | *Protein* | *Lactose* |
| **Cow** | 3.7% | 3.4% | 4.8% |
| **Goat** | 3.6% | 3.5% | 4.5% |
| **Sheep** | 7.4% | 4.5% | 4.8% |
| **Buffalo** | 7.7% | 4.5% | 5% |

*Information courtesy of American Farmstead Cheese, by Paul Kinstedt, c. 2005. Data taken from Fox et al, 2000 and from Guo et al, 2001.*

Keep in mind that fat content depends upon breed, climate, season, and so on. Jerseys, for example, have the highest butterfat content of the major dairy cattle breeds: up to 5.3 percent. That's a big difference from Holstein milk, which averages 3.6 percent!

In addition, different breeds have been raised in specific geographic areas for centuries, and these animals have as much to do with the kind of cheese made from their milk as does their location and environment. Specific cheeses, like Parmigiano Reggiano (see Chapter 4 for information on this famous cheese), have strict laws that dictate the specific type of animal milk used, the region it must be produced in, and how the cheese is made. In this way, the relationship between milk and pasture is very much like wine grape varietals and regions.

## Examining the three main milks used in cheesemaking

The three main milks used in cheesemaking are cow, goat, and sheep. Each has its own characteristics in terms of flavor, color, and texture, as well as differing butterfat contents and chemical compositions, depending upon the species and breed.

Over thousands of years, dairy animals have been domesticated and genetically selected to produce more milk. In addition, their natural lactation cycles (the period of time during which they produce milk to feed their young) have been extended to maximize milk (and thus cheese) yield and profit. The lactation periods we list in the next sections for the three main dairy species (cow, goat, and sheep) are generalities; many variables, including species, breed, climate, season, pasture, vegetation, supplementary feed or lack thereof, the herd management practices of the farmer, and so on, also impact both the quality of the milk and the length of lactation periods.

### Having a cow

After giving birth, cows can *lactate* (produce milk, also known as *freshening)* from their mammary glands (in cows and other dairy animals, it's called an udder) for as long as two years.

Cow milk ranges from deep to light, creamy yellow, depending on what the animal is eating and its breed. Its composition works well for most cheese styles. Cow milk is comparable to goat milk in terms of fat and protein content, but its composition is different, which affects how cheese is made. In general, cow milk has a medium weight in the mouth, as compared to goat milk, which is the lightest, and sheep milk, which has a slightly heftier feel.

## Saving Bessie: Heritage breeds

The advent of modern agriculture has led to the development of a few select breeds of livestock and poultry, designed for maximum output to meet global demand for commodity products such as milk.

Sounds great, right? Before you answer, consider this: These animals have likely lost many crucial genetic traits that helped the original, often ancient ("heritage") breeds they're descended from. The loss of these traits can have dire consequences in the event of a widespread epidemic: Think of foot-and-mouth disease or Mad Cow disease (bovine spongiform encephalopathy). These "factory-farmed" animals are likely to have little to no disease resistance. Making matters worse, the diseases that affect livestock populations may develop antibiotic resistance as a result of the prophylactic drugs being routinely included in the animal feed as growth stimulants.

Heritage livestock and poultry breeds are again gaining in popularity because family farmers are realizing the importance of preserving genetic diversity, as well as preventing the extinction of the historic breeds still in existence.

Many heritage animals retain traits such as disease resistance, tolerance to climatic extremes, mothering traits (sometimes lacking in modern breeds, who are often separated from their young at birth), and physical characteristics that make them better suited to specific geographical environments. Some of these breeds are so scarce their estimated global population is less than 2,000 animals.

One example is the Red Devon cow, a breed that first arrived in the United States with the Pilgrims, via Southwest England. These handsome, russet-colored cattle are small, hardy, and a good multiuse animal for draft, milk, and meat. The Red Devon fell by the wayside over hundreds of years, with the development of hybrids. Now, however, Red Devons are slowly making a comeback, thanks to enterprises such as the Rare Breeds program in Colonial Williamsburg, Virginia.

For more information on heritage breeds, go to the American Livestock Breed Conservancy, www.albc-usa.org/.

### Getting your goat

Goats can lactate for as long as 10 months after giving birth. Unlike cows, they favor brambles and thorny grasses in pasture, hence their reputation for eating anything — though in fact they're rather finicky. Bright-white goat milk is leaner and less sweet in the mouth than cow, and the cheeses are usually described as having a citrus-like tang, which is the result of the milk's chemistry.

Although goat milk has approximately the same fat and protein content as cow milk (although that also varies, depending upon breed), its fat globules are generally smaller, and its chemical composition makes it easier to digest. Goat milk is ideal for many people who have problems consuming dairy products (see the "Eating cheese when you're lactose intolerant" sidebar if you have difficulty digesting dairy).

# Recombinant bovine somatotropin, or rBST?

Recombinant bovine somatotropin (rBST) is a synthetic version of a naturally-occurring protein hormone produced by dairy cattle. This hormone, known as bST or bGH (bovine growth hormone), is produced by the pituitary gland, and its basic function is to regulate metabolism. rBST was developed (via genetic engineering) as an injectable to boost the milk production of dairy cows.

rBST was introduced into the commercial dairy industry in the early 1990s, and it soon came under close scrutiny. Cows treated with rBST have an increased likelihood of health problems ranging from lameness to *mastitis* (a serious infection of the udder). These conditions result in increased antibiotic use, which can result in antibiotic resistance.

Mounting evidence also shows that rBST has dire effects on human health, including an increase in antibiotic resistance, milk allergies, and cancer rates. The United States is the only industrialized nation to not ban the use of rBST.

U.S. consumers concerned about rBST in their milk supply haven't managed to get its use banned, but the FDA now recommends that dairy producers who don't use the hormone label their products as such. Look for the words "made from cows not treated with rBST" or similar phrasing on packaging.

## Feeling sheepish

Some dairy sheep require a lush grass environment to be profitable dairy producers, but in general, they thrive in more challenging habitats, such as lowland scrub or sparse, mountainous terrain. Sheep produce milk for the least amount of time — only up to 6 or 7 months after giving birth — and their milk is quite different from both cow and goat milk, with far more butterfat and protein.

Like goats, sheep produce milk that is white in color (rather than yellow) because they convert the carotene in what they eat into vitamin A. Not surprisingly, sheep milk and cheeses made from sheep milk often taste like the smell of a clean wool sweater. Sheep produce significantly less milk than either goats or cows, but the milk is higher in solid content.

## Exploring other milk options

In parts of Asia, the Middle East, Africa, and Europe, the milk of water buffalo, yaks (technically, only the males are called yaks; females are called *dri* or *nak*), camels, mares, jennets (female donkeys), and even reindeer is used to make cheese, usually as a subsistence food for nomadic peoples. The flavors and chemical compositions vary greatly, but the host animal is always one that is best suited to its environment. It will often supply meat, leather, muscle (power), or transportation, as well. Water buffalo milk, which is high in butterfat, is frequently used for Italian cheeses in specific regions, most notably Campania (see Chapter 11 for details).

# Mixing things up: Mixed-milk cheeses

Man has been creating mixed milk cheeses for thousands of years. While the practice doubtless was born of necessity to utilize leftover milk, our inherent need to tinker (remember all those scary concoctions you used to make in the blender when you were a kid?) resulted in what were likely some very tasty cheeses.

Today, cheesemakers mix the milk of cow, goat, or sheep (combining two or sometimes all three) for several key reasons:

✔ Flavor (because each milk has its own distinctive characteristics)

✔ Increasing production/yield

✔ Balancing flavor and texture of a cheese

Some famous mixed-milk cheeses have been made for hundreds of years. Examples include the Spanish cheeses Cabrales (a blue cheese made from cow, sheep, and goat milk, although today it's often made solely from cow milk); Valdeon (a blue cheese made from cow milk sometimes mixed with goat or sheep milk); the French cheese La Tur (a robiola made from cow, sheep, and goat milk). (A robiola is a soft cheese made with one, two, or all three milks.)

In the U.S., the more well-known artisanal mixed-milk cheese producers are Carr Valley (Wisconsin), Tumalo Farms (Oregon), Central Coast Creamery (California), and Old Chatham Cheesemaking Co. (New York) — among others.

# Going green: Sustainable dairy farming

If you've ever seen or driven past a large cow dairy, you know just how messy a production it can be. Even relatively clean dairy animals like sheep and goats create a lot of waste product in the form of manure, methane, and whey. That's why methane digesters are being looked at as a means to clean up and power dairy farms of the future. Some, such as Oregon's Lochmead Dairy, are already using technology to turn their cows' waste into fuel.

Methane digesters (also known as *anaerobic* or *biogas digesters*; kudos to the marketing team behind those names) use a tank-and-turbine system that captures the methane gas from cow manure and burns it to create electricity. Another bonus: Utilizing the manure keeps it from contaminating the groundwater supply — a serious issue for dairy and other industrial livestock farming.

A few other sustainable farming practices are implemented by the following cheesemakers:

✔ **Solar power:** Redwood Hill Dairy (California); Rogue Creamery and Pholia Farm (both in Oregon)

✔ **Water filtration and reuse:** Fiscalini Farmstead Cheese and Pt. Reyes Farmstead Cheese Company (both in California); Cedar Grove Cheese (Wisconsin)

✔ **Hydro-power:** Pholia Farm (Oregon)

✔ **Wind turbines:** Dewlay Cheesemakers (United Kingdom)

✔ **Recycling whey** as supplementary animal feed (for hogs): Juniper Grove Farm (Oregon)

✔ **Recycling and composting:** Jasper Hill Farm (Vermont)

# *Making Cheese*

Despite how technical modern cheesemaking has become — even where small producers are concerned — it all comes down to the same few basic steps:

1. Bringing the milk "up to temperature" (to simulate the animal's body temperature, which activates the starter culture) and adding the starter culture

2. Adding a coagulant, such as rennet

3. Forming and molding the curd, and draining the whey

4. Salting the cheese

5. Aging the cheese (during which rind develops, with the exception of fresh cheeses; see "Ripe for the picking" and "Rinding your business" later in this chapter)

If the milk is to be pasteurized, that step precedes everything else; it will then be cooled down and become ready for the cheesemaking process. Figure 2-1 shows the general steps in the cheesemaking process.

Sometimes, as with the production of fresh cheese, one or more steps will be omitted, but *all* cheese requires the milk to at least be brought up to temperature so that the milk can *coagulate* (when the proteins clump together to form curds). In the following sections, we discuss the essential steps of general cheesemaking.

---

## What is farmstead cheese?

You may have heard the word "farmstead" applied to a cheese or other artisan food products, such as jam. By law, where cheese is concerned, the term means a cheese is made on the farm with milk that comes from the farm's own animals.

A farmstead cheese isn't necessarily better than a cheese made from milk sourced from an outside dairy or *co-op* (a dairy collective), but it may mean that the cheesemaker — who is often the dairy farmer, as well — has more control over the quality of the milk. It also means the milk is likely to go from animal to cheese more quickly.

The more channels through which milk must travel to reach the cheesemaking vat, the greater the odds for spoilage, bacterial contamination, or loss of flavor. Ultimately, however, the safety of both milk and finished product are the result of proper testing and sanitation measures.

---

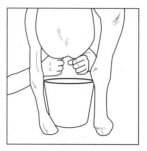

1. Milk the animal

2. Pour milk into vat and heat

3. Stir in cultures and rennet;
check coagulation

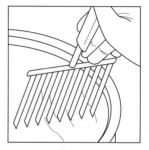

4. Cut curd

5. Pack or ladle curds into forms

**Figure 2-1:**
General
steps in the
cheesemak-
ing process.

6. Remove cheese
from form

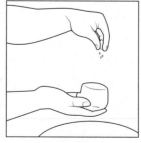

7. Salt cheese

8. Turn and care for
maturing cheese

## Preserving tradition

What was the purpose of making cheese, anyway? Like many ancient foods, it was a form of preservation, a way to make use of fresh product in order to prevent waste and/or provide a source of nutrition during the winter months, when little food was available.

Rather than dispose of surplus milk — a valuable source of protein, fat, and other nutrients — dairying cultures found ways to preserve it in the form of cheese or butter, whether through brining, drying, smoking, or burial.

Cheese is but one of many forms of preserved foods. Vegetables, fruit, meat, and seafood were pickled, potted, canned, smoked, sun- or air-dried, cured/salted, or preserved in liqueur or other alcohol. The homesteading movement that has gained momentum among urbanites and home cooks in recent years is testimony to the enduring popularity of these foods and a practical, affordable, delicious way to make use of seasonal foods — regardless whether we grow them ourselves.

# Smart starter: Heating the milk and adding the starter culture

The first step in cheesemaking is to *ripen* the milk (bring it up to a specific temperature range) in preparation for the addition of cultures and rennet. This initial ripening may in fact be the only time the milk and curds are heated.

When the milk has reached between 77 and 100 degrees (which also corresponds to the approximate body temperature of the animal), the cheesemaker adds a *starter culture*, which acidifies the milk, increasing the population of beneficial bacteria. The starter culture works by fermenting the *lactose* (natural sugar) in the milk and converting it to lactic acid. When the pH is low enough, the milk will be able to coagulate.

In case you've forgotten your high school chemistry, pH is a measure of the alkalinity or acidity of a solution — in the case of cheesemaking, milk. For coagulation to occur, the pH of the milk must be at the right level. If it's too high (that is, too alkaline), the cheese will fail to age properly and will have an excess of retained moisture. If it's too low, the opposite problem occurs, and the cheese will be dry and crumbly because of the excess acidity produced by the bacteria. Therefore, checking the pH level of the milk before moving on to the next step is essential.

Acidification can happen naturally (imagine that past-its-expiration-date milk carton in the back of your fridge), but it needs to occur in a controlled manner for a cheese to develop as the cheesemaker intends.

## Eating cheese when you're lactose intolerant

Chances are, you or someone you know has issues tolerating milk or other dairy products (Laurel does!). Although some people do have true dairy allergies, more often the problem is *lactose intolerance*, which is the inability to digest significant amounts of *lactose*, the natural sugar in milk and other dairy products.

The problem comes when a person has a shortage of the enzyme *lactase* in the gut. Lactase naturally breaks down lactose so that it can be absorbed into the bloodstream. People without enough lactase experience uncomfortable gastrointestinal symptoms after eating foods with lactose; how much they're able to consume without side effects depends upon the individual.

Fortunately, most cheeses have little lactose because it has been converted to lactic acid during the natural cheesemaking process. In general, the longer a cheese is aged, the less lactose it contains. Certain types of milk, like goat or sheep milk, are often more easily tolerated by the intolerant, due to the size of their fat molecules. Digestive aids such as Lactaid can also help ease the symptoms of lactose intolerance.

While acidification is happening, several other important things take place, including the onset of flavor production and the restriction of unwanted bacteria. Desired yeast, mold, and bacteria can also be added to the milk, which has a further impact on the taste, rind, and style of the cheese. (See "Exploring Cheese Styles," later in this chapter for more information on the importance of cheese cultures.)

Because of the presence of these organisms, cheese is a living thing, even after it's been aged. It will continue to ripen, even after you take it home. For storage tips, go to Chapter 7.

## Curd is the word: Letting the fluid milk coagulate

After the acidification process has begun, the milk is ready to be coagulated, or turned into *curds* (soft clumps of protein) and to release *whey* (a liquid by-product). The cheesemaker makes curds by adding rennet.

*Rennet* is an enzyme that occurs naturally in the stomach lining of young *ruminants* (cud-chewing animals). Instead of traditional rennet, many cheesemakers now use non-animal rennet. Non-animal rennet, also called *vegetarian rennet,* is made from microbial and yeast-derived coagulants and, in rarer instances, various species of thistle such as cardoons. Check with your cheesemonger about rennet types if you have a dietary preference. Fluid milk can also be coagulated through acidification alone, and this is how some soft, fresh cheeses are made.

## A curd is a curd is a curd . . .

All curd is cottage cheese–like in texture, right? Not necessarily. It depends upon the type of milk and cheesemaking methods used. Visually and texturally, curds vary greatly: some are goopy, with a pudding-like texture; others hold their shape when cut and resemble gelatinous cubes; and still others form distinct, rice-like shapes that are firmer.

Curds continue to change throughout the cheesemaking process. Usually, they progress from soft to more firm, and their aroma changes from sweet and lactic at the beginning to more acidic and tangy as they set.

Once coagulated, the milk *sets*. It's then cut, stirred, and sometimes heated to form the right-sized curds, as explained in the next section. Curd is considered fresh cheese and can be eaten as is, or it can be made into specific shapes and styles (see Chapter 3 for a discussion of soft cheeses).

The acidification process doesn't end after the milk coagulates. Instead, the cheesemaker has created an environment for the cheese to acidify in a controlled manner to a pre-determined range, as we explain in the later section "Ripe for the picking."

## Placing the curds in forms and draining the whey

After the curds have formed, a cheesemaker really gets down to business. The curds are scooped up or cut, and transferred into perforated *forms* (molds — not to be confused with the organism) that will determine the final shape of the cheese. These are usually in the form of wheels, *boules* (slightly flattened balls), disks, squares, or pyramids. Sometimes, cheesemakers use cheesecloth inside each form, or in place of a form, which produces a more refined, smoother rind.

How the curd is handled is all important to the cheese it will become. In general, the smaller the curd is cut, the more whey it expels. And if the curd is stacked (as in the cheddaring process) or pressed, the pressure of the weight expels more whey. Cooking the curd, too, releases more whey. To make a cheese that's soft and gooey, the curd needs to be left uncut and handled gently — usually hand-ladeled into forms — so that moisture is retained in the cheese. The opposite is true for harder cheeses, which need to have the moisture drained out of them.

## Making do

When it came to forming or protecting cheese for aging, the farmers of yore were forced to rely upon what was available in their immediate area. Examples of this are wood ash (used to keep insects off of the cheese and as a preservative), fresh leaves (popular choices were — and still are — chestnut, sycamore, grape, cherry, and maple), tree bark (which acted as a form to hold the curds in place), or reeds.

Sometimes these natural materials also left a distinct impression on the exterior of the cheese. Majorero, a goat cheese from the Canary Islands (see Chapter 12 for more information), is shaped with plaited palm leaves, which leave a diamond-pattern on the rind. Valdeon, Spain's famous mixed-milk blue cheese, is wrapped in large sycamore leaves, while Cabrales is covered in maple leaves. Livarot, a washed-rind cow milk cheese, is one of the oldest cheeses still produced in France. It's the size and shape of camembert and is made with the addition of three to five reeds wrapped around its perimeter, which keep the cheese from sinking as it sets and ages.

While these decorative touches were born of necessity, the tradition lives on, making these cheeses an indisputable reflection of their *terroir* (environment; see the section "Digging into the importance of terroir" later in this chapter). Additional factors, such as the type of soil — volcanic, limestone, clay, and so on — and what the animals eat are what give artisan cheeses their identity.

The holes in the forms also allow the whey to drain out, removing excess moisture from the curd. Other ways exist to expel moisture after the curd has drained, including stacking, salting, stretching, heating the curd, and pressing down on the formed cheese itself.

*Whey* is the liquid that remains after cheese production. It's mostly water and protein, and is generally considered a positive by-product by small-scale cheesemakers. Some cheeses, such as ricotta (discussed in Chapter 3), are traditionally made from whey.

Moisture content is important in cheesemaking because it ultimately determines whether a cheese will be soft (Chapter 3) or hard (Chapter 4). To transform curd into different cheeses, the addition or natural growth of yeast, mold, and bacteria to the milk is also usually required (with the exception of some fresh cheeses). Ultimately, these will affect the taste and style of the final product. (See "Exploring Cheese Styles," later in this chapter.)

## Worth its salt: Applying or adding salt

After the curd is set and removed from the form, the young cheese is either soaked or washed in brine (saltwater solution), or salt is directly applied to the cheese's exterior. Some cheeses, such as cheddar, are produced by salting the curds before the cheese is actually placed into forms.

> ## Whey not?
>
> Whey has been used since ancient times as a nourishing beverage or as medicine. Now, however, whey is primarily used as an animal feed supplement because of its high protein content, as a soil supplement, or as a human nutritional supplement or food additive.
>
> In past centuries, farmers fed leftover whey back to their animals — both dairy and pigs.
>
> It supplemented their diet and fattened them, making for richer milk and tastier meat. Today, many smaller farms are returning to this trend, utilizing whey from neighboring farms or what's been produced on their own property. This type of system is all part of the cycle of sustainability.

Salt plays several key roles in cheese production. It slows down enzymatic activity and enhances flavor. Salt can keep unwanted organisms away from the cheese; it can also inhibit the growth of bacteria that are essential to the final product. For that reason, salt content is crucial to good cheesemaking. In most instances, salt draws out more moisture and helps form the rind — the outside of the cheese.

## Ripe for the picking

*Ripening,* or aging, a cheese refers to the period of time required for a rind and flavors to develop, unless it's a fresh cheese. Depending on the style of cheese, aging becomes a delicate balancing act that requires strict attention. You may have heard of some cheeses being aged in caves (either natural or man-made). Regardless of where a cheese is aged, aging needs to occur in a controlled environment, within a specific temperature and humidity range in accordance with the style of cheese being produced. If these things are out of balance, the rind — which is not only part of the cheese but protects it as it ages — may crack, damaging the entire wheel or causing the rind to develop more quickly than it should.

Every style of cheese requires a different treatment with regard to rind development, moisture content, and aging. Ripening a cheese correctly and determining when it is ready to cut and eat takes experience and understanding the milk, cheese recipe, style, and how to adjust the environment where the cheese is aged. In this way, it is just like baking bread. The cheesemaker makes adjustments every step of the way.

# To pasteurize or not to pasteurize: The raw milk debate

*Pasteurization* is the process of heating (or "heat-treating") milk to deactivate or kill certain types of bad bacteria, such as E. coli or listeria. Pasteurization of cheeses is not mandatory in the United States; it's up to the cheesemaker. Currently, all mass-produced, "industrial" milk and cheese in the United States is pasteurized, but some states do permit the sale of *raw* (unpasteurized) fluid milk. *Remember:* **Raw milk cheese is legal throughout the U.S.** *provided it's been aged longer than 60 days.*

In this country, industrial cheese and many artisan or farmstead cheeses are made using *batch* or *vat pasteurization*, in which milk is heated to 145 degrees Fahrenheit for at least 30 minutes, or *HTST* (high temperature short time), in which milk is heated to a minimum of 161 degrees Fahrenheit for at least 15 seconds.

If a cheesemaker decides to produce a raw milk cheese, he or she can use one of two different production methods:

**Method 1:** In this method, milk is warmed "up to temperature" in order to activate the starter culture and rennet to make cheese. The cheesemaker may then move on to the other steps necessary to produce the cheese.

**Method 2:** In this method, cheesemakers heat the cheese to a slightly higher temperature, known in the United States as *thermalization*. There is no federal regulation that specifies the temperature or time required to thermalize milk, but it always refers to milk that has been heated to below 145 degrees Fahrenheit (the minimum temperature for pasteurization). For example, some cheesemakers thermalize milk to 131 degrees Fahrenheit for between 2 to 16 seconds

Technically, thermalization doesn't meet the legal definition of pasteurized milk, so the end product is referred to as a raw milk cheese. So why thermalize milk at all? Because doing so still destroys certain bad bacteria, while preserving many of the flavor complexities within the milk and resulting cheese.

In the U.S., the cheese must then be aged for a minimum of 60 days before it's legal to sell. Imported raw milk cheese must also have been aged over 60 days to be sold legally. (In the European Union and New Zealand, raw milk cheese aged less than 60 days, such as Brie or camembert, which we discuss in Chapter 3, are legal to sell for consumption, but Australia has regulations similar to the United States.)

Raw milk and cheese are high-demand specialty products. Some proponents believe that raw milk and the cheese made from it taste better, are more digestible, and help boost the immune system. They also believe pasteurization destroys the beneficial bacteria and enzymes that lend flavor and complexity. But there are just as many detractors, the main concern being that raw milk's ability to harbor deadly pathogens if handled incorrectly poses too great a threat to the general public and can be fatal to infants, young children, the elderly, or those with compromised immune systems. Although this is a valid concern, pasteurization doesn't guarantee product safety. Whether milk is raw or pasteurized, safety comes down to sanitation measures, dairy herd health, production practices, and proper shipping and storage. We believe that there's a place in the market to safely sell both products.

## A-list affineurs

Most cheese lovers have never heard of affineurs, but they're the behind-the-scenes celebrities of the artisan cheese industry. Affineurs work very closely with cheesemakers, purchasing their cheeses at very young ages, aging them at a different location so the cheesemaker can produce more product, and oftentimes changing the cheeses by adding herbs to the rind or altering them in other positive ways. Thus, they help support the livelihood of artisan cheesemakers, as well as work to promote the cheese industry. While affinage is primarily a European thing, it's slowly growing in popularity in the U.S.

To be an outstanding affineur, a deep understanding of microbiology and the conditions required to mature cheese is a necessity, as is a commitment to public health and safety. Some are helping to protect and preserve certain cheeses that would otherwise be an endangered species, which is changing the face of the artisan cheese world.

Look for cheeses aged by the following affineurs; you'll see their names listed on tasting notes at some cheese shops, or ask your cheesemonger: Rolf Beeler (Switzerland); Caroline Hostettler (Florida); Jean d'Alos (France); Herve Mons (France); Neal's Yard Dairy (U.K.); L'Amuse (Netherlands); Cellars at Jasper Hill (Vermont; also a cheesemaker); Luigi Guffanti 1876 (Italy); La Fromagerie (London); Formaggio Kitchen (Boston); and Artisanal and Murray's Cheese (both in New York).

In Europe, ripening is often done by an *affineur*, someone who is trained in *affinage*, or finishing a cheese. In the United States, the cheesemaker usually does the ripening. Because cheese is a living thing and continues to ripen, however, it is often handed over to those who will distribute and sell it at a slightly younger age, so retailers and cheesemongers are caretaking the cheese through its final stages.

# Exploring Cheese Styles

In the previous section, we describe the basic process by which all cheese is made. But every style of cheese has its special characteristics and properties. These are developed by making specific adjustments during the cheesemaking process. Here, we discuss what makes one cheese different from another.

## Getting cultured: Bacteria and mold

Besides the starter culture, which acidifies the milk (refer to the earlier section "Making Cheese"), other ripening agents such as bacteria, yeast, and molds (the microscopic organisms, not the forms used to shape cheese) are usually added during the cheesemaking process. These affect the flavor and texture of the cheese.

Although you've probably been taught to be afraid of bacteria and mold, the very environment we live in has many indigenous, harmless, and even beneficial species. Without them, many cheeses people know and love wouldn't exist because the original cheese styles were derived from specific molds growing organically where the cheeses were made or aged (a classic example is the *Penicillum roqueforti* mold that lives in soil of the natural caves of Roquefort-sur-Soulzon in southern France, where Roquefort cheese is aged). Although these molds are naturally present in that environment, humans encourage their growth and cultivation elsewhere for the production of cheese and other foods and therapeutic agents such as antibiotics.

Below are examples of the most-commonly used "good" molds and bacteria introduced during the cheesemaking process, although many others are available:

- *Penicillium roqueforti* (mold): Produces the blue veins in blue cheeses
- *Penicillium candidum* (mold): Produces the white mold on bloomy-rind cheeses like Brie
- *Geotricum candidum* (mold): Results in the wrinkly, mold-ripened cheeses such as St. Marcellin and crottin
- *Brevibacterium linens* (bacteria): Produces the orange-red rind on "stinky" cheeses
- *Proprionibacterium freudenreichii* (bacteria): Produces holes inside Swiss-style (also called *alpine* or *mountain-style*) cheeses such as Emmental

*Brevibacterium linens* (or *B. linens*), which is used to make washed-rind cheeses, occurs naturally on human skin. That's why some stinky cheeses have a locker room smell to them. Think about that next time you get ready to wash your gym clothes!

## Rinding your business

The rind of a cheese is its skin. It's an important part of the cheese and is the result of the surface of the cheese being exposed to the air. When combined with the bacteria and molds used in the cheesemaking process, as well as the correct temperature and humidity, the rind forms. (***Note:*** The interior of a cheese is called the *paste*, or *pâte* (pronounced "pat").

The rind helps to create a cheese's specific taste and texture, although a cheese's acidity and moisture content are most indicative of its ability to age well. The rind also protects the cheese. On certain cheeses, such as washed rinds and surface-ripened cheeses, the rind plays an integral part in the development and flavors of the entire product.

The following sections outline the main rind categories. As you read this info, keep in mind that, while writing this book, we realized that there wasn't a way to make cheese classifications fit into neat, easy squares. Some cheeses are surface-ripened but also have several additional molds added to them, so they can be cross-referenced, like Langres, which is both washed-rind and mold-ripened. That is why the basics matter when talking cheese: hard or soft; cow, goat, or sheep; buttery, nutty, or stinky. Otherwise it gets confusing — even for the experts!

## Natural rinds

These cheeses are exposed to air, and their rinds form as part of the aging process. Natural rinds develop organically on all cheeses if left to themselves, without the addition of bacteria or mold to the milk or curd. Natural-rind cheeses are usually wiped or patted down by hand, sometimes using olive oil, butter, or lard to prevent cracking. Examples of natural-rind cheeses include certain cheddar and Tomme de Savoie.

## Surface-ripened rinds

All cheeses that are ripened from the outside surface inward are *surface-ripened*. This includes the following types of cheeses:

- **Bloomy rind:** Softer cheeses like Brie can have a white, "bloomy" rind that literally ripens the cheese from the outside in. This happens because of a specific mold (*Penicillium candidum*). The rind is edible and imparts a mushroomy flavor. (See Chapter 3 for a closer look at these cheeses.)

- **Washed rind:** Salt brine, wine, beer, and spirits are all used to "wash" various cheeses so that specific bacteria (*Brevibacterium linens*) form and flourish, often — but not always — resulting in a *stinky* cheese. The rind is usually reddish and sticky with a distinct sulfurous or footy odor. The interior is less intense-smelling and, when aged, becomes soft and gooey with meaty, yeasty flavors. (See Chapter 3 for some of our favorite washed-rind cheeses.)

- **Mold-ripened:** Cheeses that are particularly wrinkly with a tangy, floral taste, like many French goat cheeses, La Tur, or St. Marcellin, are mold-ripened, which means there has been the addition of the *Geotrichum* molds (see Chapter 3). They can also be washed- or bloomy-rind, but it's the addition of *Geotrichum* mold that makes the difference — and it is always used on mold-ripened cheeses.

*Note:* Some non-surface ripened cheeses, like Gruyère, have rinds that are washed (technically, smear-ripened), but for our purposes here, we're talking about soft cheeses.

### Clothbound, waxed, or coated rinds

Wrapping, waxing, or coating a cheese is a way of discouraging molds from developing on the rind, as well as imparting unwanted flavors to the cheese itself. The wax used for cheese isn't the same wax used for candles. Instead, it's a special, non-edible, but food-safe cheese wax that remains flexible over time. It protects the cheese, allowing it to age without cracking, and inhibits unwanted molds from growing. With Gouda production, a special non-edible food-grade coating is used to stifle the development of mold. (You can find Gouda in in Chapter 4.)

Cheesecloth is also used to wrap cheese, specifically cheddar. Some cheesemakers press crushed herbs, spices, vegetable ash, or other ingredients onto the young rind of the cheeses before maturing them.

# Where in the World?

While the average consumer can't taste a cheese and tell what country — let alone what region — it's from, certain styles of cheese provide clues. Style, taste characteristics, and type of milk are indicators, because they generally reflect the geography, habitat, and climate of their place of origin.

For example, Northern Italy is the heart of that country's dairy industry because the temperate climate and fertile soil yield lush pastures. The grasses and other plants that the cattle (or other animals) eat are converted into high-quality milk that, in turn, is made into rich cheeses, such as Taleggio, Robiola, Parmigiano Reggiano, and Gorgonzola Dolce. Sheep milk cheeses, although produced throughout Italy, are more commonly found in the south because the hot, arid climate and sparse vegetation are well-suited to the indigenous breeds of sheep.

This section explains a bit more about the concept of *terroir* and how it applies to cheese. We also define what a *designation* (a locale as it pertains to specific foods) means where cheese is concerned and provide you with some examples of famous designated cheeses.

## Digging into the importance of terroir

From the French *terre,* meaning "land," *terroir* is a term most recently associated with wine. The term has no literal translation; instead, it refers collectively to the geography, soil, and climate of a specific growing region. These factors influence the flavors in the resulting grapes. Thus, a good wine is said to be an expression of its terroir.

Artisan cheese is much the same. The plants that the animals graze upon are often indigenous to the region or the result of the season. An alpine cheese such as Gruyère, for example, is evocative of the rich grass, wildflowers, and herbs that grow in the high mountain summer pastures of the Swiss Alps. Thus, Gruyère is a manifestation of its terroir. Tradition and history also play important parts in the production of this (and many other) cheeses and are an important part of their terroir.

Terroir is increasingly being used to describe other foods such as produce or meat. And we admit that perhaps the term should be used judiciously, so as to avoid the snobbery that can be associated with wine, cheese, or other "fine" foods. But we're fans of terroir, both as a belief and as a way to describe cheese. One of the most beautiful things about a local, handcrafted cheese is its ability to evoke a sense of place — even if you're on the other side of the world.

# Demystifying designations

PDO, DOC, DOP — sometimes, you see these mysterious letters on the label of a cheese, similar to what you might find on a European wine label. It may lead you to wonder: Are they the cheesemaker's initials? A secret code? Shorthand for some unsavory additive? Nope. What you're looking at are the various, country-specific and European Union (EU)–specific terms for regional foods and agricultural products such as beer, wine, honey, and so on, that have been granted a special designation.

These designations are a way of identifying and protecting regional and traditional products from imitation. It's a complex system, so we're just breaking it down to its most basic elements. Following are some of the most common labels you'll find on cheese.

The U.S. doesn't have its own laws regarding protected domain names for cheese. Some wine regions such as Napa Valley have implemented specific designations for wine. With regard to food, the lack of designation is why you'll see domestically produced prosciutto, cheddar, feta, and so on. Hopefully, as New World food purveyors begin to define our own culinary traditions, federal regulations will be put into place to protect our historic and indigenous foods, as the Europeans have done with theirs.

## PDO (Protected Designation of Origin)

*PDO (Protected Designation of Origin)* is the English language designation (in other countries, you will see different initials, as described in the later chart). It refers to a specific traditional and regional food or agricultural product (such as wine) with very strict production rules.

To help you understand what a PDO means, here's an example using Roquefort cheese: This blue cheese from southern France is made from the milk of the Lacaune, Manech, or Basco-Béarnaise breeds of sheep. The cheese must be aged in the Cambalou caves of Roquefort-sur-Soulzon, where the *Penicillium roqueforti* mold that gives Roquefort its distinctive earthy characteristics grows.

Designated cheeses usually have specific protocol for the method of production and even the type of food the animals eat, all of which contribute to the finished product's signature taste, appearance, and smell. To be granted PDO status, every cheese must be produced in the specified manner, in the designated region. Here are some examples of PDO cheeses from their respective countries:

- **France:** Comté, Pont l'Évèque, Livarot, and Époisses
- **Switzerland**: Gruyère, Tête de Moine, and Vacherin Mont d'Or
- **UK:** Stilton, Single Gloucester, and Somerset Cheddar

### Other designations

Other designations you may see in the EU include the following:

- **DOC (*Denominazione di origine controllata*), Italy:** Examples include Parmigiano Reggiano, Pecorino Romano, and Fontina.
- **DOP (*Denominación de origen protegida*), Spain and Portugal:** Examples include the Spanish cheeses Manchego, Cabrales, and Idiazabal, and the Portuguese cheeses Sera de Estrela and Castelo Branco.

The term AOC *(Appellation d'Origine Contrôlée)* was used as the designation for France and Switzerland until May 1, 2009. You may still see it used in the United States, so don't let it confuse you.

Although it may seem silly or pretentious to devote such time, energy, and paperwork to designating foods, it's a way of preserving ancient artisan traditions and ingredients that are a true expression of the terroir. Regulating the name of a product protects the reputation and livelihood of the producers of these famous foods and prevents confusion for the consumer.

# Why is artisan cheese so expensive?

When I was a rookie cheesemonger at Neal's Yard Dairy in London in the early 1990s, I asked a colleague to explain why the British and Irish farmhouse cheeses we worked with cost so much more than the commodity cheeses of the same name. By way of an answer, he showed me a photograph of a very large-scale cheese operation in the north of England.

"The cheese that's produced here in one day," he told me, "is equivalent to the annual output of *all* the British and Irish farmhouse cheesemakers put together."

That was true at the time. These days, the question of price can still be answered by comparing numbers. A pound of cheddar made at a large-scale U.S. facility, for example, costs between $0.19 and $0.21 to produce, whereas a cloth-wrapped, aged American farmstead cheddar costs approximately $4 per pound to produce.

The goal of a large-scale cheese factory is to produce consistent cheese as quickly, safely, and inexpensively as possible. It's a highly competitive market where financial success is determined by efficiency, stable shelf life, easy distribution, and economies of scale. Flavor isn't the only priority.

For the American artisan cheesemaker, success is determined almost entirely by his ability to make a delicious, high-quality cheese that differentiates itself from its competitors. Creating an excellent cheese expressive of its terroir is the main goal. Achieving this often means getting back to the basics of cheesemaking, which translates into removing much of the mechanization process and investing heavily in milk quality, skilled labor, and other production costs.

None of this comes cheaply. Quality animal feed, essential to produce good milk and therefore good cheese, is expensive. And when it comes to shipping, smaller producers rely on carrier services such as FedEx or UPS to deliver their perishable cheeses to customers as quickly as possible. Rising fuel prices add to the expense. And cheeses imported into the U.S. are subject to fluctuations of the euro. Despite how grim this all sounds, guess which is the fastest growing sector of the cheese market? Yes. Artisanal and farmstead.

—Kate Arding, ***culture:*** *the word on cheese* co-founder and veteran cheesemonger

# Chapter 3

# A Hard Look at Soft Cheeses

*In This Chapter*

▶ Covering the basics of soft cheeses

▶ Noting the difference between fresh, surface-ripened, washed-rind, and blue cheeses

▶ Discovering a variety of soft cheeses to try

*R*eal men eat soft cheese. Trust us. Despite the delicate texture and flavor and dainty appearance of some varieties, others may be milky, oozy, gooey, fluffy, salty, stretchy, or seriously stinky. Regardless of characteristics, soft cheeses command attention. They're the closest thing to fresh milk, in some instances, just days (or, if you're lucky, hours) out of the animal. And they're versatile; you can snack on them, use them for cooking or as a garnish, or serve them on a cheese plate.

Real men also eat *semi-soft* cheese. Note that this term is merely a textural description, and *not* a style of cheese. Yet it's used frequently in cheese talk, and it can be confusing. All it means is that these cheeses — Reblochon is a good example — retain less moisture than soft cheeses and more moisture than hard cheeses (covered in Chapter 4). They often make excellent melting cheeses.

As you may have guessed, we have an, ahem, soft spot for all of the cheeses in this category. Their beauty lies in their seeming simplicity. They're often meant for eating as-is and are only enhanced by the addition of an accompaniment or two (and yes, a glass of wine or beer counts!).

Soft cheeses are just what they sound like: texturally soft and often gooey or oozy. They can have different flavors and shapes. A semi-soft cheese, on the other hand, is more pliable and holds together better.

*Note:* If a cheese has a particular designation, we include that designation in our discussion. For a quick review of what the different acronyms mean, refer to Chapter 2.

# Soften Up: Understanding the Soft Cheese Basics

The main thing you need to know about soft cheese is that this category refers to various styles (which we list shortly) that are meant to be consumed fairly quickly because they have a short shelf-life. They can be made from all kinds of milk, but the common denominator for these cheeses is their texture and the fact that they're high in moisture. Soft cheeses aren't pressed to expel excess whey, nor are they made to be aged long-term. They're also not ideal if you're traveling or throwing a big party in a hot climate because they don't hold up well in extremely warm temperatures (and washed rinds quickly become odiferous).

Think of soft cheeses as more immediate expressions of the milk of the animal and enjoy them with minimal accoutrements as soon as possible after purchase. For serving and pairing suggestions, check out Chapters 7, 15, and 16.

Following is a brief breakdown on the different styles of soft cheeses. We get into more detail in each individual section, as well as provide a list of varieties and serving suggestions.

- ✔ **Fresh:** An unripened cheese, not designed for aging. Fresh cheeses may be as young as a few hours old (ricotta, for example) or preserved in brine (such as feta) after they're made, for a shelf life of no more than a couple of weeks.

- ✔ **Surface-ripened:** This term refers to all cheeses that are ripened from the outside surface inward.

The terms *surface-ripened, soft-ripened,* and *mold-ripened* are often confusing because there's no clear-cut definitive or regulatory term to define them. Some cheese professionals use the terms interchangeably, while others prefer to use each term to refer to a specific type of cheese. In the following list, we outline the three subcategories of the surface-ripened style and explain the terms and definitions we use throughout this book:

- • **Bloomy rind:** This name is pretty self-explanatory: *bloomy* refers to the soft, velvety white mold that covers Brie, camembert, and other cheeses. This mold also works its magic on the delicate curd within, forming a paste that may range in texture from soft to oozy. Specific molds are required to foster this ripening process; they also create an edible rind with a distinct, mushroomy flavor.

- **Washed rind:** Salt brine, wine, beer, and spirits are all used to "wash" this style of cheese so that specific bacteria (*B.linens*) form and flourish, often — but not always — resulting in a stinky cheese. The rind is usually reddish or orange and sticky with a distinct sulfurous, meaty, or "footy" odor. The interior is less intense-smelling and, when aged, becomes soft and gooey. This is generally an easy style to remember because the texture and smell of washed rinds is so distinctive.

- **Mold-ripened (with a wrinkly rind):** Cheeses with a rumpled rind and a tangy, floral flavor, like many French goat cheeses, are surface-ripened by the addition of *Geotrichum* mold (see the later section "Surface-Ripened Soft Cheeses" for details).

Consume soft cheeses within a week or two of buying them, tops. Their lack of aging, high moisture content (which can provide a breeding ground for bad bacteria or mold), and low salt content aren't conducive to a long shelf life. If they smell sour, fizz on your tongue, or have spots of bluish-green or pinkish-red mold, toss them. *Note:* The exception to pinkish mold are washed-rind cheeses (see the section "Washed-rind soft cheeses: An odiferous array" later in this chapter) because this is their normal color. If washed-rind cheeses are bad, they tend to smell like ammonia.

# Getting Fresh

If you've ever had fresh cottage cheese or mozzarella — the kind that comes packed in water, rather than wrapped in plastic — you've already sampled *fresh* cheese. The style simply refers to cheeses that are not destined for aging.

Fresh cheeses are perishable, so you need to eat them quickly after purchase. At their best, they're just days or hours "out of the animal," and their color, flavor, and, to a certain extent, texture, reflect that. Because they're so minimally aged, and the molds and bacteria haven't had adequate time to develop true rinds, fresh cheeses range in color from snowy white to ivory or the palest yellow. Fresh cheeses such as mozzarella and chèvre are sweet, creamy, milky, or tangy. Texturally, they may be in loose, clumpy curds or velvety smooth; fluffy and airy; satiny or somewhat runny; squeaky, crumbly, or moist; or dry or grainy. But all *good* fresh cheeses possess the pronounced rich, clean flavor of fresh milk. Many have a hint of sweetness due to the natural sugars in the milk, and some, like feta, are brined and, therefore, at least somewhat salty. Tangy flavors are generally associated with cheeses made from goat milk.

Some of the most notable fresh cheeses include the following:

- **Chèvre:** *Chèvre* means "goat" in French. It usually refers to soft young goat milk cheese that's the consistency of whipped cream cheese (see Chapter 19 for an easy chèvre recipe you can make on your own). You can find chèvre at any grocery store or cheese shop.

  Chèvre makes a great savory addition crumbled on top of pizzas, salads, and pasta, egg, vegetable, and grain dishes. Or try it in place of cream cheese.

- **Cottage cheese:** At once tangy and sweet, with rich, clumpy curds, this cheese is usually made from cow milk.

  Cottage and all of the following cheeses may be found at any decent-sized grocery store, but for artisanal versions, look at specialty grocers and cheese shops.

- **Cream cheese:** Artisanal cream cheese is made by adding a starter culture and coagulant (refer to Chapter 2) to cow milk and a touch of cream. It's not as rich as mascarpone (see the next item in this list), but it's quite thick and spreadable. Its flavor is more tangy and sour than sweet.

- **Mascarpone:** Technically, this Italian dessert favorite isn't a cheese. It's a cultured (acidified) dairy product, but it's often categorized as a cheese. Like certain types of cheese, mascarpone is a *triple-crème* (enriched by the addition of cream; see "Creamy contents: Double-versus triple-crème cheeses"). Mascarpone is satiny, sweet, and thick but spreadable. It's a key ingredient in the famous Italian dessert *tiramisu*.

- **Crème fraiche:** Like mascarpone, crème fraiche is a cultured dairy product, but it's often found in the cheese department. It can be made from either cultured buttermilk or sour cream made from whole milk. By adding an acidic component to either, the mixture thickens to form a substance that resembles a more buttery, satiny version of sour cream.

  Crème fraiche is excellent for baking, stirring into soups, or as a substitute for whipped cream on desserts. Eaten straight up with fresh berries or stone fruit, it's nothing short of heavenly (try out the Classic Crème Fraiche recipe in Chapter 19).

In addition to the specific uses already outlined in the list, these cheeses are wonderful paired with fresh fruit, spread over good-quality toasted bread, or (if you're like us) eaten shamelessly by the spoonful.

## Whey to go! Fresh cheese from leftovers

Whey cheeses are made from the residual solids left in whey after it's reheated at a higher temperature (refer to Chapter 2 for more about whey). The best-known whey cheese is ricotta, which has a soft, fluffy texture and sweet, milky flavor. This Italian specialty may be made from the solids left over from cow, sheep, or water buffalo milk. Most people associate it with lasagna.

Ricotta is wonderful for baking, in pasta dishes, or with fresh fruit and a drizzle of honey. Look for a producer local to you.

## Pasta filata: Stringy, stretchy, fresh cheeses

*Pasta filata* ("spun paste") cheeses have an elastic, chewy texture and are usually a striking white color. Some varieties are also brined or smoked. A hot-water bath at the curd stage melts the curd so that it can be stretched into the desired shape. If you look closely, you can see the stringy layers — even in the aged varieties. (You can pull your own pasta filata by following the mozzarella recipe in Chapter 19.)

You'll enjoy snacking on any of these:

✔ **Mozzarella:** A good-quality fresh mozzarella is a thing of beauty: sweet, rich, and delicate. It's usually made from water buffalo (*mozzarella di bufala*) or cow milk (*fior di latte*) and is a specialty of Campania, Italy — though there are many excellent domestic producers. The best way to enjoy mozzarella is to eat it just after it's been stretched; some restaurants make hand-pulled mozzarella to order, which is worth seeking out. But even with nothing more than a drizzle of olive oil and a pinch of sea salt, fresh mozzarella will turn you off the rubbery mass-produced stuff forever. Try it on sandwiches, pizza, or cubed into pasta.

If you purchase fresh mozzarella packed in whey and water (it's not a brine), store any leftovers back in the liquid to keep them at their best. Give them a quick rinse and pat dry before using. Some fresh mozzarella is also sold cryovaced in plastic.

✔ **Burrata:** This southern Italian cheese from Puglia hit the U.S. radar less than a decade ago, and it's now in great demand and made domestically (by Belgioioso, Di Stefano, and Gioia brands) as well as imported. Burrata is a combination of mozzarella, *stracciatella* ("the pulled curd"), and cream. Slice through the edible exterior skin, and you'll be rewarded with a decadently rich filling.

> Serve burrata as you would mozzarella, or with fresh summer fruit and honey.

✔ **String cheese:** This really is a semi-soft cheese, but we want to include it here because it's a great example of pasta filata. Children love this mild cow milk snacking cheese. Many grocery stores also carry pure-white Armenian string cheese, which often has black nigella seeds added for a touch of pungency and visual appeal. This type of string cheese is traditionally made from sheep or goat milk and braided.

# Surface-Ripened Soft Cheeses

All cheeses ripened from the outside surface inward are *surface-ripened*. On the outside, surface-ripened cheeses can be fluffy, velvety, reddish orange (or other shades coming from the bacterial growth of the washed rind), or wrinkly in texture. Although some people are rind lovers, most folks know it's what's inside that counts, and in this case, the interior is rich and rewarding. The paste of surface-ripened cheeses can be oozy, creamy, dense, or chalky, with flavors ranging from fruity, yeasty, or earthy to mushroomy or stinky.

The following factors influence the differences in style, texture (of both rind and interior), and flavor of all surface-ripened cheeses:

✔ Type of milk and species of mold used.

✔ The time of year — spring through late summer are the peak periods for milk production in most dairy species.

✔ How and where the cheeses are ripened and under what conditions. The conditions refer not only to humidity and temperature, but also the type of material they are ripened upon. Spruce boards, for example, can lend a faint woodsy essence. These are the factors that cheesemakers need to worry about most because they can create havoc in the cheese room unless skill and knowledge are applied while making the cheese.

✔ Shape, width, and depth of the cheese.

The molds added to help ripen surface-ripened soft cheeses really showcase the milk and butterfat. *Penicillum candidum* (also known as *Penicillium camemberti*) and *Geotrichum candidum* give these cheeses their distinctive, edible white to pale-yellow, beige, or grayish rinds, which often have a mushroomy flavor. *Geotrichum* cheeses are especially notable because the mold usually gives the rind a distinct, wrinkly texture.

Some surface-ripened cheeses can be cross-classified. For example, Langres has a wrinkly rind and is also a washed-rind cheese, meaning it has both the addition of *Geotrichum* and the *B. linens* bacteria. Camembert au Calvados is both a bloomy rind and a washed rind. And many soft goat cheeses are made with *Penicillium candidum* with a bit of *Geotrichum candidum* — and some are *also* washed rind! Remember that it's the species of mold and rind treatment that makes the difference in a cheese's classification. Just because a cheese is made in one style doesn't mean it can't also be classified as another.

In the following sections, we break down surface-ripened cheeses into their three main categories.

## Bloomy-rind soft cheeses: Fluffy, furry, velvety rinds

When a cheese is described as earthy, that doesn't mean you're eating the equivalent of a mouthful of soil. It just means the dominant flavor is reminiscent of what clean dirt, mushrooms, or a forest floor smells like. Other flavors you might find in an earthy cheese include beefy, tangy, grassy, herbaceous, goaty or sheepy (depending on the milk used), or musty. One of the most famous bloomy-rind cheeses in the world, camembert, fits into this category.

*Bloomy rind* and *soft-ripened* are used synonymously throughout the cheese world for a similar style of cheese. It can get confusing, but it's not all that hard to grasp if you focus on the basics. Expect a soft, white rind and interiors that range from soft and oozy to malleable and dense. For our purposes, we prefer to use only the term *bloomy rind*.

As mentioned previously, all surface-ripened cheeses ripen from the outside in, and it takes a bit of skill to know when a cheese is completely ripe. How can you tell when a bloomy rind cheese (such as Brie) is ripe, especially when cheeses vary so much in consistency?

- ✔ **Feel:** Poking a bloomy-rind cheese only tells you if it's ripe just under the rind, not the whole way through. To gauge overall ripeness, take the wheel carefully in both hands and very gently flex it. If there's a reasonable amount of give, it's probably ready to go. If it resists or is stiff, it's not ripe.

- ✔ **Fragrance:** A ripe bloomy-rind cheese should have an easily detectable aroma indicative of its flavor characteristics, be they earthy or fruity. Young Brie or similar cheeses don't give off much aroma, while an over-ripe one smells astringent and ammoniated.

- **Funk:** As with all cheese, your palate plays a big role in how you determine ripeness. As Brie ages, its flavors become stronger and often more complex, and some people prefer different stages of ripeness. There are no hard and fast rules, so just eat what you enjoy!

Small brown spots are normal, but if you notice large brown spots on the rind, if the rind is powdery rather than damp/moist, or if it has astringent flavors that burn your tongue, the cheese is past its prime. Dump it.

If bloomy-rind cheeses sound appealing, try these:

- **Camembert:** Slightly mushroomy, with a satiny, creamy, off-white interior and an edible, bloomy white rind, this French cow milk classic is from the mega-dairy region of Normandy. (An interesting aside: In the 1956 film *High Society*, Bing Crosby compares true love to "old camembert.")

- **Brie:** Brie, which comes from Île-de-France, a region adjacent to Paris, is a bit more sweet, fruity, and feminine than its earthy cousin camembert but possesses a similar creamy texture and bloomy rind.

The true, raw milk versions of both Brie and camembert are unavailable in the United States because of FDA regulations (refer to Chapter 2). However, you can find great pasteurized Bries from Rouzaire in Tournan-en-Brie and really good camemberts from Isigny Sainte-Mère and the E. Graindorge or Île de France brands. You can also find some excellent domestic versions. Try Moses Sleeper, a Brie-style from Jasper Hill Farm (VT), any of the handcrafted Brie-style cheeses from Marin French Cheese (CA), or Old Chatham Sheepherding Company's Hudson Valley Camembert (NY).

- **Mt. Tam:** Made by Cowgirl Creamery (California), this is an 8-ounce, triple-crème cow milk bloomy rind. It's buttery and creamy but doesn't seem as super-rich as some of the French triple crèmes. Pop a bottle of bubbly with this cheese for a fun pairing.

Earthy bloomy-rind cheeses are excellent with fall or winter fruit such as purple grapes, apples, or pears, or dried fruit such as figs, muscatels (wine grapes), or cherries. If you're looking for something savory, pair them with cured meats on a cheese plate. Add some country-style bread and a salad of bitter greens dressed with good extra virgin olive oil and red wine vinegar, and you have a rustic but satisfying meal suitable for guests.

## Creamy contents: Double- versus triple-crème cheeses

If you love supremely rich, creamy, or buttery soft-style cheeses, odds are at least some of them are double or triple crèmes. The terms are fairly self-explanatory: a double crème calls for double the amount of cream in its production, or a minimum of 60 to 75 percent butterfat. Triple crèmes, as you might assume, use triple the amount of cream and must be 75-plus percent butterfat. France is the only country that has legally defined these terms, but they have been widely — although not officially — adopted worldwide.

The first triple creams were developed during the Belle Epoque to meet the demands of Parisian consumers infatuated with decadent cuisine. After two World Wars, few of these cheeses remained in existence, but there was a revival during the 1950s.

The cheeses in these categories may be fresh or ripe cheeses made from any kind of milk (although cow is most common) or a mixture of milks. Here are some of the most famous — and popular — examples of double-, triple-, and mixed-milk cream cheeses.

- ✔ **Double crèmes:** St. Agur, Fromage d'Affinois, cream cheese

  Some Bries and other bloomy-rind cheeses made for export to the U.S. are double crèmes (60 percent) because that's what American consumers like. But the higher butterfat content isn't traditional for these cheeses in France.

- ✔ **Triple crèmes:** Brillat-Savarin, Explorateur, mascarpone

## *Washed-rind soft cheeses: An odiferous array*

For some cheese lovers, the earthy, savory cheeses we describe in the preceding section are as potent as they care to get. For other people, the stronger, the better.

Traditional washed-rind cheeses of all textures are for adventurous eaters who are fans of the funk. Their rinds are sticky and orange, reddish, pinkish, or brownish in color, and are often described as smelling like dirty feet or socks, or *barnyard* (with a whiff of barn, wet hay, or animal) and tasting beefy, yeasty, or meaty. Soft washed-rind cheeses are generally oozy and gooey.

Don't let the descriptions of stinky washed-rind cheeses scare you off. Despite their odorific capacities, most of these cheeses smell much stronger than they taste.

Washed-rind cheeses get their name and flavor as a result of the process of washing them with brine or other liquid during aging and the resulting bacteria that forms the rind itself. Some cheesemakers use wine, while others — most famously Belgian Trappist monks — use beer. You'll also find cheeses washed in pear brandy, bourbon, grappa, or whatever regional spirits inspire the cheesemaker.

It's bacteria that gives washed-rind cheese its signature stinky characteristics. *Brevibacterium linens (B. linens)* can exist naturally in the air where the cheese ages, but usually it's added to the brine. *B. linens* develops a distinctive flavor highly sought after by lovers of stinky cheese. It's responsible for the color, texture, and smell that are the hallmarks of most washed-rind cheeses.

Cheese of any type should never smell like ammonia, which is a sign it's over-ripe. Washed rinds in particular are prone to this characteristic. But before you decide to throw out an ammoniated cheese, give it some fresh air. Unwrap it and let it sit on the counter for an hour or so to breath and then scrape off the outer layer of the cut surfaces. That should do the trick.

Serious cheese geeks find the varieties in this category particularly exciting. There's just something about digging in (literally — you eat the first two of the following three examples with a spoon) to a heady, oozy, puddle of cheese that's irresistible:

- ✔ **Epoisses:** One of the crown jewels of French cheese, this Burgundian washed rind has a fondue-like texture within a rust-colored rind. Eat it by cutting a hole in the top and spooning out the satiny white paste.

- ✔ **Vacherin:** This famous seasonal alpine cow milk cheese is made on both sides of the Swiss/French border. Produced only in the fall and winter, the freshly formed cheeses are encased in a strip of spruce before being washed with brine and aged. The resulting cheese is a slightly pungent, smokey, oozy delight. Eat as you would Epoisses. *Note:* For domestic versions of this cheese, try Rush Creek Reserve by Uplands Cheese Company (Wisconsin) and Winnimere, by Jasper Hill Farm (Vermont).

- ✔ **Munster:** Not to be confused with the American version, spelled "Muenster," this historic French cheese was originally made by Alsatian monks. It has a bright-orange, stinky rind and a luscious, creamy white interior.

Oozy washed-rind cheeses are as versatile as their creamy cousins. Serve them with a simple salad of bitter greens and crusty bread for mopping up the cheese, and you have an easy, elegant dinner. Or pair these cheeses with fresh or dried fall fruits for a dessert plate. Sip with a good ale or fruit-driven red wine.

ASK THE EXPERT

# What's the difference between Brie and camembert?

Both Brie and camembert are flat, soft disks of white, bloomy-rind cow milk cheese. But they have distinct differences aside from how long they've been around (the first records of Brie appear in 774; camembert was created more than a thousand years later, in 1791).

Traditional Brie is large and flat, about 14 to 16 inches in diameter and between 1 to 2 inches tall; the surface area allows for more moisture evaporation during aging, which impacts both the texture and flavor of the cheese. Camembert is much smaller and more compact, around 4 to 5 inches in diameter and 1.5 inches tall; as a result, it matures faster than Brie.

Although both cheeses are made in northern France, according to PDO law, Brie must be made in Île-de-France and camembert in Normandy, two distinct regions. During production, the curd is handled in very different ways. When making Camembert de Normandie, cheesemakers preserve moisture through minimal cutting before scooping the curd with deep, perforated ladles. The molds are gradually filled, one ladle at a time, over the course of four hours. This technique, coupled with light pressing under a metal plate, makes for a more densely textured young cheese.

This step of ladling is different for Brie. The curd is cut, releasing more whey that is drained off. Cheesemakers use a special ladle that is shallow and perforated; four or five ladles of curd fill forms that are traditionally set atop a mat made of local river reeds. The forms are filled more quickly and left to drain overnight without any additional weight, making for a less dense young cheese.

These differences translate into distinguishing flavors and textures in the finished cheeses: Camembert shows a heavier density in the mouth and a flavor evocative of mushrooms, truffles, and wet hay. Brie has a slightly brighter, tangier, even fruitier flavor. But remember: When it comes to picking a favorite, it's your taste that counts, so try them both and see what you like best.

— Carlos Souffront, former cheesemonger at Zingerman's Delicatessen, Ann Arbor, Michigan (***culture:** the word on cheese*, Spring 2011)

## *Mold-ripened: Wrinkly soft cheeses*

Floral and perfumy, these cheeses range from having a chalky texture when young that evolves, becoming fluffy and gooey as the cheese ripens. They're made using *Geotrichum candidum*, a mold that lends a distinctively sweet flavor and often encourages a wrinkly rind to form on the cheese itself.

> ✔ **La Tur:** This small, surface-ripened round is a delectably creamy blend of cow, sheep, and goat milk from Northern Italy's Piedmont region. Beneath its delicate, wrinkly rind lies a mousse-like ivory paste redolent of crème fraiche, mushrooms, and grass, with a faintly tangy finish.

- ✔ **St. Marcellin:** These discs of surface-ripened cow milk cheeses from the Rhône-Alpes region of France have a delightful floral pungency and satiny to soupy ivory paste. When young, they're traditionally sold in little ceramic ramekins so that they can be heated before serving, if desired. The larger version is called St. Felicien.

- ✔ **Bonne Bouche:** This wrinkly-rinded, ash-coated goat milk disc from Vermont Butter & Cheese Creamery is soft and gooey when ready to eat, with a tangy, goaty pungency.

These cheeses are subtle, so serving them with anything too strong or complex will overpower their delicate flavor and texture. Plain crackers or a baguette are good choices, along with fresh fruit, preserves, and toasted nuts. Pilsner or a fragrant white wine like Gewurztraminer or Riesling are ideal for a beverage pairing.

# A Semi-Softie at Heart

Semi-soft, as we mentioned earlier, isn't a style of cheese. It's a textural category — just like soft or hard. But we're including semi-soft cheeses here to differentiate them from the very soft cheeses that we discuss earlier, because the term *semi-soft* is commonly used in the cheese world. Semi-soft cheeses have a pliable interior that's malleable enough for you to leave an indentation with your finger, but not without some resistance. The style — meaning what type of rind these cheeses have and how they've been produced — can vary. You'll see semi-soft cheeses that have no rind formation (that is, they're *rindless*), or they have natural, washed, or coated or treated rinds.

In the following sections, we provide examples of some popular semi-soft beauties, classified by their style (foremost) and flavor.

## Pressed, brined, and dry-salted fresh semi-soft cheeses

In brining, a cheese is soaked in an acidified saltwater solution to inhibit bacterial growth (basically, brining is a preservation method from the days before refrigeration). That's why brined cheese in bulk is still stored in its liquid. Packaged fetas are sealed in plastic so they won't oxidize and develop (unwanted) bacteria and mold. Brined cheeses like feta range from creamy to crumbly in texture.

Many pressed cheeses, in addition to being weighted down to expel excess moisture, are also brined and dry-salted to extract even more liquid. This process gives them their dry, loose, or firmer texture. Others are simply dry-salted. All of these cheeses can be made from whole milk or whey, and most have a fairly high salt content.

The most popular varieties include the following:

- **Feta:** This most ubiquitous of brined cheeses is native to Greece, but other countries such as Bulgaria, Turkey, France, Israel, and the United States also produce feta. True feta, however, is a PDO (Protected Designation of Origin) product, must come from specific regions in Greece, and must be made from sheep milk or a controlled percentage (70 percent) of goat milk. Other countries sometimes use cow milk, as well, but by law, feta made in other countries has to be designated as "Feta Style" to differentiate it from Greek Feta.

    Don't empty the brine out of your feta container. Keep the cheese refrigerated and in brine, which helps to preserve its shelf life and keep it at optimum quality.

- **Ricotta salata:** Unlike fresh ricotta, this cow, goat, or sheep milk cheese is ricotta that's aged and pressed to make it firm so that it can be used for grating or shaving over food. You can also grill it like Halloumi (we introduce you to this cheese in the next section).

- **Cotija:** This Mexican cow milk cheese ranges from moist to dry and very crumbly. In general, the drier it is, the saltier. Cotija is used in many traditional dishes including soups, salads, beans, *chile rellenos,* and *antojitos* (fried masa dough snacks).

As the name suggests, brined and pressed cheeses are salty and best used as garnishes. They add a zesty flavor to salads, grain or vegetable dishes, or pasta. If you use one of these cheeses in a recipe, go easy on the salt; you can always add more later on.

## I'm (not) melting! Fresh semi-soft cheeses that stay in shape

Cheese that doesn't melt? How is that possible? Some cheeses don't melt because of their acidity level, which affects the chemical composition of the cheese. Cheeses that are either very high or very low in acid don't melt. Most of the cheeses in this category are of a definitive ethnic origin (Greek, Indian, and Mexican, for example) and have specific applications in their respective cuisines:

- **Queso blanco:** This soft, mild Mexican cow milk cheese ranges from creamy to dry and crumbly in texture. It's an *acid-coagulated* (or acid-set) cheese, meaning that vinegar, lemon juice, or another acidic ingredient is used to set the curd, rather than rennet. Queso blanco is used as a filling or garnish, or pan-fried.

- **Halloumi:** This firm Cypriot (from Cyprus; although it's also made in Greece) goat or sheep milk cheese is traditionally served as a snack or dessert.

  Fried Halloumi drizzled with honey is a delicious treat; dredge it lightly in flour before pan-frying, or skip the dredging and just brush the cheese lightly with olive oil before placing it on a hot grill.

- **Paneer:** Fluid milk plays a role in Indian cuisine, primarily desserts. But this firm, unsalted, acid-set cheese is popular in both sweet and savory dishes. Paneer is used in curries and other saucy preparations and in desserts made with flavored simple syrups, such as rosewater.

Non-melting cheeses are ideal if you're looking for something that retains its shape on the grill or in a sauté pan, or as a textural garnish for soups, salads, curries, or stews.

## Semi-soft rindless cheeses full of buttery flavors

Texture and a rich, full flavor with a distinct buttery quality unite the cheeses in this group. They're classic table cheeses, meaning they're often served before or after a meal, but they're far more versatile than that. Sometimes these cheeses are airlocked in plastic or wax to slow down aging and molding. Here are two of our favorites:

- **Young Asiago (also known as Asiago Pressato):** From Italy's Veneto region, Asiago is usually consumed after it's been aged at least 9 months, when it's classified as a hard natural rind cheese. Young Asiago, however, is sold when it's less than 3 months of age, is rindless and white, and has a chewy, slightly dry texture, and mild, mozzarella-like flavor.

- **Pecorino fresco:** Most regions of Italy produce a version of this fresh, young (up to 3 months; *fresco* means "fresh") sheep milk cheese. Pecorino fresco has a texture ranging from stretchy (like mozzarella) to fairly dry, but it always has a mild, slightly sweet flavor.

These young cheeses love fruit, fresh or dried. They also go well with salumi, as long as the meat isn't too fatty. You can also use young Asiago and pecorino fresco as table and snacking cheeses and for melting, grating, sandwiches, macaroni and cheese, or casseroles.

## Down to earth: Mushroomy, grassy-tasting semi-softs

Savory just means the opposite of sweet, but cheeses with these flavor profiles tend to be described as mushroomy, nutty, barnyard, grassy, hay-like, sheepy or goaty (assuming that's the milk they're made from), vegetal, herbaceous, musty, or meaty. They're often rustic cheeses (frequently described as *farmhouse* style) with natural rinds that may be off-white, gray, tan, or yellowish. Their interiors range from pure white to creamy or bright yellow.

If you want the real deal, try one of these two cheeses:

- **Gorwydd Caerphilly:** This traditionally made Caerphilly is a natural-rind, Welsh farmhouse cheese made with cow milk. The cheese itself is slightly sour and crumbly and has a white-to-ivory color. The same style of cheese was eaten for lunch by coal miners, because its high salt content helped replace what the miners lost during long hours of hard, physical labor. Industrial or young Caerphilly is nothing like the real thing and is rindless.
- **Tomme de Savoie:** This smooth, fudgy French cow milk cheese has notes of mushroom and cellar, with a grayish to tan natural rind mottled with different natural molds. It hails from the Savoie region, on the eastern border near Switzerland.

Like their buttery counterparts, earthy, rustic cheeses are lovely with fruit, as long as it isn't too delicate (avoid apricots or berries, for example, and go for dried fruit, apples, pears, and grapes), or chutney. When paired with cured meats, these cheeses can stand up to something with a bit more assertiveness: Think salt and spice.

## Semi-soft washed rinds

These cheeses emit some signature pungency, and their rinds may be orange, pinkish, or gray, with ivory to yellow paste. These are masculine cheeses, with some stink and meaty flavors. All are washed with salt brine unless otherwise noted.

- **Reblochon:** A washed-rind cow milk cheese from the Franche-Comté region of France, this cheese has a semi-soft, pliable-to-spreadable texture. The rind may be white to light orange, with an ivory paste and mild, nutty aroma and flavor. Its pasteurized version is Délice du Jura.

- **Chimay:** This semi-soft cow milk cheese is made by the Trappist brewing monasteries of Belgium, just across the French border. It's washed in Chimay ale, which gives it a mild and nutty flavor, with an aftertaste of yeast and hops.

- **Taleggio:** The bumpy, sticky, pungent, orange-colored rind on this flat, square cheese from Italy's Val Taleggio region belies its soft interior, rich with flavors of fruit and cream.

- **Limburger:** Good quality versions of this German cheese are more subtly flavored, while domestic versions, like Leiderkranz (Wisconsin), are stronger, so choose according to your palate's propensity for funk. In general, these cheeses are semi-soft, supple, and pungent (too much so, for some people), with intensely rich, creamy interiors.

- **Pont l'Évêque:** A creamy, rich, pungent cow milk cheese with a distinct beefy flavor. This ancient French cheese from dairy-centric Normandy can be eaten as-is or heated in a small ramekin for dipping bread.

Fruit, a baguette, some Parisian-style ham, and a glass of rosé. You just saved yourself the cost of a plane ticket to France! For a savory supper, try pumpernickel bread, grainy mustard, cornichons (tiny gherkin pickles), pickled onions, and cured meats or a rustic pate. Serve with hoppy IPA (India pale ale), light pilsner, lambic, or other fruity beer.

## Limburger in American lit!

So legendary is Limburger's pungency that even Mark Twain was moved to write a short narrative about it, called "The Invalid's Story." In it, the protagonist is asked to take the train so that he may transport the body of his recently deceased childhood friend back home for burial. Unbeknownst to the narrator, the wooden box containing the corpse is mistakenly switched out for one full of rifles; an added complication is an unlabeled crate of Limburger placed on top of the munitions box/coffin.

The cheese begins to warm up during the journey, creating "a most evil and searching odor." Things get so bad that even the veteran expressman sharing the carriage is moved to say, "I've carried a many a one of 'em — some of 'em considerable overdue, too, — but lordy, he just lays over 'em all! — and does it easy Cap., they was heliotrope to HIM!"

Love it or hate it, there's no denying Limburger's reputation.

# Feeling Blue

You won't find any gray area with these punchy babies. People either love them or hate them, but we maintain that the haters just haven't been introduced to a really great blue.

Blues are made via the introduction of molds from the genus *Penicillum roqueforti,* which are normally added to the milk toward the beginning of the cheese-making process. After the wheels have been formed, they are *needled* — pierced throughout to form tiny holes. The holes allow air into the cheese, which reacts with the enzymes and bacteria and creates the characteristic "veins" and pockets that are the hallmark of blue cheese. ***Note:*** Needling isn't always done. Sometimes the air between the curd is enough to "blue" the cheese or, rarely, the blue mold is added to the cheese's rind.

Whether a blue cheese is softer or more firm has to do with moisture, but just because a blue is soft and creamy doesn't mean that it's mild, nor is a crumbly blue always assertive in flavor. Almost all blues fall under the soft or semi-soft categories, however. If the blue cheese has been pressed or aged longer in open air, it will be drier. In the following sections, we categorize blues into flavor categories rather than by texture or rind, note which are softer and which are more crumbly in the description, and provide serving suggestions.

## Mellow blues

These cheeses have a definite blue flavor but are fairly subtle. Even those who are not into blues might like these cheeses:

- ✔ **Blue Castello:** Rich, buttery, and very spreadable with big, blue veins, this is a triple crème made in Denmark. It's ideal for "new to blue" tasters because it's mild and minus traditionally assertive blue flavors.

- ✔ **Gorgonzola Dolce:** Sweeter, milder, and creamier than its earthy counterpart (see the section "High octane blues"), this young cow milk cheese is one of the most recognizable blues around. It's produced in Italy's dairy-rich Lombardy region.

- ✔ **Cambozola:** A cheesemonger we know likes to refer to this soft, decadent blue as "the love-child of Gorgonzola and a bloomy-rind triple crème." And indeed, that was the thought behind this Bavarian invention of the 1970s. If you're not a fan of blue, this extra-mild, creamy creation just might change your mind.

Pair these cheeses with some honeycomb, toasted nuts, and sliced seasonal or dried fruit (think peaches, apples, or pears), and you have an elegant final course that will impress your guests. Serve with a sweeter dessert wine like Sauternes.

## Blues with attitude

Not too mild and not too strong...just right! These blues are the middle of the intensity scale when it comes to flavor. They run the gamut of texture, from creamy to crumbly:

- **Stilton:** One of the United Kingdom's most famous cheeses, Stilton is a pale-yellow cow milk blue cheese. The most famous variety is produced by Colston-Bassett, near the Nottinghamshire border. Fairly crumbly and with a natural rind, it has earthy, spicy, minerally flavors.

- **St. Agur:** This octagonally-shaped cow milk blue cheese from France's Auvergne region is notable for its moist, creamy texture and mottled, creamy color. Despite the pronounced veining, this cheese isn't overly pungent, although it does have a good amount of salt and a full-fat, buttery paste (*Note:* It's a double crème).

- **Bleu d'Auvergne:** Also from France's Auvergne region, this user-friendly cow milk blue has a yellow-white paste, a medium dry texture that holds together well, and an earthy, mushroomy flavor.

- **Maytag Blue:** Made by *that* Maytag family, this cow milk American classic from Iowa is clean-tasting, milky, and almost waxy in texture. It has a decent bite but nothing too strident, and its paste is bright white with bright blue veins.

- **Caveman Blue:** This cow milk blue from Rogue Creamery is a dense, moist cheese shot through with blue-green veins, and a pale, golden to cream-colored paste. Caveman Blue is a great blue for those past the "I don't like blues" stage because of its creamy texture and appealing notes of caramel and toasted nuts, with a hint of spice.

- **Original Blue:** Made from the milk of Holstein cows that graze on the lush coastal pastures at Northern California's Point Reyes Farmstead Cheese, this sweet, milky blue with a bright white paste has a creamy texture and an earthy bite. It's just as good crumbled on salads as it is on a burger or steak.

Enjoy these cheeses with savory accompaniments like prosciutto or other hams and olives for a pre-dinner cheese plate, or pair them with deeply flavored dried fruit such as pears, figs, or dates for a memorable dessert plate.

## High octane blues

Stronger blues can be described as minerally, earthy, footy, sheepy, barnyard, salty, grassy, toasty, beefy, or spicy — depending on milk type, *terroir* (soil/environment), and how the cheese is made and aged.

We recommend the following for those with a bad case of the blues:

- **Roquefort:** True Roquefort is a PDO cheese made from the milk of the Lacaune sheep and aged in the local caves at Roquefort-sur-Soulzon in southern France. Potent, earthy, sheepy, creamy, and dreamy, with pungent, salty veins, and a rough, mottled grayish rind, Roquefort is one of the world's most famous cheeses. There are several top makers; try a few different ones to see which you prefer.

- **Gorgonzola Piccante:** Both types of this cow milk cheese (Gorgonzola Dolce is a sweet, creamy version; see the earlier section "Mellow blues") originate from Lombardy, in northern Italy. Gorgonzola Piccante is earthy and spicy with a dense, sometimes crumbly or slightly dry paste.

- **Cabrales:** The crown jewel of Spanish cheeses, Cabrales is one of the most distinctive and assertive blue cheeses around. Though traditionally made with a mix of raw cow, sheep, and goat milk (the most sought-after), today's Cabrales is more commonly made solely from cow milk (sheep and goat milk is only available seasonally). This DOP cheese is wrapped in maple leaves and aged for 2 to 6 months in the caves of the region, although most that arrive in the United States have natural rinds and are foil-wrapped. Cabrales can be soft or firm and bone-white, gray, or dark brown in color. All are accepted versions of the cheese, made to suit the varying tastes of consumers. Regardless of appearance, when fully ripe, Cabrales packs a punch, with spicy, salty flavors, a smooth paste dotted throughout with crystallization, and robust pockets of blue. Not for the faint of heart — and oh, so good.

You can serve these cheeses just as you would the drier versions introduced in the earlier sections, but they're especially nice crumbled on salads, roasted beets, or root vegetables, or onto a juicy steak.

# Chapter 4

# Grate Tastes: Hard Cheeses

*In This Chapter*

▶ Introducing hard cheeses

▶ Reviewing rind styles of hard cheeses

▶ Discovering some notable hard cheeses

**W**e need to come clean. As much as we love soft cheeses (which we praise in Chapter 3), we're just as partial to their more-aged cousins. Although soft cheeses such as ricotta and mozzarella are more blatantly and immediately expressive of an animal's milk, some hard cheeses are the sensory equivalent of a jar of summer fruit preserves on a dreary winter's day.

Just like soft cheeses, hard cheeses are most commonly made from cow, sheep, or goat milk and have a range of textures and styles and an equally diverse array of flavors. They can be dry, brittle, crumbly, supple, moist, smoky, stinky, grassy, sharp, mellow, earthy, tangy, or buttery — but regardless of variety, they're usually extremely versatile.

In this chapter, we introduce you to the different types of rinds and styles that comprise the hard cheese family. To help you navigate the myriad varieties, we break hard cheeses into categories by rind — rindless, natural rind, washed rind, and coated — as well as by flavor.

*Note:* If a cheese has a particular designation, we include that designation in our discussion. For a quick review of what the different acronyms mean, refer to Chapter 2.

# Hard to Beat: Understanding the Basics

Although soft cheeses are more varied in style, type, and production method, hard cheeses are often more layered in flavor and texture. Hard cheeses made from peak-season milk can have intensely rich, complex flavor profiles that evoke the lush pasture the animals grazed upon at the time. They're like a cheese time capsule!

Hard cheeses are excellent for the table or on a cheese platter, but this group also boasts some of your best cooking, baking, grating, and melting choices. That said, some hard cheeses have such stunning flavor, heating them would be a shame.

Hard cheeses may be classified as semi-firm, firm, or aged in texture. Here's what you need to know about these classifications:

- **Semi-firm:** Contains the highest moisture content of the hard cheese category; if you press your finger on its surface, it won't leave an indentation, but the cheese may still be supple, pliant, and have a slightly moist texture. *Note:* This term is subjective and often used interchangeably with the term *semi-soft* (see Chapter 3), which can get confusing. There is, however, a subtle difference.

- **Firm:** More-aged and less malleable to the touch than the previous category, firm cheeses are sometimes cooked and pressed (or just pressed) to help expel excess moisture. They are, literally, firm — not pliable.

- **Aged:** Aged cheeses are also hard, but they have less moisture due to longer aging (an example is an Italian *grana* style, such as Parmigiano Reggiano or other granular grating cheese, discussed in Chapter 11). Their texture may be brittle, dry, flakey, or shard-like. Some styles, like an aged Gouda, may still retain a buttery, caramelly quality.

## Listen to your elders: Why some cheeses are aged longer than others

The expulsion of moisture during the cheese-making process via cooking and pressing results in a cheese with a dry texture that's suitable for aging (the moisture level is what can encourage growth of unwanted molds and cause other problems as a cheese ages). Cheeses are aged because that process — under specific environmental conditions — enables them to develop a rind and specific flavors. In general, the longer a cheese is aged, the harder and sharper or more intensely flavored it becomes.

Cheese was originally matured as a way to preserve surplus milk produced during certain times of the year (mainly summer) so that it could be used as a food source during the leaner months. That philosophy still holds true in some areas of the developing world, such as parts of Eastern Europe and Central Asia (see Chapters 13 and 14). Among modern cheesemakers, aging is much more likely to be based on the traditions of cheese production (particularly in Europe), the whims of the cheesemaker, or the seasonal requirements (drying goats or sheep off during the winter months so they stop lactating, which gives their bodies — and the milker and/or cheesemaker — a chance to rest).

Compared to soft cheeses, which have a higher moisture content and thus shorter shelf life, hard cheeses — especially aged natural-rind varieties — are a practical and economical choice. If stored correctly (see Chapter 7 for more about storing cheese), you can generally keep a hunk of hard cheese for up to several weeks (although we're not sure how anyone can resist for that long!).

Regardless of their classification, *hard* doesn't mean difficult. These cheeses are easy to love. Trust us.

If a hard cheese smells sour or ammoniated, try setting it out on the counter to air for an hour or so without its wrapper. Use a sharp knife to shave the surface you plan to eat, removing any visible shine or sheen. Spots of blue-green or whitish mold are harmless and can be scraped away or cut off. These "triage" measures usually solve the problem. If the cheese still smells and tastes off — sour or astringent — chuck it.

# Going Topless: A Rundown of Rindless Hard Cheeses

Some cheeses aren't aged long enough to develop a rind, but they're usually soft varieties, such as fresh robiolas or Stracchino di Crescenza. With regard to hard cheeses, this category generally refers to varieties such as block cheddar, Monterey Jack, and colby (which may or may not be industrially made) that have been aged without exposure to air (that is, in plastic). While quality varies, these are economical "everyday" cheeses, suitable for snacking, cooking, or melting — and there are plenty of excellent brands to choose from.

## It's better buttery and mild

Cheeses that have a buttery quality or sweetness to them haven't been enhanced with additives. Rather, *lactase*, the natural sugar in the milk (refer to Chapter 2) gives them their buttery property. Seasonality, terroir (also discussed in Chapter 2), species of animal/breed, what the animals have been eating, production method, and style are the other factors that influence why a cheese might have a buttery texture and mouthfeel or predominantly sweet flavor, rather than tasting nutty or tangy. The same factors that influence the sweetness of a cheese can also affect its richness. "Rich" is a characteristic of texture and flavor. A rich cheese feels full on the palate; the butterfat literally coats your mouth.

Here are a couple of the most popular buttery, rich, semi-firm rindless cheeses:

- ✔ **Havarti (semi-firm):** This Danish favorite is a popular table cheese, but it's also used for slicing and melting. Ivory to pale yellow in color with small eyes, it has a smooth, pliable paste (it's sometimes classified as a semi-soft cheese), with flavor ranging from mild to slightly sharp. It's often flavored with herbs or spices such as dill or caraway.

- ✔ **Monterey Jack (semi-firm):** This California classic is perhaps the most well-known unprocessed cheese from America. White or ivory in color, with a smooth, creamy consistency and mild-to-slightly sour flavor, Jack is one of the most versatile cheeses in terms of use and preparation method. Few cheeses are better for melting. It's often flavored with aromatics such as hot peppers or spices. (***Note:*** There are also cave-aged Jacks — natural or man-made — with rinds that range from hard to aged. These are not included here.)

These cheeses are classic snacking, sandwich, and melting cheeses. Because they hold up well and aren't strongly flavored, they're also ideal for large party platters.

## *Going mild for rindless cheeses*

Although some rindless cheeses such as block cheddar can be sharp (possessing some bite), this category is dedicated to milder cheeses that can be found at many supermarkets. Like all cheeses, even in block form, the older it gets, the stronger or sharper it gets. The primary difference in flavor is that, unlike a buttery variety, they don't leave that rich, milky feeling on the palate. No matter: We always have a brick of cheddar in the fridge for nibbling and cooking.

- ✔ **Block cheddar, 6 months or younger (semi-firm):** This is the standard (commodity) cheddar you find in nearly every refrigerator case in the country. The quality, sharpness, and color may vary — some are dyed bright orange with annatto seed (a by-product of the tropical achiote shrub that is used as dye for various food products) — but they're a good, affordable option when you want an inexpensive snacking, party, or cooking cheese.

- ✔ **Colby (semi-firm):** Colby, which was developed in Wisconsin in the late 1800s, is an American original. This cow milk supermarket staple is bright orange (because it's colored with annatto) or light yellow. It's reminiscent of mild cheddar, with a faintly sour tang at the finish.

These cheeses are great for snacking, sandwiches, burgers, macaroni and cheese, or other hearty main dishes.

If you want a sharp rindless cheese rather than a milder one, go for a more aged variety. Producers in New York, Vermont, Wisconsin, Oregon, and Canada all make excellent rindless sharp cheddars.

# Looking at Natural-Rind Hard Cheeses

Natural rinds develop organically on all cheeses if left to themselves, without the addition of bacteria or mold to the milk or curd, but this particular style of cheese is intentionally exposed to air as it ages, so the rind forms as part of a controlled aging process. Natural-rind cheeses are usually wiped or patted down by hand, sometimes using olive oil, butter, or lard to prevent cracking. Examples of natural rind hard cheeses include most Basque cheeses, but there are a multitude of others.

## Buttery cheeses with natural rinds

Natural rind cheeses can be creamy, sharp, earthy, or tangy. We find it impossible to play favorites, but it's hard to dislike a cheese with a buttery texture and flavor. The full, rich mouthfeel is a pleasing contrast against salty foods, a bitter ale, or crisp white wine. Here are a few of our favorites:

- ✔ **Carmody (semi-firm to firm):** Crafted by California's Bellwether Farms, this cow milk cheese is produced in two versions: Carmody, which is pasteurized and aged for 6 weeks, and Carmody Reserve, which is raw milk and aged for 4 months. Both have a rich, buttery taste, but Carmody is more buttery in flavor and springy in texture, while Carmody Reserve is more dense and dry with tangy, grassy notes.

- ✔ **Ossau-Iraty (firm):** This smooth, supple PDO sheep milk cheese is from the French Pyrenees. It's sweet and nutty, with an earthiness that is more noticeable in cheeses made during the winter. Wheels made from summer milk have more grassy, floral notes.

These cheeses are crowd-pleasers; mild, rich, and easy to pair with a variety of foods or beverages. Pair them with fruit and toasted nuts, but they're equally nice shaved onto a salad that incorporates sweet or savory elements. You can also shave them atop grilled asparagus or other vegetables, or grate some atop potatoes that have been sautéed with leeks or green garlic and pop under the broiler until golden. See? Versatile!

## *Earthy natural-rind delights*

One of the most common flavor profiles — particularly in goat and sheep milk cheeses — is *earthy,* meaning reminiscent of fresh soil, mushrooms, and forest. Herbaceous, grassy, hay, or vegetal flavors may also fall under this category. Think of these cheeses as a savory counterpart to rich, creamy, buttery cheeses. They make a nice choice for a pre-dinner cheese plate, paired with salumi or olives.

The following are down-to-earth classics:

- **Garrotxa (firm):** Garrotxa is a Catalonian (Spain) goat cheese aged between 3 and 4 months. These 2-plus-pound wheels have a bone-white interior; thin, grey rind; and a firm, smooth, slightly supple texture with occasional small holes. The flavors are mildly herbal and earthy, with a hint of hazelnuts.

- **Cantal (firm):** This PDO-designated cheese from the Auvergne region of France is made from the milk of the Salers breed of cow. These cows are fed on hay from November 15 to April 15, during which time Cantal is produced. The summer milk from the same cows grazing on mountain pastures is used to makes Salers — named in honor of the breed. Cantal has a tangy, buttery flavor reminiscent of cheddar but more moist and crumbly.

These savory cheeses really lend themselves toward pairings with cured meat, country-style bread, and lightly dressed greens to round out the meal. Alternatively, serve them with a hearty soup for a cold-weather comfort food repast.

## What's the difference between Parmigiano Reggiano and Parmesan?

The noble Parmigiano Reggiano cheese — one of the finest in the world — has been produced by hand according to nearly the same methods since the Middle Ages. Parmigiano Reggiano is such a valuable commodity that some cheese storage vaults are managed by banks, which keep them as collateral for dairies to which they have provided loans.

To protect the product and avoid consumer confusion, all similar cheeses within the European Union and other parts of the world must be marketed as "Parmesan." Although other excellent *grana* cheese exist, including Italy's Grana Padano, none have Parmigiano's heritage.

# *Natural-rind nutty cheeses*

Perhaps the most familiar category of natural-rind hard cheeses are those with nutty flavors: alpine styles such as Comté, Italian *grana* ("grating") cheeses, and pecorinos. They're versatile, delicious, and a good choice for entertaining because they serve dual-purpose on the cheese plate and in the kitchen. Bonus: You can save the rinds (as long as you remember to remove the paper labels) to enrich soups and stews.

- ✔ **Piave (semi-firm to firm):** From the Dolomite Mountains of Italy's Veneto region, Piave is a DOP pasteurized cow milk cheese typically sold at three different ages:

  - **Fresh** (*fresco*), 1 to 2 months

  - **Medium** (*mezzano*), 3 to 4 months

  - **Aged** (*vecchio*), 6 to 12 months

  For the purposes of this chapter, we're referring to the latter two. The texture is dense, smooth, and firm, becoming harder as the cheese matures. The interior is a rich, butter-yellow color, with a full-bodied flavor and notes of citrus and butterscotch.

- ✔ **Pecorino Toscano (firm):** Though used at all ages (from fresh to very aged, for grating) this Italian cheese has a distinctively nutty flavor and aroma when aged between 3 to 6 months. All pecorinos are made from sheep milk, and Pecorino Toscano has held its own DOP since 1996.

- ✔ **Comté (firm):** This buttery, rich, slightly sweet and supple PDO alpine cow milk cheese from the Jura Mountains of France (just over the Swiss border) is made in 110-pound wheels. Fortunately, your cheesemonger or shop will do the heavy labor for you, so all you need to worry about is how big a chunk to buy (hint: more than you think you need, as you'll find this one of the most versatile cheeses around). It has a dry, beige-brown rind and pliable interior, and is a great melter as well as a table cheese.

Ultra user-friendly, these types of cheese are good for table, snacking, parties, baking, cooking, melting, and grating. Comté is also a good substitute for Gruyère (as are other Swiss mountain cheeses).

# *Bursting with flavor: Sharp natural-rind cheeses*

A sharp cheese has bite to it. These cheeses may be described as zesty, horseradishy, or pungent, and they can pack a wallop. Sheep and goat milk cheeses in particular get more sharp and intense as they age, because the inherent qualities of the milk are amplified as the moisture content reduces. If you love bright, punchy flavors, these are for you:

- **Parmigiano Reggiano (aged):** This Italian "king of cheeses" from Emilia Romagna is revered for its nutty, fruity flavor; sweet aroma; and pale golden, granular paste (it's a classic *grana* style, which refers to hard, grainy, grating cheeses) flecked with white spots. Pesto, risotto, pasta, *frico* (fried or melted into a lacy disk) — the uses for this famous cow milk cheese are many.

  Parmigiano Reggiano is a DOP cheese from Emilia-Romana (specifically, the provinces of Reggio-Emilia, Parma, Modena, and parts of Bologna and Mantua). The name Parmigiano Reggiano can be applied only to cheese made from this region, using specific breeds of cows fed a specific diet in a specific way. See the sidebar "What's the difference between Parmigiano Reggiano and Parmesan?" for details on why this cheese is so special.

- **Pecorino Romano (aged):** The most famous Italian sheep milk cheese is also sold younger, but when hard, it's an off-white colored wheel with a thick, hard rind that's often coated. Though its name shows where it originated (Rome), most producers have moved to the island of Sardinia. Shaved or grated, this cheese adds a salty, tangy punch to pasta or vegetables.

- **Grana Padano (aged):** This *grana* cheese, similar to Parmigiano Reggiano, is another important staple of the Italian diet. Made only with skimmed milk, this DOP cheese is produced in parts of Emilia-Romagna, Lombardy, Piedmont, Trentino, and Veneto — an area that is at least twice the size of the production area for Parmigiano Reggiano. Thus the cows used to produce Grano Padano graze on pastures with a more varied terroir, resulting in versions of the cheese that possess subtle nuances in its flavor.

- **Mimolette (aged):** This flaming-orange French fireball from Pas-de-Calais and Normandy has a hard, craggy, gray rind and distinctive round shape. It may look like a rock (and be about as hard to cut) when aged, but its waxy, bright interior is smooth, with a nutty finish inspired by Dutch Edam. Its earthy sweetness increases with age.

All cheeses in this category add a zesty kick when grated or shaved atop savory dishes like pasta, casseroles, soups, or salads.

# Washed-rind and Wonderful Cheeses

Salt brine, wine, beer, and spirits are all used to "wash" various cheeses so that specific bacteria form and flourish, traditionally resulting in a *stinky* cheese. The rind is usually reddish and sticky with a distinct sulfurous or footy odor. The interior is less intense-smelling. Soft washed rinds (Chapter 3) become gooey with meaty, yeasty flavors. With more aged, harder washed rinds, the cheeses become seriously nutty and earthy.

While many washed-rind cheeses are soft, others are firmer like Morbier (semi-firm) or Gruyère (firm). Technically, these are *smear-ripened* cheeses (see Chapter 2), meaning they've been smeared with a solution of bacteria or fungi, giving the cheese a stronger flavor as it ages.

## Nice and nutty

Whether you realize it or not, these are some of the world's most well-known cheeses. Frequently (and incorrectly) called "Swiss" cheese, many in this category are alpine cheeses (see Chapter 13) that hail from not just Switzerland but Italy, Austria, Germany, and France. Some, like Gruyère, Fontina, or Comté are washed with brine (thus, they're washed rind or smear-ripened), but they also have natural rinds and are often classified as such. Washing them adds great depth of flavor and character, and heightens their nuttiness. Others, like Emmentaler, aren't washed but still have nutty flavors — and require the use of similar cultures during the cheesemaking process.

Our favorite alpine delights follow:

- ✔ **Gruyère (firm):** This Swiss alpine classic beauty is complex and versatile. It has a slightly tacky, tan-colored rind and is sweet and nutty with oniony or meaty undertones. A good Gruyère should be cave-aged for at least 9 months and will be labeled as such.

- ✔ **Fontina val d'Aosta (semi-firm):** Produced in the Aosta Valley of Italy, this DOP cow milk cheese dates back to the Middle Ages. The rind is thin, with a slightly pungent aroma and ranges from orange to dark brown. The pale yellow interior is smooth, dense, and supple, with occasional holes, and savory notes of fruit, grass, and earth. (***Note:*** Danish Fontina is an entirely different cheese with a waxed rind.)

- ✔ **Beaufort (firm):** This cow milk cheese from the Haute-Savoie region of southwestern France is aged for at least 6 months so that the flavors can concentrate. It has a slightly sticky, mildly pungent, tan-to-russet-colored rind. The interior is savory and herbaceous, with notes of grass, butter, and salt.

These cheeses are ideal for snacking, cheese plates (especially with fruit or *charcuterie,* cured meat products that include sausages, ham, bacon, or salumi), or melting, grating, or sandwiches. Gruyère is a classic melting cheese, most notably for fondue (it may also be substituted for Raclette cheese — see the next section).

## Slightly stinky cheeses

If seriously smelly cheeses are your thing, you may want to head to Chapter 3 for some suggestions. But if a bit of funk is to your liking, the following will add a bit of zip to your meals and baked goods:

- **Raclette (semi-firm):** Raclette cheeses are traditionally produced in four different valleys in Switzerland's Valais region. Aged for up to 1 year, Raclette has a silky paste with a faint aroma of earth and a full, milky flavor.

  Traditionally, a half wheel would be propped up in front of the fireplace; once the surface had begun to blister, a *racler* (scraper) was used to scoop the cheese into bowls filled with boiled potatoes. You can purchase a racler from specialty kitchenware stores or websites, such as Williams-Sonoma (www.williams-sonoma.com/), or from some cheese shops. Makes winter welcome!

- **Morbier (semi-firm):** Morbier is a PDO-designated cow milk cheese from the Franche-Comté region of France. It has a sticky rind with a pungent aroma, while the supple interior is a creamy straw color, with small holes ("eyes"); flavors are redolent of grass and earth.

  After cheesemaking had finished for the day, any remaining curd from Morbier production would have a layer of ash sprinkled on top to prevent a rind from forming and ward off unwanted bacteria. The next day the remaining day's curd would be placed on top of the ash to "complete" the cheese. Today, the ash is purely decorative. You can find Morbier at larger grocery stores, as well as specialty cheese shops.

Raclette can be used in the same manner as the other alpine cheeses mentioned in this chapter: for melting, baking, cooking, snacking, and as a table cheese. Morbier is a popular addition to cheese plates and works well paired with fruit.

# Trying Out Coated-rind and Clothbound Hard Cheeses

Wrapping, waxing, or coating a cheese (with butter, oil, or lard) is a way of discouraging unwanted molds from developing on the rind, as well as protecting it from drying out and cracking. The wax used on cheese is a special, non-edible but food-safe wax that remains flexible over time and allows the cheese to breathe as it ages.

## Currying flavor: Cheeses with spiced up rinds

Many cheesemakers like to personalize their cheeses (both soft and hard) by rubbing the rind with, or rolling a fresh cheese in, everything from espresso powder or cocoa to tomato paste, herbs, or spices. Sometimes it works; sometimes it doesn't. A successful example is Barely Buzzed from Utah's Beehive Cheese Co. This unusual cow milk cheddar is rubbed with finely ground coffee and French lavender before aging. Sounds bizarre, but the flavor combination works. The end results are butterscotch, caramel, and floral notes that play beautifully against the buttery, slightly tangy cheese.

Other successful domestic examples are Vella Cheese Company's Dry Jack, coated with unsweetened cocoa mixed with cracked black peppercorns and vegetable oil, and Mezzo Secco, a "half-dry" version of the former. Brin d'Amour (or Fleur de Maquis), a semi-firm sheep milk cheese from Corsica, is coated with indigenous wild herbs that are the same as those the sheep graze upon — rosemary, savory, and thyme (these are grown in terrain known as the *maquis*). Now *that's* terroir!

Whether or not these cheeses are good is in the taste buds of the beholder. At the end of the day, it comes down to the quality of the milk and the skill (and palate) of the cheesemaker. Do a trial run before serving these spiced up cheeses at your next dinner party (some can clash with wine or beer), but do have fun experimenting!

## *Coated-rind cheeses with a nutty flavor*

As we mention in the earlier section "Nice and nutty," not all alpine cheeses are washed-rind varieties (see Emmentaler in the following list). Think of these as widely available, mellow crowd pleasers, ideal for entertaining, snacking, and cooking.

- ✔ **Jarlsberg (semi-firm):** This Norwegian cheese possesses a yellow Plasticoat "rind" (a breathable, non-edible, food grade plastic coating) and a pale yellow paste that is nutty, milky, and buttery, with large, uneven holes. Its texture is supple and somewhat springy.

  Like Emmentaler (explained in the next item in this list), Jarlsberg is a classic for ham and cheese sandwiches, although if you like this combo, you may want to try a washed-rind alpine cheese in its place for a bit more zip.

- ✔ **Emmentaler or Emmental (semi-firm):** This is Swiss cow milk cheese in the classic sense: The smooth, almost waxy, pale-yellow paste is riddled with extra-large holes. Emmentaler has several PDO designations, depending on its age, but its minimum maturing time is 4 months.

- ✔ **Manchego (firm):** Traditionally served as a snack or cheese course with *membrillo* (quince paste), Spain's most popular cheese comes from the La Mancha region. Manchego is a DOC cheese made from the raw or pasteurized milk of Manchego sheep. Young Manchego (aged 6 months or less) is more smooth and supple, and more aged versions (1 to 2 years) are drier with developed nutty and sheepy flavors. The Plasticoat rind has a distinctive herringbone pattern.

## A better cheddar

Cheddar makes everything better! The name of this traditional cow milk cheese refers to both its place of origin (the village of Cheddar, in Somerset, England, although there are also excellent versions now made in the U.S, Canada, Australia, and New Zealand), and its production method, which involves *cheddaring*.

In cheddaring, salt is added to the curds before they are kneaded, cubed, drained of whey, and then stacked and turned. The result is a dense, flavor-packed cheese that ages from 3 to 60 months. For serving, melting is about the only thing cheddar doesn't excel at. As with certain non-melting soft cheeses (refer to Chapter 3), cheddar's acidity level affects the chemical composition needed for it to melt well. If you want it to melt, grate fine or slice it very thinly.

Coated nutty cheeses lend themselves well to just about everything as long as you remove their exterior. Consider Jarlsberg and Emmentaler just right for fondue, macaroni and cheese, open-faced sandwiches (pop them under the broiler for a melty treat), snacking, and party platters. Manchego pairs well with ham (try it with Spanish *jamon* Serrano) or as a salad cheese; shave it atop greens, tossed with dried or fresh fruit, toasted nuts, and a light vinaigrette.

## *Sharp to earthy coated-rind cheeses*

Most cheese lovers can appreciate a good cheddar. In this section, we discuss clothbound (also known as bandage-wrapped) versions. The most commonly associated flavor profiles with this most traditional British cheese (and its international counterparts) are earthy, beefy, nutty qualities. Equally at home paired with sweet or savory accompaniments, we love this category for its versatility, easy availability, and flat-out deliciousness.

Clothbound cheddars aren't natural-rind cheeses even though they appear that way once they're unwrapped. They're considered part of the coated rind category, and they're wrapped to protect the cheese as it ages in a cave or maturation room.

We're fans of the following:

- ✔ **Clothbound/bandage-wrapped cheddars (firm):** The flavor profile of these aged cheddars can vary greatly depending upon the cheese's age, the type of milk used, and where it's from. For example, a 12- to 14-month Montgomery's Cheddar from the United Kingdom is rich, meaty, and robust, with fruity notes and a texture that, while not dry, is somewhat brittle. An 18-month-old wheel will be slightly drier and the flavor sweeter and reminiscent of nuts. By comparison, a 16-month bandage-wrapped cheddar from Fiscalini Farms (California) has buttery, savory notes of earth, fruit, and toast. Cabot Clothbound Cheddar (Vermont), aged for over 12 months, tastes of peanuts, butter, and earth.

✔ **Special Select Dry Jack (firm to aged):** This hard cheese, made by Vella Cheese (California), is cave-aged up to 4 years and coated with unsweetened cocoa mixed with black pepper and vegetable oil. Its flavor changes as it ages, but it's typically mellow, salty, nutty, and rich, with earthy notes. Use it for grating or a cheese plate.

Shave clothbound cheddar onto salads, layer it on sandwiches, or serve it with sliced apples or pears or as a side with soup and some crusty bread. Dry Jack is wonderful served in the same way, but its saltier flavor profile makes it the ideal foil for salumi. You can also grate it onto everything from pasta to eggs. For serving, melting is about the only thing aged cheddar isn't the best for. As with certain non-melting soft cheeses (refer to Chapter 3), its acidity level affects the chemical composition required for it to melt.

## Sweet, butterscotchy coated-rind cheeses

What's *not* to love about an aged cheese reminiscent of caramel, butterscotch, butter, bacon, or smoke, especially if it has a bit of crunch to it? That's what we thought. Tempted? Try the following:

✔ **Aged Gouda (aged):** The longer one of these spectacular Dutch cheeses is aged, the more deep gold, caramelly, butterscotchy, and crunchy it becomes. We recommend Beemster XO, Noord Hollander, and Old Amsterdam, all aged Goudas. For a slightly younger Gouda that's not as brittle, try 12-month-old Prima Donna (firm).

A good Gouda of any age is best enjoyed as-is, with thin slices of tart, crunchy apples, or on a sandwich. Like cheddar, it isn't a melting cheese. You'll find good-quality aged Goudas at cheese shops and better grocery stores.

Of course, hard cheeses are ideal for grating, but we prefer our aged Gouda and similar cheeses in shards, to be enjoyed with slices of crisp apple and toasted nuts. We recommend showcasing it on a cheese plate...although we're not against snacking on chunks whenever we get our hands on them.

# Part II
# Choosing and Serving Cheese

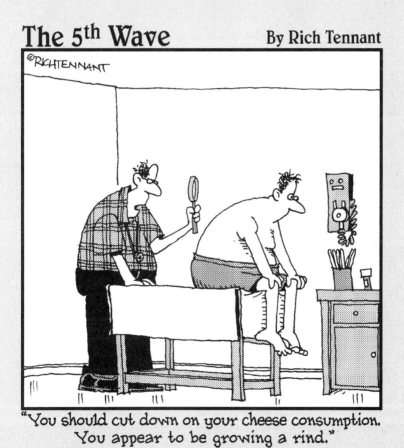

The 5th Wave                    By Rich Tennant

"You should cut down on your cheese consumption. You appear to be growing a rind."

## In this part . . .

Whereas Part I includes fundamental (but let's face it, potentially intimidating) information about cheese, like cheesemaking basics and terminology, styles, and rind types, this part is nothing but fun stuff. Here, you get to put your knowledge to good (tasting) use.

In these chapters, we show you how to use all of your senses to assess and flavor profile cheese so you can discover what you like and don't like, how to purchase cheese (including tips on how to talk to a cheesemonger like a pro), and how to serve and store cheese.

# Chapter 5

# Using the Senses to Taste and Learn about Cheese

*In This Chapter*

▶ Identifying your cheese preferences

▶ Discovering new varieties of cheese

*H*ave you ever tasted a cheese — or other food — that just lit up the pleasure center in your brain? Maybe it was the flavor, texture, or both. Perhaps it was in combination with a condiment or beverage. Whatever it was, the taste was like a little slice of heaven, suffusing you with a feeling of well-being.

We know. It's just cheese. But we believe that eating good food is one of life's greatest — and most humble — pleasures. There's just something about the combination of sweet, milky burrata with a bite of warm-from-the-garden, ripe tomato, or the satiny, hammy, salty goodness of a spoonful of Rush Creek Reserve. Sometimes, cheese is love.

A large part of the pleasure and experience of eating and appreciating cheese is attributable to its sensory components. Tasting any cheese is a combination of aroma, *mouthfeel* (the sensation it has on your palate), texture (dry, crumbly, supple, and so on), and flavor. The physical attributes of a cheese play a role, as well. Some cheeses are beautiful to behold: elegant, dainty, pretty cloaked in their velvety white rind. Others are unattractive: A really ripe Taleggio, for example, has a thick, sticky, orange rind disgorging ivory-colored ooze (absolutely delicious, for the record).

A number of factors contribute to what you may like or dislike about a certain cheese. In this chapter, we explore what those aspects are and how you can apply them to tasting and learning about cheese.

The term *organoleptic* means "relating to qualities (taste, color, odor, and feel) of a substance, such as food." It's not a cheese term per se, but the basic concept is what this chapter is about.

# *Discovering What You Like and Don't Like*

When it comes to choosing, eating, and enjoying cheese, there's no right or wrong way to do it. That said, there's a whole world of cheese out there, and you'd be doing yourself a disservice by sticking to old standbys. We frequently see repeat customers buy the same cheese over and over again because they're crazy about it. Don't get us wrong: We're happy when you adore a cheese. But by trying new things, you just might discover something you love even more.

The key to broadening your cheese horizons and finding new favorites is to figure out just what it is you like in a cheese. The first step is to identify the cheeses — soft or hard — that you love. (Take a look at Chapters 3 and 4 for a variety of cheeses in each of these categories.) Then ask yourself what it is about those cheeses that appeal to you. Focus on the following:

- ✔ **The style:** *Style* refers to the type of rind and mold, bacteria, or yeast used to make the cheese, which affects its flavor, texture, and aroma. (For more on the styles of cheese refer to Chapter 2.)

- ✔ **The milk:** The most common milks used for cheese are cow, sheep, and goat milk. Each, in combination with other factors and ingredients used in the cheesemaking process, impacts the final taste and texture. Do the cheeses you like tend to use one kind of milk over another?

- ✔ **The rind:** The rind is essentially the cheese's "skin," and it's the result of both "good" mold and bacteria and the cheese being exposed to air as it ages. Rinds fall into different categories (natural, surface-ripened, washed, and so on), and they help to create the specific taste and smell associated with a particular type of cheese. Do you find that your favorite cheeses have a particular kind of rind?

- ✔ **The flavor:** How would you describe the flavor of the cheeses that you like? There are many adjectives you can use, but a few terms, like *earthy, sharp, buttery, stinky,* and *nutty,* are pretty standard in cheese terminology. The later section "Ten 'technical' (if sometimes odd) terms used to describe cheese" provides a list of other words, complete with definitions.

- ✔ **The texture:** *Texture* refers to the consistency or feel of the cheese itself (as opposed to its mouthfeel). Some cheeses are almost rock-hard, some are soft as pudding. Some crumble, others stretch, and still others are pliable.

You may discover that what you enjoy is a particular attribute: You love cheeses that have a buttery flavor, and the texture, type of rind, and other stuff don't really matter. Or you may find that you like a particular combination of attributes: hard, natural-rind cheeses made with goat milk, for example. The key thing to keep in mind is that, by being able to identify the characteristics you like in your favorite cheeses, you have the tools to talk to your cheesemonger, as well as do a little research — and purchasing — on your own.

# Evaluating the Characteristics of Cheese

Ever heard of a *synesthesia?* It's a neurological condition in which the stimulation of one sense triggers a corresponding reaction in another sense. People with the condition (some historians suspect that Leonardo da Vinci had it) experience the world in a distinctive, emotionally evocative way. Seeing a particular color, for example, may evoke a particular smell. Feeling a particular texture may evoke a particular sound. The point? Cheese is the culinary equivalent of a synesthetic experience: A characteristic that stimulates one sense stimulates a variety of others.

## Using your common sense (s)

The following is a four-step sensory exercise designed to help you learn to evaluate the various attributes and characteristics of a cheese. Give it a try: You may be surprised by what you learn.

### The eyes have it: Appearance

Take a good look at the cheese. Does it appear hard or soft or somewhere in between? Is it gooey? Springy? Now observe the rind (or lack thereof). Once you've learned the different types of rinds and their inherent characteristics (a topic we cover in Chapter 2), you'll usually know if a certain cheese appeals to you enough to give it a try. For example, a washed rind will often be sticky-looking and red, orange, or yellow in color — even if you can't smell it, its appearance will let you know that it's going to be at least a *little* bit pungent.

What color is the paste? If it's pure white, it's likely a goat or sheep milk cheese (although aged sheep milk cheese can be straw-colored). Cow milk may be a bit more tricky to discern visually, but it often has a butter to deeper, richer yellow hue to it.

Look at (or ask about) the type of cheese: Is it blue (earthy, a bit pungent), fresh (mild, soft, with flavors ranging from sweet or salty to tangy, depending upon the type of milk and how it's made), or bloomy rind (mushroomy-tasting rind)?

### Sniffing things out: Smell

Your sense of smell is likely the first thing that will turn you on or off a cheese. If you love the earthy flavors in a wine or wild mushrooms, for example, you'll most likely appreciate a cheese like camembert, Tomme de Savoie, or certain clothbound cheddars (refer to Chapter 4), which have a distinct forest floor or musty aroma.

Some cheeses offer very little in the way of smell, especially if they're cold, so make sure you take them out of the fridge for 30 minutes before you begin these sensory exercises. Fresh cheeses such as mozzarella or ricotta may smell milky or slightly sweet, but these odors are very subtle. If you know you don't like strong, assertive flavors, and you like fluid milk, these are likely good picks for you. On the other hand, plenty of other kinds of mild yet flavorful cheeses are out there that are likely to suit your palate.

### How touching: Feel

Go ahead — you know you want to! Cut off a piece, hold it between your thumb and forefinger, and gently press down. Is it springy or solid? Does it ooze between your fingers or hold its shape? This touch test not only helps clarify whether the cheese is soft, hard, or somewhere in-between, but it also warms up a cold cheese so that it can reveal its true flavors. Kind of brings back childhood memories of Play-doh, doesn't it? We thought so.

### Taster's choice: Taste

And now the part you've been waiting for. . . *eating* the cheese. The preceding exercises have led to this moment, and it's often surprising how different a cheese can taste from the way it looks, smells, and feels.

Take the piece of cheese you've been holding between your thumb and forefinger, put it in your mouth, and push it up against the roof. What do you taste? Is it milky and buttery, sharp and salty, nutty and sweet, or something else? How would *you* describe it to someone else? What does it feel like in your mouth? And, most importantly — do you like it?

Sweet, salty, sour, bitter. There's actually a fifth flavor used when it comes to cheese (and other foods), called *umami*. It's often described as a savory, or meaty, flavor. Foods such as soy sauce, *dashi* (bonito broth used in Japanese cuisine), and Southeast Asian fish sauces are said to possess umami characteristics. It sounds complicated, but trust us: You'll know it when you taste it. We find it's most prominent in robust firm cheeses such as cheddar and alpine styles, and in gooey washed-rind cheeses like Reblochon.

## Ten "technical" (if sometimes odd) terms used to describe cheese

As you evaluate the flavor or aroma of cheeses, try to think in terms that cheese professionals use. As you read through this list, notice that some of the terms aren't technically flavors at all, but allude to sensations associated with the other senses:

- **Barnyard:** This term refers to both aroma and taste; cheeses described as barnyard are reminiscent of the scent of wet hay, earth, animal, even (yes) manure.

- **Lactic:** *Lactic* refers to cheese that has a milky, tangy quality (the result of the addition or natural acquisition of *lactobacilius* bacteria and little to no rennet, which results in a softer curd).

- **Pliable:** This term can be used to describe either the rind or interior of a cheese and is often synonymous with *supple*, meaning the paste and exterior are bendable and retain some moisture.

- **Tacky:** *Tacky* is used to describe the exterior of washed-rind cheeses. It's just this side shy of sticky.

- **Cellar:** A cheese described as *cellar* has a deep, musty, earthlike aroma or flavor, similar to how a used wine cork smells.

- **Toasty**: This term refers to aged cheeses that contain notes of toasted bread, nuts, or browned butter. It may also be present in smoked cheeses.

- **Mushroomy:** Quite literally, you'll smell and taste mushrooms. Many of the bloomy-rind cheeses — especially camembert and Brie (see Chapter 3) — have pronounced fungal flavors and aromas.

- **Stinky:** Every cheese has a smell, but some are *literally* stinky. Usually, this term refers to washed-rind cheeses (see Chapters 3 and 4), and the rind is typically the smelly part. Think yeast, meat, wet sneakers, sulphur, or feet (and we mean no disrespect; plenty of cheese connoisseurs search for cheeses that taste like dirty socks, or worse!).

- **Sharp:** This term refers to the "bite" a cheese has. Sharpness is relative, like spiciness in foods: One person's sharp is another person's mellow. Generally, though, this term is used for aged cheeses that nip at your palate a bit and leave a lasting impression.

- **Nutty:** This term is harder to define because it's one of the most-used descriptors for cheese, and many kinds of nuts exist. Roasted almonds and peanuts, sweet browned butter, and caramelized walnuts are some of the flavors this term encompasses. Not surprisingly, nuts are a great accompaniment to most cheeses, too.

The best way to get familiar with these terms is to try to apply them to the cheeses you love and any new cheeses you try. As you explore the different types of cheese, you'll build up a cheese vocabulary.

# Finding the Cheese You Like, with or without a Cheesemonger's Help

After you know what characteristics you like in a cheese, you're ready to head to your local cheese shop or grocery store and peruse the many varieties that are available. You can stay within your comfort zone — that is, look for cheeses that share characteristics with your favorites — or you can branch out farther and try varieties that differ in key ways.

For obvious reasons — mainly the expert help and the wide variety of cheeses available — a local cheese shop is the best place to go if you have one in your area. But if you don't, you can still find great cheeses to try in your local grocery store. The following sections have the details.

## Going local

Visiting your local cheese shop will help you establish a relationship with your cheesemonger. Let him or her know your preferences; by doing so, the cheesemonger can help you discover new varieties that suit your tastes.

When describing what you're looking for, focus on texture and a general flavor profile, such as earthy or buttery. Sometimes, the way a cheese is aged or the type of milk it's made from can change your perception. A semi-firm goat milk Gouda can be nutty, buttery, and not at all goaty, while a creamy blue can be sweet, velvety, and free of that trademark pungency that can be too much for some. Keep your mind, and your tastebuds, open to new experiences and rely on the expertise of the cheesemonger. He or she will most likely will be able to steer you toward a new cheese that you may have previously avoided.

If you're shopping at a cut-to-order cheese shop, don't feel like you have to buy a cheese without sampling it. Your cheesemonger should let you taste before buying. If you're dealing with pre-wrapped cheese at other cheese shops, specialty food stores, or some upscale grocery chains, a cheesemonger will usually be in attendance to answer questions — and quite possibly provide samples.

---

## Are you a turophile or a caseophile?

Essentially, *turophile* and *caseophile* refer to the same thing: one who loves cheese. Popular opinion states that a turophile (from the Greek *tyros*, meaning "cheese") is a "connoisseur of cheese," while a caseophile (from the Latin *caseo*, also meaning "cheese") is merely a "lover of cheese." Personally, we just like to say we're cheese lovers.

## Browsing the cheese section at your grocery store

Many people, often because of proximity or convenience, buy their cheese at the store where they do the bulk of their grocery shopping. These days, many supermarkets and larger grocery store chains have a cheese counter with a fairly diverse array of cheeses and someone who can help you find what you're looking for. Although they may not be able to give you samples, these employees are often familiar with the varieties of cheese they sell and can give you good advice on what to choose to suit your needs.

If you're in a place where everything is pre-cut and no cheesemonger is available, it's helpful to have a list of cheeses you'd like to try, based upon what you've discovered from reading this chapter, the lists of cheeses throughout this book, and the advice we provide in the next section.

# Taking the Cheese Challenge

Sometimes, the only thing that can nudge us out of a food rut or comfort zone is discovering that our favorite item is out of stock. If *you're* stuck on a specific style or variety of cheese, we challenge you to broaden your horizons. If you're not the adventurous type, don't worry. The short quiz in this section is designed to help you expand your cheese choices and turn you on to new types with similar flavor or texture profiles.

**Question 1:** Do you enjoy fresh, mild, milky cheeses such as mozzarella?

> **If you answered "yes":** You'll probably love burrata or pecorino fresco.

**Question 2:** If you're a fan of sharp cheddar, what about it do you like?

> A. The bite
>
> B. A beefy, savory quality
>
> C. Earthy, slightly musty characteristics

> **If you answered A:** Try Piave or aged provolone (both from Italy).

> **If you answered B:** We recommend Caerphilly (United Kingdom) or aged pecorino (Italy).

> **If you answered C:** Try clothbound cheddar (U.K. or U.S.), Toreggio (Italy), or Cantal (France).

**Question 3:** Is a stinky, sticky cheese like Taleggio your dream?

> **If you answered "yes":** Try Red Hawk (California) or Epoisses (France).

**Question 4:** Do you like smooth, buttery, mild Monterey Jack?

**If you answered "yes":** You'll fall in love with a young Gouda or boeren-kaas (Dutch "farmer cheese"), or Abbaye de Belloc, made with sheep milk (France).

**Question 5:** Are you a classicist and think Brie is the only cheese that matters?

**If you answered "yes":** Give Délices de Bourgogne or Brebiou (cow and sheep milk, respectively, both from France) a try.

**Question 6:** Do you love fresh chèvre?

**If you answered "yes":** Try other styles of goat cheese: bloomy-rind Humboldt Fog (California), Coupole (Vermont), Meredith Dairy's marinated chèvre (Australia), or Leonora (Spain).

**Question 7:** If you like blue cheese, which do you prefer?

    A.   Mushroomy, earthy flavors with a decent dose of blue

    B.   Salty and sharper blue flavors

    C.   Sweet and creamy with subtle blue notes

**If you answered A:** Try St Agur (France), Roquefort (France), Bayley Hazen (Vermont), or Big Woods Blue (Minnesota).

**If you answered B:** Try Crater Lake Blue (Oregon), Gorgonzola Piccante (Italy), or Original Blue (California).

**If you answered C:** Try Montbriac (France) or Cambozola Black Label (Germany).

**Question 8:** Are you a big fan of the sweet and nutty cheeses?

**If you answered "yes":** Try Goudas made with other milks, like Classico Reserve (Oregon) or Ewephoria (Holland). You may also love Comté (France) and cave-aged Gruyère (Switzerland), although they aren't as sweet as Gouda.

**Question 9:** Some aged cheeses get the "crunchies," which are crystallized proteins that literally crunch, like salt crystals in butter, in your mouth. Do you enjoy this quality?

**If you answered "yes":** Try an aged Gouda like Beemster XO, Noord Hollander, or l'Amuse (all from Holland).

# Behind the scenes at a cheese competition

Over 1,000 cheeses. More than 100 subcategories. That's what the judges at the American Cheese Society (ACS) face each year at the organization's annual conference. A Best in Show medal can make a cheese famous overnight, but it takes 28 judges two exhausting days of inhaling, squishing, tasting, and analyzing hundreds of cheeses.

Being a cheese judge may sound like your dream job, but the entire judging period is a formal affair that results in some serious palate fatigue. From the time cheesemakers send in their entries, labeled with only an ACS alphanumeric code (to ensure anonymity), to the moment those cheeses appear on the judge's table, the operation is meticulously run.

The process begins with nearly 300 cases of cheese arriving daily for a week before the competition. Fourteen teams of two judges — one technical judge to analyze the body, flavor, and texture of each cheese; and one aesthetic judge to survey the flavor, texture, appearance, rind development, and aroma — work together to score every cheese in a class.

Unlike other cheese competitions, where entries start with a score of 100 and are graded down for technical defects, the American Cheese Society's goal is to give positive recognition to the highest-quality cheeses. Each technical judge deducts points from a perfect score of 50, while each aesthetic judge awards points to a maximum of 50 for outstanding characteristics and qualities. The two scores are added, for up to a total of 100.

After the teams of judges examine and taste a cheese, they discuss what they've just spat or swallowed. (Seriously — have you ever tried to taste over 500 cheeses in a day? It's no picnic.)

The final task for the judges is to award the Best in Show. To do this, they conduct a second round of evaluations of all the blue ribbon winners in all the categories — between 70 and 80 cheeses and cultured products. During this round, the judges work independently, and the cheese with the most votes for first place is named Best in Show, a great honor.

After the competition, the judges' notes from the first round are sent to the cheesemakers — an incredibly valuable educational aspect. "It's not a competition; it's a judging," says David Grotenstein, chairman of the ACS competition." The goal is to assess the cheeses and give feedback to the cheesemaker on his or her work." Adds Mark Johnson, senior scientist at the Wisconsin Center for Dairy Research and a former technical judge, "This is a contest where each cheesemaker's passion for their craft is incredibly obvious. We're evaluating their life's work, and every judge on the floor takes it very seriously."

Adapted from *culture* magazine's "Go behind the scenes: The Judging," by Jeanne Carpenter, Fall 2009

# Holy smokes!

Smoking cheese isn't a new concept. It came about by accident. Ancient early shepherds built fires inside their huts during chilly nights in the mountains. They would (and in some cases, still do) hang their cheeses from the ceiling to age; it was no doubt a pleasant surprise when they discovered that the smoke added a little somethin'-somethin' to their cheese. In addition to being a method of preservation, smoking kept insects away. The process also changed the chemistry of the rind, making it undesireable to certain harmful or unwanted molds.

In Roman times, cheeses were brought to a public facility to be smoked; it's no coincidence that many smoked cheeses originated in cooler climes such as Russia, the Balkans, Germany, and regions east of the Caucaus. The tradition of Basque shepherds smoking cheese yielded a hard Spanish classic: Idiazabal, which is essentially a smoked Manchego. However, smoked cheeses are also made in warmer and more humid climates where the process also came about as a means of preservation; they were (and still are) often smoked over animal dung because wood was in short supply.

Cold-smoking is the most common modern method of producing this style of cheese, or using a smoker or a smokehouse. Note that industrial cheeses may have smoke flavoring (liquid smoke) added. if you want the real deal, talk to your cheesemonger. It's easy to find quality, artisan domestic and imported smoked cheeses like provolone (although it may not be imported from Italy), Gouda, cheddar, Gruyère, scamorza, and mozzarella. These cheeses are smoked either when very young or more aged.

The flavors of a smoked cheese are very dependent upon the type of wood used. Beech gives a light, fine smoke, whereas oak yields a longer lasting, more prominent flavor. Some cheese-makers even use nut shells to create smoked cheeses: examples include the Mozzarella Company's pecan shell-smoked mozzarella and scamorza, Rogue Creamery's hazelnut shell-enhanced Smokey Blue, and Beehive Cheese Co.'s black walnut shell and applewood-perfumed Promontory Apple Walnut Smoked cheese.

Other popular domestic smoked cheeses include Westfield Farm's Smoked Capri, a hickory-enhanced goat cheese log, and the delightful Up in Smoke from River's Edge Chevre. These little buttons of goat cheese are smoked over alder and hickory chips, wrapped in maple leaves, and spritzed with bourbon. Cheers to that!

# Chapter 6

# Purchasing Pointers

. . . . . . . . . . . . . . . . . . . . . . . . . . . . . . . . . . . . . . . . .

## In This Chapter

▶ Discovering the different outlets where you can purchase cheese

▶ Buying the best cheeses of the seasons

▶ Talking to a cheesemonger

. . . . . . . . . . . . . . . . . . . . . . . . . . . . . . . . . . . . . . . . .

*I*n this brief chapter, we cover three very essential topics: where to find cheese, when to buy certain cheeses (it is, after all, a seasonal product), and how to buy the best product you can.

We know you know that cheese comes from the store. But what kind of store? Is there a best option? What if you can only find pre-wrapped cheese? What if you live in a rural area? And when you do find a cheese shop you like, how to do you decide what to buy? Don't worry — we've got answers.

## Where to Buy: Exploring Your Options

You can purchase cheese in many places, especially if you live in a large city. What you need to decide is how you want to go about finding it. Your choices? Specialty cheese shops, grocery stores with cheese shops or counters, public and farmers' markets, online cheese retailers, and more. What's best for you? The following sections help you decide.

The busier the shop, the fresher the cheese. A general rule is that, if lots of customers are purchasing cheese, you won't find wheels or chunks hanging around getting old, ammoniated, or dried out.

### What's in store

If you're looking to purchase cheese or related items but need guidance, it makes sense to go where the professionals who can advise you are. For wine, you wouldn't hesitate to go to a wine shop, right? For cheese, head to a cheese shop!

You can find hundreds of specialty cheese shops across North America, and every month, more open. (To find a list of cheese shops, flip to the back of every issue of *culture* magazine for a Retailer Directory, or go online at www.culturecheesemag.com/cheese_stores for an interactive page that lets you look for cheese retailers in your area.)

Grocery stores and food markets of all sizes have jumped on the cheese bandwagon, increasing inventory and creating specific departments that include deli, dairy, and mid-range to high-quality cheeses.

### The benefits of going to a shop

Here are some of the benefits of going to a dedicated cheese shop or a grocery store with a special cheese section:

- **The cheesemongers know their business.** While there's no guarantee the person behind the counter has experience in cheese, the odds are good they do. If you're at a well-known shop, you can rest assured you're getting expert assistance. You should know, too, that good cheesemongers are knowledgeable about not just cheese, but food in general. They can tell you the best cheeses to use for specific recipes and what techniques work best, or how to pair cheese with beer, wine, or spirits.

- **Many of these shops are *cut-to-order*.** Some dedicated and non-dedicated cheese shops have invested in cut-to-order counters with experienced cheesemongers wielding the knives or cutting wire (basically, a primitive slicer that allows for greater ease and more accuracy and speed). This means you can sample what interests you or what your cheesemonger recommends, based on your needs and personal preferences, and the cheesemonger can portion the cheeses to your specifications (note that some cheeses, such as Epoisses, can only be sold whole, because they're too delicate to portion and lose their structural integrity by being cut).

    If you're shopping at a cheese department or shop that sells only pre-wrapped items and a cheesemonger isn't normally in attendance, you can usually count on some experienced people working behind-the-scenes (someone has to order, cut, and wrap all of those cheeses). Respect that they are busy and their role isn't to be out on the floor, but ask whether you can speak to one of them — the buyer, for example. Odds are, you'll find a great resource for inspiration, advice, and education, just as you would at a cut-to-order shop.

- **The cheese you find in a busy, reputable, and/or cut-to-order cheese shop is freshest.** Buying the freshest cheese saves you money in the long run because you won't have to throw out old product (assuming you store it properly and eat it within a reasonable period of time — be sure to ask your cheesemonger for advice).

- **Because you can purchase only what you need, shopping at these stores is often less expensive.** This also means you can indulge in costly cheeses on occasion, because you can buy smaller amounts of most types of cheese.

The Europeans have been purchasing their cheese (and bread, meat, and fish) from specialty shops for centuries. It may not be the most expedient way, but it's actually a lot of fun, as well as educational. Make an outing of it!

The downsides to purchasing at specialty stores or counters are the inevitable lines, the time it takes, and the chance that the shop will run out of the product you're looking for (always best to call and ask first). Some people love the process of seeking out the right ingredient or product, so if you approach shopping for cheese — or any other food — with a spirit of adventure and an open mind to the monger's suggestions, it's much more enjoyable.

### Finding and working with a shop

It may take a while to find a store, staff, or cheesemonger who's the right fit for you. Here's what to look for:

- **Someone who's knowledgeable and, if he or she doesn't know the answer to your questions, is willing to find out.** Many cheese shops have reference books on hand, and a good cheesemonger is always happy to do a bit of research. In addition, cheesemongers who come from a food background are often more helpful, especially if you have pairing, cooking, and entertaining enquiries.

- **Someone who's willing to work with you and cater to your tastes (as long as you're being reasonable).** Once you find a cheesemonger who knows what you like, she will be delighted to share new products that she thinks you'll enjoy.

  Avoid a salesperson who is pushy, rude, or apathetic. If the person can't answer your questions (within reason; no one can tell you *exactly* what the cows ate or guarantee that *no* pesticide residue existed on any of the pasture the animals grazed on), find another employee or a new shop.

- **A shop that looks like it sells good-quality product.** Use visual cues to clue you in on whether the product is good-quality and maintained in a safe, hygienic manager. Poorly cut and wrapped display cheeses; dirty counters, cutting boards, knives, floors, or employees; a lack of hand-washing; a lack of skill when cutting and wrapping cheeses — these are signs of a poorly-run shop, no matter how nice the staff or trappings.

For places that carry specialty cheese, find out what day their deliveries come in. That way, you'll get things when they're freshest or at their peak ripeness — or in stock. If you need a particular cheese for an event, let the cheesemonger know and ask whether he or she can hold or order it for you specially.

## Online offerings

Even cheese has gone high-tech, and if ordering online lacks the sensory experience and romance of going to your local cheese shop, several good reasons exist why online cheese shops are necessary and thriving. If you live in a rural area, are physically unable to visit retail shops, dislike dealing with crowds, or are in search of an esoteric cheese, online is a good choice. Just peruse, choose, pay, and wait for your cheese to arrive.

While the process is straightforward, online cheese shopping does have a few drawbacks:

- ✔ **You really need to know what you're looking for in a cheese.** Obviously, you can't taste the product!

- ✔ **You need to consider shipping charges and policies.** Some larger cheesemakers do offer direct shipping, but most require a minimum order, which can often be a considerable quantity, such as a full wheel (and wheels, as we discuss in Chapters 3 and 4, can be quite large). Also, shipping is mainly overnight (especially in the hotter months) which can be pricey.

- ✔ **Return policies vary.** You may be able to return a cheese due to quality, but you can't return a cheese just because you don't like it.

We recommend the following cheese retailers. Their sites are easy-to-understand and navigate and have comprehensive information. They're also trustworthy — not just in terms of security, but with regard to the quality of their products and their knowledge of how to correctly pack and ship a cheese (believe it or not, there's an art to it):

- ✔ **Artisanal (New York City):** Artisanal Bistro (www.artisanalbistro.com) is a cheese-centric eatery with a modest but well-curated retail selection of cheeses. Artisanal Premium Cheese Center (www.artisanalcheese.com) offers a curriculum of cheese education classes (note that this location doesn't have a retail outlet).

- ✔ **Beechers Handmade Cheese (Seattle):** Located adjacent to Seattle's Pike Place Market, you'll find a small selection of domestic cheeses in this café/retail shop/cheese factory — and you can watch cheese being made through the windows. A second location is now open in New York's Flatiron District. http://beechershandmadecheese.com/

- ✔ **Cowgirl Creamery (San Francisco and Washington D.C.):** Cowgirl Creamery is an excellent example of the European model (cheeses stacked on counters), with a careful selection of the best artisanal domestic and import cheeses, as well as housemade product. www.cowgirlcreamery.com

- ✔ **Di Bruno Bros (Philadelphia):** Bustling and well-stocked with specialty foods, Di Bruno's four retail locations have excellent cheese selections and the mongers know what they're doing. www.dibruno.com

- ✔ **Formaggio Kitchen (Boston):** This shop has an exhaustive array of artisan cheeses, handwritten signs, and highly educated mongers as well as lots of specialty foods. The original location is in Cambridge, with a second store in the South End. www.formaggiokitchen.com

- ✔ **Fromagination (Madison, Wisconsin):** Founded in 2007 by Ken Monteleone, this shop is located in the heart of Madison's Capital Square. With a strong focus on Wisconsin and Midwest cheeses and accompaniments, Fromagination curates a rotating selection of cheeses and food-related items. http://fromagination.com

- ✔ **Murray's Cheese Shop (New York City):** Murray's is the quintessential cheese shop, with wedges, wheels, and dry goods piled high in all directions. The original shop (now over 60 years old) is in Greenwich Village, where the store also offers educational classes. A second location is in Grand Central Station, and the company has also collaborated with Kroger supermarkets and set up Murray's Cheese counters in several states. www.murrayscheese.com

- ✔ **Pastoral Artisan Cheese, Bread & Wine (Chicago):** With three Chicago-based locations, Pastoral offers a great selection of both domestic and imported cheeses, as well as a carefully curated wine department and accompaniments for cheese. www.pastoralartisan.com

- ✔ **Zingerman's (Ann Arbor, Michigan):** Fun and delicious are the key words here (just check out Zingerman's site and catalogue, and you'll see what we mean). The shop has a fabulous deli with an assortment of cheeses, including those from its own creamery, as well as a separate bakehouse and Roadhouse eatery and a well-stocked mail order business. www.zingermans.com

Ordering online from a retailer closest to you is best, because you can save money on shipping cost and time.

## To market, to market: Buying direct

Buying directly from the producer is always the best way to go. You can ask those questions that only the cheesemaker can answer, and the lack of middlemen means a higher profit margin for them. If the cheesemaker is good, the quality of the product will be high (and fresh) and the price lower than what you would find online or in a store.

If you're lucky enough to live near a farmers' market that has good cheesemakers, shop there! And tell the cheesemakers what you like or don't like about their cheese, because they rely upon direct consumer feedback to produce the best possible product.

# Making history: Landmark cheese shops

What makes a cheese shop destination-worthy? Is it the design, the selection, the employees? In a word, yes. All are essential in creating a memorable shop, but what really solidifies a place as an institution is the role it serves (past and present) in the industry as a whole.

Here are our picks for some of the world's most important cheese shops (outside of the United States). Be sure to pay a visit if you're in town.

✔ **Neal's Yard Dairy (London):** NYD is justifiably famous for its almost exclusive selection of British and Irish farmstead and artisanal cheeses. With locations in London's Covent Garden and Borough Market, stop by for a taste of what's special that day. www.nealsyarddairy.co.uk

✔ **Poncelet (Madrid):** The first modern food shop in Spain to specialize in cheese, Poncelet focuses on domestic and international cheeses. Come here to try over 90 different Spanish cheeses you might not find in other shops. www.poncelet.es

✔ **Mons Fromager Affineur (Roanne, Paris, Renaison, Lyon, and Montbrison, France; London):** Owed by famed affineur Herve Mons, this chain of five shops in France and the U.K. does its own affinage (aging). Stock includes imports from 25 countries, as well as product from 155 French cheesemakers. www.mons-fromages.com/en/node/638

✔ **Androuët (Paris):** At just over 100 years old, the world's first dedicated cheese shop now has eight locations throughout Paris, as well as shops within Stockholm and throughout the U.K. This Old World fromagerie carries on the tradition of founder Henri Androuët by supporting small producers of very regionalized, specialized products. http://androuet.com

✔ **Fromagerie L'Amuse (Amsterdam and Sanpoort-Noord, Netherlands):** Focused on farmstead cheeses and Goudas from the Netherlands, this shop works closely with local cheesemakers and does its own affinage. www.lamuse.nl/

✔ **Fermier (Tokyo and Sapporo, Japan):** This retailer is dedicated to the sale of farmstead cheeses (over 200 of them!). www.sunnypages.jp/travel_guide/tokyo_food/cheese/fermier+atago+shop/1566

✔ **Pfunds Molkerei (Dresden, Germany):** This ornate, Baroque-style cheese shop has a massive selection. www.pfunds.de/

✔ **La Fromagerie (London):** La Fromagerie's two London shops have specialized walk-in cheese rooms stocked with an international selection of cheeses. The quality of the cheeses and the knowledge of the staff is excellent. www.lafromagerie.co.uk/

✔ **Canterbury Cheesemongers (Christchurch, New Zealand):** Started and managed by Sarah and Martin Aspinwall (NYD alums), this shop stocks a great selection of imported and domestic cheeses, and the mongers have broad international cheese knowledge. www.cheesemongers.co.nz/

# When to Buy: The Best Time to Buy Certain Cheeses

When it comes to farmstead and artisan cheese, there are definitely certain times of year — just like with produce — that cheeses are in season or at their peak.

Milk is a seasonal and constantly changing product (see Chapter 2). The components and flavors of the milk — and therefore the cheese — vary considerably according to the animal's diet as well as where it is within its lactation cycle.

If the animals are fed mainly on pasture, early-season milk (produced in the spring) is usually the richest and highest in butterfat, solids, and protein; mid-season milk (produced during the summer months) has a higher water content and therefore is lower in the other components. Late-season milk (produced in the fall) is rich but lowest in protein and, therefore, better for making hard cheeses.

In addition, seasonal climate changes (temperature, humidity, and so on) affect the cheesemaking itself. When the milk's composition changes, the cheesemaker must also adjust his or her techniques to these variables or there will be difficulties with the cheesemaking, such as rinds pulling away from the paste or overly-aggressive mold growth.

## Looking at lactation

Milk production in any mammal starts immediately after it gives birth. In industrialized dairy cow farming, where quantity and consistency are key, the common practice is to continuously milk the cow on a set schedule for many months or even years regardless of the seasons.

But in a farm setting, where the milk is destined to be made into artisanal or farmstead cheese, the focus is often more on milk quality and flavor as well as animal welfare and natural birthing cycles. In these situations, milking the animal for a certain number of months and then giving it a break for two or three months is considered good practice. This break, which is often referred to as *drying off,* occurs as the animals become pregnant again with the new seasons' offspring, allowing their bodies to recover and the maximum nutritional benefit to be derived for the unborn calf, kid, or lamb.

Without human intervention, the natural birthing cycle takes place in the spring months. *Note:* Depending upon what hemisphere the cheese is produced in, the seasons — and thus lactation cycle — may differ.

Some producers freeze milk or curd or so they have product on hand to sell during the winter, but be aware the texture of the cheese may differ from that made from fresh milk or curd. Larger dairies may keep their animals producing milk year-round.

Due to the difference in milk components, some cheeses are more desirable when released during specific times of the year. Here are some prime examples:

- ✔ In Italy, Parmigiano Reggiano wheels that are made in August and September — when the cows' milk is richest — are the most coveted.

- ✔ The first young pecorinos arrive in stores during the fall in Italy. Aged 1 to 3 months, the cheese is made from milk that was produced when grass was at its peak.

- ✔ Graskaas, a 1-month aged Gouda produced by Beemster and made from the first rich milk of spring, is a much-anticipated, short-lived seasonal treat.

- ✔ In Europe and increasingly in America, many fresh and young artisanal and farmstead goat cheeses are at their most delicious in the spring months (May and June).

- ✔ The reason why Stilton is always associated with Christmas is because the cheeses that are ready to be eaten in late December were made in the early fall, traditionally the best time for Stilton production due to the cooler weather.

If you know the age of a cheese, you can figure out what month it was made, and that will give you some clue as to what was going on weather- and pasture-wise at that time. If you really know the maker and the terroir, challenge yourself to see whether you can also make a guess as to what the dominant flavor profiles will be, based on what the animals may have been eating.

When you purchase cheese, keep these two general rules in mind:

- ✔ November and December are the busiest months for cheesemongers, because their customers are celebrating and entertaining more, so they're most likely to bring in special, hard-to-get items they may not usually carry due to their perishability and cost. Other cheeses, such as Stilton, are holiday classics, and easy to find that time of year (although they'll be in high demand).

- ✔ For any shop carrying lots of local cheeses, late spring through late fall is when you'll find seasonal offerings, with some of the inventory often changing on a weekly basis. Fresh and younger cheeses start to become available in spring, while aged and blue cheeses begin to appear more readily in the fall and winter.

# What to Buy: Making Your Dairy Dollars Count

Good cheese isn't inexpensive. As cheesemongers and consumers ourselves, we understand that you want to get not just the best product your money can buy but also the best customer service.

Cheese is intimidating to many people, as is wine. Our advice: *Relax.* Your cheesemonger doesn't expect you to possess any special knowledge, other than knowing your own palate. If you can communicate what flavors you like and don't like and what you plan to do with your purchase, you've opened the door to what can be a fun, educational experience.

## Counter proposal: Having a dialogue with your cheesemonger

A good cheesemonger doesn't just know about the cheeses: he or she also asks the necessary questions to pin down exactly what you need. Here are some examples of what you'll likely be asked or can volunteer, to help the cheesemonger help *you*:

- ✔ What's the cheese for and when? A quiet dinner in, small get-together, a sophisticated dinner party, or a no-holds-barred party?

- ✔ How many people will you be serving?

- ✔ What's the menu, and what will be served (including drinks) with the cheese?

- ✔ Is the cheese for just a nibble or a substantial part of the meal? Is it the main focus or an accompaniment? Will it be served before, during, or after the main meal?

- ✔ Will it be served indoors or out? Also, what's the weather like? (A hot climate is unkind to many types of cheese, especially pungent styles like washed rinds and blues. Fresh cheeses will also spoil quickly in the heat.)

- ✔ Are your guests adventurous types interested in experimenting with new foods or more into eating and less interested in what it is?

The most exciting thing you can say to a cheesemonger is, "Give me what you think is best right now." This opens all kinds of doors (and our hearts), and if you know and trust your monger and he or she knows your palate, then you know you're in for something special. And who doesn't love *that*? We feel the same way when a chef we know serves us a little something not on the menu.

# Telling the difference between a cheese that's ripe and past its prime

Knowing what to look for when selecting cheese will help you pick out that perfectly ripe piece. The following advice on how to judge ripeness in a cheese comes from Nathan Raskopf, the cheesemonger for Whole Foods Market, Raleigh, North Carolina, which he shared in the Summer 2010 edition of *culture: the word on cheese:*

- ✔ **When checking out surface-ripened cheeses, look at the cream line.** This translucent layer just below the rind signals where the bacteria on the surface have begun to break down the proteins in the interior — from the outside toward the center. This layer is softer and usually stronger in flavor than the middle. Remember: The wider the cream line, the riper the cheese. Left to age, the cream line would overtake the smooth, compact interior, leaving a core that is more liquid than paste. Yellow or brown spots on the exterior of the cheeses are not an indicator that a surface-ripened cheese is off.

- ✔ **Generally speaking, avoid soft cheeses that look extremely runny or watery and are wrapped in plastic.** While the interior may be just ripe, the cheese closest to the rind is likely to be overly assertive and ammoniated. This means the flavors and textures could be out of balance because the cheese has matured too much.

- ✔ **For firm cheeses wrapped in plastic, the color of the paste should be bright and fresh looking — not slimy or greasy.** Firmer cheeses tend to hold up better over a longer time. The greatest enemy for hard cheeses is either being stored at too high a temperature in plastic wrap, in which case the oils from the cheese start to pool on the surface (not pretty) or being wrapped insufficiently. In the latter case, the surface of the cheese will appear dry and cracked.

The key for you and your cheesemonger is to learn the right balance of ripeness for each cheese according to your tastes. That's why it's smart to ask for a freshly cut piece of cheese, rather than feeling obliged to choose what's already in the case, especially if it looks overly ripe or subpar. Cheese is a living and breathing product, and each one will ripen differently based on the environment in which it has been kept.

# Chapter 7

# Serving and Storing Cheese

*In This Chapter*

▶ Putting together a great cheese plate

▶ Buying better cheese

▶ Traveling with and storing cheese

Cheese is an ideal food for entertaining. It's easy to serve, and most people love it. It can be passed around on a platter, or guests can help themselves from a composed plate. Serve an interesting assortment of cheeses and accompaniments, and you've got an instant conversation piece.

Making a great cheese plate doesn't require any special skills or experience. You just need to know a few, fundamental techniques. In this chapter, we explain how to cut cheese for serving (and what kinds of cutting implements you need), what types of foods make great accompaniments to cheese, how to arrange attractive and delicious cheese plates, and more. And because storing cheese properly is an integral part of helping to maintain its flavor and prolong its life, we give you advice on how to wrap and store cheese, too.

## Cheesy Accessories: All about Knives and Boards

One of the many nice things about cheese is that you don't need any special equipment to cut, prepare, or serve it. Of course, you can invest in all kinds of gadgets — some people really love their *girolles* (blade-and-spindle devices designed to shave ribbons off the top of Tête de Moine, a firm, pungent, cylindrical cheese from Switzerland); *raclers* (special scrapers used on hot Raclette cheese to make the Swiss dish of the same name); or Zyliss cheese graters (admittedly very cool little contraptions wherein you insert a chunk of Parmigiano or other hard cheese into a metal drum, turn a crank, and — *voila!* — a veritable snowstorm of delicate cheese strands blankets your food).

At the very least, we advise investing in a classic box grater, which is invaluable for cooking and baking. We also love microplane zesters, which are fine-gauge files designed for, well, zesting citrus. But they're also useful for grating cheese, nutmeg, coconut, or ginger. Beyond a grater, what you get is up to you. In the following sections, we discuss the various types of knives and boards that are essential for cheese aficionados.

## Knifestyles of the rich and famous

If you're big on entertaining, you'll want to invest in the four main types of cheese knives. (Fortunately, they're often sold in a set.) Each of these knives, shown in Figure 7-1, serves a specific purpose that helps to maximize the flavor and amount of portions you get from a cheese:

- **Cheese cleaver:** This mini meat cleaver-like knife may have a pointed or flat head. You use it for slicing or breaking off shards from dense, very hard cheeses such as aged cheddar and aged Gouda (see Chapter 4 for more hard cheeses).

- **Cheese plane (planer):** This tool is a flat, stainless-steel triangle with a sharp-edged slot in its center. You drag the plane across the cut face of the cheese to shave off thin, even slices. A thinner slice exposes a greater amount of surface area to the air; the result is more flavor from the cheese. You use a cheese plane for firm cheeses presented in broader wedges, such as Gruyère and Manchego (also covered in Chapter 4).

- **Soft-cheese knife:** Also known as a *skeleton knife,* this offset knife has a curved tip that often has a forked tip. A soft-cheese knife has holes punched in its blade, which minimizes the surface area that makes contact with the cheese. This design prevents cheese from sticking to the knife as it's cut and served, making for a cleaner, more attractive slice with less waste left on the blade. Ideal for soft, creamy cheeses such as Brie, Délice du Jura, or Cambozola (refer to Chapter 3 for information on soft cheeses).

- **Spreader:** Ideal for chèvre, ricotta, and other soft, rindless cheeses with a spreadable consistency, you can also use this knife for butter or cream cheese.

As we note earlier, each of these knives has a particular purpose, but there's nothing wrong with cutting cheese with a paring knife (we often do it). A large chef's knife can also work if you're cutting a big piece of cheese; just be sure to use an actual cutting board to prevent damage to the knife, cutting surface, and your fingers!

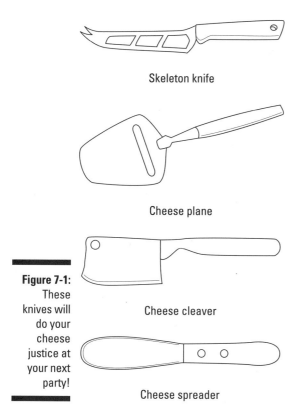

Skeleton knife

Cheese plane

Cheese cleaver

**Figure 7-1:**
These
knives will
do your
cheese
justice at
your next
party!

Cheese spreader

## *Chairman of the board*

Cheese comes in all shapes, textures, and colors, and what you serve it on *does* matter. First, think about what will keep the cheese in its best form while it sits out. We give you some suggestions for platter choices in the following sections.

Whichever type of board you buy, here's a quick clean-up tip: A diluted bleach or vinegar solution (1 teaspoon bleach to 1 quart of water, or a ratio of 1 to 5 of distilled white vinegar) is a great way to kill any residual bacteria on your cutting boards. Be sure to rinse well to avoid lingering odors or flavors.

### Stone and ceramic platters

If the day is hot, a stone platter (slate or marble/granite slab, which can be inexpensively purchased from a bathroom/kitchen supply store) is ideal because it keeps the cheese at a cooler temperature — essential for soft, oozy varieties. We think stone is the best material, but it has a few drawbacks: It can be heavy; be sure to put self-stick round felt pads on the bottom surface to protect your tabletop. It's also prone to staining, so make sure you clean it well after each use.

Ceramic platters also keep cheese cool and are easily cleaned, so they're a good — and affordable — option. Best of all, they come in a variety of colors and shapes, allowing you to be creative with your plating.

Avoid busy patterns or unappetizing colors, which won't showcase the cheese to best effect. Try things like a vivid red ceramic dish with a bright white goat milk cheese, a wedge of blue, and an herb-coated variety for some serious "wow" factor. For more tips on assembling a cheese plate, head to the later section "Serving Basics."

### Wooden boards

For a warmer, more rustic platter, look for hand-crafted boards made from different types of wood, which are often one-of-a-kind. Bamboo is also a good choice; it's eco-friendly, lightweight, and attractive. Whatever you purchase, wooden boards will quickly become your favorite go-to platter for almost everything you serve communally. They're also more gentle on knives and won't dull their edges as quickly.

Make sure the wood is treated with a food-safe finish and that the surfaces are free of splinters. And avoid boards made from wood with a scent or resin, like some species of fir, because they flavor the cheese. Also, always wash wood by hand, hand-dry, and coat occasionally with mineral oil to prevent warping and cracking.

### Metal and glass platters

Metal and glass platters are attractive choices. If you don't have a family heirloom on hand, you can score some great finds at antique stores and flea markets. With these materials, try using paper doilies or, if you can find them, paper grape leaves. They soften the look of the finished plate and make clean up easier.

When purchasing ceramic platters or bowls — especially if they're from a foreign country or are vintage — remember that the glaze may not be lead-free, so only use them for serving cold foods.

# Serving Basics

Serving cheese or making a great cheese plate doesn't require any special skills or experience. You just need to know a few fundamentals, like how to properly cut different styles of cheese, what kind of plate or board to serve it on, and basic information on how to put together a cheese plate (there *are* a few rules). In this section, we share the basic elements of serving cheese and assembling a cheese plate. For detailed information on creating beautiful and delicious cheese plates and cheese-plate recipes you'll want to try, head to Chapter 15.

## Cutting to the chase

Believe it or not, a right and a wrong way exists for serving cheese (not that anyone will be policing you, of course). In this section, we detail the ideal ways to cut each style and shape. *Note:* We don't refer to cutting whole wheels (except when quite small) or massive blocks of cheese here — that's the cheesemonger's job. Any cheese you purchase will come pre-cut and wrapped, or it will be cut to order by your cheesemonger.

After you get your cheese home, follow these instructions, which explain how to cut different styles of cheese for serving guests (you can see these techniques in Figure 7-2):

- ✔ **Small wheels, discs, pyramids, or squares:** Positioning the knife in the center of the cheese, cut into even, wedge-like slices (see Figure 7-2a).

- ✔ **Wedges of soft to semi-soft cheeses:** Cut these cheeses into thin slices, starting at the point of the cheese (see Figure 7-2b).

- ✔ **Wedges of semi-firm to hard cheeses:** Cut the wedge in half lengthwise and then cut each slice into portions crosswise (see Figure 7-2c).

- ✔ **Logs:** Slice into even cross-sections (see Figure 7-2d).

- ✔ **Blue cheeses:** Slice the wedge from the center of the thin edge to equally spaced points along the thick edge (see Figure 7-2e).

- ✔ **Cheeses that come in a box (such as Epoisses):** Cut a "lid" in the top of the cheese and set this piece aside. Then scoop out the contents with a spoon (see Figure 7-2f).

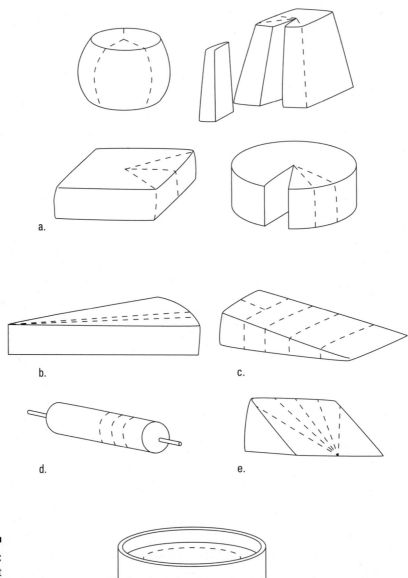

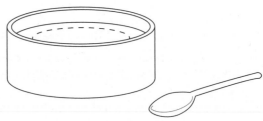

The number one rule is to have an equal ratio of rind to *paste* (interior). Resist the impulse to excavate the interior of a cheese out from the rind. Not only does it destroy the aesthetic integrity of the cheese, but it also ruins the experience for people who actually like to eat their cheese rind and all.

The rind is actually an integral part of the flavor experience of almost all cheeses, especially bloomy-rind varieties (cheeses dipped in wax or Plasticoat — a food-grade coating — are the exception). On hard cheeses, the rind generally doesn't add much to the palate if consumed. Whether you choose to eat the rind or not is a personal choice. If you don't want the rind, or if it's made of wax, just nibble around it, and discreetly spit it into a napkin.

## Serving it at the ideal temperature

Serve cheese at room temperature. Doing so allows the flavors to open up so that you can enjoy the cheese at its full potential. Removing cheese from the fridge 30 minutes (or more, depending on the ambient temperature) before serving usually suffices, unless the temperature is very hot.

Washed-rind or goat cheeses grow more pungent as they warm up. If it's hot or humid, you may want to think about serving something else, or set these cheeses out a few minutes in advance, instead of the full 30 minutes. If you're dining al fresco, keep cheeses indoors until your guests arrive because bugs love cheese, too!

## Putting together a cheese plate

When you put together a cheese plate, you probably want to do more than throw a bunch of cheeses together and set it out with a box of crackers. Instead, think about what you want to serve it with (or if you'd prefer to present the cheese(s) solo) and how to arrange things to create a presentation that's both appetizing and visually appealing, without appearing too cluttered.

As cheesemongers, we know that the biggest challenge faced by our customers is the dreaded, "What should I put on my cheese plate?" Deep breath. Cheese plates are as easy or complicated as you care to make them, but the bottom line is, you want to offer nibbles for guests — and, let's face it — impress them in the process.

# Ten great occasions to serve cheese

As far as we're concerned, there's never a bad time to serve cheese (unless, perhaps, your guests are lactose intolerant or have other dietary restrictions). But certain holidays and celebratory events seem to be tailor-made for the serving of cheese. Note too, that the holidays we've listed here are actually peak times for cheese shops, so plan your visit for opening time, when you won't have to fight a crowd and the product is in stock.

1. New Year's Eve

2. Fourth of July

3. Memorial Day weekend

4. Christmas

5. Graduation parties

6. Weddings

7. Birthday parties

8. Super Bowl Sunday

9. Thanksgiving

10. Valentine's Day

When you understand the basics of cheese styles (Chapters 3 and 4) and flavor profiles (Chapter 5), you'll be able to put together some winning picks. In Chapter 15, we provide you with specific cheese plating details, suggestions for sweet and savory accompaniments, and recipes for some of our favorite condiments.

## *Arranging your items: General principles*

Cheese — even basic varieties — is an indulgence and deserves to be center stage. When you put your cheese plate together, think aesthetics (you want it to look good and the various items to complement one another) and convenience (you want the items on the plate to be easy to remove and eat). Here are some guidelines:

- ✔ **Make sure the cheese is cut appropriately:** Don't serve every different cheese in same-size slices or chunks without rind. Not only is this presentation boring, but as we explain in the earlier section "Cutting to the chase," how you cut or slice the cheese matters. Do it improperly, and you destroy its aesthetic integrity.

- ✔ **Make the cheese the focal point:** The cheese really is the star of this show, so you want it to stand out. Avoid creating a cluttered plate, and allow ample room between the cheeses. A garnish is good; a forest of garnishes is overkill and distracts from the cheese.

Yes, everything you're serving is delicious, and people will want lots of it, but resist the temptation to pack the plate with as many goodies as you can. First, a cluttered plate is overwhelming. Second, and more importantly, you need to make sure you have enough room on the platter or board for the cheese to be cut.

✔ **Pay attention to the look of the platter or board:** Avoid busy patterns and colors that look unappetizing; you want the cheese to stand out against the background. An array of yellowish cheeses on a yellow plate, for example, is monochromatic and dull. Go for solid colors and contrasts for an eye-catching plate.

✔ **Add decorative elements (just make sure they're edible and unsprayed!):** A sprig of herbs (*not* the entire bunch), such as thyme or mint, or a scattering of small (no orchids or roses!) edible flowers add elegance and color to a plate. (Avoid strongly-scented flowers, which can clash with the aroma of the cheese.)

Give some thought to the cheese-flower/herb pairings. Citrus blossom is nice with fresh chévre, for example. Good flower-herb choices include Johnny-Jump-Up's, anise hyssop, nasturtium, borage, violets, lemon balm, cornflower, and fennel, rosemary, or sage blossoms.

Figure 7-3 shows a beautifully composed cheese plate, ideal for two people. Notice how uncluttered and elegant it looks!

**Figure 7-3:** A beautifully composed cheese plate for two people.

# Do I serve a cheese course before, during, or after the meal?

I'm often asked when, during the course of a meal, is the "right time" for the cheese plate. I ask you, when is the *wrong* time? Many cheese experts have different beliefs — rules even — as to when the cheese should be presented; wars have been fought over this very topic. But I believe that there is no right time; you heard it here first.

There are, however, some commonsense guidelines. When serving a large dinner, such as a Sunday roast of a whole venison leg with Yorkshire pudding and duck fat–fried potatoes, for example, I like to serve the cheese course before the meal with a few cocktails. Get those digestive enzymes flowing; lubricate the old intestinal tract for the feast.

If I'm planning some light, summery fare, such as a big kitchen-sink salad with lots of yummy pickled things, I like to plate the cheese alongside the entrée with a few bottles of white wine. This way, the cheese is featured as a large accoutrement to the salad, or vice versa.

For a simple pasta meal, I always prefer to have the cheese course before the dessert course, as a sort of palate cleanser that sets up a nice break between savory and sweet.

— Charlotte Kamin, co-owner of Bedford Cheese Shop, Brooklyn, New York (*culture: the word on cheese,* Summer 2011)

The same principals apply whether your cheese plate will be feeding 2 or 200 people. But when you're feeding a bunch, you may be particularly tempted to load the plate up so it lasts throughout the evening. We strongly advise you to resist this urge. Use a bigger plate or set out two (or more) and be prepared to replenish them as necessary.

Figure 7-4 shows an example of a cheese plate suitable for a party. Note how the cheeses are still cut into manageable portions (you can always put out more), and the condiments are also in small quantities. Everything is well-spaced, so the cheeses are the center of attention and easy to slice.

**Figure 7-4:**
Go for the uncluttered and easy-to-cut arrangements when hosting a party.

# On the Road or in the Cupboard: Storing and Traveling with Cheese

Cheese is best if you consume it as soon as possible after purchase — this is especially true with soft cheeses — but we understand that sometimes your eyes may be bigger than your stomach. Or maybe you stumbled across a great little cheese shop in your travels and now find yourself with a perishable item that you need to get home. If you must store your stash for later or have to travel long distances with your new purchase, this section has some tips to keep your cheese as fresh as possible.

## Putting your cheese to bed: Successful storage

The best way to keep cheese fresh is to purchase it cut to order, as opposed to already pre-cut, wrapped, and ready to go. Freshly sliced cheese tastes better and lasts longer, and you can rewrap it in the paper it's sold in. But if you're buying cheese for future rather than immediate use or you have leftovers, you need to know how to store it in a way that preserves its freshness and flavor.

The main thing to remember is that cheeses need to be appropriately wrapped for storage. You can buy the special cheese paper used by cheesemongers, which was created to keep cheese fresh. It has two layers: One is a permeable cellophane that permits the cheese to breathe, and the other is similar to butcher paper and holds in moisture. You can purchase it (Formaticum is the most widely available brand) at many cheese shops or specialty food stores, as well as online. Or you can create your own version of this handy wrap: First wrap the cheese in wax or parchment paper and then cover it in a layer of plastic wrap.

Even if you don't have special materials, you can store cheese effectively using items you likely already have in your kitchen. Here are our tips on how to preserve different styles of cheese:

- ✔ **Fresh cheeses:** These cheeses have a very short shelf life, so eat them as soon as possible. The most important thing is to prevent them from oxidizing, so keep them sealed in their original container (which may or may not contain brine) or tightly encased in plastic wrap.

- ✔ **Semi-soft, surface-ripened, semi-hard, and washed-rind cheeses:** Wrap these cheeses loosely in parchment paper, place in a plastic container with a tight-fitting lid, and store them in the humidifier/vegetable crisper drawer of your refrigerator. Because cheese continues to ripen as it ages (it's a living thing, as we discuss in Chapter 2), be sure to air out the cheese every day or so by unwrapping it and letting it sit at room temperature for half an hour.

One reason you want to keep cheeses wrapped up and/or stored in a plastic container with a tight fitting lid is because doing so keeps unwanted odors out. Odiferous foods such as cut onions can affect the smell and flavor of your cheese. Conversely, stinky cheeses can bring unwelcome aromas to items like milk or butter in your refrigerator.

- ✔ **Blue:** Wrap blue cheese in waxed or butcher paper and store it in a plastic container with a tight-fitting lid. Place it in the humidifier/vegetable crisper drawer of your refrigerator.

If for some reason you don't have a humidifier drawer in your fridge, place the wrapped cheese in an airtight plastic container, such as Tupperware.

Letting any cheese come up to room temperature and then re-refrigerating what you don't eat actually increases the aging process, expediting its demise. The best way to keep cheese fresh is to cut off a hunk (or three) and enjoy some every day!

# Tips for traveling with cheese

We both work at cheese shops in tourist-centric locations (Napa Valley and Seattle). So one of the things we most often hear from customers is "I don't have a refrigerator in my hotel room; will this cheese keep?" or "I'm leaving for the airport; how long can I keep this cheese unrefrigerated?"

Food safety experts say that two hours is the window in which it's safe to leave perishable foods out at room temperature, and we'd be remiss to tell you otherwise. That said, we've both taken cross-country flights and lengthy road trips with cheese minus ice packs and have never had a problem.

If you're going to travel with cheese, here are some suggestions that will keep you and those in the vicinity happy (sharing not required) and your cheese in good shape:

- ✔ Go for semi-firm, firm, and aged cheeses, and make sure they're kept wrapped appropriately (see the earlier section "Putting your cheese to bed: Successful storage").

- ✔ Transport your cheese in a waterproof container with an ice pack (be sure the pack is placed in a double-layer of Ziploc freezer bags to prevent leakage). Tupperware or a similar storage container is ideal, as is a collapsible/soft thermal lunchbox made of nylon, which you can purchase for about $5 at larger drugstore chains.

- ✔ Avoid fresh and surface-ripened cheeses, because they're very perishable. Buy these only if you plan to eat them immediately or are close enough to home or a refrigerator.

- ✔ Avoid taking washed-rind cheeses into a hotel room or on public transportation. The problem? It's not very considerate. These cheeses can get odiferous pretty quickly.

## Q & A with Cathy Strange, Whole Foods Market Global Cheese Buyer

Cathy Strange has a *lot* of responsibility on her shoulders. As the global cheese buyer for Whole Foods — the leading natural and organic foods retailer (308 stores in the U.K., Canada, and the U.S. as of this writing) — it's her job to source and taste cheeses from all over the world and ensure they meet criteria set by the Whole Foods company. Strange has been with Whole Foods since 1981, when she started out as a part-time employee in the specialty foods department. She progressed to a management position (known as Team Leader), then Regional Coordinator, to her present position as the company's only global cheese buyer.

*(continued)*

*(continued)*

Strange never planned a career in cheese, but she grew up in a food-loving family, and, she says, "I fell in love with artisan foods and the people who make them, especially cheese. The farmers, the herd managers, the cheesemakers motivate and inspire me to this day. The respect for the culture of food that is rapidly taking root in the U.S. today makes it a special time to be in the cheese industry. I'm fortunate to be with a company that aligns with my values and gives me an opportunity to support theirs."

We talked to Strange to find out how a cheese gets from the farm or factory to the cheese case at Whole Foods.

*Cheese For Dummies*: What makes you choose a specific cheese, and how does it go from manufacturer to one of your stores?

**Cathy Strange:** Our cheeses are selected through a process that begins with our core values. Our goal is to sell the highest quality natural and organic products, but the cheese must taste good and meet stringent ingredient standards. Farm and manufacturing practices are also reviewed: our goal is to support product produced from animals that haven't been given growth hormones.

*CFD*: Is there a different process for import versus domestic cheese?

**CS:** We're committed to preserving the tradition of European cheesemakers, while helping to establish and support New World cheesemaking by actively promoting and educating shoppers about the craftsmanship and quality of our cheeses. One example is our relationship with renown a*ffiineur* Hervé Mons, who hand-selects cheeses for us from small French producers and oversees the aging process. We also have amazing relationships with domestic regional producers and work directly with a variety of them to craft cheese to our specifications so we can offer them as exclusives to our shoppers.

*CFD*: Does Whole Foods import the cheeses?

**CS:** The company does hold an import license and participates annually in a lottery for an additional cheese license. But we also utilize the license to import a range of products. We also have wonderful import partners that work with our overall cheese program to support our regional stores.

*CFD*: What kind of team do you work with?

**CS:** Purchasing is based on a three-tier system which creates buying opportunities at all levels within the company. It allows us to offer specialty and artisan products that reflect flavors and traditions of Old World food producers, as well as local and regional gems. There is one global buyer, twelve regional buyers, and every store features local buyers. This structure provides us with the flexibility to focus on local/regional products, as well as leveraging the volume at a global level.

*CFD*: What do you see as national trends in cheese; are there marked differences in preferences across the country?

**CS:** Customers are more interested than ever before about where their food is coming from, and they directly influence our buying strategy. Our focus on farming practices, milk source, production facilities, skilled cheesemakers, and quality lead and support national trends on specialty food products. *Affinage*, small production, organic, seasonal, and more flavorful products will continue to evolve and establish roots throughout our stores.

# Part III
# Cheese Around the World

## In this part . . .

With a basic working knowledge of how cheese is made and the different styles and types of rind (the topics of Parts I and II), you're ready to explore cheeses around the world. Consider this section your handy global cheese tour guide.

Here we cover the world's major cheese-producing countries and cultures, help you better understand how and why certain types of cheese evolved, and let you discover what countries produce the styles of cheese you're most drawn to. Do you love rich, buttery, semi-firm cheeses? Delicate, oozy, washed rinds, or blues so assertive they clear the room? Read on to find out the origins of those cheeses so that the next time you're in a cheese shop or on vacation, you'll know just where to go.

# Chapter 8

## The Americas

**In This Chapter**

▶ Discovering the cheeses of the U.S. and Canada

▶ Breaking down the cheeses of Mexico, Central, and South America

*N*orth and South America are part of the New World. Both continents have indigenous cultures thousands of years old, but when it comes to cheese, it wasn't until they were colonized (mainly by the Spanish, but also by the English and French) that dairy animals were introduced and gained subsistence and economic value.

In this chapter, we provide an overview of the cheesemaking renaissance that's occurred within the United States over the last 20-plus years, as well as the emerging Canadian artisan cheesemaking scene. Then we take a brief look at Mexico and Central and South America, where cheese is often a subsistence and nutritious component of the regional cuisines.

## American Cheese, Please

The Pilgrims may have had cheese stored in their rations on the Mayflower, but the first commercial cheese factory didn't open in the United States until the mid-19th century. And while fresh "farmer's cheese" was routinely made for home consumption using milk from the family cow, the U.S. has historically never had the diverse cheese culture of continental Europe and the United Kingdom.

While America's first cheese factories were established in the Midwest and on the East Coast, cheese wasn't considered an exotic or romantic foodstuff. The vast numbers of Northern and Eastern European immigrants in those regions established them as a driving force in the industrial cheese industry; today, California, the Pacific Northwest, Wisconsin, and New England are home to some of the nation's finest cheese artisans.

The modern U.S. artisan cheese movement is fairly recent, beginning in the early 1980s. Only in the last 20 years has a truly profitable market for domestic cheese that isn't mass-produced existed. In the last decade, the demand for specialty cheese — both domestic and imported — has reached epic numbers and shows no sign of slowing.

The U.S. produces more cheese than any other country. Not more types, mind you — France carries that distinction (see Chapter 10). A 2009 study by the Agricultural Marketing Resource Center stated that America produced over 900 million pounds of *artisan* cheese alone in 2006. And that's not accounting for the vast quantities of factory cheese produced in America.

Figure 8-1 shows the major domestic cheesemaking regions in the U.S. Bear in mind that not all states produce artisan cheese (or enough artisan cheese to include in this general overview. Our goal in this chapter is to give you ideas on what to look for at your local cheese shop or specialty grocer. You can also visit regional farmers' markets, where you can often meet the cheesemakers themselves, as well as taste their products.

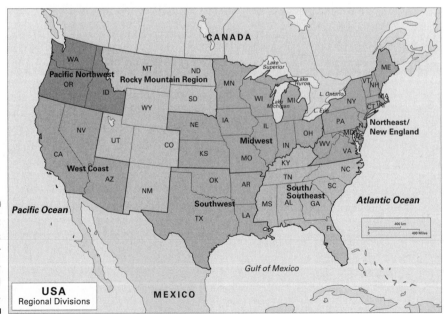

**Figure 8-1:**
The U.S.'s major cheese-producing regions.

# The West Coast

Spanish missionaries brought the first cows to Alta, California, in the 1700s (goats preceded them by 200 years). Their milk was turned into cheese by Franciscan friars. Not until the Gold Rush, however, did dairying become a bona fide economic enterprise. With most of the men seeking their fortunes in the mines, their wives used the family cow to produce butter and cheese for profit. Thus, the Sacramento Valley, Mother Lode country, Sierra Nevada foothills, and, eventually, the Bay Area (due to its population boom) became the heart of California's dairying heritage, which was initially based on butter production.

By the beginning of the 20th century, European dairy goat breeds began growing in popularity, and today goat cheese is almost synonymous with California artisan cheese production (see the sidebar "California dreaming: How goat cheese changed the way America eats").

Artisan cheese (regardless of milk) wasn't "invented" on the West Coast, but as with so many trends — many of them culinary — California played a key role in the popularization of domestic cheese, especially chèvre. And the West Coast, in general, has been and remains a driving force in the artisan cheese movement. It also produces or provides milk for much of the nation's commercial cheese and other dairy products.

## California

California is ideal for dairy cattle, goats, and sheep because of its mild, Mediterranean climate and the diversity of terroir, which ranges from lush coastal pasture to flat agricultural land or hilly scrub. These factors, in addition to its size, explain why it's the nation's top milk-producing state. Northern California is the heart of artisan cheese production, primarily Marin and Sonoma counties, which receive abundant rainfall in winter, making for rich pasture through the spring.

Diversity with regard to style and influence is also a hallmark of California cheesemaking. Consider the varieties that hail from some of the best California cheesemakers: Gouda (Winchester Cheese and Central Coast Creamery); French and other Old World European styles (Marin French Cheese Company and Andante Dairy); fresh Peruvian styles (Yerba Santa Goat Dairy); Basque-style sheep milk cheeses (Barinaga Ranch); Original Blue (Pt. Reyes Farmstead Cheese Company); buttery, Italian-influenced sheep and cow milk cheeses (Bellwether Farms); Portuguese and Mexican style cheeses (Matos Cheese Factory and Fagundes Old World Cheese); and fresh Italian style cheeses (Gioia and Di Stefano Cheese).

## California dreaming: How goat cheese changed the way America eats

Although small-scale goat cheesemakers and factories have existed throughout the United States since at least the early 20th century, California usually gets the credit for putting chèvre on the map. In the late 1970s and early 1980s, inspired chefs such as Alice Waters and Jeremiah Tower of Berkeley's Chez Panisse and Wolfgang Puck of Beverly Hills' Spago became public figures for their use and promotion of locally grown-and-sourced ingredients.

They developed a style of cuisine that reflected the agricultural and ethnic diversity of California. It's become cliché, but goat cheese, sundried tomatoes, and arugula were, at the time, the holy trinity of California cuisine. Goat cheese appeared rolled in breadcrumbs, baked, and served on baby greens, or paired with smoked salmon on pizza. Today, domestic chèvre is ubiquitous on menus, from coffee houses to fine dining restaurants.

Iconic cheesemaker Laura Chenel was one of the new wave of food artisans who paved the way for the birth of California cuisine when she launched her goat cheese business in Sonoma County in 1979. The rest, as they say, is history. Chenel opened the door for the first wave of California goat dairies — Cypress Grove, Redwood Hill, Goat's Leap — and turned chèvre from cottage industry to profitable business. Other successful goat dairies such as Indiana's Capriole, Vermont Butter & Cheese, and New York's Coach Farm followed suit, and today, you can find hundreds of goat dairies and artisan cheesemakers throughout the U. S.

Following are some of California's most notable artisanal cheesemakers:

- **Cowgirl Creamery:** Not only is Cowgirl one of the best loved artisanal cheesemakers in the country, but it also serves as supporter and mentor for cheesemakers, cheesemongers, and restauranteurs nationwide. Cowgirl Creamery is best known for Red Hawk, an award-winning, cow milk washed-rind cheese and a superlative cottage cheese (it will ruin you for the supermarket stuff). See Chapter 21 for more information. www.cowgirlcreamery.com

- **Bellwether Farms:** California's first sheep dairy (started in 1992), Bellwether Farms creates some of the nation's finest cheeses, including the award-winning San Andreas, Pepato, and sheep milk ricotta, and yogurt. Bellwether's line now includes a few varieties made from cow milk (sourced from a neighboring Jersey dairy) like the buttery Carmody and crème fraiche. www.bellwetherfarms.com

- **Pt. Reyes Farmstead Cheese:** The dairy's Original Blue, California's first table blue, has become one of America's best-known artisan cheeses, with a clean, milky flavor, creamy white paste, and earthy bite on the finish. Great on salads and burgers. They also make a buttery, firm cow milk cheese called Toma. www.pointreyescheese.com

- **Vella Cheese Company:** Known for its cocoa-rubbed Dry Jack and other aged cheeses, this company also created its Oregon Blue Vein cheese to great acclaim (see Chapter 21 for more details). www.vellacheese.com

- **Fiscalini Farms:** Although it could be described as a large artisanal operation — over 3,000 cows — Fiscalini turns out top-quality, aged, raw milk cheeses, the most famous of which is a Bandage Wrapped cheddar that's aged 18 to 30 months. San Joaquin Gold, aged 16 months, is another renowned Fiscalini cheese. www.fiscalinifarms.com

- **Cypress Grove Chevre:** Cypress Grove is one of the most beloved goat cheese producers in the country. Humboldt Fog and Purple Haze — the company's most popular offerings — are known nationwide. Chapter 21 has more details. www.cypressgrovechevre.com

- **Redwood Hill Farm:** Redwood Hill has been a leader in the American goat cheese industry and produces a line of excellent products — including cheeses, yogurt, and kefir (a drinkable yogurt). Recently, the company launched Green Valley Organics, a brand of lactose-free cow milk products. www.redwoodhill.com

# The Pacific Northwest

Oregon and Washington have been quietly establishing their presence as major players on the artisan cheese scene over the last 20 years. Sally Jackson (now retired) was one of the first artisan cheesemakers to make a name for herself in the Pacific Northwest (PNW), selling rustic, leaf-wrapped cow, goat, and sheep milk cheeses made on her eastern Washington farm. Idaho (which is often considered part of the Pacific Northwest) is beginning to emerge as an artisan cheese-producing state, most notably for sheep and goat milk varieties.

Today cheese of all types and production levels is big business in this part of the country; together, the two states boast approximately 70 cheesemakers. From giants like Oregon's Tillamook Cheese (which grew from humble beginnings over 100 years ago and today produces over 170 million pounds of cheese a year) and Washington's mid-sized Beecher's Handmade Cheese, to micro-dairies of just a few cows, PNW cheeses are diverse in milk type, style, and flavor.

In the following sections, we take a look at the standout cheesemakers from the Pacific Nortwest.

## Oregon

The rainy climate prevalent along Oregon's coast yields lush pasture that's reflected in the richness and flavor of the milk. The other thing giving Oregon a leading edge in today's artisan cheese industry? Progressive thinking with regard to alternative energy sources and sustainable business practices.

Oregon primarily produces cow and goat milk cheeses, in four main regions:

- **Portland/Willamette Valley:** Abundant rainfall, with rolling hills and verdant pasture, this is also Oregon's major wine-producing area.

- **The Coast:** Foggy, rainy, and cold, but the payoff is prime pastureland.

- **Central Oregon:** Much of the central and eastern part of the state is high desert and more conducive to raising goats than cows.

- **Southern Oregon:** A diverse region with rich, volcanic soil, and heavy rainfall tempered by blistering summer heat. The topography ranges from high-desert peaks and grassland to evergreen forest and river valleys.

The Oregon State University Creamery in Corvallis — which has been closed since 1969 — has reopened and released its first cheese in November 2011. The dairy center operates as an educational program and incubator for aspiring artisan cheesemakers.

Oregon standouts:

- **Rogue Creamery:** This producer of exquisitely crafted blue cheese has twice been named Best in Show by the ACS for its Rogue River Blue. The influence of Rogue Creamery on PNW cheesemakers can't be overstated; its presence and subsequent success have helped to put the region on the map where the artisan cheese industry is concerned. www.roguecreamery.com

- **River's Edge Chèvre:** Famed for its exquisite farmstead goat cheeses (both plain and flavored), River's Edge is best-known for beauties like Up in Smoke, an elegant, maple-leaf-wrapped young chèvre spritzed with bourbon, and Siltcoos, an ash-coated surface-ripened cheese imprinted with a fresh fern frond. Truly a taste of Oregon terroir. www.threeringfarm.com

- **Pholia Farms:** Pholia Farms is notable not just because it's a fully sustainable operation running on solar power and other green dairy systems, but because it also produces some of the finest cheeses in the PNW from a herd of Nigerian Dwarf goats. Of note: Elk Mountain, a firm, 6 to 8 month raw milk tomme-style (a small wheel), is full of nutty goodness. www.pholiafarm.com

- **Tumalo Farms:** If you think you don't like goat cheese, the cheeses produced here will likely change your mind. Best-known for aged goat cheeses such as Pondhopper (washed in locally brewed Mirror Pond Ale), Classico Reserve, and Capricorns (studded with cracked peppercorns), these smooth, buttery, Gouda-styles are pure love, encased in signature yellow and orange waxed rinds. www.tumalofarms.com

Other award-winning, influential creameries located in the central and northern parts of the state include Juniper Grove Farm (goat) and Willamette Valley Cheese Company (cow and sheep). Oregon is also home to some excellent producers of artisan Mexican cheeses, such as Ochoa Cheese Factory in the Willamette Valley, which produces Froylan brand cheese, makers of a velvety queso Oaxaca.

## Washington

Like Oregon, Washington has garnered a reputation for excellent goat cheeses, although it also has dairy cows and a fledgling sheep milk industry. Washington has a number of prime cheese-producing regions, which include the following:

- **Puget Sound:** The abundant rainfall and salt air in this region make for exceptional pasture, which is why many cheesemakers can be found here.

- **Olympic Peninsula:** Home to one of the only temperate rainforests in the United States, the coastal regions are comprised of more mild micro-climates ideally suited to dairy farming, particularly cattle.

- **Southwest:** Fertile soil and a temperate climate attract cheesemakers *and* winemakers.

- **Eastern:** Washington's bread basket is high desert and grassy hill country, excellent for dairy goats. It's the state's fastest growing cheesemaking region, primarily for farmstead goat cheese.

- **Central:** This is wine and apple country, east of the Cascade Mountains. Yakima and Wenatchee are high-desert, with rich, volcanic soil: great for goat dairying.

- **Skagit Valley/Whatcom County**: Because of its close proximity to Puget Sound, this region has a mix of lush valley pasture and marine air — ideal for producing rich, flavorful milk.

Some of Washington's "early" artisan and farmstead cheesemakers such as Pleasant Valley Dairy (1960s), Quillisascut Farm (early 1980s), and Port Madison Farm (also early 1980s) are still in operation. But a new wave of mostly farmstead and, often, second-careerist producers has been steadily arriving on the scene for the last decade. Today, Washington is home to approximately 50 cheesemakers. Some of the best-known include

- **Beecher's Handmade Cheese:** Sourcing milk from a local dairy, Beecher's Handmade Cheese produces a variety of aged and flavored cheddars, including the tangy, clothbound Flagship Reserve and Flagsheep made with — you guessed it — sheep milk. www.beechers handmadecheese.com

- **Mt. Townsend Creamery:** This immensely popular artisan creamery and retail shop sources milk from a nearby dairy and turns it into clean-tasting fresh and soft varieties such as bloomy-rind, ash-coated Seastack and Cirrus, a camembert-style. www.mttownsendcreamery.com

- ✔ **Black Sheep Creamery:** Located in the Chehalis River Valley between Seattle and Portland, this sheep dairy produces a variety of styles but is best known for its natural-rind aged cheeses (look for Queso de Oveja and Mopsy's Best), yogurt, and fresh curd. www.blacksheepcreamery.com

- ✔ **Willapa Hills Cheese:** This family creamery makes excellent cheeses (mainly blue) from the milk of its own sheep, as well as from a local cow dairy. http://willapahillsfarmsteadcheese.blogspot.com/

### *Idaho*

Move over, potatoes. Besides being one of the largest agricultural states (wheat, cattle, sheep, hay) in the nation, Idaho is also the third largest milk-producing state and the third largest manufacturer of natural and processed cheese in the U.S., according to the United Dairymen of Idaho.

Idaho's topography and climate are diverse, ranging from high-desert grass-lands and evergreen forest to the craggy peaks and high altitude valleys of the central Rockies. Idaho, like all of the Western states, has a long history of subsistence cheesemaking amongst the early settlers, who usually kept at least one dairy cow. Beginning in the mid-19th century, an influx of Basque immigrants came to Idaho to work the Gold Rush, but many became loggers and shepherds (English and Scottish immigrants already living in the region had large flocks) instead. Today, many of their descendants own sheep oper-ations, as do shepherds of Latin American or Mongolian descent.

There is still a thriving Basque community in Idaho, most notably in Boise, although the annual Trailing of the Sheep Festival in Central Idaho (www.trailingofthesheep.org) is a nod to the state's northern Spanish heri-tage. There's no definitive answer on whether Basque culture has had influ-ence on the emergence of sheep milk cheeses now being produced in Idaho, but it certainly established it as one of the nation's main sheep ranching states.

In recent years, Idaho has started to see a number of farmstead producers of cow, goat, and sheep milk cheeses crop up, some of which are garnering national awards. Here are some top cheesemakers:

- ✔ **Lark's Meadow Farms:** Located on the flanks of the Tetons, this small, family-run cow and sheep dairy produces quality raw milk cheeses, including signature cheese Dulcinea — a rustic Basque-style full of earthy, buttery flavors. www.larksmeadowfarms.com

- ✔ **Rollingstone Chevre:** Idaho's first goat cheese producer has been making fresh, surface-ripened, and aged farmstead chèvres and an award-winning blue (Blue Agé) for nearly 20 years. www.rollingstonechevre.com

- ✔ **Ballard Family Dairy and Cheese:** This family dairy sells milk and ched-dar, halloumi, and cheese curds made from the milk of its small herd of Jersey cows. www.ballardcheese.com

# *The Southwest and the Rockies*

While the Southwest and Rockies states have a long tradition of sheep and cattle ranching, their artisan cheese scene has only recently taken off and found retail outlets outside of local farmers' markets and state-wide specialty food shops. The cheeses of these regions have their own distinct terroir, from the alpine pastures of the Rockies to the high-desert forage that perfumes the cheeses of the Southwest.

## *Southwest*

In such a climatically-harsh, high-desert landscape, it's not difficult to understand why this part of the country isn't teeming with cheesemakers. Nevertheless, in Arizona and New Mexico, you can find handfuls of small, highly regionalized farmstead goat dairies that produce cheese — mainly fresh chèvre, feta, and surface-ripened varieties.

Texas, primarily the regions around Austin and Houston, is bubbling up with cheesemakers. The progressive influence of Whole Foods (the mega-green grocery chain with a global and regional cheese buyers) and Austin itself makes for a cheese-hungry customer base, and the booming craft beer scene here is rising right along with the artisan cheese movement.

In Dallas, Paula Lambert of the Mozzarella Company (www.mozzarellaco.com) has created an empire from her tiny downtown factory, where in addition to mozzarella, an array of other cow and goat milk cheeses are produced. Cheesemaking and pairing classes are also offered.

## *The Rockies*

As you'd expect, many of the cheeses made in this mountainous region (primarily Colorado and Utah) are alpine styles and are made with cow milk. The two best examples of this are the longer-aged, hard-rind alpine cheeses of the European Alps and the Basque-style varieties of the French and Spanish Pyrenees. Cheeses made at high elevations are almost always larger in format (size) and, as noted previously, are aged longer and have firm rinds. (For these cheeses to survive a harsh climate and endure the rigors of travel to market, they need to be sturdy and have a long shelf life.)

The short growing season in the high-altitude areas of the Rockies poses a challenge — largely financial, due to abundant snowfall — for cheesemakers, but it also results in some wonderful hard cheeses, such as those produced by Rockhill Creamery (Utah) and James Ranch (Colorado).

Soft and fresh varieties also abound, however, as evidenced by the washed rinds and blues made at Utah's first sheep dairy, the high-altitude Snowy Mountain Sheep Creamery (which includes some mixed cow milk varieties) or southwestern Montana's Amaltheia Organic Dairy, with its variety of fresh and flavored chèvres and goat ricotta and feta.

Following are some of our picks for the best the Rockies has to offer:

- ✔ **James Ranch (Colorado):** Exceling at cow milk Dutch-style cheeses, the Ranch's signature cheese, Belford, is creamy and tangy when young (2 to 4 months) and rich and caramel-like with age. Leyden is spiced with cumin seed, while Andalo has a spicy bite to it after spending 6 months to 2 years in the aging room. www.jamesranch.net

- ✔ **Haystack Mountain Goat Dairy (Colorado):** Although no longer a farmstead operation, Haystack Mountain continues to produce consistently good fresh, surface-ripened, and aged goat cheeses. Look for Queso de Mano or Red Cloud, both former ACS winners. www.haystackgoat cheese.com

- ✔ **Avalanche Cheese Company (Colorado):** Avalanche Cheese Company produces award-winning cheeses such as Midnight Blue, clothbound cheddar, chèvre, and a surface-ripened robiola-style. www.avalanche cheese.com

- ✔ **Rockhill Creamery (Utah):** Located near the Idaho border, this tiny, historic farm with a handful of Brown Swiss cows produces some of the finest alpine and Dutch-style cheeses in the Rockies. Our picks: Snow Canyon Edam and Wasatch Mountain Gruyere. www.rockhillcheese. com

- ✔ **Beehive Cheese Co. (Utah):** One of the dairies that put modern Utah cheesemakers on the map, the Beehive Cheese Co. makes pasteurized and raw cheddar and other pressed cheeses from its herd of Jerseys and Holsteins. Look for Barely Buzzed, a hard cheese rubbed with espresso and lavender (a true American original), and SeaHive, which is rubbed with local wildflower honey and sea salt. www.beehivecheese.com

## *The Midwest*

Is anyplace in the U.S. more synonymous with cheese than Wisconsin (it is, after all, the "Dairy State")? The nation's number one cheese-producing state makes more than 30-percent of all U.S. cheese, including the most cheddar, Colby, Monterey Jack, blue, brick, and Muenster, totaling over one billion pounds of cheese annually. Although much of this cheese is factory-made, Wisconsin has some of the nation's finest farmstead and artisan producers, such as Hidden Springs Creamery and Fantome Farm, in addition to the high-quality, larger-production cheeses from BelGioioso Cheese and Sartori.

Wisconsin produces nearly 95 million pounds of specialty cheese styles per year such as Brie, camembert, edam, feta, gorgonzola, Havarti, and ricotta, most of which are made on an industrial scale.

Wisconsin isn't the only Midwestern state producing artisan cheese. Illinois, Indiana, and Iowa also have a small number of cheesemakers, including the well-regarded Prairie Fruits Farm and Marcoot Jersey Creamery, both in Illinois.

The Midwest's tradition of cheesemaking was influenced heavily by the Swiss, German, Dutch, Belgian, Italian, and Scandinavian immigrants who populated the region. Today, even Hispanic cheeses are made in the Midwest, but what this part of the country is best-known for are artisan and farmstead semi-firm to hard cow milk cheeses and washed rinds (this is Limburger and Liederkranz country, after all), as well as larger scale factory cheeses of all types.

Today, the Midwest is home to a number of artisan and farmstead goat and sheep dairies as well. Goats are a particular favorite for fledgling cheesemakers because they're less expensive and more efficient to keep than dairy cows. Regardless of milk type, one thing is certain: the Midwest shows no signs of slowing down when it comes to making hand-crafted cheese.

Here are some of the Midwest's MVPs of cheesemaking:

- **Uplands Cheese Company (Wisconsin):** One of America's best producers of farmstead cow milk cheese, Uplands Cheese Company creates Pleasant Ridge Reserve, a nutty, grassy, raw milk alpine delight (the only cheese to win the Best in Show three times from the ACS), and Rush Creek Reserve, made only from rich, hay-based fall milk. Inspired by French Vacherin Mont d'Or, Rush Creek is a creamy, satiny, smoky raw milk washed-rind cheese wrapped in spruce bark; it's best described as tasting like "ham butter." We love. www.uplandscheese.com

- **Hook's Cheese Company (Wisconsin):** Sourcing its milk from nearby small dairies, Hook's produces large-scale, handcrafted artisan cow milk cheddars, Colby, and Jack, and signature blues including the popular Tilston Point. The outstanding 15 Year Cheddar is worth the price tag. www.hookscheese.com

- **Bleu Mont Dairy (Wisconsin):** Dedicated to maintaining a sustainable dairy operation, Bleu Mont Dairy produces organic alpine cheeses and an award-winning clothbound cheddar from the milk of mixed-breed dairy cows. (Sorry, no website.)

- **Capriole Farmstead Goat Cheeses (Indiana):** A herd of over 500 goats on this family farm produce the milk for a wide array of styles, including award-winning Old Kentucky Tomme and Wabash Cannonball. www.capriolegoatcheese.com

- **Crave Brothers (Wisconsin):** This acclaimed creamery produces a variety of styles but is most well-known for its outstandingly creamy mascarpone and Les Frères, a washed-rind Reblochon-style cow milk cheese. www.cravecheese.com

- **Carr Valley Cheese (Wisconsin):** Using Wisconsin cow, goat, and sheep milk, Carr Valley produces a vast array of affordable, quality cheeses in various styles, but it's the company's aged cheddars and other natural- and washed-rind cheeses that continually win top awards. www.carrvalleycheese.com

## Maytag: Not just appliances

It's not often that the name of a famous washing machine company is also synonymous with a pioneering cheesemaking facility. Mention Maytag, however, and you have the exception to the rule. Frederick Maytag, the son of German immigrants, settled in Iowa in the 1860s. After establishing a successful farm implement company, he designed a washing machine that eventually catapulted the company to fame and fortune.

Frederick's son, Elmer, however, found joy in establishing a herd of award-winning Holstein-Friesian cows at Maytag Dairy Farms in Newton, Iowa. His son, Frederick II, inherited both the farm and his grandfather's business acumen, and Maytag Blue was created in 1941.

Aged for 4 to 6 months in man-made caves dug into the hillside, the texture of Maytag Blue is firm, moist, waxy, and slightly crumbly, with an ivory colored paste shot through with sapphire blue veins. Flavors are rich and cream-like, with an assertive salty note and a savory finish. If you're looking for a cheese to top those other American classics — a hamburger, Cobb salad, or iceberg wedge — this is the blue for you. www.maytagdairyfarms.com

## The South

The deep South is still very much in a beginning stage of artisan and farmstead cheesemaking, but in recent years, states like Virginia, North Carolina, Georgia, and Tennessee are producing some excellent cheeses.

The regions where dairies or cheesemakers proliferate — the Shenandoah Valley, the Great Smoky Mountains, and western North Carolina's Blue Ridge Mountains — are excellent dairy country and home to a number of small-scale farms. The majority of the cheeses produced here are found only at local farmers' markets or cheese shops, but some, like those mentioned shortly, have garnered a national reputation. The future is looking bright.

Historically, the deep South doesn't have a tradition in cattle or cheese production because the hot, humid climate wasn't conducive to dairying in the days before refrigeration, and not all of the topography is suitable for cattle (this is why the new generation of cheesemakers often use goat or sheep milk). Some Southern standouts:

- **Blackberry Farm (Tennessee):** Located in the Great Smoky Mountains, Blackberry Farm produces excellent sheep milk cheeses: Singing Brook, a pecorino-style with a full, hazelnut-buttery richness; Brebis, a fresh, slightly sweet cheese similar to chèvre but with a richer flavor and texture; and Trefoil, a semi-soft washed-rind cheese that's slightly pungent. www.blackberryfarm.com

- **Everona Dairy (Virginia):** Everona Dairy produces fantastic sheep milk cheeses. Look for Piedmont, a natural-rind cheese aged 2 to 10 months, and Pride of Bacchus, a natural rind soaked in red wine. www.everonadairy.com

✔ **Meadow Creek Dairy (Virginia):** Using the milk from a herd of Jersey cows, Meadow Creek produces a small selection of raw milk cheeses including Grayson, a delightfully stinky Taleggio-style washed rind. www.meadowcreekdairy.com

✔ **Sweet Grass Dairy (Georgia):** Sweet Grass produces a diverse array of cheeses, most notably Georgia Pecan Chevre (a 3-week-old bloomy rind goat milk pyramid coated with ground pecans), Greenhill (a camembert-style cow milk cheese), and Thomasville Tomme, a semi-soft, raw cow milk cheese with a natural rind. www.sweetgrassdairy.com

# The Northeast and New England

You might say that the East Coast is the birthplace of the American cheese industry. As soon as the first English Puritans arrived in the New England colonies in the 17th century, their cheesemaking and dairying skills were put to good use. From a basic subsistence food, they established a valuable commodity and artisan marketplace that continues to this day.

The first major American cheese factory opened in New York in 1851. At the same time, waves of European immigrants — primarily Germans, Swiss, and Italians — also arrived in America, bringing their respective cheesemaking styles and traditions with them. Although many moved to Wisconsin and other nearby states, others opted to remain in the Northeast and start dairying.

Vermont, Maine, New Hampshire, New York, Massachusetts, and Connecticut have many artisan cheesemakers and industrial producers of note, the majority of which have been established in the last 20 years. In this section, we cover just the major centers of cheesemaking in the northeastern United States.

Farm tours to visit cheesemakers are growing in popularity across the country. In the Northeast, Taking Root Artisanal Adventures (www.takingroot us.com) works to design private tours and, in collaboration with New York City's Saxelby Cheesemongers, to visit the region's best cheesemakers; some tours also include cheesemaking workshops and visits to other food artisans and producers.

Despite the number of farmstead cheesemakers in this part of the country, the pattern of farming is significantly different than that of the Midwest and Western United States. There's less land-base: These are smaller states, many with large urban populations. The terrain is also hilly in places and may not be well-suited to dairy farming. Winters are harsh, resulting in a shorter growing season and smaller farms and field patterns, which equals lower milk yield. Yet the quality of the milk is uniformly high, because the majority of these farms are located in regions where the terroir makes for prime pasture.

## Vermont

Vermont has more cheesemakers per capita (44 as of this writing) than any other state, and a major portion of its economy comes from dairy products (milk, cheese, eggs), including high-quality factory cheddars from Grafton Village Cheese Company and Cabot Creamery (which also produces an artisan clothbound cheddar, aged at The Cellars at Jasper Hill; see later in this section).

The state is also the home of the Vermont Institute of Artisan Cheese and the Vermont Cheesemaker's Festival, hosted at Shelburne Farms (a nonprofit environmental education center, 1,400-acre working farm, and National Historic Monument located on Lake Champlain; they also make a delicious raw milk cheddar).

Following are noteworthy Vermont cheesemakers:

- ✔ **Vermont Butter and Cheese Creamery:** Originally dedicated to crafting European-style dairy products, including butter, crème fraiche, mascarpone, and cheese, Vermont Butter and Cheese has gone on to produce an expanded range of excellent cow and goat milk cheeses (seek out Coupole and Bonne Bouche), as well as mentor new cheesemakers. See Chapter 21 for more information. www.vermontcreamery.com

- ✔ **Vermont Shepherd:** This dairy produces signature raw sheep milk cheeses, including Vermont Shepherd, a natural rind with a smooth, earthy, slightly sweet paste, and Queso del Invierno, a firm, buttery natural rind made from the winter milk blended with that of Jersey cows from a neighboring farm. www.vermontshepherd.com

- ✔ **Jasper Hill Farm & The Cellars at Jasper Hill:** One of America's most influential dairies, creameries, and aging facilities, Jasper Hill produces several award-winning cheeses, including Winnimere and Bayley Hazen Blue. The company also matures cheeses made by other New England cheesemakers in its custom-built underground cave system. For more information, go to Chapter 21. www.jasperhillfarm.com

## New York

New York is the other great artisan cheesemaking state of the East Coast, home to some of the nation's most influential modern cheesemakers. The proximity to such a major metropolitan marketplace as NYC, combined with prime farmland (the Hudson River Valley and the Finger Lakes Region) are why the state continues to be a hub for a new generation of cheesemakers such as 3-Corner Field Farm, Sprout Creek Farm, and Nettle Meadow Farm.

Here are a couple of New York's notable cheesemakers:

- **Old Chatham Sheepherding Company:** The largest sheep dairy in the country, Old Chatham is renowned for its Hudson Valley Camembert. The company's distinctive kelly-green and black logo has become iconic amongst cheesemakers and consumers alike. www.blacksheep cheese.com

- **Coach Farm:** One of America's landmark goat cheese producers, this Hudson Valley dairy now makes everything from ricotta and fresh and aged cheeses to fluid milk and yogurt. www.coachfarm.com

New York City is home to some of the nation's finest cheese shops. In Brooklyn, the "cheese borough," Stinky Bklyn and Bedford Cheese Shop are must-visits. In Manhattan, don't miss Fairway Market, Saxelby Cheesemongers, Murray's Cheese, Ideal Cheese, Artisanal, and Eataly.

Master cheesemonger and *Cheese Primer* author Steven Jenkins began working at the cheese counter of Fairway Market's flagship store on West 74th and Broadway as a complete neophyte in 1980, before launching the store's landmark cheese program in 1996. At that time, artisan cheese shops were few and far between, as were American cheese experts. Prior to Fairway, Jenkins established the cheese businesses at Dean & Deluca in 1977 and 1991. Although written in 1996, the *Cheese Primer* continues to be one of the most well-respected and comprehensive books on the subject.

### Connecticut and Massachusetts

Like New York and Vermont, the winters in these states are harsh — but great terroir makes up for climatic hardship. Notable producers include Great Hill Dairy (www.greathillblue.com), Cricket Creek Farm (www.cricketcreekfarm.com), Rawson Brook Dairy, and the following:

- **Cato Corner Farm:** This small family farm in Connecticut produces a variety of aged cheeses from the milk of Jersey cows. Standouts include Brigid's Abbey, a smooth, creamy Trappist-style with a tangy finish, and Hooligan, a pungent washed rind. www.catocornerfarm.com

- **Westfield Farm:** Located in central Massachusetts, Westfield Farm sources goat and cow milk from local dairies to produce standouts like Hubbardston Blue and Classic Blue Log (both unusual, surface-ripened blue cheeses, rather than the standard veined format), and Smoked Capri, a small chèvre log cold-smoked over hickory wood. www.chevre.com

# Oh, Canada!

Given its early French, English, and Dutch heritage, what's most surprising about Canadian cheese production is that it's taken so long for a modern artisan scene to emerge, both domestically and nationally. Some excellent cheeses are made throughout Canada, most notably in Quebec — the problem is that they're often difficult to find outside of their own provinces.

Canada's cheesemaking roots began in much the same way as in the United States, influenced by dominating colony or immigrants. As with other cold-climate cultures throughout the world, cheese was a subsistence food, and cheesemaking was a way to preserve milk and provide a valuable source of nutrients and protein throughout the lean winter months. Due to Canada's vast and varied terrain and harsh climate, agriculture is primarily practiced in the southern portion of British Columbia, Alberta, Ontario, and Lower Canada (southern Quebec, and for the purposes of this book, Nova Scotia, New Brunswick, and Prince Edward Island). Most of the country's estimated 180 cheesemakers are located within the provinces of Quebec, Ontario, and British Columbia.

The Canadienne Cow is the only "native" North American dairy breed. It was developed in French Canada from cattle brought over from Normandy in the early 17th century, and it resembles a dark brown Jersey cow (hence its nickname, "Black Jersey"). The elegant Canadienne is a high butterfat producer, making it ideal for a variety of styles, but very few purebred animals remain after extensive cross-breeding with Brown Swiss. Fortunately, conservation efforts and breeding programs have been initiated to help protect and preserve this symbol of Canada's dairy legacy. For more information, go to www. vachecanadienne.com.

During the 17th, 18th, and 19th centuries, cheese production in Canada was influenced by the French or the British. While the French inspired the production of a variety of styles, including the monastic cheeses that are still made in parts of Quebec, early British immigrants brought the technique of *cheddaring* (see Chapter 4) with them, leading to the production of that type of cheese. By 1840, Upper Canada's first commercial cheese factory opened. By 1900, over 2,000 cheese and dairy cooperatives existed throughout Canada, most of them small and farmer-owned.

By the 1950s, new government food safety and quality standards, in addition to low profits, forced many of the small, farmer-owned cheese factories to shut down or regroup into larger collectives. It wasn't until the 1980s that Canada began to experience a new wave of independent, artisan cheesemakers — many of them "back to the land" types or second careerists — which continues to flourish today.

Canadian artisan cheeses are less a reflection of their terroir (think of the alpine styles made in the European Alps or the fresh cheeses produced in hot, arid climates), and more about the whim of the cheesemaker. That said, every region has its microclimates and distinct terroir, so one can't say that well-crafted Canadian cheeses aren't specific to their locale.

Canada is a vast country with a fairly recent artisan cheesemaking scene largely unknown in the United States; in the following sections, we touch briefly upon the cheesemaking epicenters (see Figure 8-2).

**Figure 8-2:**
Key cheese-making regions in Canada.

# British Columbia

The diverse terroir found in British Columbia (BC) allows for an array of agricultural crops from wine and orchard fruits to dairy. The Fraser Valley wine region is comprised of hills, floodplains, and lakes that feed its vineyards and pastures, while the sunny, dry Okanogan Valley wine region tends toward scrubby vegetation well-suited to goats and sheep. Evergreen-lush Vancouver Island (which also produces wine) is also part of BC's cheese-producing regions.

Of note:

- ✔ **Kootenay Alpine Cheese Company:** Located just 10 minutes from the Idaho border, Kootenay Alpine Cheese Company produces excellent farmstead alpine-style cow milk cheeses. Using a number of sustainable management practices, Kootenay relies primarily on solar power for its cheese production, and the temperature of the aging caves is managed through geothermal cooling. www.kootenayalpinecheese.com

- ✔ **Farm House Natural Cheeses:** Natural Cheeses produces a variety of excellent aged, blue, surface-ripened, and fresh cow and goat milk cheeses. www.farmhousecheeses.com

## Alberta and Ontario

Ontario is home to a growing number of specialty cheese producers (approximately 40), and Toronto, Canada's largest city, is known for its food-loving populace. Proximity to a major marketplace, as well as Ontario's accessible, high-quality agricultural land, is a key factor in galvanizing the artisan cheese industry.

Alberta's cheese scene is less well-developed, but, like the rest of the country, is growing steadily. Alberta has more mountainous, rugged terrain than Ontario, so there may be more alpine-styles emerging in the future. Stay tuned.

Here are some regional highlights:

- ✔ **Sylvan Star Cheese:** Great farmstead cow milk Gouda from Red Deer, Alberta. Popular varieties include Old Grizzly (an extra-aged Gouda spiced with cayenne and green peppercorn) and Medium Smoked Gouda. www.sylvanstarcheesefarm.ca

- ✔ **Mariposa Dairy:** This Ontario goat dairy rocked the 2011 ACS Awards with its Lindsay Bandage Wrapped Cheddar, an 18-month aged wheel of goaty goodness. It, and Mariposa's other cheeses, are marketed throughout Canada and the U. S. under the brand name Celebrity International. www.mariposadairy.ca

- ✔ **Glengarry Fine Cheese:** This Ontario creamery sources local cow milk for its artisan cheeses, including award-winning Lankaaster Aged. It also sells all kinds of cheesemaking and dairy supplies. www.glengarry finecheese.com

- ✔ **Back Forty Artisan Cheese:** Back Forty is known for its small line of handcrafted sheep milk cheeses, including Highland Blue (which is allowed to develop a natural rind) and Madawaska, a creamy bloomy rind. www.artisancheese.ca

## Canada's cheesemaking isles

Canada is a nation of archipelagos on both its Pacific and Atlantic coasts, in addition to the *thousands* of islands dispersed throughout the Great Lakes region. Many of these have strong dairy economies and some cheesemakers of note. Vancouver Island, near Washington State, is delineated by the Vancouver Island Ranges, which make for a wet west coast full of meadows, pasture, and evergreen forest. The eastern side is drier and less rugged. Agriculture is a large part of the island economy and a handful of cheesemakers throughout the region use local milk or produce farmstead varieties. Îles de la Madeleine (or the Magdalen Islands) is a peaceful fishing community that's actually part of Quebec. Prince Edward Island (PEI) is probably best known throughout the Americas for its exceptional mussels. In Canada, however, the island's nickname is the "Garden of the Gulf" because of its pastoralism and agricultural economy.

Here are our picks for dairy-centric island hopping:

✔ **Little Qualicum Cheeseworks (Vancouver Island)** is known for its alpine-style and washed-rind cheeses. The farm is open to the public for tours and tastings. www. cheeseworks.ca

✔ **Fairburn Farm (Vancouver Island)** is a working water buffalo dairy; the milk is sent to the island's Natural Pastures Cheese Company, where it's turned into mozzarella di bufala. If agritourism is of interest to you (even if it's not, the adorable buffalo calves may change your mind), we highly recommend a stay at this lovely retreat, run by two generations of the Archer family. www. fairburnfarm.bc.ca

✔ **Fromagerie du Pied-de-Vent (Îles de la Madeleine)** crafts glorious washed-rind cheeses from its herd of 75 endangered Canadienne cows imported from the mainland. Try Pied-de-Vent, a Reblochon-style, and Tommes de Demoiselles. The cheese factory is open to the public. http:// fromagesdici.com/repertoire/ pied-de-vent

✔ At **Cows Creamery (Prince Edward Island)**, cheesemaker Scott Linkletter practices a centuries-old British tradition that had all but vanished from Canada: bandage wrapping cheddar. His Avonlea Clothbound cheddar is mild, with a gentle tang and hints of grass and earth. www.cowscreamery.ca

# Quebec and the Maritimes

Quebec is Canada's cheesemaking — and culinary — capital: Montreal is home to a thriving fine dining and localized food movement, galvanized in no small part by the city's French roots. Unsurprising, then, that Quebec is where Canada's artisan cheese movement began. Whether it's the French and monastic influences or the immensity of this flat, agriculturally rich province (and its abundant fresh water supply), Quebec is home to the majority of the country's cheese artisans. Whatever the reason, Québécois cheeses are high in quality, and a number are gaining fame throughout North America. (**Note:** If you're lucky enough to go to Montreal, look for *poutine*. It's a Quebecois invention of French fries, squeaky cheese curds, and gravy that's become a national obsession.)

The Maritimes provinces of New Brunswick and Nova Scotia are lush and fertile, and thus prime dairy land, particularly for cattle. This region produces large quantities of Gouda and cheddar.

The following are some of the most notable cheesemakers:

- ✔ **Fromagerie du Presbytère:** Its Louis d'Or, a Gruyère-style raw cow milk cheese made from a herd of 85 Jersey, Holstein, and Canadienne cows, always wins top awards. www.fromageriedupresbytere.com

- ✔ **Fromagerie Le Détour:** This Quebec creamery produces outstanding cow, goat, sheep, and mixed milk cheeses, including Le Clandestine (a cow and sheep milk washed-rind cheese) and Grey Owl (an ash-coated, surface-ripened goat milk variety). http://fromagerieledetour.ca/

- ✔ **Abbaye Saint Benoît du Lac:** Established in 1912 in Quebec by exiled French monks, this monastery started a cheese factory in 1943 and produced Canada's first blue cheese, L'Ermite (Ermite) Blue. Today, among other styles, it also produces an award-winning blue called Bleu Bénédictin.

In 1893, monks living near in the village of Oka, southwest of Montreal, established the tradition of monastic cheese in Canada with the creation of Oka, a semi-soft washed-rind cheese inspired by French Port Salut cheese. Oka is still made, although today it's produced by a commercial company after the monastery sold the rights to its production in 1996.

- ✔ **That Dutchman's Farm:** This Nova Scotia cheesemaking business specializes in cow milk Goudas, including an aged version, Old Growler Gouda, as well as a popular (and perhaps aptly named!) Dragon's Breath Blue. www.denhoek.ca

# Mexican Cheeses: Taste and Tradition

Mexico is one of the world's largest consumers of cheese, despite a relative lack of diversity in styles and varieties. While approximately 50 percent of the domestic cheese is factory-made, the remainder (mostly fresh cheeses) are produced in the home, small *queserias* (creameries), or *ranchos* (farmstead operations), primarily for personal, local, or regional consumption. From aged, crumbly Cotija to creamy *requeson* (ricotta), Mexican cheeses are mainly used as garnishes, for cooking, or at the table.

Dairy wasn't a part of traditional Mesoamerican culture. The Spanish conquistadors brought cows, sheep, and goats to the New World and introduced dairying and ranching to Mexico. Besides the Spanish influence, in more recent times, cheesemaking is believed to have been inspired by immigrants from Italy and Eastern Europe.

In the last few decades, Mexico has started to develop something of an artisan cheese movement, but most of these are only available locally at markets. (Some industrial cheeses are distributed to the United States; most traditional Mexican-style cheeses, however, are produced in Hispanic-owned factories in the U.S., mainly in California. There are some producers of fine artisan Mexican cheeses in the U.S., most notably in California, Oregon, and Wisconsin.)

Following are the most well-known varieties of Mexican cheese (all are made with cow milk unless otherwise indicated):

- **Añejo (semi-firm/hard):** A pressed, aged version of queso fresco, traditionally made from skimmed goat milk. It can be quite firm and salty and is usually used as a garnish. Similar to Pecorino Romano in flavor.

- **Asadero (soft/semi-soft):** A popular white melting cheese, mild in flavor with a slight tang. It's often used to make *queso fundido*, a fondue-like appetizer, or quesadillas.

- **Cotija (semi-firm/hard):** Traditionally a raw cow milk cheese that today is produced industrially all over Mexico. It's dense and crumbly in texture and has a pronounced sour-milk aroma balanced with a pleasant lactic tang. It's often referred to as Mexican feta or Parmesan.

- **Crema (fresh):** A cultured thickened cream with the consistency of a more silky crème fraiche; it's used as a garnish (to help ease the singe of spicy food) or incorporated into sauces or soups.

- **Queso Blanco (fresh):** A creamy, mild cheese made from skimmed milk, frequently served sliced and panfried because it doesn't melt. It's also used as a filling.

- **Queso Fresco (fresh):** A pressed cheese, with a crumbly, grainy texture and slight tang. It's used as a garnish atop *anjojitos* (little, fried masa dough–based snacks), beans, salads, soups, and entrees. The aged version of this cheese is called Anejo.

- **Queso Panela (fresh):** A soft, white, smooth, and moist cheese that's popular as a snack or sold flavored or wrapped in leaves. The best versions are from the village of Tapalpa, in Jalisco.

- **Queso Oaxaca (quesillo) (soft/semi-soft):** A pasta filata cheese that resembles a ball of ribbon and can be pulled apart for snacking, melting, or cooking.

- **Requeson (fresh):** A soft, ricotta-like cheese primarily used as a filling for dishes such as enchiladas.

# Getting Fresh in Central and South America

With the possible exception of Argentina, most people don't associate Central or South America with cheese. Like all of Latin America, these countries are a mix of indigenous cultures, colonizing forces, immigrant influence, and varied terroir, climatic extremes, and levels of industrialization. As a result, the cuisine and agricultural practices of each country have developed accordingly.

Despite the different cultures and cuisines in each country and the variations in how cheese is made and used, it's possible to generalize:

✔ Central and South Americans in general don't have a long tradition of producing aged cheeses for home use. Cheese is ubiquitously made in a variety of fresh or soft styles.

✔ Most cheese uses cow milk: queso blanco, queso fresco, and related styles (which may have many different regional names and variations). The curds may be soft and crumbly, resembling a firm, moist feta, or they may be smooth, semi-soft melting varieties.

✔ Various types of fresh, semi-soft, and sometimes even semi-firm or aged factory-produced cheeses are very popular and supermarket staples in cities, although cheese shops are extremely rare.

In this section, we focus on the countries with the most significant levels of cheese production and consumption.

Central America has similar cheese styles as the subtropical and tropical and/or Andean highlands regions of parts of Venezuela, Colombia, Ecuador, Peru, Bolivia, and Brazil. In rural communities, many families keep a cow for fluid milk and fresh cheese, which provides an immediate source of nutrients.

The fresh and soft melting cheeses produced in these regions are used as garnishes or fillings in street food and dishes of humble origins. Cheese is also used as a garnish in soups, stews, or salads, or mixed into sauces, as well as served at the table and eaten with tortillas, grains, rolls, or boiled corn. The variations all depend upon the terroir, country, and climate.

Here are some more specific examples of South American cheesemaking:

✔ **Ecuador:** Ecuador's sizeable German-speaking community has impacted the country's dairying culture, most notably with the introduction of aged cheeses. Hacienda Zuleta (www.haciendazuleta.com), in northern Ecuador, is a farmstead producer of fine semi-firm and washed-rind cheeses including Andino, which is available at select cheese shops in the United States.

✔ **Argentina:** Argentina is one of the world's top ten producers of cheese — primarily Parmesan, although *provoleta* — grilled slices of domestic provolone, seasoned with dried oregano — is a national dish.

In Buenos Aires — internationally known for its dining scene — cheese shops are growing more popular, and the province's La Ruta del Queso (the Cheese Route) is a self-guided tour that includes a stop at a cheese and wine shop and two *queserias* (cheese factories). For more information, go to `http://rutadelqueso.com.ar/`.

✔ **Brazil:** Like Argentina and Uruguay, Brazil's strong cattle ranching heritage and terroir has lead to the production of harder artisan and factory cheeses in the grasslands regions. Warmer, more humid climates yield fresh and soft cheeses.

Despite being the only industrialized nation in South America, Chile doesn't have a notable artisan cheese industry, and it's not as central to the diet as it is in the less-developed countries.

# Chapter 9

# The British Isles and Ireland

*In This Chapter*

▶ Demystifying the cheeses of England, Scotland, and Wales

▶ Discussing the diversity of Irish farmhouse cheeses

*F*rance is usually the first place to come to mind when thinking about ancient cheese heritage, but the United Kingdom has a long, historic tradition of cheesemaking. Although artisan cheese production was nearly extinct by the middle of the 20th century, today it's thriving and more vibrant than ever before. Read on for a tour of the robust cheeses of the British Isles and Ireland.

# Oh, Britannia! Cheeses of the United Kingdom

Although France often overshadows it, the British Isles have an ancient, noble tradition of artisan cheesemaking. The pre-Romans in Britain practiced dairy farming and cheesemaking over 2,000 years ago, and by the 1700s, Somerset (in the southwest) and Cheshire (in the north-central) had become significant cheesemaking centers, putting the U.K. on the map as a world-renowned producer of fine cheese. Yet by the 1980s — as a result of wartime mandates and the resulting era of industrially produced cheeses — traditional cheesemaking in the U.K. became nearly extinct.

Fortunately, thanks to a few notable families and individuals who helped revive the British Isles traditional cheesemaking industry, today the number of British cheesemakers has increased dramatically; new cheeses have been introduced to the marketplace, and new generations of farmers and cheesemakers have carried on the legacy of producing regional cheeses. Lucky us, because many of these cheeses are now sold in the United States.

In the following sections, we describe the general characteristics of cheeses that come from the United Kingdom and explain what cheeses hail from the country's different regions, shown in Figure 9-1.

We're only just scratching the surface of the cheeses the British Isles have to offer; for further detail, we recommend going to the Neal's Yard Dairy website, (www.nealsyarddairy.co.uk), or *culture* magazine's online Cheese Library, which provides an alphabetical compendium of many of the world's great cheeses, including those of the British Isles (www.culturecheesemag.com).

**Figure 9-1:**
Key cheese-
making
regions in
the United
Kingdom.

# Key characteristics of British cheeses

British cheeses tend to be natural rind or clothbound (see Chapter 4), with a fairly moist texture and high fat content that's ideal for conveying the flavors of the grasses, wildflowers, herbs, and other plants the animals are feeding upon. Following are a few other general points to know about cheese from the U.K.

# The rocky history of cheese in the British Isles

Strong evidence suggests that folks in the British Isles were making cheese even before the Romans took a fancy to the region in 43 AD. During the Middle Ages, cheesemaking in the U.K. was both a means of subsistence and barter. In the feudal system, peasants kept their own animals, and while the men tended to the field and livestock, the women made fresh and surface-ripened "farmer-style" cheeses that were used to pay rent, taxes, and other monetary dues.

The Agricultural Revolution that began in Britain in 1700 led to the production of harder, aged cheeses, which were more practical for the larger retail market because they kept longer and traveled better. Dairying and *farmhouse* (farmstead) and artisanal cheesemaking became industries in their own right, and Britain's cheese revolution had begun. World-renowned cheesemaking centers developed in Somerset and Cheshire, which would later become critical regions to modern-day artisanal cheesemaking.

Despite its remarkable cheesemaking history, things took a turn for the worse in the 20th century, for a variety of reasons:

- ✔ **Fallout from two World Wars:** Many dairies were forced to close following World War I because the labor force had been nearly decimated. Rationing food shortages and subsequent government legislation during WWII required the remaining dairy farmers to sell fluid milk for immediate consumption rather than converting it into cheese.

- ✔ **Adverse agricultural legislation:** These laws resulted in a massive decline in the number of cheesemakers in Britain. By way of example, in 1914, there were 2,000 producers of farmhouse Cheshire cheese, and in 1979, just one.

- ✔ **The era of industrial commodity food:** In the 1950s, after years of wartime hardship, the populace wanted food in abundance and a "modern" lifestyle. The popularity of supermarkets increased while small, independent cheese shops declined, taking with them the connections to the artisan and farmhouse cheesemakers themselves.

Despite the considerable obstacles, a few diehards — such as the Kirkham family of Lancashire soldiered on (you can read about this family's contribution in the later section "Cheeses from Northern England").

## Terroir

The British Isles share a similar temperate, wet climate. Thus, although every region produces its own signature cheeses, the styles aren't as varied as they'd be in places with greater climatic or geographical/elevational extremes. Far more important is the fact that much of the British Isles are dairy heaven with regard to terroir. Pastures may remain lush year-round, and the cool temperatures allow for the long maturation of cheeses.

The fact that the British climate is so suited for long maturation times is why a country so well-known for its heavenly single, double (containing a higher butterfat content), and clotted cream didn't traditionally produce oozy, gooey varieties such as those seen in France or Italy (discussed in Chapters 10 and 11, respectively). Today, of course, this is no longer true. The new generation of British cheesemakers have embraced the production of a more diverse array of styles and types of milk, now that a receptive retail audience exists both domestically and overseas. (Here's a bit of related trivia: If you look at a map of the world, you'll find that harder, larger format cheeses have traditionally been made in northern climes.)

The U.K.'s revival in farmstead cheesemaking has in turn sparked an interest in resurrecting specific heritage dairy breeds to add further flavor complexities to the final product. As a result, British cheeses are every bit as much an expression of their terroir as a Swiss alpine cheese or a runny French washed rind.

### Size: Bigger is better!

Why are aged British cheeses so hefty? We asked *culture* magazine co-founder and cheese director Kate Arding, a native Brit. Her answer: "It's not just a British thing, actually. When the size of a wheel increases, the ratio of surface area (rind) to volume changes dramatically. This means that larger wheels take much longer to mature than smaller ones, but the general thinking is that flavor development on larger wheels is better because the cultures work more slowly, over a longer period of time. It's also cost-effective, because during production and maturation, it takes much less time and labor to attend to, say, 5 large wheels rather than 20 small ones."

Many cheesemakers that produce large wheels often make smaller ones for the holiday market, although these are rarely under 5 pounds. If you're planning to do a lot of entertaining or gift giving, look no further.

---

## Time for tea: What's clotted cream?

Afternoon tea wouldn't be nearly as much fun if not for clotted cream. This thick, unsweetened treat is also known as Devonshire cream or Cornish clotted cream (the latter has a PDO designation and must be a minimum of 55 percent fat) because it's most associated with the counties of Devon and Cornwall in southwest England. Clotted cream is traditionally eaten with scones and jam, although we're not ashamed to say that we love it straight up by the spoonful. It's made by heating heavy cream over very low heat for at least 12 hours. The cream forms clots (hence its name) during the cooking process, after which it must be refrigerated overnight. The final product has a distinctive slightly caramelized, milky flavor and is outrageously good dolloped onto berries or other fresh summer fruit, as well as pie or tarts.

You can find imported, jarred Devonshire cream in specialty shops in the United States, but it's not the same as the real, fresh deal. Fortunately, clotted cream is easy to make; for a recipe, go to *culture* magazines's website: www.culturecheesemag.com/recipes/clotted_cream.

## Neal's Yard Dairy: A cheese industry legend

Founded in 1979 in London's Covent Garden district, Neal's Yard Dairy was originally created as a tiny creamery with the primary goal of producing fresh cheeses and Greek-style yogurt to sell to local residents. At the time, Britain's farmhouse and artisanal cheese industry was at its lowest point in modern history, and the handful of remaining traditional British cheesemakers struggled to sell their handcrafted cheeses alongside cheaper commodity versions of the same name.

During this time, 19-year-old Randolph Hodgson took over Neal's Yard Dairy. Frustrated at the lack of availability of British farmhouse cheeses via brokers and distributors (French cheeses, by contrast, were sold everywhere), he visited cheesemakers on their farms and brought their cheeses back to sell at Neal's Yard alongside housemade fresh cheeses. Interestingly, early customers who came into the shop found it hard to believe that British cheeses could taste so good. Sales grew, allowing Neal's Yard to focus attention on the producers, raising awareness of British cheeses in the process. Starting in the late 1980s, British cuisine began to come into its own, largely thanks to a handful of well-respected British chefs who were buying quality regional ingredients — including cheese.

Today, Neal's Yard consists of two retail stores and a large warehouse where British cheeses are exported across the globe. The dairy has also influenced and helped the start-up of cheese businesses around the world including in the U.S. In addition, Neal's Yard alumni have gone on to create their own cheese businesses, both in the U.K. and as far afield as New Zealand. Long may it continue.

— Kate Arding, *culture* magazine co-founder and cheese director

## The Southwest and West

Consisting of undulating hills, moorland, and rocky coastal cliffs, this southwestern and culturally rich corner of England generally maintains a temperate climate due to the presence of the Gulf Stream. In addition, this region has mineral deposits in the soil and plenty of salt-laden Atlantic rain, which combine to provide good pasture: a dream for dairy farmers and cheesemakers because the animals can graze outdoors year-round.

Although cheddar is made throughout the Southwest in Devon, Cornwall, and Dorset, Somerset and Mendip Hills produce the most renowned versions. The limestone in these areas promotes the healthy and varied growth of grass in the Southwest and gives the cheeses a distinct flavor.

Following are a few of the most famous cheeses of these regions, beginning with the cheddars of Somerset; the two listed here are the most traditional clothbound English varieties available. The cloth wrapping protects the cheeses and prevents them from cracking during the maturation process, which can range from 6 to 18 months (or, in rare cases, up to 3 years).

✔ **Keen's Cheddar:** The Keen family has been dairying at Moorhayes Farm since the end of the 19th century. This raw cow milk cheddar is one of our favorites: golden-hued, buttery, and rich, with a spicy bite on the finish. It's made in 30-pound half wheels or 56-pound traditional wheels. We know — it makes our backs hurt, too!

✔ **Montgomery's Cheddar:** Considered by many to be the *other* member of the Royal Family, this noble, beefy, fruity cheddar is made by James Montgomery and Steve Bridges of Manor Farm. The Montgomery family has been making cheese for three generations from raw cow milk. "Monty's" is aged for a minimum of 12 months and up to 24 months.

✔ **Ticklemore:** This firm, pasteurized goat cheese was created and originally made by Robin Congdon of Ticklemore Dairy in Devon; he's also the master behind several of the region's blue cheeses. Ticklemore is pressed by hand into a colander, which gives it a distinctive, flying saucer shape. This cheese is slightly crumbly and moist with milky and mushroomy flavors.

✔ **Single and Double Gloucester:** Admittedly one of the more mild cheeses out there, Gloucester is a white or pale orange raw cow milk cheese that's usually eaten young — between 2 and 9 months. (By the way, it's pronounced "*gloss*-ter." Now you can amble up to the cheese counter and request it like a pro.)

Single and Double Gloucester are very different from one another. Single Gloucester refers to the version made from skimmed milk, which gives the cheese a drier, more crumbly texture than Double Gloucester, which is made with whole milk and cream. Thus, Double Gloucester is the longer aged of the two, with a slightly creamier, less sharp flavor.

# The Southeast and East

Historically, this region of England is one of the most interesting; its proximity to London and the rest of Europe means it's always been heavily influenced by trade and foreign affairs, the results of which can be seen in the architecture and by the fact that it's widely regarded as the wealthiest area of Britain.

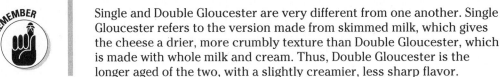

## What's in a name?

Call us silly, but one of the things that really delights us about British cheeses are the names. Many are given the surname of the cheesemaker, but others sound so lyrical to our American ears that we consider the name alone another reason to like these cheeses! There's Ticklemore, Cornish Yarg, Stinking Bishop (we cover that one in Chapter 20), Ogleshield, Woolsery English Goat, Flower Marie, Stumpies, Duddleswell, Lord of the Hundreds, Blacksticks Blue, Crowdie, Cooleeney, Knockdrinna, and T'yn Grug.

Climate and topography play a large role in this region's success. The southeast — Kent in particular — has a microclimate and soil structure highly suitable for small-scale and arable farming (primarily hops, for you beer lovers). These factors, combined with the nearby London market, made the region predominantly geared to crop production rather than dairying. In addition, the influx of wealth over the last three decades has resulted in the eradication of much of the farmland in favor of development.

Yet, all is not bleak on the dairying front. Thanks to the artisanal food movement, a number of significant cheesemaking operations have sprung up and are flourishing, largely due to the same influences that helped small-scale farmers survive for centuries: namely, proximity to major economic demand.

Here are some of the notable cheeses from this area's emerging cheesemakers:

- **Wigmore:** Anne and Andy Wigmore's Village Maid Cheese Company is located in a converted garage in their garden: no ancient dairy farm here! The couple also produce Spenwood (raw, natural rind, sheep milk) and Waterloo (raw, cow milk, semi-soft), which are famous in their own right. Wigmore is a bloomy-rind sheep milk cheese with a clean, lactic flavor with hints of grass and citrus.

- **Tunworth:** This raw cow milk camembert-style cheese is another departure from traditional aged English cheeses. Cheesemakers Julie Cheyney and Stacey Hedges made their first batch in 2004; today they produce approximately 250 cheeses a day — proof that Britain can't get enough of French-style bloomy-rind cheeses that reflect the local terroir.

- **Golden Cross:** This family dairy owned by Kevin and Alison Blunt has been producing hard and surface-ripened raw goat and sheep milk cheeses since 1989. They make a traditional, ash-coated goat cheese log reminiscent of France's St. Maure that's delicate, tangy, and earthy.

## The Midlands

The Midlands area of England is well-known for its mineral-rich soil. These factors weren't lost on Victorian entrepreneurs: from the late 18th century until the 1980s, this region was at the heart of Britain's coal mining, heavy industry, and steel manufacturing. Although a significant proportion of the landscape reflects these now-defunct factories and mines, it's counterbalanced by large expanses of hauntingly beautiful moorland and the surviving agricultural farmland.

Due to its wet and windswept weather, the Midlands are better suited to livestock farming than arable crops. In recent years, efforts have been made to restore and enhance areas of grazing and pasture, most of which had been stripped of nutrients — the result of mining activities. In addition to traditional beef production, the area has become increasingly attractive to dairy farmers and cheesemakers. Here are some cheeses that come from the Midlands:

- **Cheshire:** Believed to be England's oldest cheese, Cheshire dates back to at least Roman times. This cow milk cheese is one of the great classics of Britain, notable for its pinky-orange hue (from the addition of annatto, a dye made from the seed of the achiote shrub), crumbly texture, and mild, tangy flavor that grows more pronounced and savory with age. Although waxed versions are available, our favorite Cheshire is the clothbound version from Appleby's Farm in Shropshire.

- **Shropshire Blue:** This cow milk cheese originally hails from Scotland, but in the 1970s, its production was moved to Nottinghamshire and Leicestershire after the closure of Castle Stuart Dairy in Scotland. It's atypical of most blues due to its bright orange paste (annatto, again). It's creamy, sharp, and spicy; try it with a glass of dessert wine.

- **Lincolnshire Poacher:** These 44-pound cylinders of raw cow milk cheese have been made by fourth-generation farmers and brothers Tim and Simon Jones since 1992. Based on a traditional Somerset Cheddar recipe, the Joneses have tweaked things a bit, combining fresh, warm morning milk with cooled milk from the previous evening and allowing the development of a natural rind. Aged between 1 to 2 years, this cheese has a smooth texture and fruity flavors with hints of grass and toasted nuts.

- **Stilton:** Often called the "king of English cheeses," this cylindrical PDO blue has been around since the 18th century. It can be produced only in the counties of Nottinghamshire, Derbyshire, or Leistershire (from local milk), but there are additional strict production laws. Stilton's trademark earthy, meaty, full flavors make it an ideal pairing with port or dried fruit. It's often thought of as a holiday cheese because the wheels, which are made in September or early October (the best time for producing this type of cheese) are mature at Christmastime.

Stilton was traditionally made with raw milk, but in 1989, a listeria outbreak — which, it's worth noting, was never definitively traced back to the cheese — resulted in changes in Stilton's production. Since then, it's been made with pasteurized milk; one of the best producers is Colston-Bassett Dairy.

## The North of England and the Borders

The North of England and the Borders (refer to Figure 9-1) is a traditional stone mining region with a varied terrain that ranges from rolling hills and moors to rugged rocky upland. The rural landscape has changed relatively little; the fields enclosed by dry stone walls and the stone farmhouses and cottages that dot the foothills of the larger mountains look much the same as they did hundreds of years ago.

Due to its chilly climate and topography, this area, which includes Yorkshire, Northumberland, and Lancashire, was traditionally suited to sheep farming and dairying.

The North of England and Border regions were home to some of Britain's oldest traditions of cheesemaking, which were at one time associated with the monasteries built by Jervaulx monks newly arrived from Normandy in the 11th century. Unfortunately, many of the region's cheeses have been lost to history, due in part to the Reformation and subsequent dissolution of the monasteries by Henry VIII in the 16th century. In other cases, it was because the cheeses were primarily made for home consumption and the recipes were lost. Although many farms might have had one or two cows to provide milk for home cheesemaking, it wasn't until the mid-1800s that cow dairying on a commercial scale began to have an impact.

The cheeses of this region have a very distinct terroir, which can be tasted in Northern England's most famous examples:

- ✔ **Wensleydale:** The greatest success story of any of the cheeses of this region, Wensleydale was introduced by the Normans and managed to survive the chaotic centuries of war, disease, poverty, and industrialization. Today, it remains one of Britian's better-known farmhouse cheeses — and Wallace & Grommit's love for it has certainly helped spread the name far and wide. Hawes Creamery produces one of the more traditional versions, using raw cow milk (sometimes, sheep milk is used) and binding the cheese in cloth. Wensleydale is usually eaten young, when it's finely textured, flakey, and moist.

- ✔ **Lancashire:** This raw cow milk cheese is wrapped in cloth and then rubbed liberally with butter to seal it and prevent unwanted molds from developing. It's aged for at least 6 weeks, resulting in a mild, buttery, crumbly cheese redolent of the wildflowers and herbs the cows graze upon, with a lemony tang on the finish. Lancashire's texture is so rich and creamy that locals refer to it as "buttery crumble," but cheesemaker Graham Kirkham prefers to call it "fluffy monster."

## Cheeses from Scotland and Wales

While both of these countries produce cheese, it's not in significant enough amounts or well-known enough outside of the U.K. to cover in this brief chapter. Here, we highlighted the most famous cheeses from each country, to give you a taste of what's out there:

✔ **Scotland's Isle of Mull cheese:** Scotland doesn't produce a vast array of cheese, but arguably its most famous is Isle of Mull Cheddar. It's produced on, er, the Isle of Mull, located in the Inner Hebrides, off the west coast of Scotland. The Gulf Stream makes for a mild climate that produces rich pasture on this otherwise hilly island that boasts 300 miles of coastline. Made from raw cow milk on Sgriob-ruadb Farm, the 50 pound wheels are clothbound and have a delicate acidity and a moist texture and may develop blue veining as they age.

✔ **Caerphilly from Wales:** From the lunch pails of Welsh coal miners centuries ago to a sought-after treasure at today's cheese shops, Caerphilly cheese has traveled some distance. Although the very first Caerphilly — a fresh, moist farmstead curd that workers carried into the mines — has nearly vanished with the advent of factory-made versions (which are rindless, acidic, and bear no similarity to the aged, natural-rind version we discuss here), a new artisanal interpretation of old-fashioned Caerphilly has put this quirky cow milk cheese in front of connoisseurs.

Gorwydd Caerphilly, made by the Trethowan brothers of Gorwydd Farm in central Wales, debuted in 1996 to the delight of cheese aficionados. With little resemblance to the Caerphilly still made in British factory dairies, the Gorwydd version redefines Caerphilly and raises the prestige of the lowbrow cheese. Today, this aromatic, aged cheese with its furry gray rind and mushroomy flavor has become the benchmark for what this cheese can — and should — be.

# Cheeses from the Emerald Isle

Like the United Kingdom, Ireland has a centuries-long history of cheesemaking. The prodigious amount of rain, mineral-rich soil, and temperate climate from the Gulf Stream make this island a dairy haven the likes of which has few other counterparts on the planet. The combination of Celtic history, climate, proximity to continental Europe, and the influences of itinerant monks and the Catholic church over the centuries have all influenced the cheesemaking, as evidenced by the variety of styles, which include washed rinds, blues, and aged cheeses, as well as butter of exceptional quality.

In the 1970s, a back-to-the-land movement brought several cheesemakers to the south and southwest of Ireland (County Cork and Kerry) which have become primary cheesemaking centers, particularly for washed rinds. Westerly ocean breezes spray the abundant pastures with salt, which introduces flavors to the milk, giving it a true Irish terroir. Other key cheese-producing regions include County Clare, in the northeast and Tipperary, in Central Ireland. Figure 9-2 shows the main cheese-producing areas in Ireland.

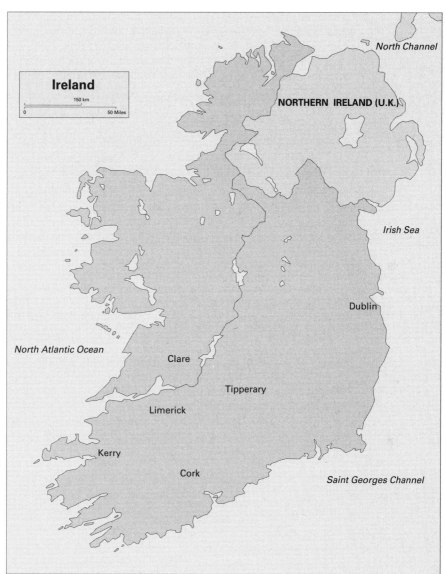

**Figure 9-2:**
Ireland's
main
cheese-
producing
areas.

The following list offers a brief overview of Irish cheeses from the Republic of
Ireland (not included are the cheeses of Northern Ireland, which has smaller
production that isn't well-known in the U.K. and beyond):

- ✔ **Gubbeen:** This 3-pound disc of semi-soft, pasteurized, washed-rind cow milk cheese is a great example of modern Irish farmhouse cheesemaking. Giana and Tom Ferguson began producing this slightly pungent, earthy, buttery cheese in 1979, using milk from their mixed herd, that includes Ireland's only native breed, the Kerry cow.

- ✔ **Cashel Blue:** Ireland's most famous blue is produced in County Tipperary by the Grubb family. Named after the Rock of Cashel, an outcrop overlooking the Tipperary plains, Cashel Blue is made from the family's herd of Friesian cows. After aging for up to 6 months, this rich, creamy beauty develops well-marbled veins and a clean, lactic flavor; more mature versions are mellower, with a hint of nuttiness.

- ✔ **St. Tola Original:** Located in County Clare is St. Tola Organic Goat Cheese, a 65-acre organic dairy. The goats graze outdoors in summer on buttercups, meadowsweet, and wild garlic, which result in fresh, soft, and hard cheeses of exceptional flavor. This namesake cheese is a mild surface-ripened number with a rich mouthfeel that makes it ideal for a cheese plate or cooking.

- ✔ **Dilliscus:** This most unusual farmhouse cow milk cheese from County Kerry is made by Maja Binder. Her farm is located on the Dingle Peninsula, where the coastal pastures are washed by sea spray, which gives the milk — and thus the cheese — potent herbal and gamey flavors. Dilliscus contains *dillisk* (or *dulse),* a North Atlantic species of red seaweed. Seaweed, prepared in various ways, is a traditional food of the Irish diet. Dilliscus is an ugly cheese, without question: Its rind is rust-colored and pitted, and it has a smoky brown paste marked by small eyes. Binder wraps her cheeses in brown paper tied with string (to allow them to breathe without getting wet). The result is a potent cheese that pleases some and frightens others: but it's definitely got terroir!

# Chapter 10

# France

**In This Chapter**

▶ Discovering France's dairying history and its cheesy past and present

▶ Covering key cheese regions, from Normandy to the Midi-Pyrenees

**C**heese, wine? *Ooh la la*! Even dairy-phobes know that France and cheese are practically synonymous. Why? Because the French have been making cheese for centuries, and that kind of practice makes perfect. France is the top exporter of cheese worldwide and domestically produces over 1,000 varieties of farmstead, artisanal, and industrial cheese (46 of them PDO-designated, see Chapter 2).

It's easy to devote an entire book to the cheeses of France, and many authors have. Alas, we have only this one chapter, which is why we just skim the surface: But fear not. We provide you with a general overview of how the history and terroir of this dairy-obsessed country have conspired to create an unprecedented, fabulous cheese culture, and introduce you to some wonderful French cheeses.

In this chapter, we only just scratch the surface of the cheeses France has to offer. For more in-depth reading on Gallic dairy goodness, we recommend *culture* magazine's online Cheese Library, which provides an alphabetical compendium of many of the world's great cheeses, including those of France (www.culturecheesemag.com/cheese-library). We also recommend these books: *Cheese: Exploring Taste and Tradition,* by Patricia Michelson (Gibbs Smith); *French Cheeses,* by Dorling Kindersley (DK Publishing); and *Cheese Primer,* by Steven Jenkins (Workman).

# Fancying France

Cheese holds a sacred place in everyday French life, as evidenced by the sheer volume of cheeses produced domestically, the number of dedicated cheese shops (*crèmeries*), the key role dairy (primarily butter and cream, but also cheese, depending upon the region) plays in the cuisine, and the ubiquitous *cheese course.* This course is a part of most meals and is served directly after the main course with salad and before the dessert, or in place of dessert.

## Becoming the King of Cheese

Each region of France (there are 22 metropolitan plus 5 overseas regions) produces its own specific cheeses, carefully and mindfully protected by government and proprietary regulations, designated by the acronym PDO (Protected Designation of Origin; see Chapter 2 for more information).

With so many cheeses being produced in a country that's geographically smaller than the state of Texas, you may wonder how that much variety is possible. The reasons:

- **Multiple microclimates:** Many of France's regions have specific microclimates, which result in cheeses with a very distinct terroir. The topography of these areas ranges from salty coastal marsh, to grasslands and lush valleys comprised of vineyards, orchards, and pasture, to the extreme elevations and snowy peaks of the Alps, Jura, and Pyrenees mountains. The map in Figure 10-1 shows France and its mountain ranges.

    A word about regions: France uses the term *département* to describe its administrative regions; think of them as comparable to a county in the United States. Historic regions are contained within the larger, contemporary regions (think of these as you would the Pacific Northwest or New England). It gets confusing, and we clarify as needed throughout this chapter.

- **Cultural and cheesemaking influences from bordering countries:** Some of France's regions are adjacent to and interconnected to Spain, Italy, and Switzerland, while others border Belgium and Germany. These border regions have a rich, diverse culture of cheesemaking and well-defined local cuisines that are influenced by their neighbors.

- **History and tradition:** The Loire Valley and Poitou, for example, are known specifically for their goat milk cheeses, because invading Saracens brought both goats and goat cheese recipes with them in the 8th century. Monasteries in various regions have produced renowned washed-rind cheeses such as Munster and Livarot for centuries, and the Basque Pyrenees, with its tradition of shepherding, yields aged sheep milk cheeses like Ossau-Iraty.

## Shopping for French cheeses in the States

As wonderful as French cheeses are, you may face a challenge or two when you try to buy certain varieties in the United States (and we're not just talking about pronunciation!).

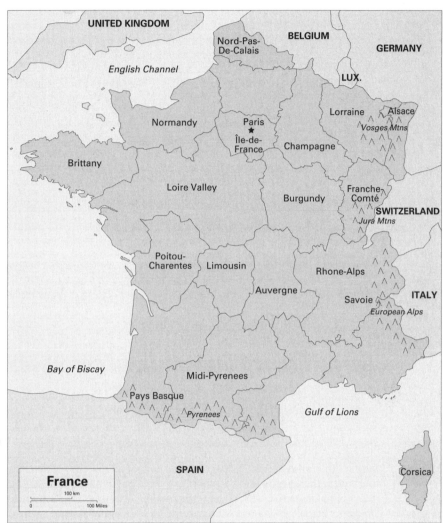

**Figure 10-1:**
France and
its mountain
ranges.

Seventy-percent of France's PDO cheeses are made with raw milk — and
many of those are aged less than 60 days, the minimum amount of time
required by U.S. regulations for import. That's why you can't find authentic
versions of cheeses such as Camembert de Normandie, Brie de Melun or Brie
de Meaux, and Selles-Sur-Cher in the United States (see Chapter 3 for info on
soft cheeses). For export to countries that don't permit the sale of raw milk
cheeses under 60 days of age, pasteurized milk is used (the same law applies
to raw milk cheeses made in the United States). For more information on raw
milk and raw milk cheese, head to Chapter 2.

Another hurdle to buying French cheeses is being able to pronounce the name of the cheese. One of the most frequent questions we hear at our respective cheese counters from customers perusing the French cheeses? "Can I please get some (*indistinct mumble*)?" Trust us, most cheesemongers aren't fluent in French either; we have to learn how to say those complicated names and regions, too. Don't be embarrassed if you mangle the name, but the easiest thing to do is point to the cheese you're interested in and ask, "I'd love to try some of that. How do you pronounce it?" Next time, you'll sound like a pro!

# Cheeses from the North

The northern part of France is — pardon the pun — a melting pot of cheese culture. Most of the varieties produced here have been influenced by the surrounding countries, and the best known cheeses of these regions include Brie, camembert, Livarot, and Mimolette. We discuss these, and more, in the following sections.

One of the other reasons this part of France is well-populated with cheese-makers is because it's near Paris. The proximity of a major retail, wholesale, and export center means cheesemakers have an almost immediate outlet for their cheeses — especially crucial for fresh or otherwise perishable varieties.

## Île-de-France and its fabulous cheeses

Located adjacent to the region of Champagne and home to Paris, Île-de-France is one of the most populous and affluent regions in France. This green, lush area is ideal for dairying and is also the birthplace of Brie, one of the world's most beloved cheeses.

In the 7th century, this region became known as Brie, and the cheese itself garnered the moniker in the 11th century. Brie cheeses were initially produced on farms and monasteries for the personal use of farmers and monks. Brie is the closest cheese region to Paris, and in the Middle Ages, Brie cheeses were sold at the great fairs of Meaux and Melun to supply Parisian markets via rivers. By the end of the 18th century, the Courts of Europe always finished gala dinners by serving this favorite cheese of the Parisian elite.

# Why does France produce so many different cheeses?

In the 19th century, France produced 300 different varieties of cheese; today, it produces over 1,000. Why so many? We asked Cécile Delannes, who runs the American-based French Cheese Club, her opinion.

"The fact that the French are very food-obsessed explains why most villages develop their own specialty, whether it's a pastry, candy, main dish, wine, or cheese," she explains. "If you go to a French farmers' market, you can see how proud the vendors are of their respective products. When it comes to making cheese, every producer has their own way of differentiating their product, so it's very distinct to their dairy as well as the terroir. It can be quite funny, because even family members will argue over who makes the best, say, Cantal, even though they're all produced in the same village — just by different cheesemakers."

She adds, "The fascinating thing is that this isn't all marketing hype. I was shocked when I visited E. Graindorge (a cheese producer in Normandy). Every cheese not only had a lot and batch number assigned, but they could even name the woman who hand-ladled the curds into the forms. Proprietor Thierry Graindorge explained that each woman has a special *coup de main* — the way the curd is hand-cut and dropped — that makes their final camembert slightly different. Consumers will specifically request cheeses made by "Marie" or "Colette." Talk about artisanal!"

There are various types of Brie cheeses — some of which are PDO, while others are not. Thus, a Brie produced in one village may differ in flavor than a Brie made in a village nearby: the reasons for this difference are terroir, breed of animal, or production technique. See Chapter 3 for more information on Brie. The following list gives you the lowdown on the best of Brie:

- **Brie de Meaux:** Made in Meaux, a municipality in the Île-de-France region, this is one of the two PDO-protected Brie cheeses. Aged on straw mats, this bloomy-rind cow milk cheese weighs about 6 pounds and is approximately 15 inches in diameter. The white rind comes from the use of *Penicillium candidum* mold, and it often becomes reddish brown as it ages. The paste is deep, creamy yellow. Aromas and flavors are of mushrooms, truffles, almonds, and hay.

If you want to try a cheese as close to Brie de Meaux as possible and aren't planning a trip to France, try Fromage de Meaux. This cheese is made in Île-de-France and is produced in a manner identical to that of Brie de Meaux, with one key difference: Fromage de Meaux is made from pasteurized milk, whereas its PDO-designated cousin can only come from raw milk.

✔ **Brie de Melun:** Made in the larger Île-de-France municipality of Melun, this is a stronger flavored, more rustic cow milk Brie than its sister, Brie de Meaux. It's also smaller, weighing just over 3 pounds.

Brie de Melun and Brie de Meaux are actually made differently (they vary in coagulation methods and time), so their PDO regulations are adjusted accordingly.

 ✔ **Brie de Nangis:** Even smaller in size than Brie de Melun (Nangis is about 2 pounds) and *not* PDO-regulated, this cow milk cheese hails from the municipality of Nangis. Almost extinct, Brie de Nangis was brought back into production very recently. It's creamy, full-flavored, and very mushroomy.

Unless Brie is clearly labeled with *Meaux, Melun,* or *Nangis,* it's not produced in these areas. There are many Brie producers worldwide but only a few that make the real thing. Quality does vary between producers, so perform your own taste test or ask your cheesemonger for suggestions.

Note that the following cheeses are not true Bries, but they are made in a similar style:

 ✔ **Coulommiers:** This small, bloomy-rind cow milk cheese probably predates Brie — and quite likely inspired its production. It's, in essence, a small format Brie but, because of its size, doesn't fit the criteria for a PDO. It's creamy, mushroomy, and more dense than Brie and is often served slightly underripe.

 ✔ **Fougerus:** Named for the fern (*fougère*) that adorns its surface, this bloomy-rind cow milk wheel is slightly larger than Coulommiers and similarly made. Rouzaire created this cheese and is the sole producer. Fougerus is buttery, earthy, and slightly grassy in flavor and aroma.

 ✔ **Explorateur:** Buttery and luscious, this cow milk triple crème has the same white rind as Brie and Brie-style cheeses but it's richer and more velvety. As it ages, the flavor becomes stronger.

Sometimes a piece of Brie, camembert, or other bloomy-rind cheese has an ammoniated aroma when you first open it. This is due to the ripening cheese's natural gases that are trapped inside its wrapping. Let the cheese air out for a few minutes, and the smell should dissipate. Note that the cheese will still have a sharper, tangy odor, which is not only normal, but appropriate. That said, bloomy-rind cheeses are supposed to be flavorful, mushroomy, earthy, and oozy — but never ammoniated or with a runny, watery texture. If your cheese displays these characteristics, toss it out. See Chapter 7 for more information on serving and storing cheese.

# *Normandy's cheeses*

Known for its verdant pastures, distinctive Normande dairy cows, prolific apple orchards, and 360 miles of dramatic coastline, this region in northwest France has been producing outstanding milk and dairy products since the 10th century.

The regions of Isigny and Brittany have long been famous for butter and cream, but the Pays d'Auge, the green, fertile dairy country in the heart of Normandy, is known for its cheese. Pont l'Évéque and Livarot — both washed-rind cheeses — are also produced here and are two of the most famous in France.

Normandy is excellent dairy country because the warm waters of the Gulf Stream sweep its coastline, yielding a mild climate, warm southwesterly winds, abundant rainfall, and salt-sprayed pastures. Normande cows also produce one of the richest milks (in butterfat content, minerals, proteins, and vitamins).

Here are a few of the signature cheeses of the Normandy region:

- **Camembert de Normandie:** One of the best known French cheeses — and perhaps the most widely copied cheese in the world — Camembert de Normandie is basically a small version of Brie made in a different area. The real deal must come from this exact place: It's made from the milk of the Normande cow, weighs 8 ounces, and is about 4½ inches wide. See Chapter 3 for more information.

  Look for 45 to 50 percent butterfat on the labels of your camembert and Brie cheeses: The higher the butterfat content, the milder the flavor. If you want a butter-bomb, go for a triple-crème like Brillat-Savarin (included later in the list).

- **Livarot:** Known as "the poor people's meat," this small, reddish-orange, washed-rind cow milk cheese was originally made by monks; today, E. Graindorge is the only cheesemaker in the town of Livarot. The cheese has a strong, beefy taste and aroma. The raw milk version is hand-wrapped with loops of a reed harvested from local lagoons, while pasteurized Livarot is wrapped with strips of paper.

- **Pont l'Évèque:** Made in a square or rectangular shape, this PDO washed-rind cow milk cheese was originally produced in monasteries. Its weight varies widely, from 6 ounces to 3.6 pounds. It's beefy and nutty, with a texture similar to a ripe camembert. The rind, like that of Livarot, can be bitter and sometimes gritty, so many choose not to eat it, but oh, what glorious flavor the interior possesses!

- **Brillat-Savarin:** Originally created in Normandy during the 1930s by renowned cheese affineur and retailer Henri Androuët, this much-loved triple crème was named after the famous 18th century politician and epicure. It's made from pasteurized cow milk on a fairly large scale, and production now also occurs in northern Burgundy and Brie.

✔ **Mimolette:** Also known as *Boule de Lille* ("ball from Lille"), Mimolette is produced in the Flanders area of Pas-de-Calais, in northern France, as well as in Normandy. This aged, raw cow milk cheese is similar to Dutch Edam, with caramel, butterscotch, and sweet, toasted nut to sharp, cheddar-like flavors. The waxy paste is bright orange because of the use of annatto (a seed from a South American shrub), but it's the rind that makes Mimolette famous.

The rind is very dense, thick (up to half-an-inch) and hard. It's not uncommon to see a coating of brown dust on the outside, which is a sign of age and the action of mites munching on the rind. The mites' digestive enzymes are said to contribute to the flavor of the cheese (we know . . .). Although edible, the rind itself isn't appealing in flavor or texture. Yet, a good Mimolette is also a thing of beauty: a moonscaped cannonball of a cheese that, when cut, makes for a striking addition to the table or cheese plate.

While the species may vary, cheese mites are little insects (Mimolette harbors the species *Acarus siro,* to be specific) that are just barely visible to the naked eye. They're generally considered pests because they feed upon the rind of a cheese, resulting in a pocked appearance, a residue of brown dust (this is actually an accumulation of both live and dead mites, cheese, and excreta . . . not exactly appetizing), and signature musty aroma. Cheese mites aren't harmful if consumed, but they can render a cheese unsalable. Yet, sometimes, as with Mimolette, the nibbling action of the mites is considered beneficial.

✔ **Neufchâtel:** Neufchâtel (the real thing, *not* the cheese of the same name sold in the United States as a low fat version of cream cheese) is a surface-ripened cow milk cheese that's been made in Normandy for over 1,000 years. It's made into various shapes, including hearts, logs, and squares; its nickname, *Coeur de Bray* ("heart of Bray"), comes from the name of the oldest market town in Normandy, Bray.

# Cheeses from Western France

France's western side faces the Bay of Biscay, running from the mouth of the Loire River down to the border it shares with Spain. Much of the coastline is comprised of long, sandy beaches interspersed with estuaries and inlets, but in the agricultural inland, some of the country's best-known cheeses (and wines) are produced.

# Loire Valley

Incredibly fertile land paired with mild temperatures have garnered this major wine, goat cheese, and crop-producing region the moniker, "Garden of France." The namesake Loire River and its tributaries create microclimates ideal for agricultural pursuits. The loveliness of this pastoral region attracted kings and nobility, who built magnificent country châteaux that still stand today.

The Loire is the land of goat cheese (chèvre). Because of its large size — approximately 300 square miles — it produces 70 percent of France's goat cheese (the country is also the top producer of goat cheese in the world).

The Loire produces high-quality goat cheeses in all shapes and sizes (although most are small format), ranging from logs and discs to pyramids and tiny cylinders called *crottin*. The wine, too, is abundant here; much of it is crisp and bone-dry, like Sancerre, which conveniently pairs well with the local cheeses.

Following are a few notable cheeses from this region:

- **Chabichou:** Its name is derived from the ancient Saracens who once lived in the area with their goats (*chebli*). These petite goat milk cylinders can be eaten quite young or aged for several months, which makes them very firm and strong-flavored. Try grating them on top of salads or pasta.

- **Crottin de Chavignol:** Excuse the French sense of humor: *Crottin* means "animal droppings," which refers to the shape and appearance of these little, wrinkled — dare we say adorable — goat cheese cylinders. Don't think that something this small won't have much flavor; crottin have incredibly rich, complex flavors with hints of coconut, hay, and sweet cream.

- **Sainte-Maure de Touraine:** Made in a log shape with a piece of straw, wheat, or a thin stick inserted down the center to hold it together as it ages, this PDO goat cheese is easy to serve (remove said straw and slice crosswise). It may be coated with ash (for aesthetics) or will often grow a blueish mold, which is harmless.

- **Selles-Sur-Cher:** This small, PDO goat milk disc (or *rond*) is traditionally coated in ash and often eaten at a few weeks of age, rather than more matured. Like most of these regional cheeses, it's named for its place of origin — "on the (river) Cher." The town of Berry is the epicenter of the local goat cheese production.

- **Valençay:** Made in an eye-catching pyramid-shape, this goat cheese is well-known throughout France and widely imitated elsewhere. According to legend, the flattened top of the pyramid came about after a French diplomat (Talleyrand) lopped it off to ensure that Napoleon, who was visiting Talleyrand's chateau, wouldn't take offense after his failed conquest in Egypt. Now *that's* deference!

## C'est chèvre

The French word *chèvre* (pronounced "shev") translates literally as "goat." When referring to cheese, however, it means "goat milk cheese" and, in particular, the fresh or mold-ripened varieties that come in an array of sizes, shapes, and flavors.

Chèvre — as in goat milk cheese, be it fresh, dried, smoked, or otherwise fiddled with — is made all over the world. The French, however, are the unspoken titleholders for being the world's most skilled and most prolific producers of goat milk cheeses. The Loire Valley in mid-western France, in particular, is known for its heavenly chèvres.

In its most simple form, chèvre is soft and fresh, similar to cream cheese, with a delicate, slightly tangy flavor. In a global sense, it's eaten straight up, rolled in herbs or spices, used as a filling for pasta or meat, made into spreads or dips, or crumbled on salads, sandwiches, or soups. It's one of the most versatile types of cheese around. In France, the most popular way to use chèvre is as a table cheese or on a cheese plate. *Chèvre chaud* is a popular French dish made by placing fresh or aged chèvre on top of toasted bread and broiling it (*chaud* means "hot"). It's used as a garnish for dressed salads.

The age at which many of the preceding goat cheeses are eaten is largely a matter of preference. Some prefer young cheeses that are soft and very mild, while others enjoy them harder and more pungent (they're even grated over food as a garnish). The smaller the cheese, the faster it ages (because there's more surface area to dry out and less density). Experiment, and you may discover a new favorite!

## Pays Basque

The western Pyrenees create a natural border between France and Spain. The northern side (Iparralde) is the French portion, formerly known as Gascony. It's now the Pays Basque and Bearn regions; the southern side (Hegoalde) is in Spain. The entire region as a whole is a true melting pot of cultures, the result of thousands of years of intermittent combat and politics. The Basque language and culture here are decidedly independent, and the locals pay no attention to the border and cross back and forth without a care.

Rolling hills — pastureland — are scattered throughout the isolated Pays Basque. The region is known for its food (both the seafood from the coastal access on the western side, as well as the rustic, farmhouse cuisine of the mountains). With regard to dairy, there's a long tradition of sheep milk cheeses made here.

The PDO cheese of this region is Ossau-Iraty-Brebis Pyrenees (details coming up), but there are many similar, semi-firm sheep milk cheeses produced by small cooperatives. These cheeses are called *Fromage de Brebis*. There are also 100-percent cow and mixed milk (cow and sheep) cheeses made here, all of excellent quality. Most are similar in weight (8 to 12 pounds) and appearance (natural rind with the cheesemaker's initials imprinted into them), although smaller wheels (2 to 3 pounds) of longer aged sheep milk cheeses are also produced.

Here are the best of the Pays Basque cheeses:

- **Ossau-Iraty-Brebis Pyrenees:** More commonly known as Ossau-Iraty, this cheese is named for the region's Ossau Valley and is one of two sheep milk cheeses granted PDO status (the other is Roquefort). It's made in various sizes, primarily from the milk of the local Manech ewes. Ossau-Iraty is the name reserved for those cheeses made under the strict PDO regulations. Other sheep milk cheeses made here that are not PDO-controlled are called *Fromage de Brebis.*

- **Abbaye de Belloc:** Made from local sheep milk, this cheese has been made by the Benedictine monks at the Abbaye de Notre-Dame de Belloc since 1960 and is based on the Ossau-Iraty recipe. The natural rind is covered with naturally occuring brown and gray molds, and the interior is firm, sweet, and buttery, and velvety in the mouth.

- **Bleu de Basque:** This lovely, natural-rind sheep milk blue is delicate and luscious, although it grows in intensity with age. Its texture is slightly waxy yet creamy, and it's an extraordinary pairing with a late-harvest dessert wine or Sauternes.

- **P'tit Basque:** This newer sheep milk cheese (1997) is widely distributed and wildly popular because it's brought a taste of the Pays Basque to the rest of the world. These firm, nutty little cylinders weigh in at about 2 pounds and are ideal for cheese plates and snacking.

- **Gabietou:** Made from a rich mixture of cow and sheep milk, this lightly pressed cheese is washed with brine, which gives it a reddish hue. It's creamy but has a bite, especially when aged. The younger versions (under 4 months) are soft and spreadable.

- **Bethmale:** Traditionally weighing about 10 pounds and made from cow milk, this washed-rind cheese can also be made with goat milk. It's a delight, with a deep yellow-orange rind and a cream or bone-white (if goat) interior marked by small eyes, a smooth texture, and pronounced nuttiness with a hint of funk.

# Cheeses from the South and Southeast

This area includes the south central regions of France just east of the Pays Basque, continuing on to the southeastern border shared with Switzerland and Italy. The topography is quite diverse, and much of it is less-travelled than other parts of the country due to the mountains and high plateaus. Regardless, some of the nation's most popular cheeses come from these regions.

## Midi-Pyrenees

Part of the southern Massif Central, the Midi-Pyrenees is an elevated plateau (about 3,600 feet) of ancient lava floes and granite that have been eroded by several glaciations. Cattle breeding is a large part of the local economy, dominated by the Aubrac breed (initially used for meat and, more recently, dairy).

Following are a few notable cheeses from this area:

- **Roquefort:** Few cheeses carry the intrigue, nobility, or respect commanded by Roquefort (pronounced "roque-*for*"). It's indisputably one of the world's most famous — and oft-poorly imitated — cheeses. True Roquefort is a PDO raw milk blue cheese produced in the Midi-Pyrenees region. It is made primarily from the milk of the Lacaune sheep, although the Manech and Basco-Béarnaise breeds are also used. The cheese must specifically be aged in the Cambalou caves of Roquefort-sur-Soulzon, where the mold that gives Roquefort its distinctive character (*Penicillium roqueforti)* is found. The resulting cheese is rindless and wrapped in foil; the interior is white and slightly moist, with distinctive veins and pockets of blue mold. Potent, earthy, salty, sheepy. . . dreamy.

  There are currently seven Roquefort producers, the largest of which is Roquefort Société, made by the Société des Caves de Roquefort, which owns several caves and allows visits from the public. Roquefort Papillon is also a well-known brand; the other five producers include Carles, Gabriel Coulet, Fromageries Occitanes, Vernières, and Le Vieux Berger.

- **Laguiole:** Laguiole is a 100-pound, 4-plus month-old raw cow milk cheese made in Aveyron, a mountainous, isolated area. Local history notes that it was first made in a monastery and dates back to the 12th century. The recipe and technique were then taught to the local people, who to this day make the cheese in their *burons* (stone huts) every summer.

*Aligot,* anyone? Laguiole cheese is made into a regional dish (other cheeses, like Cantal and tommes are also used). Hot mashed potatoes are whipped up with butter (and sometimes crème fraiche) and seasoned with garlic, salt, and pepper for a rib-sticking French favorite that resembles a thick, elasticky fondue. Talk about comfort food!

## Auvergne

Just south of the center of France lie the extinct volcanoes and high plateaux pastures of Auvergne. The soil of the region contains magnesium and potash, and the abundant supply of pure, high-altitude water feeds meadows carpeted with various species of grasses and herbs. Despite the harsh climate, there's a long tradition of dairy farming and cheesemaking (and cheese consumption, for breakfast, lunch, and dinner) using ancient, resilient breeds of cattle indigenous to the region — Salers (dairy), Aubrac (beef and dairy), and Charolais (beef, draft, and dairy).

Following are the most amazing cheeses that Auvergne has to offer:

- **Bleu d'Auvergne:** With centuries of tradition and technique, this cow milk blue is one of the most reliably excellent blue cheeses made in France. Sold wrapped in foil, the entire cheese is edible — rind and all. The flavor is strong but not overpowering or too salty, with a texture halfway between creamy and crumbly. The earthy notes release hints of the fertile pastures where the animals graze.

- **Saint-Nectaire:** Made high up on the volcanic mountains of the region, this quintessentially French cheese was served to King Louis XIV in the 17th century. It's a semi-soft, washed-rind cow milk cheese with deep, mushroomy, beefy aromas and flavors. Traditionally, it was aged on rye straw — and the cheese itself was used as currency.

- **Cantal:** A popular cheese from this region, Cantal is the sister cheese to its raw milk version, Salers (see the next item in this list). This dense, firm cheese is made from the milk of the native Salers cow and is shaped into hefty cylinders and cut into wedges for sale and serving. It's eaten at various ages: *jeune* (less than 60 days); *entre-deux* (between 3 and 7 months); and *vieux* (more than 8 months). Although slightly sharp, Cantal also has a nutty, buttery quality that makes it a great partner for lighter red wines as well as many beers.

- **Salers:** Possibly the oldest recorded cheese in the world, Salers has stricter production rules than its sister cheese, Cantal, which is why it's something of a rarity. Salers must be made exclusively from the milk of the Salers cow and only between May to October. The cheese is produced using the same cheddaring technique as the eponymous cheddar (see Chapter 4 for details).

- **Fourme d'Ambert:** Mild yet full-flavored, this moist cow milk blue is another ancient cheese from the mountains of Auvergne. It has a natural, brown-colored rind, with deep blue veins, and an earthy, intense flavor.

# Rhône-Alpes and Haute-Savoie

Bordering both Switzerland and Italy on the eastern side (via the Jura Mountains and the Alps), this small region (Haute-Savoie is a department) is both pastorally rich and staggeringly mountainous: bona fide alpine cow dairying country. Like the Basque region on the opposite side of France (and other mountain areas the world over), transhumance is an essential practice for cheesemakers and dairy farmers due to the climatic extremes and high elevations (see Chapter 12 for more information on transhumance).

Some standouts from the Rhône-Alpes:

- **Reblochon:** Reblochon is from the Montbéliard, Abondance, and Tarine breeds of cow and is produced in either one of 20 small factories or in 180 farmhouse (*fermier*) facilities in Haute-Savoie. Beneath the reddish orange, velvety rind lies a smooth, supple, ivory paste with fruity, meaty flavors.

  Rebolochon comes from *reblocher*, which means "twice milked" in the local dialect. It was an invention of Savoie herdsmen in the 13th century, when farmers were completely dependent upon landowners, who insisted that all of a herd's milk was their property. At milking time, the herdsmen would leave a small amount of milk in the udders of their charges and, after their bosses were gone, would return to extract the rich, creamy held-over milk to use for themselves.

- **Tomme de Savoie:** This skimmed cow milk cheese comes in many viariations throughout the Savoie, all of which can be called Tomme de Savoie. They possess tan, natural rinds with a cellar-like aroma, ivory-to-pale yellow paste with small eyes, and intensely earth flavors. The only PDO of this cheese is Tome des Bauges, because its manufacture is strictly regulated (it must be made only from the milk of certain cattle breeds in a limited area, adhering to traditional cheesemaking practices).

  A *tome* or *tomme* is a general term used for a smaller, round wheel of cheese made on the farm. These wheels are meant to be eaten at the table and are made from whatever milk the cheesemaker has on hand.

- **Beaufort**: Made from the milk of the local Tarentaise cattle, this rich, buttery alpine cheese (Chapter 13 has details on alpine cheese) is, like Gruyère, a great melter with exceptional depth of flavor — sweet, nutty, and fruity. Yet it commands attention served straight-up at the table.

  Beaufort comes in three classifications, based on the time of year or how the cheese is produced: Beaufort d'Hiver (winter); Beaufort d'Été (June to October); and the highly-sought-after Beaufort Chalet d'Alpage, made twice a day in mountain huts located above 3,000 feet and using milk from a single herd. If you can find a cheesemonger carrying this stuff, stock up!

## The cheeses of Corsica

The Mediterranean island of Corsica is volcanic and mountainous, but it's best-known for the *maquis* — the local name of the dense, scrubby underbrush comprised of wild herbs and flowers. The climate ranges from hot, dry, and coastal, to snowy on the highest peaks. This is sheep and goat country, and these animals forage upon the *maquis*, resulting in delicate cheeses redolent of the native plants.

Standout Corsican cheeses include the following:

- ✔ **Fleur du Maquis (also known as Brin d'Amour):** This cheese is a young, soft, sheep milk square coated with the same wild herbs, flowers, and spices eaten by the animals (rosemary, thyme, lavender, fennel seed, juniper . . . even red bird's eye chilies). The cheese itself is sweet and rich, infused with the flavor and aroma of the *maquis*.

- ✔ **Brocciu:** Prounounced "brooch," Brocciu is one of the national foods of Corsica. This fresh, rich sheep or goat milk cheese is similar to ricotta, although it may also be aged. The fresh cheese is used as a spread, in cooking and baking, and as a stuffing for eggs, pasta, or seafood.

# Cheeses from Eastern France

Some of the most beloved cheeses come from the eastern side of France, which includes the northeastern Champagne region, Alsace-Lorraine, Burgundy, and the mountainous Franche-Comté. Landlocked and highly agricultural, these areas have distinctly different terroir and food traditions based on location, inhabitants, topography, and geology. Champagne and Burgundy are top wine-producing regions, while Alsace-Lorraine and the Franche-Comté bear the influence of their bordering countries (Germany and Switzerland, respectively).

## Burgundy

When it comes to cheese, Burgundy produces these top two treats:

- ✔ **Epoisses:** One of France's most iconic cheeses, Epoisses is a soft, oozy and utterly delicious cow milk PDO cheese. It traditionally comes in a small, round wooden box, although small and large versions (the bigger of the two is known as *Perrière*) are now available. It's washed with *marc,* an eau de vie made from grape skins and seeds, which turns its rind orange and gives it a meaty, barnyard smell. Inside, however, the paste is creamy white and satiny.

# A few of France's finest fromageries

France has many excellent cheese producers. The ones we list here are industry standouts that have distribution in the U.S. Look for them!

- **Fromagerie Rouzaire:** This fromagerie is a third-generation, family-owned operation in the heart of the Brie region. Fromagerie Rouzaire collects milk from some 25 dairies in the region and produces some of the better Bries, as well as several cheeses of its own creation, including Fougerus, Gratte-Paille (cow milk double crème), Pierre-Robert (cow milk triple crème), and Jean Grogne (large format, cow milk triple crème).

- **Lincet:** Lincet, a fifth-generation cheese-making family, expanded its base in île-de-France after it acquired a dairy in northern Burgundy. Look for its Délice de Bourgogne, Brillat-Savarin, and Chaource.

- **Berthaut:** The Berthaut family was farming in Burgundy for generations and started to produce cheese in 1956. The recipe and production of Epoisses was almost extinct when Jean Berthaut's parents revived the tradition. Jean studied the process and carried on the family business, carefully modernizing production methods. Today, Berthaut is one of the top producers of Epoisse and other Burgundian washed-rind cow milk cheeses such as Affidelice au Chablis (washed in Chablis wine), Soumantrain (a larger version of Epoisses), and the tiny Trou de Cru (smaller versions of Epoisses).

- **E. Graindorge:** Eugène Graindorge began making Livarot cheese on his farm in Normandy in 1910. By 1927, he had taught his dairy farmer neighbors how to make the cheese; he also built aging caves. Today, his grandson, Thierry Graindorge, oversees the much larger, modernized cheesemaking operation. The business produces excellent cow milk camembert flavored with Calvados (a local apple brandy) and Grain d'Orge, a Livarot washed with Calvados.

When it comes to affinage (see Chapter 2), look for cheeses aged by Hervé Mons, Rodolphe Le Meunier, and Jean d'Alos, which can be found at better cheese shops and dairy departments throughout the United States.

The proper way to eat Epoisses is to cut a hole in the top and spoon out the luscious interior: try it paired it with dried fruit. Be sure not to smother the cheese in plastic or keep it too long: It will, literally, create a stink.

- **Délice de Bourgogne**: This cheese is like butter in a rind. If that's your thing, you'll want to take this sexy, bloomy-rind, triple-crème cow milk cheese home with you. It's basically a larger version of Brillat Savarin (see the earlier section "Normandy's cheeses"). Try it with a glass of bubbly and let the party begin!

## Champagne

As Winston Churchill said in World War I: "Remember, gentlemen. It's not just France we are fighting for, it's Champagne!" And so it goes . . . fight for your right to bubbly, and the cheese will follow.

Champagne, adjacent to Île-de-France (and thus close to Paris), is the north-ernmost winemaking region in France. Its cool climate and chalky soils yield grapes — and thus wine — that are high in acid, making them ideal for added carbonation (hence the invention of sparkling wine: what's produced here is authentic Champagne, a PDO beverage). The cheeses that pair beautifully with the local bubbly are the same ones produced in the region.

Some of Champagne's greatest hits, cheesewise:

- ✔ **Langres:** Pronounced "*lahn*-gruh," this soft cow milk cheese resembles a round, orange brain (trust us, it's apt). It's medium-size (about 3 inches wide and 1½ inches deep) with a wrinkled, concave top that traditionally serves as a happy holding tank for Champagne or *marc* (eau de vie made from grape seeds and skins). The orange color comes from the addition of annatto (the seed of the achiote shrub) and has nothing to do with the pungency of the cheese itself. In reality, it's quite mild and similar in consistency to cream cheese.

- ✔ **Chaource:** Despite taste and appearances, this PDO cow milk cheese isn't a triple crème (see Chapter 3 for details). Although it does have a creamy white center, bloomy rind, and velvety mouthfeel, its butterfat is 50-plus, rather than 75 percent — the result of excellent pasture and milk.

## Alsace-Lorraine

Bisected by the Vosges River and bordered by the Rhine on its eastern side (adjacent to Germany and Switzerland), this region is gorgeous, green, and interspersed with dense forests. It has plentiful rainfall and fairly cold, snowy winters, yet it receives ample sun, making it agriculturally exceptional. Accordingly, the food and drink culture is also extraordinary, abundant with produce as well as meat, freshwater seafood, and — of course — dairy.

Alsace-Lorraine became German territory in 1871 after thousands of years of shared languages and intermittent occupation. At the end of World War I, it reverted back to France and has remained part of the country ever since (although there was brief moment during World War II when Germany annexed it). Because of this, there are strong ties to both countries.

Munster is the most famous Alsatian cheese. The word itself means "monas-tery," which is where Munster was first made to sustain the local populations throughout the winters. A creamy, pungent washed-rind cheese made from the milk of the native Vosges cattle, Munster is traditionally consumed with heavy rye bread or boiled potatoes and cumin (sometimes the cheese itself is spiced). (***Note:*** Munster bears no similarity to the American Muenster cheese, which is very mild in comparison and made quite differently.) Even if you shy away from stinky cheese, give this a try — you'll thank us!

Try Munster with a fruity Gewurztraminer or Riesling wine from the same region: this is a great example of a "terroir match." These sweet white wines provide an ideal counterbalance to the meaty, saltiness of this cheese.

# Franche-Comté

Ah, the Alps! This region is one of the country's most lucrative cheesemaking areas, a vast amount of which is Comté.

Sharing a border with Switzerland, this steep region has the Vosges Mountains to the north and the Jura Mountains to the south. The overall terrain is that of vast pastures and dense, yet accessible forest. Approximately 40 percent of the local agriculture is dairy, and the long, hot summers and high precipitation (rain and snow) ensure there's plenty of rich grass and wildflowers to fatten the cattle.

Following are the noteworthy cheeses from this area:

- **Comté:** Made from the milk of the local Montbeliard cow, Comté is one of the most popular table cheeses in France. Like its sister cheese, Gruyère (made on the Swiss side of the border), Comté shares the same production methods (see Chapter 13), but is longer aged. Sweet and nutty with spectacular melting capabilities, this semi-firm washed-rind cheese (technically it's smear-ripened; see Chapter 2) is a staple on local cheese plates and is the secret ingredient of many French chefs. Each 90-pound wheel requires the milk of about 30 cows.

- **Vacherin Mont d'Or:** A soft and creamy cow milk cheese that's gooey and spoonable when ripe, Vacherin Mont d'Or is made from raw milk and available only from mid-September to mid-May. When the cheese develops an orange rind (at around 3 months), it's packed in round spruce boxes that lend it a characteristic resiny flavor. If seasonally unavailable at your local cheese shop, look for Edel de Cléron, a pasteurized version.

- **Morbier:** This is a washed-rind, stronger-flavored cheese that, like most from this region, is a great melter.

   This ancient, semi-firm cow milk cheese was traditionally made in two steps, using the milk from both morning and evening. The cheese from the evening was protected from dirt and insects by a layer of spruce ash, and then the curds from the next morning's milking were placed on top, which left a fine, dark, horizontal line through each wheel of cheese. Today, the ash is used solely for aesthetic purposes.

- **Bleu de Gex:** Also known as Bleu du Haut Jura or Bleu de Septmoncel, Bleu de Gex is made from the milk of the local Montbeliard cattle. This fairly robust blue dates back to the 14th century. Today, it's produced using the same traditional methods, resulting in a cheese with a buttery aroma, soft texture, and peppery finish.

# Chapter 11

# Italy

● ● ● ● ● ● ● ● ● ● ● ● ● ● ● ● ● ● ● ● ● ● ● ● ● ● ● ● ● ● ● ● ● ● ● ● ● ● ● ● ● ● ● ● ● ● ●

## In This Chapter

▶ Exploring dairy-centric northern Italy

▶ Understanding the importance of sheep cheeses in central and southern Italy

● ● ● ● ● ● ● ● ● ● ● ● ● ● ● ● ● ● ● ● ● ● ● ● ● ● ● ● ● ● ● ● ● ● ● ● ● ● ● ● ● ● ● ● ● ● ●

*I*taly, the world's leading producer of wine and one of the primary producers of cheese, has a history of cheesemaking that goes back thousands
of years. Evidence indicates that cheesemaking was practiced in Italy well
before the rise of the Roman Empire and seems to date back to at least the
Bronze Age.

Sheep in particular are essential to Italy's cheesemaking traditions. Although
cows predominate in the alpine and fertile lowland pastures of the northern
third of Italy, sheep are better-suited to the rocky, hilly, arid terroir of central
and southern Italy, and are a critical part of the economic, culinary, and
cheesemaking culture. Although goats (introduced by invading Arabs) never
fully caught on as dairy animals in their adopted homeland, the new generation of cheesemakers today are using goat milk more frequently.

The Italians' pride in both their cheesemaking traditions and dairy animals
have resulted in the preservation of both recipes and breeds that might
otherwise have been lost to antiquity. The result is a vast array of cheeses,
numbering to over 1,000, many of which are regional specialties.

In this chapter, we focus on Italy's primary cheesemaking areas and highlight
the country's most famous or otherwise notable cheeses.

Like France (Chapter 10) and Spain (Chapter 12), Italian cheeses are usually
named for their place of production and/or the type of milk, style, other ingredients, or technique used, rather than for the producer or local landmarks.
In addition, many have different regional names or slight variations, which is
why you see so many bearing similar prefixes or suffixes such as *formaggio*
(cheese), *pecorino* (*pecora* means sheep), *caprino* or *capretta* (*capra* means
goat), or *affumicata* (smoked).

# Cheeses from the North

Northern Italy (see Figure 11-1) is the heart of the country's dairy industry. The River Po extends from the Apennine Mountains to the Alps, before draining into the Adriatic Sea in the east, nourishing some of Italy's richest agricultural land en route. Most of the cheeses here are made with cow milk (sometimes blended with sheep or goat milk), and the styles tend to be rich and creamy or pungent (primarily surface-ripened, washed rinds, and blues). This region also produces some fresh styles, as well — Lombardy's ricotta and mascarpone come to mind — but young cheeses requiring immediate consumption are more closely associated with the hot, arid south.

**Figure 11-1:** The key cheese-making regions in Italy.

The alpine regions of Valle d'Aosta, Friuli-Venezia-Giulia, Piedmont, and Lombardy are heavily influenced by their respective bordering countries of France, Switzerland, and Austria. These alpine styles (refer to Chapter 13), are generally made from raw cow milk and are larger in format, traditionally designed to preserve surplus milk and provide sustenance throughout the harsh winters.

## Valle d'Aosta and Piedmont

Both Valle d'Aosta and Piedmont are alpine regions, nestled in Italy's northwest between France and Switzerland. Valle d'Aosta is miniscule, however, while Piedmont — perhaps Italy's most prolific cheese-producing region — stretches from the Swiss border in the north, south to the Apennines which border Liguria. Because three sides of Piedmont are dominated by these ranges, almost half of the region is mountainous.

The topography and climate of these regions are what you'd expect from the Alps, but Valle d'Aosta has a particularly bitter climate. Piedmont has more diversity in the form of lush mountain pasture, fertile agricultural land in river valleys, and harsh winters in the higher elevations.

Here are some regional specialties worth seeking out:

- **Fontina Val d'Aosta:** Produced in the Aosta Valley near the Italian/Swiss border, this classic DOP washed-rind alpine cheese is made with raw cow milk from the native Valdaostana cows and aged over 90 days. The cheese is dense and supple, with occasional eyes, and a pale yellow, nutty, faintly pungent paste. It's ideal for melting, baking, or snacking, and is most famously used in *fonduta*, a fondue-like dish enriched with butter, eggs, and white truffles.

- **Blu del Moncenisio:** This raw DOP cow milk blue from the Moncenisio Pass is dense, intense, and moist, with a faint hint of the barnyard. Divine paired with a rustic salumi.

- **Castelmagno:** Dating back to the 13th century, Castelmagno is a semi-firm DOP cheese made with cow milk, although 10-percent sheep or goat milk or a blend of the two is sometimes added. The milk is inoculated with *Penicillium* mold to help develop the flavors; some producers also pierce the aging wheels with mold to encourage veining as with blue cheeses. Castelmagno is aged 5 to 24 months in natural caves; the resulting cheese is dry, with a brittle, mild, nutty paste that finishes with a slight tang.

- **Toma Piemontese:** Toma Piemontese are some of the oldest styles of cheese in Italy and produced by many small cheesemakers and farms throughout the region. They can be made from whole or skimmed cow milk, are semi-soft to semi-firm, and have a nutty, earthy flavor.

As with French-style tommes (see Chapter 10), *toma* is a general term used to refer to round cheeses from specific areas. These cheese are produced in Lombardy as well as Piedmont.

✔ **Robiola Piemonte:** This cheese is very different from the Robiola from Lombardy (refer to the next section). Robiola Piemonte is a style of fresh cheeses that develop thin rinds and are made from raw or pasteurized cow, sheep, or goat milk, or a mixture of the three. Depending on the type(s) of milk used, the cheese is usually very creamy and delicate, with flavors redolent of crème fraiche, mushrooms, or grass, with a tangy finish. Look for Robiola della Langhe (cow and sheep milk that has been thermalized; refer to Chapter 2) in the United States; in Italy, the Robiola Roccaverano (goat or a combination of all three milks) and Murazzano (sheep) made from raw milk are worth seeking out.

The world's largest cheese festival is held every other year in the city of Bra, south of Turin. For more information on the Bra Cheese Festival, turn to Chapter 22.

## Lombardy

Italy's dairy heartland is also one of the country's most industrial, populous regions because its capital is the cosmopolitan city of Milan. Lombardy is topographically diverse, with alpine peaks along the northern Swiss border, a substantial lakes district, the smaller Apennine range south of the Po River basin, and the famous agricultural Plains of Lombardy. The lowlands — Lombardy's major agriculture and dairying region — has a milder climate conducive to the growing of Mediterranean crops such as olives and citrus. The highest quality milk, however, comes from the wildflower and grass-rich alpine pastures of the north.

Here are Lombardy's most famous cheeses:

✔ **Taleggio:** This distinct, square-shaped, washed-rind DOP raw cow milk cheese from the Val Taleggio dates back to the 10th century. Beneath a ripe Taleggio's striated, orangey rind lies a pungent, yet delicate interior that is creamy, buttery, and fruity. Truly one of Italy's great contributions to cheese.

Due to high demand, the production area for Taleggio has extended to the Po Valley and led to the start-up of small and medium scale dairies that have successfully balanced traditional methodology with modern technology. It's also produced in Piedmont.

✔ **Gorgonzola:** Unquestionably Italy's most famous blue, Gorgonzola is actually two separate blue cheeses (differentiated primarily by their age):

• **Gorgonzola Dolce** is aged for about 2 months and is sweeter, milder, and much creamier than the more earthy Gorgonzola

Piccante. Dolce was developed after World War II, largely in response to a demand for milder cheese.

- **Gorgonzola Piccante** is aged for a minimum of 3 months and is a more earthy, spicy version with a dense, often crumbly or slightly dry paste. It's also referred to as Gorgonzola Montagna or Naturale.

Both varieties are DOP and must be made in Lombardy or Piedmont, in approximately 60 different dairies ranging from small, family operations to giant industrial concerns.

✔ **Stracchino:** Also known as Crescenza or Crescenza di Stracchino, this fresh, mild, milky, rindless white cheese is rooted in the tradition of transhumance (see Chapter 12). It was traditionally made during the fall and winter months, when the cows made their way down from alpine pastures. The physical exertion (*stracca* means "tired") increases the butterfat content of the milk, and the cool air helps to preserve the cheese.

Stracchino is also made in Piedmont and Veneto. In the United States, Bellwether Farms and BelGioioso make domestic versions that are worth seeking out; this is an elegant addition to salads or fresh summer fruit, or try it on freshly grilled bread drizzled with extra virgin olive oil.

✔ **Robiola Lombardia:** Unlike the Robiola of Piedmont, this term refers to regional cheeses that resemble small Taleggios — meaning they're washed rind and almost always made with cow milk. These cheeses are pungent, nutty, and slightly salty; regional varieties include Robiola Brescianella, Robiola Rustica, and Robiola Valsassina. Unwashed versions are now being produced; in the United States, look for Robiola Nostrana.

✔ **Ricotta:** This sweet, milky-tasting fresh cheese of peasant origins was a way to make use of the residual solids left in the whey from cow, sheep, or water buffalo milk, so they would have sustenance after producing whole-milk cheeses for market. It's wonderful for baking, in pasta dishes, or with fresh fruit and a drizzle of honey.

Although classically associated with Lombardy, ricotta is produced throughout Italy and is an important staple in the south; see the later section "Cheese from Southern Italy" for more details.

## Friuli-Venezia Giulia and Veneto

Friuli-Venezia Giula is Italy's northeasternmost region, sharing alpine borders with Austria and Slovenia, and its southern border with the Adriatic Sea. Friuli is notable for its hams (most notably *prosciutto di San Daniele*) and rustic mountain cuisine influenced by its bordering countries.

# The pecorinos of Italy

What would Italy be without its sheep? Cheese-deprived, for starters. Despite the excellent cow-country of the north, sheep milk cheeses, or *pecorino* (*pecora* means "sheep") are the mainstay of Italian cheese production because the animals are so well-suited to the mountainous — and often sparsely vegetated and arid — terrain throughout much of the country. Economically and practically, sheep make sense for other reasons, as well. They provide wool, leather, milk, meat, glue, pelts, soaps, and candles, and the horns can be made into buttons, utensils, and other useful objects. Compared to cows, they reproduce faster, require less shelter, and are able to forage. They're also an integral part of subsistence farming and barter trade.

Not all Italian cheeses made with sheep milk are pecorinos (robiolas, for example), but the flavors of a pecorino also vary depending upon breed, season, terroir, style, size, and age.

Pecorino generally refers to semi-soft *(fresco)* to about 3 months, to hard, aged cheeses *(stagionato)*.

The four main pecorino-producing areas are Tuscany, Lazio (where Rome is located), Sicily, and Sardinia, but these cheeses are eaten throughout Italy at the table as well as used in the various regional cuisines. Visit an Italian cheese shop, and you'll be staggered by the array of different varieties, only a handful of which make it outside the country or overseas. Generally, northern pecorinos tend to be milder, smoother, and sweeter, while their cousins to the south are harder, more robust, and salty. Bear in mind that similar pecorinos may be made in different regions of Italy, but specific versions may be famous — whether due to terroir, producer, breed, or a combination of these factors.

Here are some of our Italian pecorino picks:

| Pecorino | From | Notes |
| --- | --- | --- |
| Formaggio di Fossa | Umbria | Coated with wild herbs, aged in a sack for 5 months, buried in a natural hollow *(fossa)* for 90 days, and returned to the cellar for 60 days prior to consumption. (Never let it be said the Italians take short cuts when it comes to their food.) |
| Pecorino Affinato in Vinaccia in Visciola | Umbria | Macerated in Visciola cherries |
| Pecorino di Pienza Rosso | Tuscany | Rubbed with tomato paste |
| Pecorino Foglie di Noce | Tuscany | Rubbed with olive oil and wrapped in walnut leaves |
| Pecorino Pepato | Sicily | Flavored with black peppercorns |
| Pecorino Peperoncino | Tuscany | Flavored with fresh red chilies |
| Pecorino Romano | Lazio | Today produced primarily in Sardinia due to production cost |

Sweet yet piquant, Bohemian Blue is especially good when drizzled with honey. (Blue, semi-soft, sheep milk, Wisconsin)

For more information on the cheeses included in this insert, consult *culture* magazine's online cheese library:
http://culturecheesemag.com/cheese-library

A blue to please all palates, Blaues Wunder is mild, creamy, and utterly delicious. (Blue, semi-soft, cow milk, Switzerland)

With dense blue veins and a crumbly paste, Gorgonzola Piccante packs a blue Italian wallop. (Blue, semi-firm, cow milk, Italy)

Aged only a few days, Brebis Blanche is fresh, sweet, and tangy with full, cream-like flavors. (Fresh, soft, sheep milk, New York)

Meaning "little bell" in French, Clochette is a wrinkly rinded goat cheese produced seasonally from late March through autumn. (Mold-ripened, semi-soft, goat milk, France)

A PDO cheese, Pouligny St. Pierre coats your palate with flavors of hay, grass, cellar, and earth. (Mold-ripened, semi-soft, goat milk, France)

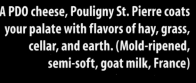

For more information on the cheeses included in this insert, consult *culture* magazine's online cheese library:

Tarentais is a good example of a cheese that ages from the outside in. (Mold-ripened, semi-soft, goat milk, France)

Formed by hand, using cheesecloth, Capricious is an aged goat milk cheese with a natural rind. (Natural rind, aged, goat milk, California)

The natural rind of Twig Farm Tomme is mottled with natural molds encasing an ivory-white paste. (Natural rind, semi-firm, goat milk, Vermont)

A close look reveals the thin layers of pulled curd within Caciocavallo Podolico. (Pasta filata, firm, cow milk, Italy)

Made in a variety of shapes, this aged Provolone has an assertive and firm bite, quite different from the younger versions. (Pasta filata, firm, cow milk, Italy)

These freshly stretched balls of mozzarella are briefly smoked over hickory, coloring the outside and infusing the cheese with flavor. (Pasta filata, soft, cow milk, New York)

For more information on the cheeses included in this insert, consult *culture* magazine's online cheese library: http://culturecheesemag.com/cheese-library

By aging their cheeses in plastic, Tony and Julie Hook of Hook's Cheese Company can mature some cheddars for up to 15 years, resulting in extra-sharp flavors. (Rindless, firm, cow milk, Wisconsin)

Pungent and stinky, Grayson's bark is worse than its bite. Pairs brilliantly with beer and dried fruit. (Washed rind, semi-soft, cow milk, Virginia)

With its distinctive horizontal layer of edible ash, Morbier stands out on any cheese plate. (Washed rind, semi-soft, cow milk, France)

Encased in a bright-white, velvety rind, Bent River Camembert has rich, buttery flavors with hints of mushroom. (Bloomy rind, soft, cow milk, Minnesota)

An American goat milk original, Humboldt Fog has bright lemony flavors when young that intensify with age. (Bloomy rind, soft, goat milk, California)

Chili peppers, together with a 12-hour smoking process, give the rind of Smoked Ricotta Peperoncino its vibrant color and piquant, meaty, and smoky flavor. (Coated rind, firm, sheep milk, Italy)

For more information on the cheeses included in this insert, consult *culture* magazine's online cheese library: http://culturecheesemag.com/cheese-library

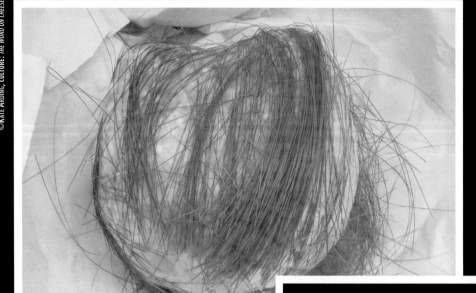

This comb-over look-alike, Saras del Fen, is made from mixed milk depending on the season and is wrapped loosely in green hay. (Rindless, soft, cow, sheep, and goat milk, Italy)

Designed for grating, Belper Knolle is rolled in a spicy mix of powdered Himalayan salt, local garlic, and Oberland pepper. (Coated rind, aged, cow milk, Switzerland)

A mild washed-rind cheese, the flavors of ColoRouge are buttery, rich, and smooth with a clean, milky finish. (Washed rind, soft, cow milk, Colorado)

Made only in autumn and early winter, Rush Creek Reserve is wrapped in spruce bark and hand-washed with a salt brine and yeast solution. (Washed rind, soft, cow milk, Wisconsin)

©Kate Arding, culture: *THE WORD ON CHEESE*

©Kate Arding, culture: *THE WORD ON CHEESE*

Each wrinkly wheel of Langres is washed with salt brine and Marc de Champagne plus a touch of annatto (natural red dye). (Washed rind, soft, cow milk, France)

Wheels of Hoch Ybrig are washed with brine that contains white wine, creating a concentrated, sweet finish. (Washed rind, semi-firm, cow milk, Switzerland)

©Kate Arding, culture: *THE WORD ON CHEESE*

For more information on the cheeses included in this insert, consult *culture* magazine's online cheese library:
http://culturecheesemag.com/cheese-library

Tilsiter's pungent aroma belies the mild, milky flavors of the cheese itself. Pair this with Belgian ale. (Washed rind, semi-firm, cow milk, Switzerland)

Dark porter is added to the curd after it has been formed and the whey drained off, adding distinctive color and flavor to Cahill's Irish Porter Cheese. (Coated rind, semi-firm, cow milk, Ireland)

Hillis Peak's rind is repeatedly rubbed with vegetable oil and smoked Spanish Paprika. (Coated rind, firm, goat milk, Oregon)

This Gouda-style cheese, made by nuns at Our Lady of the Angels in Virginia, is coated with wax to protect its interior while aging. (Coated rind, semi-firm, cow milk, Virginia)

A dense, natural rind protects matured Caerphilly, a cheese that was traditionally eaten in the Welsh coal mines. (Natural rind, semi-soft, cow milk, Wales)

Traditionally, many long-aged cheeses were wrapped in cheesecloth, a practice that continues today. Cloth protects the wheels while allowing them to breathe and mature without drying out. (Coated rind, firm, cow milk, U.K.)

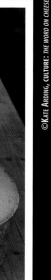

For more information on the cheeses included in this insert, consult *culture* magazine's online cheese library: http://culturecheesemag.com/cheese-library

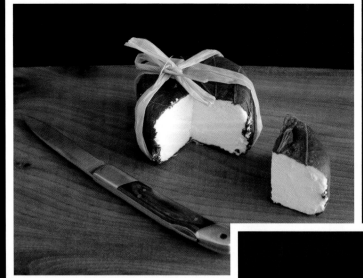

Mexican pepperleaf (Hoja Santa) are wrapped around cheeses and secured with raffia, imparting desired flavors and providing a beautiful presentation. (Coated rind, soft, goat milk, Texas)

Reminiscent of the moon's cratered surface, Mimolette's rind is left to the natural devices of cheese mites that munch away until asked "politely" to leave by the monger. (Natural rind, aged, cow milk, France)

Though offering cheeses made from a variety of milks, this cheese plate is monochromatic and has an overload of bloomy rind styles. Adding different cheese styles will liven the plate up.

Varied in cheese styles and textures with easily nibbled accompaniments and wedges turned outwards for simple cutting, this plate would make any party happy.

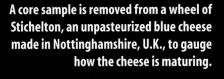

Cheeses from different producers mature in Guffanti's underground aging caves in Arona, northern Italy.

A core sample is removed from a wheel of Stichelton, an unpasteurized blue cheese made in Nottinghamshire, U.K., to gauge how the cheese is maturing.

For more information on the cheeses included in this insert, consult *culture* magazine's online cheese library: http://culturecheesemag.com/cheese-library

Sheep at Lovetree Farm, Wisconsin, are brought in from the pastures for milking.

After spending the summer in high Alpine pastures, Bavarian cows return to the lower slopes in a celebration known as Viehscheid. Here the lead cow wears a garland of flowers to indicate a successful season.

Jersey cows, such as these at Dancing Cow Farmstead in Vermont, are renowned for producing high-butterfat milk, ideal for younger soft cheeses.

Cheesemaker Karen Weinberg drains whey out of the vat of cut curd at 3-Corner Field Farm, New York.

Fresh chèvre is placed in cheesecloth to drain off excess whey at Rawson Brook Dairy, Massachusetts.

Ricardo Huijon and co-author Thalassa Skinner, happy cheesemongers at the cut-to-order Oxbow Cheese Merchant in Napa, California.

For more information on the cheeses included in this insert, consult *culture* magazine's online cheese library: http://culturecheesemag.com/cheese-library

With its temperate climate, Marin County, located on northern California's Pacific Coast, provides an ideal dairying and cheesemaking environment.

During the summer months, Brown Swiss cows graze in the high altitude summer pastures of the Bavarian Alps. These fields are renowned for their rich flora resulting in highly prized milk and cheese.

In addition to wine making, Tuscany's rolling landscape provides an ideal environment for sheep milk cheeses.

Known as the Dairy State, Wisconsinites may well have milk running through their veins. The rolling hills and lush pastures are an ideal environment for dairy cows, resulting in a plethora of dairy farms and cheesemakers.

| Pecorino | From | Notes |
| --- | --- | --- |
| Pecorino Tartufo | Tuscany | Flavored with black truffles |
| Pecorino Toscano | Tuscany | Sold at several different ages |
| Pecorino Vinaccia | Umbria | Macerated in grape must |

Veneto, which encompasses the northern Padana Plain (see Tuscany) and the River Po delta, is vast and fairly populous, particularly around its coastal capital of Venice on the Adriatic. Since the late 20th century, Veneto has become a wealthy agricultural export region; its primary crops include wine grapes and other fruit, cereal grains, and to a small degree, cattle.

Together, these regions produce many different varieties of cheese, but only a handful are well-known outside of Italy. The following are the best-known cheeses from Italy's northeast:

- ✔ **Asiago:** Asiago is from Veneto. It's usually consumed after it's been aged at least 9 months and is classified as a hard, natural-rind cheese, ideal for grating. Young Asiago (sold at around 3 months of age) is rindless and white, with a chewy, slightly dry texture, and mild, mozzarella-like flavor. Originally made with pure sheep milk, today Asiago is 100-percent cow milk.

- ✔ **Montasio:** Made from semi-skimmed, raw cow milk, Montasio is a pressed, cooked (meaning the curd is heated during production) DOP cheese from Friuli. First made in the 13th century at an abbey called Moggio, the cheese is now made in a number of dairies and factories in the region. The cheese is generally released at one of three different stages: 2 months, 4 months, and 12-plus months for aged versions, when it resembles Piave or Asiago (also in this list). Montasio is quite aromatic and supple yet mild, with hints of grass and fruit. With age, it grows firmer, with notes of butterscotch and nuts.

*Frico* is a staple of Friuliano cuisine; it's essentially a crisp made from shredded Montasio. A couple of versions of *frico* exist: One is hot, made with potatoes and lightly cooked onions; the other is the classic *frico croccante,* which is a crunchy version. Either way, it's irresistible.

- ✔ **Piave:** Piave is a DOP pasteurized cow milk cheese from Veneto, typically sold at three different ages: fresh (*fresco*), 1 to 2 months; medium (*mezzano*), 3 to 4 months; and aged (*vecchio*), 6 to 12 months. The texture is dense and firm, becoming harder with some crystallization as the cheese matures. The interior is a rich, buttery-yellow color, with a full-bodied flavor and notes of citrus and butterscotch. Great for snacking, melting, or grating.

- ✓ **Provolone:** True provolone (the American deli version is but a pale, bland shadow compared to the real thing!) originated in Basilicata in the south, but today, the majority of this pasteurized cow milk pasta filata cheese is produced in Veneto and Lombardy. Provolone isn't finished until it's been brined and coated in wax for aging, sometimes for years. It may be classified as a soft or hard cheese, depending on its age; it's sold *dolce* (technically, "sweet") at 2 to 3 months of age, or as a more aged version known as *piccante*. Provolone may also be smoked. However it's sold, the cheese is traditionally molded into a pear, log, or ball and hung from the ceiling by a rope.

- ✓ **Sottocenere:** This semi-firm truffled cheese from Veneto is made with milk from four cattle dairies in the region. After the curd is blended with black truffles and truffle oil, the wheels are rubbed with ash, herbs, and spices, and aged 3 to 4 months. Fragrant, heady, and decadent, Sottocenere has hints of cream and vanilla that balance its predominantly earthy flavors and aromas.

- ✓ **Ubriaco (or Umbriaco):** The name of this raw or pasteurized cow milk cheese from Veneto means "drunken" in Italian. It refers to the practice of bathing the cheese in grape *must* (the stems, seeds, and skins) or fortified wine for three weeks before washing it in brandy made from the residue of pressed black grapes. The result is a delicately fruity cheese, with a firm, moist, slightly crumbly texture.

# Cheeses from Central Italy

The central regions of Emilia-Romagna and Tuscany (refer to Figure 11-1) have a Mediterranean climate and are comprised of fertile rolling hills and flat plains bisected by the Po River. Both are major agricultural regions for wine, fruit, olives, rice and other cereal grains, cattle (meat and dairy), and sheep, which do well in Tuscany's terroir.

## Emilia-Romagna

Emilia-Romagna is home to some of Italy's oldest food traditions as well as its culinary epicenter, Bologna. The region is also the origin of Italy's most famous cheese, Parmigiano Reggiano, which is made from cow milk.

In addition to being the place known for introducing Parmigiano Reggiano to the world, Emilia-Romagna is Italy's leading producer of wheat and the origin of its finest ham, *prosciutto di Parma*. The city of Modena is known worldwide for its Balsamic vinegar, while the city of Bologna — nicknamed *La Grossa* ("the fat one") — is renowned for its chocolate, salumi, and pasta.

## Parmigiano Reggiano: The King of Cheeses

Parmigiano Reggiano is a DOP cheese from Emilia-Romagna (specifically, the provinces of Reggio-Emilia, Parma, Modena, and parts of Bologna and Mantua). This noble *grana* cheese — one of world's finest — has been produced by hand according to nearly the same methods since the Middle Ages. The name Parmigiano Reggiano can only be applied to cheese made from this region between the months of April and November, from specific breeds of cows fed a specific diet. There are approximately 406 producers of the cheese — both dairies and factories — that are regulated by a *Consorzio* that works to uphold regulations and promote the cheese worldwide.

Parmigiano Reggiano is such a valuable commodity that some cheese storage vaults are managed by banks, which keep them as collateral for dairies to which they have provided loans. To protect the product and avoid consumer confusion, all similar cheeses within the European Union and other parts of the world must be marketed as Parmesan. Although other excellent *grana* cheeses exist, including Grana Padano, none possess Parmigiano's heritage.

Both dairy cattle and sheep are used as dairy animals in Emilia-Romagna, but cow milk is more common because the pasture is so exemplary in much of the region. If you love food as well as history, a visit to this pastoral place is a must.

- ✔ **Parmigiano Reggiano:** Parmigiano Reggiano is made with raw skimmed evening milk combined with whole morning milk. The curds are then cooked and pressed to extract as much moisture as possible, which is what gives the cheese its signature shard-like texture. Parmigiano is renowned for its rich, nutty, fruity aroma and flavor, which is redolent of pineapple. Its pleasantly crunchy texture varies with age; most Parmigiano is between 14 months and 2 years of age, but *stravecchione* wheels may be up to 4 years old.

So revered is Parmigiano Reggiano that the Italian writer Bocaccio, in his 14th century novella, *Decameron*, wrote of a mythical paradise called Bengodi, where the common people lived atop a "mountain of grated Parmesan cheese."

- ✔ **Grana Padano:** This widely produced DOP *grana* cheese is made only with skimmed cow milk and aged up to 6 months. Flavors are redolent of butterscotch and tropical fruit. It's best used as a grating cheese.

Grana Padano is produced in parts of Emilia-Romagna, Lombardy, Piedmont, Trentino, and Veneto — an area that is at least twice the size of the production area for Parmigiano Reggiano. Thus the cows used to produce Grano Padano graze on pastures with a more varied terroir, resulting in a cheese that possesses subtle nuances in its flavor.

## Serious salumi

Although the Umbrian town of Norcia is known as Italy's epicenter of cured meats (primarily pork and wild boar, or *cinghiale*), the rest of Italy is no slouch when it comes to salumi and other cured meats. Here are a few notable ones:

✔ **Culatello di Zibello (Emilia Romagna):** A silky delicacy made from the prized rear muscle of a ham.

✔ **Prosciutto di Parma (Emilia Romagna):** Italy's most famous ham has been produced for over 2,000 years. It's sweet and delicate, with supple ribbons of fat — a classic duet with Parma's Parmigiano Reggiano.

✔ **Salame Toscano (Tuscany):** A highly seasoned, moist pork salami studded with cubes of fat. If you want to deviate from the classic combo of an aged pecorino Toscano, substitute Fiore Sardo for a more piquant pairing.

✔ **Finocchiona (Tuscany):** A firm salame spiced with fennel. Wonderful with pecorino fresco or a fresh, tangy chèvre.

✔ **Coppa (Calabria):** Made from whole, dry-cured pork neck and shoulder and more similar to ham in flavor and texture. Have some with Beaufort or Comté for a sexy, salty, buttery duet.

✔ **Sopressata (Basilicata, Puglia, and Calabria):** A firm, dry, rustic pressed salame, traditionally made from pork although beef may also be used. Plays well with sliced apples and a slightly sweet cheddar. A very different, uncured version is made in northern Italy.

✔ **Bresaola (Lombardy):** Air-dried, salted beef. It's lean and slightly sweet; try it alongside a creamy, mild blue such as Gorgonzola Dolce.

## Tuscany

The Tuscan landscape is famed worldwide: rolling hills that are a patchwork of vineyards, olive groves, and slender cypress trees, and ancient walled cities perched on hilltops. The Po Valley/Padana Plain is Italy's largest agricultural region within Tuscany and is known for its rice and other cereal grains, stone fruit, vegetables, and livestock.

Sheep rule the landscape in Tuscany; the region's pecorinos are considered among the best in Italy, and here you'll find all manner of cheeses, but it's the hard, aged cheeses that are the true treasures. Here we offer two of Tuscany's top hits:

✔ **Pecorino Toscano:** Though used at all ages (from fresh to very aged, for grating) this DOP Italian sheep milk cheese has a firm texture, distinctive, nutty flavor, and mild, peppery finish, with flavors and aromas that become more pronounced with age. Pecorino Toscano can be made from raw or pasteurized milk, from animals that graze on pasture or are fed hay or dried grasses; the cheese is aged between 3 to 6 months, depending upon the producer.

- ✔ **Pecorino Pienza Gran Reserva:** This hard DOP cheese hails from the city of Pienza, which is famed for its pecorinos. It's made with raw milk sourced from local dairies. The rind is rubbed with olive oil to prevent cracking and reduce unwanted mold and bacterial growth. The resulting cheese has a smooth, firm texture and brownish-gray rind; the flavors are sweet and nutty, balanced by sharp and salty notes, and slight crystallization that increases with age. Pienza is also known for both its younger and more aged pecorinos, as well as a version rubbed with tomato paste (see the sidebar "The pecorinos of Italy" for details).

# Cheeses from Southern Italy

Although southern Italy (refer to Figure 11-1) suffers scorching summer heat and has rocky terrain, it also possesses rich, volcanic soil and a more varied climate that includes abundant seasonal rainfall and even some snow at the higher elevations in winter. The topography (this includes the large, mountainous islands of Sardinia and Sicily) makes farming on a large scale difficult, as does the heat, but the soil yields spectacular crops — particularly wine and olives (for both oil and the table), and the area has a rich culinary heritage.

The exception to the rocky terrain are the marshy areas outside of Naples in Campania, used for the cultivation of both rice and water buffalo (their milk is used for cheese). Because transportation is difficult in the rural south, the traditional cheeses of these regions have tended to be either fresh, for immediate consumption, or hard and robust, to withstand longer maturation and the rigors of travel.

## Campania

This arid, hilly, volcanic region — home to Naples and Mt. Vesuvius — has a network of rivers that make for agricultural land famed for two things: tomatoes and water buffalo. The animals are well-suited to the marshy soil of the river valleys outside of Naples, and their milk is used for mozzarella di bufala and other fresh and soft styles of cheese. Cow and sheep milk cheeses are also found throughout Campania. Here are a few notables:

- ✔ **Mozzarella:** Cheese lovers know that Campania means mozzarella! A good-quality fresh mozzarella is a thing of beauty: sweet, milky, and delicate. This DOP pasta filata cheese is traditionally made from water buffalo milk (mozzarella di bufala), which makes for a more rich, buttery cheese, although cow milk is now a popular (but non-DOP) alternative.

## How water buffalo arrived in Italy

Asiatic water buffalo are believed to have been introduced to southern Italy in the 2nd century AD. After the Roman Empire fell, the rivers south of Naples grew clogged with silt, and the buffalo, which have broad hooves that prevent them from sinking in marshy soil, were well-suited as beasts of burden. It was only a matter of time before the animals were used for their milk.

Buffalo milk is creamy, rich, and snowy white in color; at 7- to 9-percent butterfat, it's richer than even sheep milk, but because of its chemical composition, it's more digestible than cow milk and milder in flavor than goat or sheep milk.

Historical references vary as to how long buffalo cheese has been made in southern Italy. Records indicate production has occurred since at least the 12th century, but it's been widespread since at least the late 1700s. Italy's most well-known buffalo cheese is mozzarella di bufala, a DOP product from Campania (non-DOP versions are also produced in Lazio and Puglia). There are also excellent buffalo cheeses produced in northern Italy, such as Lombardy's Quadrello di Bufala, a Taleggio-style made by Gritti.

Authentic mozzarella di bufala is produced under strict regulations across seven provinces in central and southern Italy. Fresh mozzarella is sold in small (approximately 1½-ounce) balls called *bocconcini* or in 4- or 8-ounce balls packed in a whey-and-water mixture in a tub or sealed bag.

The best way to enjoy mozzarella is to eat it just after it's been stretched; some restaurants make hand-pulled mozzarella to order, which is worth seeking out. But even with nothing more than a drizzle of olive oil and a pinch of sea salt, eating the fresh version will turn you off the rubbery mass-produced stuff forever.

- **Fior di Latte:** Cow milk mozzarella is also made throughout Campania and Puglia (and indeed, the rest of Italy). This name literally means "milk's flower."

- **Scamorza:** A slightly drier pasta filata cousin to mozzarella that may or may not be smoked.

## Puglia/Sardinia and Sicily

Despite the rich, volcanic soil, southern Italy is very rural and relatively poor, with a fiercely hot summer climate. Thus, Puglia's farmers practice smaller scale agriculture, primarily the cultivation of wheat, wine grapes, olives, fruit, and sheep.

Sicily and Sardinia are much the same as Puglia with regard to terroir and agriculture, but seasonal tourism is also an important economic staple. Sheep are essential to the way of life in southern Italy, for their wool, meat, and milk (for making cheese).

Some examples of cheese from this region include the following:

- **Caciocavallo Podolico:** This hard-to-find but famed pasta filata cheese comes from the milk of the rare Podolica cow, a breed native to Puglia (the cheese is also produced in Campania, Molise, and Basilicata). Caciocavallo has a smooth, thick rind, and dry, hard texture with occasional eyes; flavors are of smoke, herbs, toast, and barnyard, balanced by fruitiness and a lactic tang. There are also other, less esoteric versions of Caciocavallo produced throughout southern Italy, including Puglia.

  Between November and June, the herds graze in lower elevation pastures before being herded up to nearly 10,000 feet, where they feed on a summer diet of native grasses, fruits, and berries — flavors that are inherent in Caciocavallo Podolico.

  *Caciocavallo* roughly translates as "cheese on horseback" and is believed to have originated from the way the cheeses were suspended like saddlebags across a horse's flanks during transit back down the mountain.

- **Burrata:** Burrata ("buttery") originated in Puglia around the 1920s, because cheesemakers were looking for a way to make use of the leftover scraps from producing other cheeses. Burrata is essentially mozzarella made with the addition of cream. Cut through its stretched, edible skin, and you'll be rewarded with a rich, sweet, creamy curd (*straciatella*) that's the essence of summer.

  Although finding imported burrata year round is possible in the U.S., its extreme perishability has inspired several domestic producers — Belgioioso, Di Stefano, and Gioia — to make their own excellent versions.

- **Fiore Sardo (Pecorino Sardo):** Traditionally a raw DOP sheep milk cheese sourced from native Sardinian animals of a single flock, industrial versions may now use pasteurized milk or blend it with cow milk. Artisan Fiore Sardo is still made in *pinnette*, small mountain huts belonging to the shepherds. The cheeses are aged between 2 to 8 months; the smoke from open fires gives the cheese its signature smoky overtones and dry, hard rind. The interior is firm, dense, and straw-to-ivory colored, with a sweet, nutty paste with notes of burned caramel and salt.

  One of the world's most ancient cheeses, Fiore Sardo is believed to date back to the Bronze Age.

✔ **Pecorino Romano:** Italy's most famous pecorino cheese originated in Lazio, the region where Rome is located. Today, however, due to mainland production expenses, most producers are now located in Sardinia. We're including this DOP cheese here because Lazio isn't a major cheese-producing region, although a few producers do still make *genuino* Romano in Lazio (Fulvi is an imported brand to look for). Pecorino Romano may be sold younger, but it's usually an aged, off-white colored grating cheese with a thick, hard rind; it adds an intense, salty punch to pasta or vegetables.

✔ **Ricotta salata:** Unlike fresh ricotta, this salty, pure white Sicilian sheep milk cheese (it may also be made from cow or buffalo milk) is aged and pressed to make it firm to hard, so it can be used for grating or crumbling over food. It's a nice addition to salads or pasta, or as a substitute for feta.

# Chapter 12

# Spain, Portugal, and Other Mediterranean Countries

## In This Chapter

▶ Exploring the cheese legacy of Spain and Portugal

▶ Discovering the historical and cultural roots of Turkey, Greece, and Cyprus, through cheese

*T*o many, the Mediterranean countries are synonymous with sexy; miles of sun-drenched coastline and azure sea; flower-bedecked, whitewashed buildings; vineyards; olive and almond groves; and in southern Spain and Portugal, the subtle culinary and architectural influences of North Africa.

Yet cheese is also inextricably linked to the identities of these countries, most notably that of sheep and goats, which have adapted to thrive in the geographical and climatic extremes of specific regions. Turkey, Greece, and Cyprus are just as dependent upon dairy (in some instances, for subsistence) and have an ancient legacy of shepherds and nomadic herders. Here, we take a brief look at these different countries by way of their shared cultural obsession: cheese.

# Simply Spain

Spain is a country of extremely diverse climate and topography, with a centuries-old tradition of cheesemaking. In the verdant northeast and northwest, spicy blues are traditionally made with cow milk, while the Arab influence in the south has made goat the animal of choice — first for meat and now, among the new generation of cheesemakers, for milk.

Also available are the hard sheep milk cheeses from the plains of La Mancha and the mountainous Basque Country, as well as fresh requeson, a ricotta-like cheese made from the solids left over from cow, goat, or sheep milk. In addition, some famous cheeses are produced on the islands belonging to Spain, as we explain in later sections. Figure 12-1 shows the cheesemaking regions of Spain.

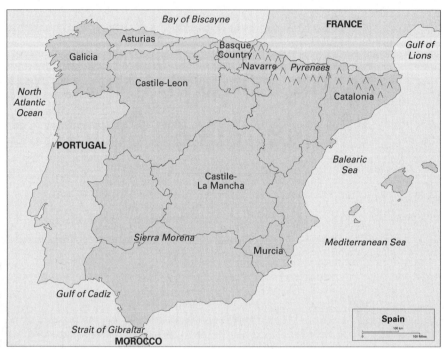

**Figure 12-1:**
Cheese
regions
of Spain.

While cheese in general was traditionally used for the table, contemporary use of both domestic and imported cheeses for cooking and serving
with tapas is very popular. Prior to the 1980s, however, Spanish cheeses
were really only produced for home consumption or a very localized retail
market. The cumulative effects of the Spanish Civil War, two World Wars,
and Franco's regime significantly delayed the country's agricultural and commercial progress. It wasn't until after Franco's death in 1975 that Spain began
to embrace its agrarian culture and open it up to a wider retail market that
included the rest of Europe and export markets.

Although specific Spanish cheeses such as Manchego and Cabrales are now
recognized worldwide, Spain still has relatively few cheese shops, although
farmstead and artisan cheeses are widely available at the country's many
public and farmers' markets. Fortunately, there's a growing interest in
Spanish (and Portuguese) cheeses in the United States, and an increasing
number of small-production varieties are finding their way into U.S. cheese
shops.

Check out Poncelet cheese bar and retail shop in Madrid (www.poncelet
cheesebar.es) and Formatgeria La Seu in Barcelona (www.formatgeria
laseu.com) for the finest in Spanish cheeses.

ASK THE EXPERT

## Transhumance: A revitalized way of life

In the 1990s, I moved to the French Pyrenees from the United Kingdom, where I had studied photojournalism, and there I found these mountains, rising as high as 10,000 feet, full of stories just waiting to be told.

For centuries, farmers have herded their animals (cows, goats, and sheep) up and down the mountains to different pastures each spring and fall, a journey they call the *transhumance.* After World War II, trucks gradually replaced the traditional ways of moving livestock, and young people left the mountain valleys for jobs in towns.

But about 20 years ago, shepherds in the Pyrenees (whose sheep are used for meat, wool, and cheesemaking) revived the twice-yearly practice of transhumance as a way of breathing life back into the mountains. Since then, they have opened these marathon hikes to all comers, attracting visitors from near and far. They pack the cafes, stay in the guesthouses,

and relish the local cheeses. The welcome is genuine.

To join a transhumance is to be part of this revitalizing expedition. A typical transhumance may cover 40 miles or so, spread over three days, and climb to 6,000 or 7,000 feet. There's a strong feeling of solidarity. Each farmer is helped by his friends and family. In due course, he will return the favor.

At the end of the day is a village party with enough food to feed a small regiment — everything locally produced, of course. I've come to be a part of mountain society, living here rather than just observing from afar. I want to record this life in case it ever disappears, and without the least desire to be pretentious, I like to think that I can help these people tell their story.

— Martin Castellan, contributor and photojournalist (*culture: the word on cheese,* Summer 2010)

Spain produces so many wonderful cheeses — 16 of them DOC (Chapter 2 explains designations) — that we can't possibly devote space to all of them. Instead, we provide a brief historical and geographical overview of the country so that you can learn some of the most notable varieties.

## *Cheese regions in the north*

The top third of Spain varies dramatically in terrain and climate. There's the temperate Atlantic climate and lush, mountainous, "green"' northwestern regions of Galicia and Asturias and the rugged, high-altitude peaks of the Pyrenees in the heart of Basque country. In Catalonia, the climate ranges from mild and Mediterranean along the coast, to harsh in the inland and mountainous areas.

In the following sections, we introduce you to these northern regions of Spain and share some of their most notable cheeses.

### Galicia

Galicia is known for its distinctive, cone-shaped cheeses:

- **Tetilla:** Perhaps the most famous of the cone-shaped cheeses, Tetilla, a DOC, is traditionally made from the pasteurized milk of the Rubia Gallega cow (however, because Tetilla is so popular, milk from other, more popular breeds is used to supplement the Rubia Gallega milk). Mild, with a soft, spreadable paste, this cheese is often served with cured meats, olives, or used for melting.

- **San Simon:** This cone-shaped, raw DOC cow milk cheese is smoked over green birch and aged for approximately 2 months. Although some cheeses are factory-made using forms, artisan versions — such as those made by third-generation cheesemaker Javier Pineiro and his wife Sonia of Queixeria Fontelas — are shaped and trimmed by hand. San Simon is a rich, ochre color with a semi-firm, smooth, pale yellow paste flecked with small eyes. Flavors are mild, sweet, and earthy, with notes of butter and delicate smoke.

- **Arzúa Ulloa:** Sometimes referred to as *queixo do pays* ("cheese from the land"), this DOC pasteurized cow milk cheese is made in both farmstead and industrial versions, with the handmade variety increasingly hard to come by (they're usually sold at local markets). Despite this, Arzúa Ulloa is one of the most classic and popular cheeses of Galicia. Its rind is smooth and waxy, and the paste is pale yellow, flecked with blue or white dots of mold and occasional eyes, with a velvety texture. The aroma and flavor are fresh, lactic, and tangy.

### Asturias

Asturias is home to Spain's most famous artisan, farmstead, and blue cheeses. The region has many natural limestone caves that have traditionally been used for aging these cheeses, which are made predominantly with cow milk (the vast amount of pasture available is well-suited to cattle), although some cheeses may also be mixed with a lesser amount of goat or sheep milk. The valleys and mountains receive a lot of rainfall and are more humid than those of neighboring Cantabria, which yields similar cheeses.

Following are a few notable cheeses from Asturias:

- **Cabrales:** Cabrales is the crown jewel of Spanish cheeses. It's the best-known cheese of Spain and one of the most distinctive and assertive blue cheeses around. Although traditionally made with a mix of raw cow, sheep, and goat milk (the most sought-after), today's Cabrales is more commonly made solely from cow milk (sheep and goat milk is only available seasonally). This DOC cheese has been made for hundreds of years; today, production takes place on small-scale dairies in the 20-odd villages in the Cabrales and Penamellera Alta districts.

Wheels are wrapped in maple leaves and aged for 2 to 6 months in the caves of the region, although most that arrive in the United States have natural rinds and are foil-wrapped. Cabrales can be soft or firm, and bone-white, gray, or dark brown in color. All are accepted versions of the cheese, made to suit the varying tastes of consumers. However it comes, when fully ripe, Cabrales packs a punch, with spicy, salty flavors, a smooth paste dotted throughout with crystallization, and robust pockets of blue. Not for the faint of heart, but oh, so good.

Other notable cow milk blues of the region — without leaves — include Monje and La Peral.

✔ **La Chivita:** This natural-rind, raw goat milk cheese is considered one of the finest in Asturias, produced along the Cares-Selles River in the far eastern part of the region by husband-and-wife farmers Jesús and Josepha Schiano-Lomoriello. La Chivita is semi-firm, with a creamy, mushroomy flavor.

✔ **Los Beyos:** Depending upon the maker, these rustic, pasteurized cheeses may be made from cow, sheep, or goat milk. In warmer weather, they're produced in the mountain huts of the shepherds and in farm kitchens during the winter. They possess a distinct, chalky texture and mineral flavor that melts into a buttery creamy finish with a hint of acidity.

Asturias' self-proclaimed nickname is *El Parque Nacional de Quesos*: "The National Park of Cheeses."

## Cantabria

Similar to Asturias in terroir but less humid, this green region of limestone karsts and deep river valleys also yields quality cow milk blues:

✔ **Picón:** Made just ten minutes over the Asturian border, this DOC raw milk blue is nearly identical to Cabrales, although it may have some sheep or goat milk mixed in to its cow milk base. It's ripened in the caves of the Liébana area surrounding the villages of Bejes and Tresviso.

✔ **Queso de Cantabria Nata:** Creamy, soft, and smooth, with a sour tang, this beloved cheese's qualities are reflected in its name (*nata* means "cream"). Made from the milk of Frisona cows, it's been around since at least the mid-17th century and is used as a spread, filling, or in cooking.

### Catalonia

In Catalonia, in the northeast, the climate ranges from hot, arid, and Mediterranean along the coast, to harsh — with fog, freezing rain, or snow in higher elevations in the inland river valleys and mountainous areas. This region is populated by the new generation of artisan cheesemakers, many of whom use goat milk. Here are some cheeses from Catalonia:

- **Garrotxa:** Glorious Garrotxa (pronounced "gah-*roach*-ah") is a pasteurized young goat cheese, aged between 60 to 70 days. It was virtually extinct by the 1980s until a handful of fledgling cheesemakers — part of Spain's "new wave" of cheese artisans — revived it. Garrotxa has a thin, suede-like gray rind — the result of natural mold — called *pell florida* ("flowering skin") in the Catalan dialect. These 2-plus pound rounds have a white interior with smooth, supple paste. The flavors are mildly herbal and earthy, with a hint of hazelnuts. If you can find a cheese shop with a young wheel on hand (often difficult to come by with imports), snatch some up! As of this writing, a DOC is being formed.

- **Nevat:** A relatively new creation, Nevat is made by esteemed cheesemaker Josep Cuixart, from the milk of Murcian and Grenadine goats. The wild herbs and plants the goats forage upon give the cheese notes of rosemary, thyme, and olive, even though the milk is pasteurized. *Nevat* means "snowed" in Catalan and refers to the white, bloomy rind and bone-white interior of the cheese. The texture can range from soft to almost runny along the rind; flavors are clean, lactic, and bright with an underlying sweetness that appeals even to those who aren't fans of goat cheese.

## Cheeses of the Basque Country

The temperate Basque Country resembles a snapshot from another century. Ancient villages, shepherds tending their flocks, farmers toiling in the fields, shimmering olive groves, and rolling hills are the hallmarks of this agricultural region, famed for its hard sheep milk cheeses:

- **Idiazabal:** One of the most famed cheeses of the Basque region, this cheese (pronounced "ee-dee-ah-*zah*-bahl") is made from the raw milk of the Latxa or Carranza sheep. Named for a village in the Goierri valley, this DOC cheese originated in the mountain pastures of the Pyrenees, where nomadic shepherds made it during the summer months and aged it in the rafters of their huts until they descended back to their villages in fall. The result? Cheeses that had a distinct, smoky flavor from the hearth fires. Today, artisan Idiazabal is smoked over beech or hawthorne wood before being aged. The resulting cheese is dense and slightly waxy, with small eyes and a dry, yet supple texture and a lightly smokey flavor. Idiazabal may also be made unsmoked.

✔ **Roncal:** Made from the rich, raw milk of the Latxa and Aragonesa sheep of the region, Roncal is an exceedingly nutty, semi-firm cheese. Depending upon the season, the animals may graze in the high Pyrenees or the Bardena area of Navarre; either way, Roncal is made in one of seven villages in the Valle de Roncal in northeastern Navarre. Aged for a minimum of 4 months, the cheeses are best consumed from November to July when they're at their peak, with a firm, meaty texture and notes of hay and tartness. You may notice a sheen of oil or butterfat on the interior of the cheese, which is normal.

The reason sheep milk cheeses leave grease spots on their wrapping paper at room temperature or collect droplets on their surface is because the milk is so high in butterfat. They're perfectly safe to eat, but be aware of this if you're planning to serve them for a party and set them out just prior to the arrival of your guests.

## Cheese from central and southern Spain

Central and southern Spain is the land of the legendary Don Quixote. Less diverse than northern Spain, the regions here range from hilly (parts of Castile-Leon) to the sparse, arid plains of La Mancha. Cheeses are also produced on the volcanic Canary Islands, off the northwestern coast of Africa. Because of the climate and topography, goat milk cheeses are increasingly popular here, as are the ubiquitous sheep milk varieties.

Some thistle rennet cheeses, most notably from Extremadura (Torta del Casar and Torta la Serena, both of which are DOC cheeses, and Torta de Barros) are also made in this part of Spain (head to the later section "A thorny situation: Thistle rennet" for info). Cheeses made in this manner tend to be more lactic and tangy in flavor and are often creamy or oozy. They're difficult to find outside of their native regions or countries but are definitely worth seeking out.

### Cheeses from Castile-Leon

This diverse region consists of the northern half of the arid Meseta Central plateau and includes mesas, mountains, valleys, lakes, and lagoons. The area has little rainfall but plenty of reservoirs fed by snow, rain, and glacial melt. Following are a few noteworthy cheeses from Castile-Leon:

✔ **Zamorano:** Named after Zamora, the principle city of the region from which it comes, this DOC raw milk cheese is very similar to Manchego (see the next section). The exceptionally high butterfat milk of the Castellana sheep from which Zamorano is made yields a firm, buttery, slightly sweet and lactic cheese scattered with small eyes; with age (over 6 months), hints of butterscotch, cooked butter, and nuts are noticeable.

Because of its similarity to Manchego, Zamorano was actually known *as* Manchego until the latter became a DOC (designations are explained in Chapter 2), and Zamorano was defined as a raw, seasonal cheese that must be produced in Castile-Leon from the milk of Churra and Castellana sheep. For details on Manchego, see the next section.

✔ **Valdeon:** The most famous cheese of the region after Zamorano, this pasteurized, mixed-milk (20 percent goat milk and 80 percent cow milk) blue used to be called Cabrales (refer to the section "Asturias") until Cabrales was established as a DOC. Because this cheese was being produced outside of Asturias and its production differed, it was branded Valdeon. Unlike Cabrales, Valdeon is aged in man-made facilities and inoculated with *Penicillum roqueforti.* Most traditional Valdeon is still produced wrapped in *plageru*, or sycamore leaves, which allow certain bacteria to penetrate and add flavor to the cheese. An assertive blue, but with underlying sweet, caramel-like notes, it's an excellent addition to a cheese plate.

✔ **Monte Enebro:** Made by legendary cheesemaker Rafael Baez and his daughter Paloma, this pasteurized goat milk log was the first of the new wave cheeses to be produced in Spain. *Penicillium roqueforti* is added and allowed to develop on the rind (usually it's what forms the veins in blue cheese), which contributes to Monte Enebro's flavor complexity and distinctive appearance. Slightly chalky in texture, younger cheeses are mild, bright, and tangy, with citrus and earthy notes. The paste under the rind can become gooey with age and the flavors much more assertive and goaty.

✔ **Leonora:** This lovely, bone-white, mold-ripened goat milk log is made from the milk of native Murciana goats in the mountainous part of Leon. It's a fairly new cheese, made by hand-kneading the curd, and its dense, almost chewy paste is tempered by bright, lemony notes.

### The Man (chego) from La Mancha

La Mancha is a sparsely vegetated, windblown place of climatic extremes (2,600 feet above sea level) and the native wooly Manchega sheep are ideally suited to the environment. These hardy animals graze on dry pasture between the cities of Toledo, Albacete, Ciudad Real, and Cuenca. The most notable cheese produced from this milk? Manchego.

Manchego is a semi-firm to hard, raw or pasteurized cheese, and its production is believed to date back thousands of years. Traditionally, it's made using braided forms (molds) of native *esparto* grass, which leave a distinctive herringbone pattern on the sides of the coated rind (see Chapter 2). The small wooden boards used for pressing the cheese embed a wheat ear pattern into the top and bottom of the eight-pound wheels.

Manchego may be artisan or industrially-produced. The cheese is matured between 60 days and 2 years; depending upon its age, it will be known as *semi-curado* (3 months, the minimum aging required to achieve DOC); *curado* (5 to 7 months); *viejo* (8 to 11 months); and *anejo* (1-plus year). Young Manchego is relatively moist and supple, with a cream-colored paste and grassy, fruity notes. As it ages, the cheese becomes drier and mellow, with hints of caramel and nuts.

Manchego is traditionally enjoyed with *membrillo* (quince paste) and, in the south, a glass of Sherry. The cheese is served rind-on and cut into wafer-thin triangles. In the United States, Manchego is often enjoyed with the same accoutrements (an idea we've borrowed from the Spanish), but it's also a favorite addition to cheese plates and works well in cooking, as a snack, or grated atop soups or salads.

### Murcia

Spain's bread basket yields all manner of fruits, vegetables, and flowers, as well as wine and olive oil, thanks to its warm climate. While not a historical dairy region, Murcia has an increasing number of cheesemakers, with an emphasis on goat milk. Here are some Murcian cheeses:

- ✔ **Caña de Cabra:** Also known know as Mitcaña de Cabra, this mold-ripened log of creamy chèvre has a fresh, mild, lemony tang and is a versatile, user-friendly cheese.

- ✔ **Queso de Murcia and Queso de Murcia al Vino:** A soft, moist, mild cheese made from the milk of the native Murcianao goat, Queso de Murcia is emblematic of this arid, barren region that is used primarily for the cultivation of rice. In 1986, the DOC cheese Queso de Murcia al Vino was born. Washed in the local *vino tinto* (red wine) known as *doble pasta* — a strong, fortified DOC-style made with Monastrell grapes — this mild cheese has a pleasing, fruity aroma and distinct, plum-colored rind. (It's known as "Drunken Goat" in the United States.)

Michele Buster, co-founder and president of Forever Cheese — an American importer and distributor of Spanish and Italian cheeses — coined the famous brand name "Drunken Goat." She felt the traditional name was a mouthful, and thanks to her marketing savvy, Drunken Goat has become one of the best-known cheeses amongst consumers outside of Spain.

## Spain's island cheeses

The Canary Islands are located 62 miles off the coast of Africa. Their farming heritage goes back well over a thousand years, but it was the island of Fuerteventura that put this Spanish archipelago on the radar of cheesemongers in search of the esoteric. Check these out:

✔ **Majorero:** This DOC natural-rind semi-firm cheese is made from the raw milk of the native Majorera goats. They graze on the scrub and wild marjoram that grows in the mineral-rich volcanic soil, and the result is a milky, nutty, buttery cheese. There are two different types of Majorero, both of which are excellent examples of their terroir:

- **Majorero pimenton** has oil and dried, ground *pimenton* (a Spanish variety of pepper) rubbed on its rind, giving the finished cheese a spicy, smoky flavor.

- **Majorero gofio** is rubbed with *gofio* (roasted cornmeal).

Both cheeses have a distinct diamond pattern on the rind, the result of woven palm fronds used as forms (molds). Majorero is traditionally served with *membrillo* (quince) or guava paste as a table cheese. Alongside a glass of sherry, it's a sexy little slice of multicultural heritage.

While there are some industrial versions, most Majorero is handcrafted.

✔ **Mahon:** Mahon hails from Minorca, the most northerly of the Balearic Islands off Spain's eastern coast. Named after the main port, this cow milk cheese is sold both young (2 months) and aged (10 months). Artisanal versions are made with raw or thermalized milk (see Chapter 2) and often have a superior flavor that only improves with age, although industrial cheeses are also available.

This pillow-shaped cheese is made by wrapping the curds in cloth and tying the ends to help drain the excess whey. The cheeses are rubbed with a blend of olive oil, butter, and paprika as they age, giving them a rust-colored rind. When young, Mahon is dense and crumbly yet moist, with occasional eyes and a buttery, fruity, tart flavor. Aged cheeses have intensified flavors and are drier, sharper, and more salty.

# Portugal

Portugal is Europe's westernmost country, along with its two Atlantic archipelagos of Madeira and the Azores (see Figure 12-2). With regard to terroir and climate, mainland Portugal can be bisected into north and south by the Tagus River, the longest waterway on the Iberian Peninsula.

The northern part of the country is more green and lush, marked by river valleys and a mountainous interior that receives occasional snowfall. This is a prime wine-producing area. The hot, arid south is mostly flat, famous for the Atlantic resort regions of the Algarve and western Alentejo. But it's also Portugal's bread basket, yielding wine grapes, orchard crops such as olives and almonds, cork, and sheep for meat, wool, and dairy. There are also Roman ruins, as well as an Arab influence visible in the architecture and cuisine. Fishing is also a major industry along the coast.

**Figure 12-2:**
Cheese-
making
regions of
Portugal.

All of the cheeses mentioned in this section are made with cardoon thistle as the coagulant unless otherwise noted.

## *A thorny situation: Thistle rennet*

Thistle rennet is used primarily in Portugal. Cardoons, artichokes, butterwort, and Lady's bedstraw are just some of types of thistle used to coagulate milk.

Cardoon is an edible relative of the artichoke and perhaps the most commonly used thistle for rennet. The use of cardoons in cheesemaking dates back to at least the ancient Romans, although the shepherds of the Iberian mountains (now known as the Serra da Estrela, which is also the name of Portugal's most famous cheese) also made their cheeses using cardoon because it was indigenous to Southern Europe and thus readily available.

Cheeses made using thistle rennet have a very distinct, slightly bitter flavor. Its use isn't widespread globally because it's a temperamental way of coagulating cheese, yielding inconsistent results. Despite the difficulties, cheesemakers of this region prefer it because of its availability and the flavor it imparts to the cheese.

Thistle rennet isn't used only by Portuguese cheesemakers; it's also seen in some cheeses from Western Spain (Torta del Casar and Queso de Sierra) and, in rare instances, the French Pyrenees and Northern Italy.

## *North and central Portuguese cheeses*

The temperate climate of northern Portugal provides enough rainfall to keep the land green and fertile, which is why it's prime wine-producing and dairying country and conducive to the production of specific styles of cheese:

- ✔ **Serra da Estrela**: Named for the mountain range that divides the Dão and Mondeog Rivers, this DOC cheese has been produced for over 800 years, using raw milk from the local Bordaleira or Churra sheep. The curds are placed in cloth-lined molds and hand-pressed, which helps give the cheese its dense, elastic texture. The use of thistle rennet creates a citrusy, earthy, almost sour flavor. Young versions (30 to 45 days) known as *amanteigada* ("buttery") are consumed like Epoisses (see Chapter 10): you cut a "lid" out of the top and scoop up the luscious interior. Cheeses aged up to 6 months are known as *velho* and have a firmer texture.

- ✔ **Castelo Branco:** From the verdant central Portuguese municipalities of Castelo Branco, Fundão, and Idanha-a-Nova come three types of this DOC sheep milk cheese. The milk for these cheeses comes from the Merino da Beira Baixa sheep; the results are pale, semi-soft, tangy varieties with a slightly spicy, sour finish; more aged versions are firm and slightly brittle.

## Cheeses from the Azores

The Azores Islands form a lush, volcanic archipelago located in the North Atlantic, 930 miles west of Lisbon. The main industry on these nine remote islands is agriculture, primarily dairy farming to produce milk for cheese and butter products. No surprise, then, that the Azores are home to one of Portugal's most famous cheeses: São Jorge. São Jorge, produced year-round on the island of the same name, is a raw DOC cow milk cheese that is pressed, cooked, and then aged for a minimum of 90 days. It has a hard, inedible natural rind, and a sharp, cheddar-like paste marked with tiny eyes.

So beloved is São Jorge that many Portuguese and Azorean immigrant cheesemakers in the United States make their own versions as a tribute to their homeland. Two of the best-known of these cheesemakers are Joe (a fifth-generation cheesemaker from São Jorge) and Mary Matos, of California's Matos Cheese Factory, in Santa Rosa, an hour north of San Francisco.

Here's an interesting bit of trivia: São Jorge is such an important part of the island's economy that the *Confraria do Queijo de São Jorge* was established to promote and protect the sale and reputation of the cheese.

## Cheeses from southern Portugal

Sparsely populated and primarily agricultural (wine, olives, almonds, dairy), southern Portugal has two faces: one features the ancient villages and Roman ruins of the interior Alentejo, Portugal's bread basket; the other is home to the upscale coastal resorts and low-key fishing villages of the western Alentejo and southern tip of the Algarve. Here are some cheeses from both of these areas:

✔ **Azeitão:** The wine region of Azeitão is known primarily for its red wine and this famous DOC raw sheep milk cheese. Although made year-round, the best season for producing Azeitão tends to be between April and September when the sheep are foraging summer vegetation. The texture of Azeitão is smooth and velvety when ripe, becoming harder and drier as it ages. Despite a pungent, sheepy aroma, the cheese has the sour-to-bitter flavor characteristic of thistle rennet cheeses, although it's well-balanced with herbal, savory notes.

Produced by a small number of farmstead dairies in the Arrábida Mountains, the origins of Azeitão can be traced to Serra da Estrela (see the earlier section "North and central Portuguese cheeses"). Cheesemakers from that area brought their skills and technique to the Azeitão, Sebutal, Palmela, and Sesimbra regions where the cheese is made.

✔ **Nisa:** A firm, raw milk DOC cheese from the Alentejo, Nisa is made predominately from the milk of the Saloio sheep which are related to the more popular Merino. Produced by approximately 20 small-scale artisans and farmstead operations, Nisa is also made in limited quantities by a handful of small factories. With a rust-colored rind and smooth, firm, dense ivory paste dotted with small eyes, Nisa is slightly sweet compared to most cheeses made with thistle and has hints of cream and walnuts.

✔ **Evora:** Named after the village of Evora, a UNESCO World Heritage Site (well-worth the trip should you visit Portugal), this small, firm, round DOC cheese is from the Alentejo region. It has grassy, lanolin notes and small eyes throughout the paste. Traditionally, it was preserved in olive oil in stoneware pots, but now it's more often enjoyed young and soft, or aged over 60 days, when it becomes shard-like.

✔ **Serpa:** From the lower Alentejo comes this DOC cheese named for its village of origin. It's made in a manner similar to that of Serra da Estrela, but with the raw milk of the native Merino sheep. Slightly pungent when young, Serpa becomes firmer and somewhat spicy when aged.

# The Magnificent Mediterranean

While mostly unknown in America, the cheeses of Turkey and Greece are plentiful and an essential part of the culinary, economic, historical, and social culture of these countries. The Turks produce nearly 200 different types of cheese — most of which are intensely regional — and the Greeks are the top cheese consumers per capita in the world (averaging around 68 pounds per person annually).

While this is just a brief overview of the cultural and geographical factors and cheeses of these two countries, we'd be remiss not to include them. Tasting most of these cheeses, however, requires a trip to their place of origin. . . not such a hardship when you consider that these countries possess some of the most beautiful and well-preserved islands, villages, coastal regions, and archaeological sites on earth.

## Turkish cheese, please

Turkey stands at the crossroads of Europe and Asia, which makes its cheese production all the more interesting (for more on Central Asian cheeses, see Chapter 14). Many of its cheeses aren't known outside of their area of production because large portions of the country (primarily eastern and central Turkey) still have remote, albeit dwindling, populations of the nomadic peoples who make them.

The European (Thrace) part of Turkey is quite small, making up only 3 percent of the country. East of the Bosphorous Strait (which bisects İstanbul) is

Anatolia, the Asian part of Turkey. Geography and climate vary dramatically from fertile lowlands to scruffy highlands, and temperate Mediterranean weather to frigid eastern winters.

Turkish cheeses from rural areas are rustic, made from raw, unpasteurized cow, goat, or sheep milk (or a combination of two or all three), using recipes and techniques passed down through many generations. Goats in particular thrive on the highland vegetation that makes up much of Turkey's arid, rugged landscape. Sheep are more suited to lowland pastures. Eastern and central Anatolia produce the most distinctive cheeses, sold in strings, rounds, or braids, often annointed with herbs or hot red chilies.

A number of cheeses are linked to either their cities or regions of production, much the way Parmigiano Reggiano (see Chapter 4) is in Italy. On a larger scale, Turkey has a well-developed dairy and cheese industry, so some of the best-known cheeses, like the Greek-style feta, are mass-produced and widely distributed. These are exported around the world.

What follows are the best-known cheeses produced in Turkey (note that (*peynir* is the Turkish word for "cheese"):

- ✔ **Beyaz Peynir:** This white cheese is similar to feta and is primarily served with breakfast. It's also eaten with salads or in a grilled cheese sandwich known as *tost*.

- ✔ **Kaşkaval:** Spelled *kashkaval* in Greece, Bulgaria, Hungary, and other Central European countries, this is a mild, yellow, cheddar-like cheese.

- ✔ **Mihaliç Peynir and Kelle Peynir:** These are mild, semi-firm grating cheeses made from goat or sheep milk, used much the same as Parmesan. Locals prefer them as a breakfast cheese, but because they're great for melting, they're also used on top of pizzas or baked dishes.

- ✔ **Örme Peynir:** This irresistible, large braided cheese made from sheep or goat milk (or both) is often mixed with parsley and local herbs (*ot*) and eaten at various ages up to about 2 years of age. It has a snowy, white color, is chewy and milky, and is eaten for breakfast and snacks.

In the foothills of Mt. Erciyes are scores of dairy farming villages. The cheeses they produce — such as Erciyes Peynir, a nutty, yellowish variety — are available in local farmers' markets. Cheeses of this region are very diverse, and include varieties with light, musty rinds, which are unusual for Turkish varieties.

Nearly all kids love string cheese but the processed, mass-produced stuff we get in America can't compare to the Middle Eastern varieties. If you really want to hook your offspring on cheese (as well as keep them occupied for a while), try giving them Armenian string cheese or its equivalent. You'll find it at ethnic markets and some grocery chains and specialty shops. The "strings" can be up to three feet long, and even adults (namely, us) have a hard time resisting these satisfyingly chewy, mild ropes of pure dairy goodness.

# Greece

The Greeks consume more cheese per capita than any other country in the world. It's surprising — at least, to Americans — because with a handful of exceptions, Greek cheeses are virtually unknown in this country. Besides Feta, which is nearly as ubiquitous as goat cheese, you may find Myzithra, Kefalotyri, Kasseri, and halloumi (which is actually a Cypriot cheese) in larger grocery stores and cheese shops. Unusual and tasty cheeses all, but the true treasures of Greek cheesemaking are to be found in the most unprepossessing of villages or on the smallest of the country's approximately 1,400 islands (only 227 of which are inhabited).

Despite being one of the most mountainous countries in Europe, Greece has a mostly Mediterranean climate. The exception to this are the high-altitude regions of the northwest, which receive heavy snowfall in winter. Thus, cheesemaking is a seasonal endeavor in this part of the country.

The Greek tradition of cheesemaking has been traced back to the 8th century; Homer even referenced it in both the *Iliad* and *Odyssey*. While the Greeks have had thousands of years to hone their craft, most of their cheeses are rustic and simple and made from the milk of goats and sheep, which are well-suited to the terrain — 75 to 80 percent of which is mountainous or semi-mountainous — and Greece's hot, arid climate. Cows are raised to a small degree on the mainland; cow milk cheeses are fairly uncommon and are usually mixed with sheep or goat milk.

Literally hundreds of cheeses are produced in Greece, but the production can be limited to an island or the area surrounding a village. In fact, Greek cheeses are known less for their differences than for their specific regionality; even their names are based upon locale and root words. For example, Kefalotyri is a giant, fresh sheep milk cheese; *kefa* means "head" and refers to the cheese's size. Ladotyri of Mytilinis is a hard, cylindrical cheese preserved in olive oil: *lado* means "oil," *tyri* means "cheese," and *Mytilinis* is the capital city of Lesbos, the island on which this cheese is made.

In the following list, we describe the most classic and widely available Greek cheeses. All are made from goat or sheep milk, or a mixture of the two:

- ✓ **Kefalotyri:** Like Feta and Manouri, Kefalotyri is a whey cheese made of sheep milk. It's fairly salty and may be eaten young and fresh like Feta, or aged, which gives it a more piquant flavor. It's used as a table or grating cheese, or as a sweet pastry filling. It may also be fried, like halloumi (see the next section).

✔ **Myzithra:** This hard, snowy-white whey cheese has been produced for thousands of years. The cheese is salted, dried, and used for grating (try it over pasta for a more zesty alternative to parmesan).

✔ **Manouri:** Another whey cheese, Manouri differs in that it also has milk or cream added to it. The result is a mild, semi-soft cheese that is tangy and fresh.

✔ **Kasseri:** This soft to semi-hard pasta filata-style cheese is stringy, mild, and used as a table cheese or in cooking.

✔ **Feta:** What we know as feta in the United States — white, crumbly, salty, creamy — usually comes atop a Greek salad, but in Greece, it's far more than mere garnish. In 2002, Feta was granted PDO status. True Feta (note the capital *F*!) can only be produced in Greece, on the island of Lesbos and the mountains of Macedonia, Thrace, Epirus, Thessaly, Sterea, Ellada, Peloponnesus, and Mytilini. It must be made from sheep milk or a controlled percentage (70 percent) of goat milk. Other countries sometimes use cow milk, as well, but by law, feta made in other countries has to be designated as "Feta Style" to differentiate it from Greek Feta.

If you get the chance to buy the real stuff, you'll see it's nothing like dry, oversalted industrial versions. Creamy, dreamy, and just as delicious tossed with orzo and grilled vegetables as it is on a pizza, Feta is one of our favorite cheeses as far as versatility and culinary compatibility are concerned.

## Hello, halloumi: A famous Cypriot cheese

Cyprus, the third largest island in the Mediterranean (after Sicily and Sardinia), is east of Greece and south of Turkey. Through central Cyprus runs a low-lying mountain range, the Troodos; near sea level are Cedar and Aleppo pine forest and scrubby vegetation. Drought is also a constant problem at lower elevations. Sheep and goats thrive in these conditions, so Cyprus has its share of subsistence farmers and shepherds, as well as a commercial dairy industry for its famous national product: halloumi cheese.

Halloumi is a fresh, brined non-melting cheese made from nothing more than unpasteurized milk and animal rennet. Mint leaves are traditionally pressed between the blocks of salted cheese to act as a preservative. Halloumi can be eaten fresh, because of its mild and milky flavor, but it's most often fried or grilled. We love it as an appetizer, but it's also delicious drizzled with honey.

## A country divided

Cyprus has played a pivotal role in its history, and remains the source of an ongoing territorial conflict that has raged since the early 1970s.

The Republic of Cyprus is a country divided. The southern portion of the island is under the control of the Republic (citizens are known as Greek Cypriots, and the international community recognizes the island as a whole as the Republic of Cyprus), while the northern half is under Turkish control and refers to itself as the Turkish Republic of Northern Cyprus (Turkish Cypriots).

Despite the political instability, Cyprus is a popular tourist destination amongst Europeans, who are seduced by the semi-arid subtropical climate, beaches, outdoor recreation, and Mediterranean cuisine, which, as you might expect, is similar to that found in Greece and Eastern Turkey.

# Chapter 13

# The Rest of Europe

. . . . . . . . . . . . . . . . . . . . . . . . . . . . . . . . . . . . . . . . . . .

## In This Chapter

▶ Discovering the tradition behind Swiss and German alpine cheeses

▶ Exploring cheese from the Netherlands to the Nordic countries

▶ Touching on the little-known cheese culture of other European regions

. . . . . . . . . . . . . . . . . . . . . . . . . . . . . . . . . . . . . . . . . . .

Consider the great mountain ranges that span the European continent: the Alps, the Pyrenees, and the Caucasus. Then think of the smaller ranges: the Scandinavian Mountains, the Dinaric Alps, even the Stara Planina — the "new" part of the Alp-Himalayan chain that extends into Central Asia. This mountainous topography should give you an idea of what you'll find in this chapter: mountain cheeses, baby!

In addition to these hard, alpine styles, you can also find the mild, semi-soft cheeses of Scandinavia and buttery Goudas and farmhouse cheeses of the Netherlands. In this chapter, we highlight a variety of cheeses and cheese-making regions in Switzerland, Germany, the Netherlands, and provide a brief primer on dairy cultures in Eastern Europe.

# The Hills Are Alive: A Brief Primer on Alpine Cheeses

One of the highest and largest mountain ranges on earth, the Alps cross Switzerland, France, Italy, Germany, Austria, Liechtenstein, and Slovenia. As we note elsewhere in this book, there's an intrinsic — and integral — link between dairying and cheesemaking amongst mountain cultures. Cheese, while originally produced on family farms or from milk from a token animal for subsistence, gradually became a local source of commerce, and eventually, a major economic entity. In the case of alpine cheeses (mountain cheeses indigenous to the Alps), they've achieved global fame, and those that aren't produced according to the same recipes and artisan methods used for hundreds of years are often imitated with industrially made versions.

Also shared with other global high-altitude cultures is the practice of trans-humance, which is, in essence, following the seasonal cycle of the mountain regions. After the spring thaw, shepherds lead their animals high up into the *alpage* (mountain pastures) to graze upon the rich, nutritious summer grasses and wildflowers. While the animals eat their fill, they're milked, and the resulting cheese is made in the shepherds' nearby mountain huts.

Here are some common characteristics of alpine cheeses:

- ✔ **They traditionally are made in *large format,* meaning they're big (20 pounds and up).** This enables them to have a longer shelf-life. It also makes them more durable for transport down from the mountains.

- ✔ **Made with cow milk, alpine cheeses are always semi-firm to hard, with natural or washed-/smear-ripened rinds.** Some of the best examples of true alpine cheeses are Beaufort, Abondance, Gruyère, Appenzeller, and Comté.

Alpine styles are re-created in places other than the Alps, and the procedure (sometimes minus the transhumance) is similar.

To make these cheeses, milk is heated in large copper cauldrons over open fires. The curds are then "cooked," meaning they are reheated to a higher temperature, and pressed. These two steps remove excess moisture, which enable the cheeses to age as long as several years. At summer's end, farmers, cows, and cheeses descend from the mountaintops with great fanfare, and the cheeses are then aged in cooperative maturing facilities.

Because seasonal food traditions are still a major part of alpine (and other mountain) cultures, these regions conduct annual festivals dedicated to send-ing the animals and shepherds off into the mountains, as well as celebrations to welcome them back home in the early fall. Few sights are more charming than seeing 5,000 garland-and-bell bedecked dairy cows walking down the main street of a village, and the local festivities that accompany such events ensure that this ancient tradition thrives.

# *Holey Cheese! Styles from Switzerland*

Switzerland is the homeland of "Swiss" cheese, one of the best-known "styles" in the world. The term, however, is a generic American catch-all to describe alpine cheeses, a very distinct, complex category (see the preceding section). That we tend to associate Switzerland with alpine cheeses makes sense if you consider that the European Alps cross parts of France, Italy, Austria, and

Germany, but Switzerland lies smack in their path. In fact, the high Alps make up one-fourth of the entire country.

Switzerland, shown in Figure 13-1, produces 75 percent of its cheeses with raw milk, and of these, most (about 85 percent) are made with cow milk. The bovine breeds used are best-suited to the plentiful mountain pastures and harsh winter climate, and they yield the high butterfat milk that's necessary to produce large format alpine cheeses. Today, however, goat and sheep milk cheeses are becoming more popular, and soft, mixed-milk, "non-traditional" cheeses are on the rise.

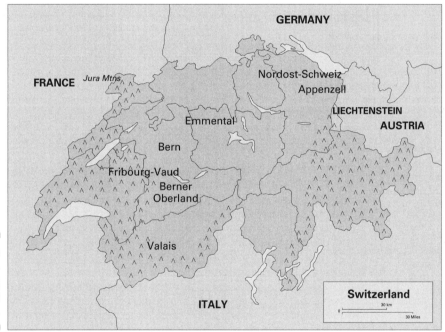

**Figure 13-1:**
Cheese-producing regions in Switzerland.

In the following sections, we take you on a brief tour of Switzerland's key cheesemaking regions and best-known varieties.

## Good eats from Berner Oberland and Emmental

Envision the Swiss Alps, and you're picturing the regions of Berner Oberland and Emmental with their tiny, picturesque villages perched on mountainsides or nestled within narrow valleys; snowy peaks; and wildflower-carpeted meadows full of tawny cows with large, clanging bells adorning their necks. The scenery is dazzling and still unspoiled in many parts of these two regions, which lie in the southwestern part of Bern; even tourist villages like Grindelwald retain authentic charm.

And then there's the cheese. . . ! Following are some of the top picks you can find from these areas:

- **Hobelkaese (shaving cheeses):** Perfect as an accompaniment with the region's rich and hearty cuisine, these are harder, aged varieties such as Berner Oberlander Hobelkase and Tête de Moine.

- **Sbrinz:** This PDO cheese is perhaps the best-known cheese from the Berner Oberland. Each 88-pound wheel is made from raw Brown Swiss cow milk that comes from 30 small, local dairies. Sbrinz is aged between 2 to 4 years and has a dense, grateable paste that is strong and spicy, with a hint of butterscotch.

- **Emmentaler (also known as Emmental):** This cheese is marked by extra-large holes — the result of introduced *Proprionibacterium freudenreichii* bacteria, which creates carbon dioxide gas. It is Swiss cow milk cheese in the most classic sense and has a smooth, almost waxy, pale-yellow paste with a pronounced nutty, slightly sweet flavor. It's a PDO cheese and has several designations in various areas depending on its age, but the minimum maturation time is 4 months. Regardless of where it's made, PDO regulations stipulate that Emmentaler must be produced within dairy co-ops that use raw cow milk sourced from within an 18-mile radius from animals that haven't been fed *sileage* (fermented grass and other crops). Now *that's* what we call a local, sustainable cheese.

The salt water that sometimes leaks from a cut Emmentaler cheese is called "tears of joy" by the Swiss, because it indicates that the cheese is high-quality.

## *Fondue cheeses from Fribourg-Vaud*

Fondue. That's what the region Fribourg-Vaud is famous for, and who doesn't love a pot of molten cheese? The region's three main cheeses — Gruyère, L'Etivaz, and Vacherin Fribourgeois — are PDO-regulated and traditionally used in fondue, but this is a major cheese-producing area regardless:

- **Gruyère:** This famous alpine beauty is complex yet versatile. Made from the milk of the Fribourgeois (Holstein, to Americans) cows owned by local dairy co-ops, a good Gruyère should be aged for at least 12 to 16 months, although younger versions can be excellent. Technically a washed-rind/smear-ripened cheese (see Chapter 4), Gruyère is wiped regularly with brine during aging; this process, combined with the rich native grasses upon which the cows feed, makes for high-quality milk and thus one of the world's great cheeses: simultaneously sweet, nutty, and earthy, with oniony or meaty undertones. Use it for just about anything.

✔ **L'Etivaz:** This was developed in 1932 by former Gruyère-producing families who wanted to continue to make the most traditional version of Gruyère after the PDO-production rules were relaxed. L'Etivaz is an alpage cow milk cheese made the old-school way, in copper cauldrons over an open wood fire, only during the summer months. It's similar to Gruyère, but more smooth and creamy, with fruity undertones.

✔ **Vacherin Fribourgeois:** One of the earliest recorded cheeses used to make fondue (approximately 1,000 years ago), this PDO raw milk cheese is made only with the milk of the local Fribourgeois cow. Only a small number of local artisanal cheesemakers produce this cheese, and it's become something of an endangered species. Firm, yet relatively soft compared with other typical Swiss cheeses, Vacherin Fribourgeois has pronounced aromas and flavors of milk, freshly cut hay, and nuts.

## Raclette from Valais

The Valais area may ring some bells at the mention of its two most famous landmarks: the Matterhorn and nearby village of Zermatt. This stunning region provides a more stereotypically Swiss landscape in summer: goats grazing in alpine meadows, bells tinkling, small chalets with flower-bedecked balconies, and, like most of Switzerland, a cheese-centric regional cuisine.

Besides the many alpage cheeses indigenous only to this region, Valais' most famous export (and dish) is Raclette. Traditionally produced in four different valleys in the area, Raclette cheese has a silky paste with a faint aroma of earth and a full, milky flavor, even after 12 months of aging. Traditionally, a half wheel would be propped up in front of the fireplace; once its surface had begun to blister, a *racler* (scraper) was used scoop the cheese into bowls filled with boiled potatoes. You can purchase a racler from specialty kitchenware stores or websites and some cheese shops. There are also electric heating devices meant for tabletop raclette-making.

## Specialties of the Jura Mountains

Straddling the French border, the Jura Mountains form a hilly, rural region of pasture and pine forest. The yellow limestone that's distinct to the terroir is believed to be a contributing factor as to why Jura cheeses show different flavor profiles than all other Swiss cheeses. The French influence can be strongly felt in the regional cuisine and in the Jura's most famous cheese: Vacherin Mont d'Or, one of Switzerland's few traditional deviations from firm alpine cheeses, described in the following list:

- **Vacherin Mont d'Or:** This seasonal raw, cow milk alpine cheese is made on both sides of the Swiss/French border. Produced only in the fall and winter months, the freshly formed cheeses are encased in a strip of spruce bark before being washed with brine and aged for 6 weeks. The resulting cheese is an earthy, smokey, milky delight that's sold in a little wooden box. To eat Vacherin Mont d'Or, cut a hole in the top of the cheese and shamelessly spoon up the satiny cream within. Did we already say *yes, please*?

- **Tête de Moine:** Like Hobelkaese, Tête de Moine (which means "monk's head") is a smear-ripened cylindrical cheese, aged for a minimum of 3 months, that is shaved into curly ribbons by a *girolle* (a blade and spindle device designed specifically for this cheese). First created by the monks of Bellelay Abbey (thus, it's also known as Bellelay), the recipe was passed on to local farmers. Today, it's produced in nine small dairies within the region.

  Traditionally Tête de Moine, a particularly great table cheese for the holidays, was made only from summer milk and sold from when the first leaves of autumn began to fall until March, but today it's made and sold year-round. Tête de Moine is fairly pungent; try it on soups and salads or with cured meats.

## Cheeses from the "bread basket": Nordost-Schweiz

Located in the northeast near Zurich, Nordost-Schweiz is Switzerland's bread basket: flat, fertile agricultural land that includes vineyards, orchards, and dairy, as well as industrial economies. The following cheeses of this region, which include Appenzeller and Tilsiter, are still made in the style of alpine cheeses:

- **Appenzeller:** Produced in Appenzell and St. Gallen, this smaller format (15 pound) mountain-style cheese dates back over 700 years. Today, local dairy co-ops provide the milk (from Simmenthaler and Brown Swiss cows) used to make the cheese. Appenzeller was traditionally made using raw milk, but regulations have become less stringent and now some dairies prefer to thermalize instead (see Chapter 2). The cheese is routinely washed in a "secret" brine of white wine, herbs, and spices — and occasionally herb brandy — which give it a distinct rind and flavor. The result is a firm, supple cheese with small eyes and a robust complexity with herbal, floral, and grass notes. The grated cheese is favored for a regional dish, *chaeshappech*, a savory fried pastry served with salad.

✔ **Tilsiter:** Although today it's produced in several areas of Nordost-Schweiz, the recipe for Tilsiter came to the town of Tilsit in the 19th century via Germany (an area that was technically East Prussia at the time) where emigrant Dutch farmers traditionally made this cow milk cheese. Young cheeses are aged up to 3 months and are smooth, mild, and milky, despite a sometimes pungent aroma. Raw milk versions may be aged up to 8 months and are quite strong. Tilsiter is traditionally used as a table cheese.

# Looking at Cheeses from Germany

Germany has less mountainous regions conducive to sheep and goats, and because cattle were used mainly for meat and manure (fertilizer), and milk was almost an afterthought, cheesemaking didn't follow the same trajectory seen in Switzerland, France (covered in Chapter 10), or Italy (Chapter 11).

Cheesemaking using rennet likely came to Germany with the ancient Romans in the first century AD but, like much of Europe, fell by the wayside in the following centuries with the exception of some monastic cheesemaking. Subsequently, cultured cheese only resurfaced in areas where dairy farming was established enough to ensure a surplus of milk: mainly on the north (Baltic) coast and in the Allgäu — the foothills of the Alps located in the south.

Germany's dairying industry began in earnest in the second half of the 19th century, and in the last 20 years, a specialty cheese scene has emerged. These new German cheesemakers can be found throughout the country and, like their American counterparts, are often pursuing a second career. Goats and sheep are the preferred dairy animals (as a way to avoid the milk quota dairy cows are subject to). Figure 13-2 shows key cheesemaking regions in Germany.

In the following sections, we cover the styles of cheesemaking and most notable cheeses found within Germany.

## Cheeses from the North

With regard to cheesemaking, this area consists of the flat marshland of the Baltic Coast, and the rich pasturelands of the states of Niedersachsen, Schleswig-Holstein, and Mecklenburg-Vorpommern. Although industrial cheeses such as Tilsiter and Butterkäse are made in the north, there's also an emerging artisan cheesemaking scene, but production tends to be low.

**Figure 13-2:**
Key cheese-
making
areas in
Germany.

✔ **Tilsiter:** Although the name may be the same as the Tilsiter produced in
Switzerland, German Tilsiter is a fundamentally different cheese.

Here it's a semi-soft, pasteurized, washed-rind cow milk cheese that is
not pressed. It can range from creamy, buttery, and mild to extremely
pungent and sharp, depending upon its age. (If you prefer a more mellow
cheese, however, just remove the sticky red rind.) Tilsiter is sometimes
made with herbs, black peppercorns, or caraway. Traditionally, it's
eaten on rye bread with butter: we like that kind of double-dairy punch!

✔ **Aschekäse:** About an hour north of Hamburg, cheesemaker Tobias
Schüller produces a cow milk cheese the same shape and size of Tilsiter,
but softer. His Aschekäse is enriched with cream and marbled with thin

layers of ash (similar to Morbier; see Chapter 10). This contemporary cheese combines creaminess and crumble, and mellowness and pungency with a bit of tang.

✔ **Deichkäse:** *Deichkäse* is a pressed hard cheese that combines Tilsiter cultures with mountain cheesemaking practice (*Deiche*, or dikes, are a prominent feature of the flat, marshy landscape where this cheese is produced). It has a natural rind and is made from raw cow milk. Look for the Milbenkäse version (see Chapter 20), in which cheese mites are allowed to provide the finishing touch, making for a more. . . intense flavor.

# Cheeses from Bavaria and Allgäu

The alpine topography in southern Germany give residents of this area more of a historical cheesemaking foundation — one that, like Switzerland, is based upon the practice of transhumance (covered in the earlier section "The Hills Are Alive: A Brief Primer on Alpine Cheeses"). Two areas of the south are of special note: Bavaria and Allgäu, both of which have became known for hard alpine cheeses (both young and aged) made from high-quality raw milk.

State, country, and cultural borders between Austria, Switzerland, and Germany in this corner of the Alps are virtually unnoticeable once you're up in the mountains. Hence, the cheeses are very similar in nature.

## Handkäse and quark

Historically, in the home, the residual sour skimmed milk from buttermaking was turned into *Handkäse* — small, rustic cheeses. Today, these Handkäse have developed into a small industry in some areas. In the Pfalz (also known as the Palatinate) region in southwestern Germany and in the Harz region in the north, Handkäse — also known as Harzer — is popularly consumed with beer or wine. It's often served *mit Musik* (with music), meaning it's been marinated with plenty of raw onion, oil, and vinegar, and sometimes seasoned with caraway seeds.

Handkäse may be shaped into small, flat discs or finger-thick sticks; with aging, it goes from crumbly, white, and mild, to gooey, yellow, and pungent. The most notable Handkäse comes from Nieheim, a small town in Westphalia (in the north). Nieheim is also home to the *Deutscher Käsemarkt* (German Cheese Market). Held every other year, this festival draws artisan cheesemakers from all over the world.

Another traditional German cheese is quark. Throughout Germany, *quark* — a fresh, soft farmers-style cheese — is served with unpeeled boiled potatoes; fresh herbs or other aromatics are often added. The many regional variations have names ranging from *Bibbeleskäse* to *Glumse*. Quark is also essential for *Käsekuchen* (cheesecake).

✔ **Bavaria:** The state of Bavaria provides the mental postcard many people associate with Germany. It's home to vast swaths of evergreen forest, at the eastern end of the magnificent Alps.

✔ **Allgäu:** The southern heart of German cheesemaking is in the region of Allgäu — an alpine region comprised of fertile pasture and pristine lakes located at various elevations. Although best-known for its alpine cheeses, the Allgäu is also famed for Limburger and Romadur. Both of these small format, semi-soft washed rinds were developed in the 1830s through the influence of a Belgian dairy worker.

In the following list, we provide a brief look into the cheeses of note that come from these regions:

✔ **Spicherhalder Alpkäse:** Third generation dairy farmers, the Vogel family make the transhumance circuit from their home on the German-Austrian border to the Allgäu Alps each summer, with their herd of 30 Brown Swiss cows. The milk — sweet from rich pasture grasses and alpine flowers, is turned into two wheels of cheese each day, made the old-school way in copper vats. Washed in brine solution and aged for at least a year, the result is a truly special alpage cheese with floral, earthy, and smoky notes and a smooth, buttery finish.

✔ **Weisslacker:** Also known as *Bierkäse* (beer cheese), Weisslacker is a Bavarian specialty of surface-ripened cow milk cheese specifically designed to be consumed with beer; some people even dip it into their drink before consuming! It's also used to make their *Käsespätzle* ("cheese noodles"). Weisslacker is ripened under high humidity, which contributes in part to its extremely pungent aroma; paradoxically, it's fairly mild in taste.

✔ **Allgäuer Bergkäse:** Literally "mountain cheese," this bold, raw cow milk alpine cheese is somewhat similar to Gruyère in flavor. In the best versions, nutty and herbal aromas are enhanced by ripe fruity notes. Eat Allgäuer Bergkäse at several months of age for a snack. Aged over 12 months, the flavors are much more complex, making for a truly special cheese.

✔ **Romadur:** This pungent, washed-rind cow milk loaf cheese is similar to Limburger, and both have their origins in Belgium. Romadur was introduced to Bavaria in the mid-19th century and is one of the most popular German cheeses today. It's used in cooking and the condiment *Obaztda* (combined with butter and herbs, spices, and/or onion or garlic), or consumed with pumpernickel bread and a sturdy lager.

✔ **Limburger:** This famously pungent cheese originated with Trappist monks in the Limburg region of Belgium in the 19th century. It was immensely popular and copied shortly afterwards by the Germans, who began production in 1830 in the Allgäu. Germany is now the leading producer of Limburger, although it's also produced in the United States (notably, Wisconsin), Belgium, and the Netherlands. Although there are few artisanal producers left, the Allgäu is considered to yield some of the best versions.

Limburger is milder than its aroma suggests, with earthy, mushroomy flavors and a faint tang. Anton Holziner and his daughter Luise of Käserei Zurwies specialize in excellent soft cheeses since taking over a former co-op dairy in 1990; their Limburger is available in the U.S.

✔ **Cambozola**: First produced in 1900, Cambozola has been patented and produced in large amounts by the German cheesemaking company Champignon since 1970. This mild blue is like the love child of a buttery triple-crème cow milk cheese and Gorgonzola Dolce. It's a crowd-pleaser, even amongst non-blue lovers.

# Exploring Cheeses from the Netherlands

Whether you call it Holland or the Netherlands (the Dutch are amenable to either, although "Holland" is technically a region in the western part of the country), even cheese neophytes know that this low-lying, flat-as-a-dime country on the North Sea is famous for at least one dairy product, Gouda. But Gouda isn't the only cheese produced in the Netherlands (shown in Figure 13-3), as the following sections show.

In the following sections, we outline some of the best-known Dutch cheeses. Many are similar in style, although the milk type may vary.

## Gouda

Most of the cheese produced in the Netherlands is Gouda. It can be raw milk or pasteurized and can range in size from 1- to 176-pound wheels! The rind may be natural, coated, or waxed (see Chapter 2 for information on rinds), and the cheese may be plain or flavored with herbs or spices. Gouda may be aged from 2 months to 5-plus years. (Aging for that length of time can only be done in cooled cellars, or the cheese will taste bitter. Done correctly, it's butterscotchy and crunchy with crystallized proteins.) The one characteristic shared by most Goudas the world over? Their flattened wheel shape.

Only a very small minority of Gouda is a farmstead cheese. Today, Gouda is primarily known as an industrial cheese, which makes it difficult for artisan and farmstead cheesemakers to earn a living or start a cheese operation. The name Gouda isn't protected but it's widely recognized that true Gouda comes from Holland and is made from cow milk. Regardless, excellent Goudas are also produced in the U.S. and other countries (including Holland), from cow, goat, or sheep milk.

**Netherlands**

Wadden
Sea

Friesland

Drenthe

Emmen

North Holland

North Sea

Beemster

Amsterdam

Gouda

Utrecht

**South Holland**   **Utrecht**

Rotterdam

GERMANY

BELGIUM

**Figure 13-3:**
The
Netherlands.

Noord-Hollandse Oplegkaas is the only Gouda with a PDO. Made of pasteur-ized cow milk from the northwestern part of the country, Oplegkaas (*opleg* means "aged") is a cheese made to mature; they're usually sold at a minimum of two years old, when they possess caramel and butterscotch flavors, and crunchy, crystallized proteins.

The correct pronunciation of Gouda is "*how*-duh." We're not suggesting you sashay into your local cheese shop or grocer and ask for it in Dutch, but it's good to know should you be lucky enough to try it in its place of origin.

## Boerenkaas

Boerenkaas, which means "farmer's cheese," is essentially Gouda, with regulations imposed upon it. Both Boerenkaas and Boeren Goudse Oplegkaas are regulated names so the milk must always be raw, from a single, smaller-scale farm to ensure artisanal production. Boerenkaas may be made from cow, goat, or sheep milk, but never mixed.

Like Gouda, it can have many variations in color and flavor, depending upon the type of milk used, where it's from, and how long it's been aged. Because it acquires flavor and textural development with maturation, Boerenkaas is aged for several months and generally eaten "middle-aged" or aged. The following are two well-known Boerenkaas cheeses:

- **Boeren-Leidse met sleutels** is a PDO raw cow milk cheese with cumin (*met sleutels* means "with keys" and refers to the city's coat of arms). To much of the world, this cheese is also known as *Leyden* because, historically, it was produced in the Leiden area in the south. (Leyden is also industrially made, but only the farmstead versions meet PDO regulations.)

- **Boeren-Goudse Oplegkaas:** Perhaps the best-known Boerenkaas produced in the Netherlands, this cheese is made in the Green Heart region, using only raw summer milk produced by cows grazing in pasture rich in peat moss. The cheese is made in the traditional style, in wooden forms lined with linen, and weighs a minimum of 44 pounds. The wheels are aged for 2 to 4 years, resulting in a rich, creamy, caramelly cheese that, in our opinion, is the only thing that can compete with chocolate for our favorite dessert.

## Edam

This PDO cheese is well-known in America — think of the red wax-coated wheels or balls often served at holiday parties. Not to burst your cheese bubble, but this isn't true Edam. The real deal was first made in the 14th century from cow milk that came from a restricted region around the town of Edam in northern Holland. It was aged longer and thus harder and sharper in flavor than the mild, semi-soft Edam that's exported; these cheeses were coated in red or yellow wax to preserve them, as well as make them identifiable to the consumer. These days, Edam is pasteurized and produced only in Friesland. Check with your cheesemonger for aged and artisanal versions. There are also some nice domestic Edams.

Because Edam was so sturdy and resistant to spoilage — as well as delicious — it's believed to have been the world's most popular cheese from the 14th to 18th centuries, when the Dutch were doing much of their seafaring expeditions and trading.

## Graskaas

Graskaas is produced by Beemster, one of Holland's oldest and most renowned cheesemakers. This rare, raw cow milk cheese is produced from the first milkings of the year, when the cows return to spring pasture after a winter spent indoors. Graskaas is handcrafted according to the original recipe, which was developed in 1901. Because the milk quantity is so limited, only 2,000 wheels are produced annually. The cheese is aged for 1 month, released with great fanfare, and shipped around the world.

Graskaas is softer and creamier in texture than most Goudas because it's so young and made with richer milk. Buttery and semi-soft, this mild cheese makes for a fabulous pairing with bubbles and pilsner-style beers. Look for it in June. In addition to Graskaas, Beemster produces exceptional aged Goudas, including Beemster XO.

# Cheeses from the Nordic Countries

While dairy production in the sub-arctic chill of northern Finland or Iceland may seem at odds with the seasonal nature of milk, the truth is that these countries, as well as Denmark, Norway, and Sweden, have an ancient history of cheesemaking.

In the following list, we outline some popular Nordic cheeses, arranged alphabetically:

- **Danbo (Denmark):** A popular, loaf-shaped, waxed cheese that is smooth and dry, with a supple interior marked by small eyes. It's most commonly used for breakfast, on sandwiches, and for snacks.

- **Danish Blue (Denmark):** A mild blue invented in the early 20th century by a Danish cheesemaker bent on creating a domestic Roquefort-style.

- **Danish Fontina (Denmark):** A semi-soft, smooth, and mild cheese, with a coating of red wax. It bears no similarity to Italian fontina, which is an alpine cheese.

- **Esrom (Denmark):** A creamy, moist, Trappist-style cheese also known as Danish Port-Salut.

- **Gjetost (Norway):** A fudgy goat or cow milk whey cheese with a sweet, caramel-like flavor.

- ✔ **Greve (Sweden):** A semi-firm cheese similar to Swiss Emmentaler (holes included). Aged about 10 months, it's buttery, tangy, and zesty.

- ✔ **Havarti (Denmark):** A semi-soft cow milk cheese with a dense, buttery, ivory-colored paste riddled with small eyes, and flavors that range from mild to slightly sharp.

- ✔ **Jarlsberg (Norway):** This famous Norwegian cheese has a yellow wax rind and a pale yellow paste that is nutty, milky, and buttery, with large, uneven holes ("eyes"). Its texture is supple and somewhat springy — great for melting and sandwiches.

- ✔ **Skyr (Iceland):** A cultured, fat-free dairy product that is technically a soft cheese. It has a high protein content and the consistency of very thick yogurt. Although all modern skyr is made with cow milk, sheep milk was also used until the 19th century.

- ✔ **Kryddost (Sweden):** A semi-firm cheese studded with cumin and cloves. Considered a delicacy, it's best enjoyed with smorgasbord or on dark rye with aquavit. *Skål!*

- ✔ **Lappi (Finland):** A firm, exceedingly mild cheese made from partially skimmed milk.

- ✔ **Leipäjussto (Finland):** A rather delightful fresh, "squeaky" cheese often made with reindeer milk. Chapter 20 has more details.

## Going a little farther east

In the last couple of decades, monumental changes have taken place in the former Soviet Union and in Eastern and Central Europe, and things continue to evolve. Yet we can't include the "rest of Europe" without mentioning the Balkans, Transcaucasia, and the former Soviet states. Here's a short-and-sweet tour through some of the cheeses from Central and Eastern Europe, arranged alphabetically:

- ✔ **Armenia:** Briny young cheeses like Lori and Chanakh are popular eaten with flatbread, while string cheese (braided and often studded with black nigella seeds) is a favorite snack. Aitsi panir is a fresh, brined goat cheese packed into little clay pots. The preference for salty cheeses is said to be both a matter of preservation and to replace body salts lost due to a hot climate.

- ✔ **Bosnia and Herzegovina:** Livno is a dry, yellow cheese from western Bosnia; also popular is a feta-like cheese called Travnički in central Bosnia and Herzegovina. Sir iz Mijeha ("cheese in a sack") is made by aging raw cow, sheep, or goat milk or a combination of the three in a full-size sheepskin (talk about unwieldy!) for 2 to 12 months.

- ✔ **Bulgaria:** Sheep milk feta is extremely popular and more creamy than the Greek variety; it can be found in American specialty shops and groceries. Kashkaval, a traditional Turkish cheese, is also found

*(continued)*

*(continued)*

throughout the Balkans, including Romania, where it's spelled *Cascaval*.

✔ **Croatia:** Croatia just may be the next big thing in cheese if Paški sir, a pasteurized, natural rind cheese made from the milk of indigenous sheep, is any indication. In appearance, Paški sir has a maroon rind but is similar to Parmigano Reggiano in its interior: straw yellow, with a visible crystallization. It has a smoky, salty, nutty complexity.

✔ **Czech Republic:** Abertam is a traditional farmhouse cheese made from sheep milk. Shaped into balls with a punchy flavor, it has a firm texture, thin yellowish rind, and is a favorite for snacking or melting.

✔ **Georgia:** Suluguni, a soft, brined cheese from the Samegrelo region in the west, made from goat, sheep, or cow milk, is used for the beloved dish *khatchapuri*, or cheese bread. A thin dough is wrapped around the flat cheese and fried until the interior is molten.

✔ **Hungary:** Túró is fresh cheese similar to quark (refer to the earlier sidebar "Handkäse and quark"); although usually made with cow milk, sheep or goat milk is sometimes used.

In the classic Hungarian spread *körörzött* (also known as *Liptauer*), it's seasoned with sweet paprika, garlic, onions, salt, and caraway seeds. Trappista is another favorite cheese, made with cow milk from the same recipe used by the 18th century French monks who created Port-Salut.

✔ **Poland:** Ocszypek is an oval, smoked, salty pasta filata shepherd's cheese (see Chapter 3) from the Tatra Mountains. Made from raw sheep milk, it's pressed into hand-carved wooden molds that give it a pattern unique to each producer. Twaróg (quark) is frequently used in the cuisine, while Bryndza Podhalanska is a PDO sheep milk (sometimes mixed with cow milk) cheese from northeastern Poland; it's salty, strong, and sometimes has a faintly sour flavor.

✔ **Romania:** Telemea is a traditional semi-soft cheese made with sheep or cow milk. Creamy and tangy, it's used as a table cheese, for snacking, and in salads or other dishes. It may also be aged for sharper flavor or spiced with cumin seeds. Brinza is a ubiquitous, feta-like cheese that's also found in Russia.

# Chapter 14

# Off-the-Map Cheesemaking

## In This Chapter

▶ Examining the cheese industry potential in Australia and New Zealand

▶ Understanding the economics of cheese in Central Asia

▶ Exploring the nomadic cheese culture of the Middle East

*A*ustralia, New Zealand, and *cheese* — four words most people don't often associate with one another. In the last decade, however, Australia and New Zealand have, in their typical understated way, been gaining ground for their artisan (what they call *specialty*) cheeses, much of it farmstead. In this chapter, we explore how immigration influenced cheesemaking in these two countries and where their artisan cheese movement is now (let's just say the forecast is sunny).

Farther afield, we take a look at subsistence cheesemaking in Central Asia and how the Middle East's dairy culture has changed little in thousands of years yet remains a fundamental part of daily life.

# Antipodean Artisans: Australia and New Zealand

Australia is one of the most geologically, geographically, and climatically diverse places on the planet. This vast continent the size of the mainland United States supports flora and fauna found nowhere else on Earth. There are tropical rainforests, 16,000 miles of coastline, and cattle stations (ranches) the size of Texas. Yet while much of Australia is barren Outback, it has swaths of fertile dairy land as well, particularly in the states of Victoria, South Australia, and Tasmania.

Blessed with plentiful rainfall and abundant grazing crops, New Zealand is known for its dairy and meat animals (cows and sheep), which are generally raised outdoors and grass-fed year-round, resulting in more flavorful, nutritious meat and milk, loaded with conjugated linoleic acids (CLA), Omega-3 fatty acids, and beta carotene (see Chapter 1).

## Aussie ingenuity

Cheesemaking is still a fairly new commercial enterprise in Australia, but given the nation's agricultural and immigrant history, it's not surprising in the least that a cheese revolution is taking place.

Granted, Australia isn't a cheese destination the way France or Italy are (see Chapters 10 and 11), but it's exciting to see Australian cheesemakers come into their own, especially in a country better known for culinary wonders such as pie floaters and Vegemite. Because Australia — like America — is a young country, it doesn't have the history and tradition that have guided European cheesemakers for hundreds of years, influenced as they were by their terroir, invading cultures, and other factors. Thus, Australia's cheesemakers are mostly forging their own identity.

The potential for a thriving Australian artisan cheese industry unique to the country is ripe. The purity of environmental conditions and the indigenous flora that nourish dairy animals make for a distinct terroir, which is of great interest as artisan cheesemaking and craftsmanship progress. There are, however, some hurdles to industry growth:

✔ The country's rigid quarantine and production laws — similar to those in the United States — that prohibit production and importation of raw milk dairy products (see Chapter 2 for details on the raw milk debate and import restrictions).

✔ Little infrastructure and few educational outlets for artisan cheesemakers, which places limitations on what they can accomplish.

Fortunately, consumer demand for artisan cheese — both domestic and imported — in Australia's cosmopolitan capital cities is booming, and we expect to see its domestic cheese industry grow dramatically in the years to come.

Large and small production cheese is being made around Australia. In the following sections, we highlight the most prolific areas for artisanal cheesemaking in the country (see Figure 14-1) and a few top producers within each region.

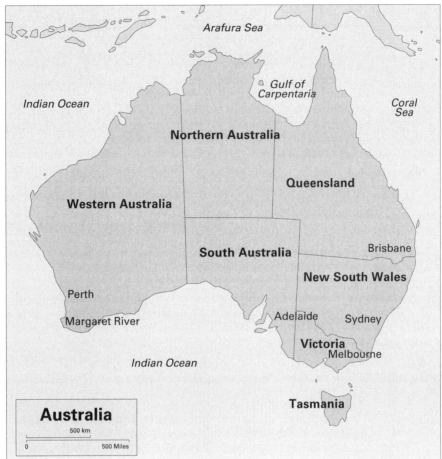

**Figure 14-1:**
Australia's
cheese-
producing
regions.

### Victoria

Victoria could best be compared to the American Rockies due to its mountains, seasonal snowfall, river valleys, and prime pasture and agricultural land. Rainfall here is plentiful, and the climate is more temperate, although the central and northern parts of the state are hotter and flatter.

TECHNICAL STUFF

# A walk(about) down memory lane

Australia was originally settled by the British as a penal colony in 1788. The *First Fleet* refers to the 11 ships that sailed from England to Botany Bay to establish the country's first European colony. Onboard the ships were five cows and two bulls, but the animals escaped soon after landing. The colony soon found itself with a small population of feral cattle, and more cattle — mostly oxen — were later exported from India and England for labor.

Until the first commercial dairy was established in Sydney in 1805, the settlement suffered from a serious lack of dairy products (which alone is cause for felonious behavior, in our opinion!). In 1820, commercial cheesemaking finally took off in New South Wales, and by the 1830s, a small export market existed. Tasmania also began commercial cheese production in the 1820s.

The interest in artisan cheesemaking that began in the late 20th century is largely the result of Australia's well-traveled populace growing inspired by the foods they've tasted overseas. The other major cheesemaking influences are the waves of immigrants that have flooded Australia off and on since its settlement.

Australia's melting-pot culture has resulted in thriving ethnic enclaves and a vibrant, eclectic cultural and culinary scene in urban areas like Sydney and Melbourne. With regard to cheese, the immigrants from traditional cheese-consuming cultures such as the Middle East, Mediterranean, and other parts of Europe have resulted in cheesemakers replicating the styles of cheese from their homeland. That's why you see so many aged Italian-, Dutch-, and alpine-style, and fresh, brined, and surface-ripened cheeses and yogurt being made in Australia.

Victoria's dairy industry began in the 1830s and quickly prospered. By the late-18th and early-19th centuries, dairy co-ops became the norm, supplying milk for commercially produced butter and bulk cheddar for the domestic and export markets. Today, Victoria is a major producer of fluid cow milk and artisan cheese. Following are some notable cheesemakers:

- **Yarra Valley Dairy:** This third-generation farm in the heart of wine country produces excellent farmstead cheeses, including luscious, Persian-style cow milk feta marinated in olive oil and herbs (available in the U.S.) and surface-ripened cow and goat cheeses.

- **Sutton Grange Organic Farm:** Sutton Grange Organic Farm, the home of Holy Goat Cheese, is located in the Goldfields region (so-named because it was the site of the Victorian Gold Rush in the 1850s and '60s). Holy Goat Cheese is considered by domestic cheese experts to be some of Australia's best. The makers specialize in French-style farmstead chèvres and mold-ripened goat milk cheeses.

- **Meredith Dairy:** Located 60 miles west of Melbourne, Meredith Dairy is the largest farmstead producer of goat and sheep milk cheeses in Australia. This dairy is equally famous for its custardy sheep milk yogurt and surface-ripened cheeses. You can find some of Meredith Dairy's products, such as marinated feta, at select cheese shops and grocers in the United States. The dairy and cheese factory are dedicated to sustainable land management and run entirely on biodiesel.

- **Milawa Cheese Company:** In northeast Victoria's King Valley, a noteworthy wine region, Milawa Cheese Company was founded in 1988 by Dave and Anne Brown in what was originally the local butter factory. This creamery has become a destination for cheese-lovers who want to sample and purchase Milawa's wide variety of artisan cow and goat cheeses and housemade bread.

- **Tarago River Cheese Company:** One of Australia's best-known creameries, Tarago River Cheese Company is located in Gippsland, the heart of Victoria's dairy country. The dairy produces one of Australia's first farmstead blue cheeses, Gippsland Blue, made from cow milk.

- **Shaw River Buffalo Cheese:** The nation's first water buffalo dairy (the herd was started with animals imported from Italy and Bulgaria), Shaw River Buffalo Cheese produces mozzarella and other fresh cheese styles, a washed-rind cheese, and yogurt.

## Gabrielle Kervella: The First Lady of Australian goat cheese

Although she's from New Zealand, Gabrielle Kervella became known as the "Australian doyenne of goat cheese" after she kicked off the country's caprine cheesemaking movement. Kervella got her first herd in the 1980s because she was interested in the homesteading movement and established a dairy in Western Australia.

From the milk of her 200 goats, Kervella produced a highly successful commercial line of excellent fresh and aged cheeses, including a lush fromage blanc; the tangy, clean, lightly aged, mold-ripened Affine; and Cabecou, a traditional-style chèvre from southwestern France that she marinated in olive oil and herbs.

In the early 2000s, Kervella and her partner, Alan Cockman, completed a new cheesemaking facility and classroom for visiting chefs and cheesemaking classes. In 2008, the couple retired to Kervella's native New Zealand, after selling all the farm and creamery equipment and goats to a start-up cheesemaker.

Although no longer making cheese, Kervella is responsible for not only fostering Australia's interest in goat cheese, but also advancing the country's burgeoning reputation as a producer of quality farmstead and artisanal cheeses and dairy products.

## South Australia

Much of South Australia (SA) is desert. Wine production, dairy, and other agriculture are restricted to coastal areas in the south, but the pay-off is fertile soil, although the near-ideal growing conditions are hampered by an ever-present water shortage.

While the following are among the better-known cheesemakers in SA, the southern part of the state has a handful of other small farmstead and artisan cheesemaking operations:

- ✔ **Alexandrina Cheese Company:** This farmstead dairy and creamery is owned and run by Dan and Krystyna McCaul and some of their children. Combining dairying with cheesemaking, the company produces Dutch-style flavored cheeses, rinded cheddars, ricotta, and other excellent dairy products.

- ✔ **Barossa Valley Cheese Company:** The brainchild of winemaker-turned-cheesemaker Victoria McClurg, this much-loved SA cheese producer hand crafts cow and goat milk cheeses in a tiny creamery adjoining its retail shop in the town of Angaston — right in the heart of wine country.

- ✔ **Woodside Cheese Wrights:** Located in the Adelaide Hills, Woodside Cheese Wrights is one of SA's first artisan cheese companies, at just over a decade old. Longtime second-owner Kris Lloyd produces over 20 styles of goat and cow milk cheeses, many of which are only available seasonally.

- ✔ **Udder Delights:** Udder Delights has a retail shop and café in the Adelaide Hills and makes a variety of goat and cow milk cheeses ranging from creamy goat curd to cow milk blue.

## South Australia's cheese and wine trails

Several of SA's top wine regions have taken the guesswork out of pairing wine and cheese. On each of the three different Cheese and Wine Trails (in McLaren Vale, Adelaide Hills, and the Barossa Valley), you'll need to self-drive, but the regions are well-mapped and rural, for those nervous about driving on the left-side of the road.

Each route includes a picnic hamper of regional cheeses and accompaniments to be picked up at your starting point (local cheese shops). An enclosed map includes driving instructions to specific wineries, as well as a "menu" telling you what wines to pair with each cheese and condiment. What's not to love (besides driving, that is)?

Following is a list of details and starting points; if you prefer to do it yourself, each sells a selection of local cheeses and other accompaniments:

- ✔ **McLaren Vale:** Blessed Cheese café and retail shop, McLaren Vale, www.blessedcheese.com.au.

- ✔ **Adelaide Hills:** Udder Delights Cheese Cellar, Hahndorf, www.udderdelights.com.au.

- ✔ **Barossa Valley:** Barossa Valley Cheese Company, Angaston, www.barossacheese.com.au.

---

## King Island: Australia's export cheese

Although part of Tasmania, King Island has become a dairy destination of sorts, thanks to enterprising cheesemaker Ueli Berger of King Island Dairy. Located off the main island's western coast, King Island lies at the entrance of the Bass Strait, right in the path of the notorious "Roaring Forties" that whip straight up from Antarctica. The winds make for ideal dairying conditions. The island has a moderate climate and low rainfall, and the rich pastures are sprayed by the rough coastal waters.

The first farmers came from Victoria at the beginning of the 20th century, and a dairy cooperative was formed soon after. King Island Dairy opened in the 1970s and is now the employer of 150 of the islands 1,500 inhabitants and buys milk from its 16 different dairy farms.

Berger, a Swiss immigrant in his 50s, moved to Tasmania when he was 20 to work for a different cheese company. He started at King Island Dairy in 1998, and today, he and his team produce bloomy-rind, washed-rind, cheddar, and blue cow milk cheeses. Some of King Island's cheeses—mostly notably Roaring Forties Blue—are available in supermarkets (including in the U.S.), but the company's handcrafted artisan line, Black Label (which includes Brie, a double Brie, a blue triple-crème, and a waxed and clothbound cheddar), is sold only in domestic specialty shops and to restaurants. While production is hardly small scale, the cheeses still retain an artisan quality: Each is crafted from island milk and named after a local landmark, and the factory itself is in a rural location in this most remote of places.

— Adapted from *culture* magazine's "King Island: Australia's Export Cheese," by Lucy Barbour

---

### Tasmania

Despite being Australia's smallest state, Tasmania's location south of the mainland gives much of this island a cool, wet, lush climate ideally suited for dairy cows (although goat and sheep milk cheeses are also produced). Like Victoria and SA, Tasmania also produces wine — including almost all of the Pinot Noir used in Australia's sparkling wines — and is emerging as a well-known region in its own right.

Artisan cheese (and other foods) are so ubiquitous in this isolated, self-sufficient state that they can be purchased at the *farm gate* (the dairy or creamery), in specialty shops, and even, in some instances, at gas stations. (Tasmania has brilliantly re-envisioned the Kwik-ee mart as a purveyor of local artisan foods.)

Top producers in Tasmania include the following:

✔ **Pyengana Cheese Factory:** The Pyengana Cheese Factory is situated in the far northeast of the state in the town and valley of Pyengana, which comes from an Aboriginal dialect and means "the meeting place of rivers." Fourth-generation dairy farmer/cheesemaker Jon Healey produces Australia's oldest artisan cheese — traditional clothbound farmhouse cheddars — from their herd of Friesian cows.

- ✔ **Tongola Goat Products:** This Swiss immigrant cheesemaker produces just a handful of seasonal cheeses — fresh, surface-ripened, and washed rind — in southern "Tassie" from a herd of approximately 30 goats.

- ✔ **Grandvewe Cheeses:** Grandvewe Cheeses in Birchs Bay, in the southern part of the state, is the only sheep milk cheese producer in Tasmania (it's also organic).

- ✔ **Bruny Island Cheese Company:** Owner Nick Haddow is one of Australia's most original and outspoken cheesemakers, producing an array of fresh, surface-ripened, washed, and aged natural-rind goat and cow milk cheeses made from local milk.

### Where's the rest of Australia?

While not major cheese-producing states, the following do have a handful of cheesemakers and counting:

- ✔ **Queensland:** Most dairy farming is in the southeast because the far north is tropical rainforest. Industry deregulation also depleted the number of dairy farms, as did a long-term drought, but small farmstead and artisan producers — mostly of goat cheese — are on the rise and popular with consumers. Also in Queensland is an excellent Swiss-style cow milk cheese producer, Fromart.

- ✔ **New South Wales (NSW):** Despite being Australia's oldest dairy state, industry deregulation has resulted in farm decline in NSW. Sydney has an amazingly diverse and progressive food scene, however, and as a result, interest in domestic and import cheeses is growing, making small-scale cheesemaking more viable. Sydney, like Melbourne, also has several well-regarded cheese shops.

- ✔ **Western Australia (WA):** Australia's largest state is mostly Outback. The Mediterranean climate in the remote southwestern portion makes it a prime agricultural region for dairy and home to the famous Margaret River wine region. And while WA's capital, Perth, is very cosmopolitan with an impressive dining scene, it's simply too difficult and expensive for WA's small cheesemakers to ship their cheese, so consider cheeses from here truly localized products.

## New Zealand: A new era for Kiwi cheesemakers

The Commonwealth country of New Zealand lies 1,400 miles across the Tasman Sea from Australia. Comprised of two islands, the North and the South, most of New Zealand's microclimates are a haven for dairying. The top of the North Island is sub-tropical, and the land remains fertile and lush until the distinctly arctic weather at the bottom of the South Island puts a stop to pastoral agricultural economies. The prevailing Westerly weather system also makes for a wet west coast and a dry east coast, which creates further agricultural diversity.

Sheep are the most common agricultural crop produced by New Zealand, although they're primarily raised for meat and wool. Dairy cattle are also abundant.

New Zealand's traditional dairying areas are Taranaki (in the midwest), Waikato (central), and Northland, all in the North Island. In recent years, Canterbury and environs (east coast of the South Island) has also become a major dairy producer, as has the Kapiti Coast area of southwestern South Island. Figure 14-2 shows New Zealand's notable cheese-producing areas.

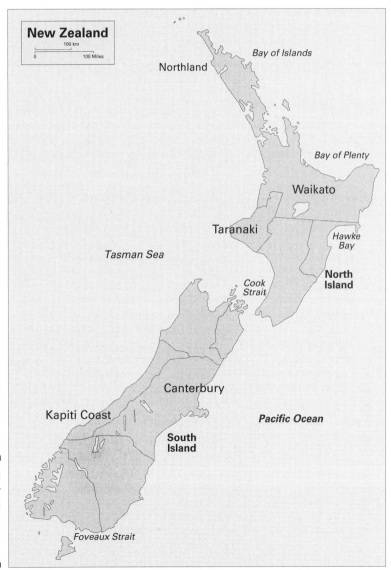

**Figure 14-2:** New Zealand's cheese-producing regions.

## Ready, set, raw

One of the crowning achievements for Kiwi cheesemakers and cheesemongers is the recent (2009–2010) change in laws regarding the production of raw milk cheeses and the import and sale of any cheese licensed for retail sale in the European Union. Today, any raw milk cheese, regardless of how long it's been aged, can be sold within the country. Although costly for Kiwi cheesemakers to put in place the risk-analysis assessments necessary to produce raw milk cheese, some have gone the distance and done just that. It's a giant leap forward for the future of New Zealand's fledgling artisan cheese industry and a boon for consumers, who will now be able to taste many of the world's benchmark cheeses at home.

In other words, Kiwis can now have their raw milk and eat it, too.

### Kiwi cheese, in a nutshell

Like so many New World countries, New Zealand had no cheeses when the first European — mostly British — settlers arrived at the end of the 18th century. (Dairying wasn't a part of the indigenous Maori culture.)

The first cows arrived in 1814, as did the recipes for cheddar and Cheshire, the most popular cheeses from "back home." As early as 1850, Port Cooper, a semi-soft, sweet, medium-aged cheddar, was exported from New Zealand to Australia and became a huge hit among the miners toiling in the goldfields.

The first domestic dairies, established at Edendale (on the south coast of the South Island) and Flemington (on the South Island's east coast) in 1882, produced cheddar. With the advent of refrigeration, more than 400 dairy cooperatives set themselves up throughout New Zealand to bolster the burgeoning cheddar industry, which was wholly focused on export to Britain.

Today, New Zealand's biggest cheese company is Fonterra, a farmer shareholder co-op structure that encompasses nearly 90 percent of the country's milk production, making New Zealand the largest dairy exporter in the world (pretty astounding for a place the size of Colorado). Most of New Zealand's milk is made into commodity block cheese or sold as fluid milk, although a vibrant, if micro, artisan and farmstead ("specialty") cheesemaking industry is springing up throughout the country.

### NZ's emerging specialty cheese industry

Over the last 30 years, an artisan cheesemaking scene has been percolating in New Zealand, but only in the last decade have these cheeses — especially those made with goat and sheep milk — hit both the domestic and international radar. While just a handful of Kiwi cheeses are exported to the United

States, in their homeland, they're available from specialty retailers, farmers' markets, and at the farm gate (the dairy or creamery).

New Zealand's new generation of specialty cheesemakers have a few other key assets: The quality of the native pasture and resulting milk, and a traditional understanding of animal husbandry learned from their British ancestors. These factors have helped facilitate small-scale production of various styles of cheeses from cow, goat, and sheep milk.

Here we list two of New Zealand's most influential modern cheese producers:

✔ **Kapiti:** Kapiti was founded in 1983 by Kiwi cheesemakers who returned home from their overseas travels armed with knowledge gleaned abroad. Determined to expose the public to a more diverse and high-quality type of cheese, they started a creamery on the southwestern section of the North Island. Today, Kapiti has two factories in the Kapiti Coast region, where they produce hand-crafted, high-quality dairy products ranging from tangy goat milk cheeses to creamy blues, sharp cheddar, and ice cream made with cow milk. The company is now owned by Fonterra but maintains its own brand and line of distinct cheeses.

✔ **Puhoi Valley Cheese:** Puhoi Valley Cheese was founded in 1983 in the sub-tropics 40 minutes north of Auckland on the North Island. The Puhoi Valley itself was settled over 140 years ago as a farming/dairying region by Bohemian immigrants from the Czech Republic. The namesake creamery produces goat and cow milk cheeses, including blues, Brie-styles, feta, cheddar, Parmesan, and a variety of yogurts. This artisan cheesemaking facility has done much to educate the public and locals about cheese and smaller scale dairy production.

# Subsistence and Barter: Cheese in Central Asia

Quick — form a mental picture of stereotypical dairy land. Depending upon what part of the U.S. you're from, your imagination may lean toward the rolling green hills of Wisconsin or New England or perhaps the foggy coastal pastures of Northern California. More likely — and less aesthetic — are massive, muddy farms crowded with Holsteins.

Now picture the vast emptiness of the Mongolian steppe, or the dramatic foothills of the Himalayas. Even if you've never been to this part of the world, the characteristics of the landscape and the images conjured by the words that describe it challenge our archetypal American view of dairying.

As with much of Europe, the types of cheese produced in Central Asia (as well as parts of the Middle East such as Pakistan and Afghanistan) correlate directly to elevation and terrain. Yaks, for example, are commonly used at higher altitudes because they're genetically adapted to that environment (see "Yakkety-yak" sidebar in this section). Cheese and other dairy products such as butter and yogurt may be made from sheep, goat, yak, cow, or mare milk, depending upon the country and region.

## More than a luxury item

In Central Asia (and the Middle East, which we get to later in this chapter), dairying is more than just an occupation, and cheese isn't the luxury product it is in the industrialized world. It's an essential dietary source of protein, fat, and other nutrients. For the rural inhabitants of the Central Asian countries of Mongolia, Tibet, Nepal, Bhutan, Northern India, and Northern China (see Figure 14-3), cheese or other dairy products are frequently used as barter or a source of income. A commercial dairy industry has even emerged in Nepal in recent years; milk is purchased from co-ops, and the production is primarily fluid milk, yogurt, ice cream, and cheese (mozzarella, paneer, and processed cheese) made from cow and yak milk.

*Note:* Of these countries, Mongolia is the largest because only a small area of China and India, relatively speaking, produce and use cheese in this manner or as a substantial part of their diet.

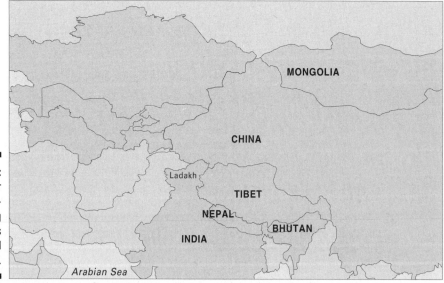

**Figure 14-3:** Major cheese-producing countries of Central Asia.

# *Cheese that transcends borders: Part 1*

The cheeses of Central Asia don't vary greatly, due to the similarities in terroir, nomadic culture, cuisine, and cheesemaking methodology. The names and sometimes the type of milk may differ, but many of the cheeses in the following list have counterparts in other countries in this part of the world:

- **Qurut (also called *qurt, kurut, aaruul*):** Made from drained sour milk or yogurt, this cheese is traditionally formed into balls or chunks, or sliced into strips, and dried; it may also be salted. It's consumed from Turkey and Azerbaijan to Inner Mongolia, where it's sometimes flavored and eaten as candy. Qurut is usually made from cow, yak, or camel milk.

- **Shosha (or *churul*):** Shosha is a pungent Tibetan cheese made from cream and the skin that forms on top of milk.

- **Chhurpi (called *byaslag* in Mongolia):** Fresh, slightly sour, with a loose, lumpy curd, this cow or yak milk cheese is also dried, cubed, and smoked over a fire until hard so that it can be sucked on.

- **Eezgii:** Eezgii is a slightly sweet Mongolian cheese similar to *byaslag*, but cooked until golden brown and dry. It's stored in sackcloth and eaten as a snack.

- **Urum:** A Mongolian clotted cream made from yak or camel milk, this high-fat, nutrient-rich food is eaten as a snack, added to milk tea (a dietary staple made with milk, tea, and salt), or used to make a caramelized pudding called *khailmag*.

- **Juju dhau:** Juju dhau is a Nepalese delicacy made from very fresh water buffalo milk that has been heated on a wood stove. After milk solids and spices have been added, the milk is curdled in a clay pot with older juju dhau (the culture). More milk is added, and the mixture is left to further develop until the appropriate flavor and texture have been reached.

- **Chal (*shubat*):** This fermented camel milk drink is slightly effervescent and popular in Turkmenistan and Khazakhstan. A similar beverage called *kumis* is made with mare milk in Kyrgzstan and elsewhere on the Central Asian steppe.

This is but a brief overview of the primary cheese-producing countries and regions; it's not by any means all-inclusive. Other Central Asian countries such as Uzbekistan, for example, produce cheese. A fresh cheese called *tvorog* — variously described as similar to quark or fromage blanc — is common and also used in Russian cuisine. In addition, Uzbeks consume a strained yogurt called *chaka* — also common to Afghan cuisine — which illustrates how many of these dairy products cross borders, although their names are usually different and their uses may vary.

## Yakkety-yak: A very versatile animal

The yak — a massive, wooly bovine — is one of the world's oldest domesticated animals. It's adapted to extreme altitudes and crucial to the survival of the peoples of northern India, Mongolia, Tibet, and the northern Chinese province of Qinghai. Domesticated yaks are used in Nepal and Bhutan, as well.

Yaks are used for milk, meat, fiber, hide, fuel (the dung), and as a pack and work animal. They fatten upon the alpine vegetation during the short summers and provide sustenance throughout the long, harsh winters, when little other food is available.

Yak milk contains higher levels of heart-healthy conjugated linoleic acid than cow milk and is sweet and rich in flavor. The milk is used to make butter and fresh and aged cheeses. It curdles naturally when transported in animal-skin bags via horseback. The resulting cheese may be eaten fresh, dried in the sun, or smoked.

# Nomad's Land: The Middle East

Many historians and cheese experts believe that cheese was accidentally discovered in the Middle East (see Figure 14-4). Regardless of its origins, the first peoples of this region, the Sumerians, are believed to have become a non-nomadic, agricultural society around 8,000 BCE. The rich soil nourished by the Tigris and Euphrates rivers permitted them to grow crops, including barley, wheat, and other grain and seed plants, and to raise cows and sheep for their meat, hides or wool, and milk. Cheese and other dairy products have been an important part of the subsistence diet ever since; even in urban areas, fresh cheese or yogurt is a part of nearly every meal. (Head to Chapter 1 for more on the history of cheese.)

In the following sections, we discuss the role cheese plays in a large portion of the Middle East.

## The lifestyle and terrain of the pastoralists

Many of the peoples of the Middle East are descended from a culture of nomadic herders known as *pastoralists,* people who moved with the seasons to find pasture to feed their flocks. These people are deeply dependent upon their animals for survival and, as such, connect to them on a sociological, status, and cultural, as well as economic, level. While the pastoralists' numbers have decreased dramatically since the 20th century, there are still millions of nomadic peoples worldwide, including in much of the Middle East.

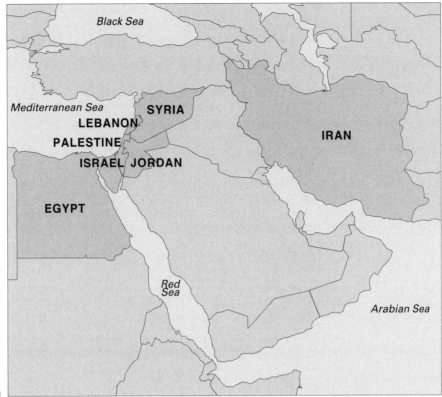

**Figure 14-4:**
The primary Middle Eastern cheese-producing countries.

Sheep, goats, and camels were traditionally important sources of food, milk, wool or hide, dung, and muscle power. In rural areas today, not much has changed: Shepherds still tend to their flocks and sell or barter the animals' by-products for other food or material goods.

Although many tend to view this part of the world as consisting mostly of desert, the Hindu Kush — a sub-range of the Himalayas — runs through central Afghanistan and northern Pakistan. The nomadic peoples of the mountains also make cheese. In Afghanistan, shepherds make a sheep milk cheese called *serat* that's smoked and dipped in wax as a preservative. Kadchgall, a cylindrical, salty-sweet sheep or camel milk cheese, has its origins with the Pashtun people of Afghanistan and Pakistan.

Thousands of years of climate change, soil erosion, and development have changed many traditional Middle Eastern grazing landscapes. There are fewer grasslands (one reason sheep and goats are used rather than cows) and thus less room — culturally and physically — for nomadic pastoralists.

Fortunately, these proud, resilient people are dedicated to keeping their culture alive, and one can only hope that environmental and political factors and urbanization don't force them into extinction.

## Cheese that transcends borders: Part 2

The nomadic subsistence diet includes significant quantities of fresh, soft, and semi-firm rindless cheeses and other cultured dairy foods. In the following list, we focus on the various cheeses shared by different Middle Eastern cultures, due to their similarities among nomadic groups and their cuisine and styles of cheesemaking. Keep in mind that significant differences exist between the various countries and cultures of the Middle East (for a more comprehensive list, we suggest reading Saad Fayed's "Middle Eastern Cheese Varieties" at www.about.com):

- ✓ **Labneh (also known as *lebni* or *labni*):** This strained yogurt may be eaten fresh, dried, or shaped into balls that have been preserved in olive oil. Labneh is ubiquitous throughout the Middle East, including Jordan, Lebanon, Syria, Israel, and Iran. It's eaten with breakfast or for a snack, or used in cooking.

- ✓ **Nabulsi:** A popular Jordanian and Palestinian cheese, nabulsi is made of brined goat or sheep milk and used at the table, fried, or included in the Palestinean pastry *knafeh*.

- ✓ **Ackawi:** Although its origin is Palestine, this semi-firm, slightly salty cow milk cheese is also made in Syria, Lebanon, and Turkey. It's a popular table cheese and is also used to make shanklish, a fresh-to-aged sheep or cow milk cheese flavored with local wild herbs.

## Got camel milk?

Fresh cheeses made from camel milk are produced in limited amounts by nomadic tribes in the Middle East and Central Asia, but because camel milk lacks an enzyme that enables curdling, cheesemaking on a wider scale is impractical. Tiviski, a camel dairy in Mauritania (Africa), produces camel milk cheeses (see Chapter 20), but the sale of camel milk is currently banned in the U.S., unless it's for personal consumption. A Danish company has created a rennet coagulant called *camel chymosin*, or CHY-MAX, developed by isolating an enzyme in the stomach of a camel calf and replicating it in a lab. CHY-MAX has enabled experimental versions of hard cheese to be developed, but don't expect to see cows, goats, or sheep out of a job anytime soon.

# Part IV

# Eating, Drinking, and Cooking with Cheese

The 5th Wave                    By Rich Tennant

"Honey, do you remember me mentioning not to use the Humboldt Fog in the fondue pot?"

## In this part . . .

Cooking and drinking (wine, beer, spirits, or non-alcoholic drinks) are just as big a part of cheese education as eating the stuff straight up. If you want to expand your cheese repertoire, these chapters explore the basics of cooking with cheese — and provide you with many menus' worth of simple, seasonal, sophisticated recipes — as well as the fundamentals of pairing cheese with various beverages.

We also show you, step-by-step, how to create an impressive cheese plate (easier than you think) and give you a handful of basic cheese recipes and tips should you be inspired to try cheesemaking at home.

# Chapter 15

# Making Cheese the Life of the Party

## In This Chapter

▶ Knowing what goes into (and onto) a memorable cheese plate

▶ Discovering what condiments compliment cheese

▶ Making your own condiments

### Recipes in This Chapter

▶ Chile-Citrus Olives
▶ Buttermilk-Oat Crackers
▶ Cherry Preserves
▶ Caramelized Shallots in Port Wine

**W**e get it: Cheese plates can be intimidating, even to experienced home cooks. But it needn't be so. Once you understand a few general rules, putting together a great plate is a snap — and fun, to boot. In this chapter, we show you how to make cheese the star of the show.

## Creating Great Plates

Unlike learning to cook, which takes time and repetition to achieve a level of comfort, composing a cheese plate is fast and easy after you grasp the basics. Whether you're dining alone or hosting a party for 100, the rules are the same, give or take a few adjustments.

In the following sections, we offer our tips on how to assemble a plate that makes a lasting impression.

### How much is enough? Deciding on serving size

Planning serving amounts can be tricky. Although you don't want to over-feed your guests (or have piles of untouched food), you don't want to leave them feeling deprived, either. So how do you strike the perfect balance? It all depends on how you're serving the cheese. Here are some guidelines:

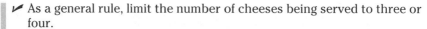

✔ As a general rule, limit the number of cheeses being served to three or four.

   Serving more than three or four cheeses can lead to *palate fatigue,* which is the tastebud equivalent of what happens when you smell too many perfume samples; your nose becomes immune to the complexities in each new fragrance. With palate fatigue, you simply can't discern the subtle differences between different cheeses.

✔ If you're providing cheese along with other hors d'oeuvres at a party or as a pre-dinner appetizer, allow approximately 1 ounce of each cheese per person.

   A pound has 16 ounces, so a half-pound of each cheese usually suffices for a dinner party of eight.

✔ If the cheese constitutes a main accompaniment to a light meal, plan on up to 2 ounces of each cheese per person.

✔ If the cheese is main focus of the meal, up to ¼-pound per person is reasonable (but realize that serving cheese as a main course can get costly with large dinner parties; instead, reserve it for intimate groups who truly love and appreciate cheese).

Some cheeses, like Manchego, Brie, or cheddar, are popular, so you may want to serve a bit more of these varieties and provide smaller portions of stronger flavored or more pungent cheeses, like blues or washed rinds. Although a small portion of extremely rich cheeses like triple crèmes go a long way, they're quite affordable, making them good party fare. Look for varieties such as D'Affinois or Brillat Savarin.

## Selecting cheeses for a plate

One of the things to consider when selecting what kinds of cheese to serve depends on how many guests you anticipate. Some cheeses aren't ideal for small portions (think of a very delicate washed-rind cheese, which won't hold up well), or perhaps the cheese is sold only by the half-wheel or wheel (which is the case with small format cheeses like Epoisses or St. Marcellin). Conversely, an extremely expensive cheese can be affordable, if you're only purchasing a small amount.

Tell your cheesemonger how many people you're entertaining. He or she will likely have a different suggestion if you say you need a cheese for a party with 20 guests versus a picnic for 2.

Another thing to take into account when selecting the cheeses is how dense or rich they are. A creamy, high-butterfat cheese tends to fill up guests more quickly than something stinky, blue, or sharp, which most people will consume in smaller quantities (of course, this really just comes down to your guests and how much they love cheese).

Whatever you select for your plate, choose cheeses that increase in intensity. Anything works: You can do all blues, sheep, or surface-ripened. Just make sure you serve them from lightest in flavor and salt to heaviest, always ending with the blue (which can obscure your palate when tasting the other cheeses). In the next section, you can find advice on how to present the cheeses so that your guests know in what order to eat them.

For the most diverse, well-rounded plate, try the following (refer to Chapters 3, 4, and 5 for specific cheese ideas):

- ✔ One creamy or mild cheese
- ✔ One semi-soft or semi-firm cheese with a bit of bite or a washed rind or surface-ripened
- ✔ One hard or blue cheese

---

# Easy sweet and savory ideas from your pantry to spice up your cheese plate

If you find yourself with unexpected guests, the following foods are compatible with most styles of cheese, and you're likely to have at least a few of them already in your pantry:

- ✔ Almonds, hazelnuts, walnuts, or pecans (roasted is ideal, or you can toast them yourself in the oven prior to serving, to bring out their full flavor and aroma)

- ✔ Chunky fruit preserves

- ✔ Chutney or *mostarda* (a sweet and savory Italian fruit mustard)

- ✔ Olives

- ✔ Cured meats or paté

- ✔ Pickled vegetables

- ✔ Dried fruit such as apricots, figs, dates, pears, peaches, or muscatels

- ✔ In summer, fresh, ripe peaches, nectarines, figs, cherries, strawberries, or raspberries

- ✔ In fall or winter, sliced apple or pear, or pomegranate seeds

- ✔ Honeycomb or good-quality honey (avoid anything too strong or medicinal like chestnut or eucalyptus honey, which can overwhelm or clash with many cheeses)

- ✔ A day-old baguette or country-style bread thinly sliced, brushed with olive oil, and toasted.

**Tip:** It's always a good idea to have a few things on hand for just these types of situations. Keep some dried pasta, too, because you can always make a good, last-minute meal out of pasta tossed with sautéed garlic, good olive oil, and grated cheese.

## Arranging your plate

As we explain in the preceding section, on your cheese plate, you want to present a variety of cheeses that increase in intensity from lightest in flavor and salt to heaviest. So how do you avoid having to stop a guest mid-bite with, "No, not *that* one. Eat this one first!"?

If you're serving individual cheese plates or a plate for a small gathering, arrange the cheeses clockwise, in order of how guests should taste them. For a party situation, don't worry about the order. A nice touch in this situation is to label the cheeses, including where they're from, so guests know what they're eating. Go online or to a local cheese shop or cooking store to buy cheese tags or non-disposable ceramic signs that you can write on with a dry-erase pen.

Ask your cheesemonger to carefully label each cheese so that you can either reuse the label for your guests or rewrite them (cheesemonger's handwriting can be as indecipherable as a physician's!). Although they'll often include the maker or dairy and origin of the cheese, feel free to request it just to make sure.

# Picking Sides

One of the most frequent questions we hear from customers is, "What do I serve with this cheese?" The best way to answer this question is to think about how you intend to serve the cheese(s). Is this for a cocktail party or pre-dinner appetizer? Do you want to focus exclusively on one type of milk? Is it a dessert plate? After you've decided how you want to use the cheese, you can begin thinking about accompaniments.

And when it comes to choosing sides, keep these two things in mind:

> ✔ **Follow the KISS method — Keep It Simple, Stupid.** (Chefs are fond of using this acronym with regard to plate garnishes.) Less is always more on a cheese plate. You don't need olives *and* cornichons *and* artichoke hearts *and* roasted peppers *and* nuts *and* fruit *and* five types of crackers. A foofy, cluttered plate just detracts from the cheese. Instead, you want to let the cheese shine.

> Honing your accompaniments down to one, two, or three high-quality options can be intimidating, but avoid the temptation to turn your cheese plate into a smorgasbord. It takes away from the cheese, which, after all, is the star of the show, and can be overwhelming to the palate.

✔ **Always provide some type of flavor balance with regard to a cheese plate.** You don't want all sweet or all salty, for example. Items that provide specific flavor profiles include salty olives, vinegary pickled foods, bitter greens or cheese rind, smoky or salty cured meat, sweet fruit. This rule also applies when you use cheese in salads or use a salad as a side dish with a cheese plate.

In the next two sections, we offer some simple and satisfying ideas for the two main categories of cheese plates: savory and sweet. (***Note:*** We make suggestions about what kind of drink to serve with these plates; for details on pairing both alcoholic and nonalcoholic beverages with cheese, head to Chapter 16.)

# Savory

For a savory plate, serve a bowl of dry-cured or crunchy, briny green olives such as Picholines or Lucques — don't forget a small dish for the pits — *or* cornichons, and one or two different types of cured meats. Slice up a loaf of crusty bread and set out a little bowl of some grainy mustard and a spreading knife. This type of plate goes especially well with beer.

You can also mix things up a bit for a fall or winter cheese plate. Serve cured meat with some grapes, slices of apple or pear, pomegranate seeds, dried fruit, or chutney (sweet with savory), *or* pickled vegetables or a simple salad (to add balance try to incorporate a sweet element, such as citrus segments or candied nuts in the salad).

# Sweet

For a dessert plate, you can never go wrong with some beautiful seasonal fruit and some toasted hazelnuts, almonds, walnuts, or pecans. (Locally grown fruit is best because, in addition to supporting regional farmers, it will also be ripe, taste better, and be higher in nutrients.)

If the weather is cold and dreary, serve any of the following: thin slices of apple or pear, or pomegranate seeds; dried fruit and a bit of honeycomb; or good-quality preserves with toasted nuts and slices of toasted walnut or sourdough bread.

In warmer weather, think berries, or try cherries and other stone fruit such as peaches, nectarines, or plums. Served with plain crackers or a baguette, these fruits are an elegant match for bloomy-rind, goat, or fresh cheeses.

# How I got into cheese — Laurel's story

People often ask what inspired me to become a food writer and cooking instructor, and more specifically, how I came to focus on cheese. I think they expect to hear heartwarming recollections of a childhood spent beside my mother at the stove, and reminiscences of glorious holiday repasts, table groaning with the bounty from our garden. They anticipate my memories of milking goats and tangy chèvre on homemade bread for an after-school snack. They imagine my Russian grandmother frying *latkes* for breakfast (using eggs I'd collected from our flock of Rhode Island Reds).

And, to a certain degree, there is truth in these examples. Looking back, I'm quite certain my formative experiences with food and, in particular, dairy, are what shaped my career. But the reality is that, while I grew up on a small ranch where we primarily raised dairy goats and mules (really), the daughter of a large animal veterinarian and a former barrel-racing-champion-turned-homemaker, my own culinary education had a few . . . inconsistencies.

I used to watch my brother milk his goat, eagerly awaiting the day I was deemed old enough to do it myself. And I did observe my mother cooking sometimes; she still has a way with instant mashed potatoes and cracks open a mean jar of Prego. Our neighbors had a garden, and at the age of ten, I established a roadside produce stand, yet Birds-Eye was a staple at my own dinner table. The eggs I gathered each morning (when I wasn't being held hostage in the henhouse by our sadistic, child-hating rooster) my mother whisked in a microwave-proof bowl, before nuking them into rubbery oblivion. I was in college before I learned that scrambled eggs aren't really "made" in a microwave.

The one time my mom tried making yogurt and cheese from goat's milk (she was having an early 1970s back-to-the-land moment), the results were not exactly edible (in retrospect, I don't think she realized the milk required starter cultures). So we instead drank goat milk by the gallon, and in the process, my family became huge caprine aficionados. We bred our Nubian doe, Go-Go, every year, and ended up keeping several of her doelings. For my part, I adored our goats. Even when I fed Go-Go an uninflated balloon, it was with the best of intentions (it was Easter, and I thought she'd appreciate its pretty pink color).

In sixth grade, I decided to follow in my older brother's footsteps and raise goats for a 4-H project. I bounced out of bed each morning to milk Rose, a distant relative of the late Go-Go (who died of natural causes, not from ingesting peony-hued rubber). Despite my rural upbringing, our property was located in a peaceful canyon only a couple of miles from what is today a populous bedroom community of Los Angeles. There were a few other families with children up the road, but I was the only one living on a ranch. Needless to say, I got picked on a lot, as my classmates didn't share my goaty enthusiasm; they dubbed me "Goat Girl," much to my humiliation (today, I think it's the coolest nickname ever, although I still wish my dad had never told my college roommates, in all seriousness, "Laurel always had a way with cows").

I honestly never had a real cheese epiphany at a young age. I remember always having a shameless lust for dairy, especially butter and whipping cream straight from the carton. I think the first time I ever paid attention to cheese was when I was snacking on some Longhorn my mom was grating. I asked her what kind of cheese it was, and from there I moved on to gobbling Laughing Cow and Babybels. The first "gourmet" cheese I ever tried was Laura Chenel's chèvre in my early 20s, and I suppose that connection to my inner Goat Girl was what sealed the deal. From then on, I was committed to educating people about where their food came from, and taking them to visit a dairy has always been my favorite way to do it.

If you have a big party, avoid serving cut fruits that oxidize easily, like apples, pears, peaches, or nectarines; instead, save them for a small gathering and slice right before serving. (Don't be tempted to use the old lemon-juice-and-water wash, which changes the flavor and increases the acidity.)

## How I got into cheese — Lassa's story

I come from an adventurous family, one that travels to strange places and forages for food. When I turned 10, my parents cooked up elk burgers for my birthday party and served them on my mother's homemade, wholegrain bread. Needless to say, that experience still remains in my friends' memories, but at the time it was just short of mortification for me. I now know my ability to willingly try all things and enjoy a wide spectrum of tastes came from my parents . . . as well as my ongoing fear of not fitting in socially.

Cheese, however, was something my parents knew nothing about. We ate it but not in the research-laden, labor-intensive way that we attacked most foods and wine (I've been drinking wine with dinner since I was little ... my father is Australian). So when I wrangled my way into a summer job at a start-up gourmet food store in Boston at age 19, I was delighted to be tapped for the cheese counter. This was in the 1980s, when much of the cheeses that came from Europe were raw milk, too. I accompanied the cheese manager, Bonnie Brown, on trips to a main specialty food importer. Heaven! There was an entire warehouse, chilled and criss-crossed with massive shelving units that were laden with cheeses from all over the globe. We bought enough to make an excellent cheese counter.

I had no idea that cheese was made from anything other than cow milk. In fact, the idea of goat milk was off-putting to me, and I couldn't even contemplate sheep milk, though I'd eaten more lamb and mutton than beef at that point (again, Aussie roots). Bonnie gave me several samples to take, and I scurried home and unwrapped them. The one that intrigued me most was a wrinkled, white round the size of a large plum and shriveled up like a prune. It was made with goat milk and came from the Perigord region of France. I was scared and incredibly intrigued; the smell was exotic, animal-like, and the skin was so strange. This was cheese?

I cut it open and the inside was bright white. There was a distinctly darker layer just below the wrinkled rind, and the rind itself was harder than the center. I cut off a piece and poured myself a glass of cold, crisp white wine, which I sipped first for fortitude. Then I tasted the cheese.

Wham! Just a small morsel was packed with flavor, ranging from milk to meat to summer's hot grassy fields with the high-pitched buzz of crickets. This wasn't like anything I'd ever eaten before. It was intense but not in an unpleasant way. The texture was dense and rich, and the flavors just kept on coming. One small piece made me long to know how this was made.

That simple crottin opened up the whole new world of cheese to me — and to my family, who were then forced to taste everything I brought home. For me, it was instantaneous adoration. For them, it took a little while. But for all of us, life had definitely changed forever.

# Composing the Components

In this section, you get down to the nitty-gritty: actually putting the plate together. No one is going to judge you on how you assemble your cheese plate. But if you A) want it to look professional, and B) want people to remember you as someone who knows his or her way around a cheese plate, take an extra minute to read this section.

## Keeping it simple and other tips

The key to a professional-looking cheese plate is to keep things simple, spare, and elegant. Here are some other suggestions:

- **Have a good backdrop.** Using the right plate, platter, or cheese board can make the cheese stand out. See Chapter 7 for ideas.

- **Don't crowd the food.** Leave space between the cheeses so they're the main focus on the plate. An uncrowded plate also leaves room for guests to cut the cheeses without making a mess.

- **If you're adding condiments to the plate itself, don't let them touch the cheese.** You can fan out slices of fruit, or you can add a *small* handful of toasted nuts or dried fruit (avoid big, heaping piles).

  We prefer to use preserves, honey, or honeycomb only on very small or individual cheese plates, because, while wonderful as an accompaniment, they get too smeary and unattractive on a party plate.

- **For savory or wet sides such as olives or pickled vegetables, serve them separately.** Place them in small bowl or on a decorative plate next to the cheese plate . . . and don't forget a bowl for the olive pits.

- **Layer cured meats directly onto the cheese plate, but be sure to keep them separate from the cheese.** This keeps things looking tidy.

- **Fan sliced bread or crackers onto the plate or place them in separate (preferably lined) baskets or bowls.** It really just depends on how formal or casual you want to be, how many guests you have, or what type of plate (dessert or appetizer, for example) you're serving. For dessert plates, thin slices of toasted walnut bread are a nice accompaniment.

If you have a very simple plate — say, just one or two cheeses and maybe one condiment — add some greenery for a bit of visual interest. If you're doing a cheese plate with sweet elements, perhaps a few edible flowers tucked against the cheese. On a savory plate, you could do a few stalks of flowering chive or two or three springs of thyme or rosemary. Maybe you have some beautiful maple, chestnut, or oak leaves (just be sure they're clean — gently wipe them with a damp towel and pat them dry, first) that you can place beneath the cheese.

Whatever you use, be sure it's from a source free of pesticides and hasn't been contaminated by pollutants and/or animals. Some flavors simply aren't compatible on any plate — cheese or otherwise!

## Complimentary condiments you can make yourself

Sure, you can buy all the condiments you need, but it's also fun, inexpensive (usually), and easy to make your own. Homemade condiments also make great gifts (given, of course, with cheese!). In the following recipes, we share three of our favorite cheese plate accompaniments.

# Chile-Citrus Olives

*Prep time:* About 10 min  •  *Cook time:* 5 min  •  *Yield:* Serves 4 as hors' d oeuvres

These dressed-up olives always impress guests, despite how ridiculously easy they are to make. Pair them up with a sturdy blue or aged pecorino.

| Ingredients | Directions |
|---|---|
| 10 ounces dry-cured black or green olives (such as Picholine and/or Lucques)<br><br>3 to 4 strips of orange peel | **1** Combine all ingredients in a medium sauté or frying pan over low heat, adding a bit more olive oil if the mixture is too dry. |
| 2 cloves garlic, gently crushed | **2** Warm the mixture until it's completely heated through. |
| 2 pinches red chile flakes<br><br>1 to 2 tablespoons extra virgin olive oil | **3** Remove the mixture from the heat and place it in bowl for one hour at room temperature before serving to give the flavors time to develop. |

*Per serving: Calories 198 (From Fat 158); Fat 18g (Saturated 1g); Cholesterol 0mg; Sodium 567mg; Carbohydrate 5g (Dietary Fiber 0g); Protein 0g.*

***Note:*** Don't make these olives more than a few hours ahead; if you refrigerate them, they'll lose their subtly nuanced flavors. Be sure to provide a small bowl for guests to dispose of pits.

***Tip:*** Remove the orange peel with a vegetable peeler instead of a citrus zester. You want those big strips in there for more flavor and aesthetics; zest gets soggy.

***Vary It!*** You can substitute lemon peel for the orange or add sprigs of fresh thyme or rosemary.

*Source: Laurel Miller, The Sustainable Kitchen*

# Buttermilk-Oat Crackers

***Prep time:*** 45 min • ***Cook time:*** 12 – 14 min • ***Yield:*** About 72 small (1¾ inch square) crackers

Rustic, yet delicately flavored, these crackers from ***culture*** magazine look especially pretty shaped with the aid of a cookie cutter. They pair well with cheddars, blues, and alpine-style cheeses.

| *Ingredients* | *Directions* |
|---|---|
| **1 stick unsalted butter (¼ pound)** | *1* In a medium saucepan, melt the butter. Remove from the heat and stir in the buttermilk; set aside. |
| **⅓ cup buttermilk** | |
| **1½ cups quick-cooking rolled oats, divided** | *2* In a food processor or blender, grind 1¼ cups of the oats to make a coarse-textured flour. Transfer the oats to a large bowl and stir in the flour, sugar, wheat germ, baking soda, salt, and the remaining ¼ cup of the oats. |
| **1 cup all-purpose flour** | |
| **¼ cup sugar** | *3* Whisk the butter mixture to blend and add this mixture to the oat mixture, stirring until a soft dough forms. Divide the dough into two balls and let them rest in the bowl for 10 minutes (this allows the oats to absorb some of the moisture, making the dough easier to handle). |
| **¼ cup wheat germ** | |
| **1 teaspoon baking soda** | |
| **¾ teaspoon salt** | |
| | *4* While the dough rests, heat the oven to 325 degrees. On a lightly floured surface with a lightly floured rolling pin, roll out one ball of dough to an 11-inch square, about ⅛-inch thick. Cut six strips horizontally and then vertically to make 36 small crackers. (Alternatively, cut the dough into whatever shape you desire.) Transfer the shapes to a baking sheet and bake for 12 to 14 minutes, or until the edges of the crackers are golden. Transfer the crackers to a wire rack to cool. If you're making shapes with a cookie cutter, reroll the scraps to make more crackers. |
| | *5* Repeat Step 4 with the remaining ball of dough. Let the crackers cool completely before storing them in an airtight container. |

*Per 9-cracker serving: Calories 29 (From Fat 13); Fat 2g (Saturated 1g); Cholesterol 4mg; Sodium 43mg; Carbohydrate 3g (Dietary Fiber 0g); Protein 1g.*

*Source:* **culture:** the word on cheese *(Summer 2011)*

# Cherry Preserves

*Prep time:* 30 min • *Cook time:* 20 – 40 min • *Yield:* 1½ quarts

This recipe comes from our friend, chef Ryan Hardy, formerly of The Little Nell in Aspen, Colorado. He's big on putting up food for the winter, and by following this recipe, you can also relive summer with this ruby-colored condiment in the colder months. Serve with fresh or mold-ripened chèvre, double- or triple-cremes, or blue cheeses.

| *Ingredients* | *Directions* |
|---|---|
| 4 pounds ripe sweet or sour cherries, washed, stemmed, and pitted<br><br>4 cups plus 2 tablespoons granulated sugar<br><br>2 to 3 lemons, juiced<br><br>2 to 4 tablespoons apple pectin powder<br><br>3 pint-sized canning jars, with lids | *1* Combine the cherries and four cups of the sugar in a large, heavy-bottomed pot large enough to hold double the volume. Bring the mixture to a boil over medium-high heat and simmer until the cherries release their liquid and begin to foam across the top of the pot.<br><br>*2* Skim off the foam to maintain clarity and simmer for 20 minutes more, or until all of the cherries soften; then stir in the juice of two lemons. Taste to see whether the flavors are balanced. Add more lemon juice, if necessary.<br><br>*3* In a separate bowl, combine 2 tablespoons of the apple pectin with 2 tablespoons of the sugar to prevent the pectin from seizing up when added to the preserves. Ladle ¼ cup of the sugar-pectin liquid into the cherry mixture and whisk to form a slurry.<br><br>*4* Return the slurry to the preserve pot and continue to simmer until the mixture has a slightly thickened, syrupy consistency. (If necessary, repeat Step 3 to make a second batch of the slurry mixture and return it to the preserve pot.) Remove the preserves from the heat. (Note that they will thicken more as they cool.) Store the preserves in the refrigerator for up to a week. |

*Per 2-tablespoon serving: Calories 94 (From Fat 4); Fat 0g (Saturated 0g); Cholesterol 0mg; Sodium 0mg; Carbohydrate 23g (Dietary Fiber 1g); Protein 0g.*

***Note:*** If you're familiar with canning practices and have the necessary equipment, consider canning these preserves. Doing so lets you store them at room temperature for several months. A good guide is *Canning & Preserving For Dummies, 2nd Edition,* by Amelia Jeanroy and Karen Ward (Wiley).

***Tip:*** At many farmers' markets, you can find frozen, pitted cherries sold by the farmer as a way of selling surplus fruit before it spoils. But because thawed fruit loses water and volume, be sure to measure the fruit before freezing and make a note of the quantity on the storage container. Thaw fruit in the refrigerator.

***Tip:*** Apple pectin powder is available at most drug stores and pharmacies.

*Source: Chef Ryan Hardy (***culture:*** the word on cheese, *Spring 2009)*

# Caramelized Shallots in Port Wine

*Prep time:* 30 min • *Cook time:* 30 min • *Yield:* 1½ – 2 cups

For a savory cheese plate, serve *culture* magazine's rich, winey shallots with a hearty loaf of bread (try walnut or rye), cured meat, and gloriously stinky washed-rind or buttery cheeses such as Gouda, Beaufort, Carmody, Cabot Clothbound Cheddar, or Stilton.

| Ingredients | Directions |
|---|---|
| **2 tablespoons bacon fat or olive oil** | **1** Heat the bacon fat or oil in a saucepan over medium heat. Add the shallots, salt, and pepper and cook until the shallots are very tender and caramelized. |
| **1½ cups finely minced shallots** | |
| **1 teaspoon kosher salt** | **2** Add the port, reduce heat to low, and cook the mixture until the liquid has mostly evaporated (you want to create a viscous syrup around the shallots). |
| **Freshly ground black pepper** | |
| **½ bottle (750 ml) port wine** | **3** Remove the mixture from the heat and allow it to cool. Store in the refrigerator for up to 2 weeks. Serve at room temperature. |

*Per ¼-cup serving: Calories 72 (From Fat 33); Fat 4g (Saturated 1g); Cholesterol 4mg; Sodium 252mg; Carbohydrate 7g (Dietary Fiber 0g); Protein 1g.*

*Source:* **culture:** the word on cheese *(Fall 2009)*

# Chapter 16

# Having a Drink with Your Cheese

## In This Chapter

▶ Learning rules for pairing alcoholic and non-alcoholic beverages with cheese

▶ Exploring wine grape varietals, beer styles, and spirits

▶ Mixing things up with cheese-friendly cocktail recipes

**Recipes in This Chapter**

▶ The Widow's Kiss
▶ The SweetWater
▶ Blueberry Cobbler

Cheese before dinner with a glass of wine; a picnic featuring frosty beer and good cheese; a mug of claret-colored cherry cider with a hunk of earthy blue. This is the stuff dreams (ours, at least) are made of.

Pairing wine, beer, and non-alcoholic beverages like the aforementioned cider is perhaps the most intimidating part of cheese education for the novice. But it shouldn't be. Although there are some definite do's and don'ts, pairing cheese with drinks is mostly about common sense, as you'll see. Plus, practice makes perfect, and it's a lot of fun to practice!

For all your wine basics, go to *Wine For Dummies,* 4th Edition, by Ed McCarthy and Mary Ewing-Mulligan. For beer basics, read *Beer For Dummies,* 2nd Edition, by Marty Nachel. *Whiskey and Spirits For Dummies* by Perry Luntz covers the rest.

# The Noble Grape

Wine and cheese are classic partners, but to get the pairing to really work, you need to think about matching the qualities of the wine with those of the cheese. Just because a wine is excellent and a cheese delicious doesn't mean the two will be wonderful together. In the following sections, we offer expert tips on how to pair wine with cheese, and introduce different styles of wine and the cheeses that tend to go well with them.

Before you launch into the details of how to pair wine and cheese, keep these general points in mind:

- **Know your priority:** If you're planning to drink a specific bottle, pair the cheese to suit the wine. If you want specific cheeses, choose the wine that best complements them.

- **Know the wine you're drinking:** When pairing cheese (or any food) with wine, the wine characteristics you need to work with are the fruit, acidity, oak, alcohol, and *tannins* (the organic compound that gives certain wines that mouth-puckering quality). Because these are the components that stand out in a wine, they become the dominant features to focus on when choosing a pairing.

- **Keep in mind that there's no way to say definitively, "This grape varietal will go with this cheese."** Why? Because even the same kinds of wines differ for a bunch of different reasons. A Cabernet Sauvignon blend from Napa, California, made in 2006, for example, isn't going to taste the same as a Cabernet Sauvignon blend made in 2006 from Bordeaux, France. The best thing to do is taste the wine and decide whether it's intense or subtle and what flavor components it has (bright, tannic, acidic, sweet, or fruity) and let that determine your cheese selections.

## A few rules and tips to get the best matches

We asked Natalie Fryar, winemaker at Jansz Tasmania, for her wine and cheese picks. Her answer will appeal to even the biggest wine or cheese neophytes: "I've never met a wine that doesn't go with Parmigiano Reggiano or Comté, from sparkling or Sauternes to those of Alsace, Burgundy, Bordeaux, Italy, Provence, Spain, or Portugal. The only real thing is that the wines have to be good. Bad wine goes with nothing but heartbreak."

We agree, but the next sections give you some other rules of thumb and tips to help you make the most of your pairings.

### Matching intensities

The number one rule for pairing wine with cheese (and anything else, for that matter) is to match intensities. For example, if you have a big, bold, young Cabernet Sauvignon, you need a cheese that will stand up to it; otherwise, you lose the flavor complexities in the cheese. Likewise, you don't want to pour a lovely, soft, 1966 Burgundy when you've got a wedge of extra sharp cheddar; the wine's subtleties will be lost. The wine and the cheese should both be present, and neither should overpower the other.

Oak (used in barrel aging) and tannins can be problematic when pairing with cheese, and salt tends to enhance them. But matching intensities matters most here. When you've got a bold, tannic red such as Cabernet Sauvignon or certain Zinfandels, try it with a full-flavored clothbound cheddar or a hunk of Parmigiano Reggiano. The sharper flavors of the cheese should soften the tannins and allow the fruit in the wine to pop.

### Aiming for similarities or contrasts

Another rule is to aim for either similarities or contrasts in flavors. When a cheese is extra buttery and rich (such as a triple crème or Brie), think about what type of wine might possess those same qualities. Chardonnay that has undergone *malolactic* fermentation (a process that converts the tangy malic acid into buttery lactic acid) makes it a good fit for those cheeses. But *too* much butteriness in the wine paired with these cheeses just might be overkill, so strive for some balance.

Alternatively, a bright, lemony flute of sparkling wine, which has a higher acid content, will cut through the richness of a triple crème. That type of contrast results in an instant party on the palate . . . and on the table.

When a wine is fruit- (rather than tannin or oak-) driven, it needs a cheese that will complement that fruit. A cheese with salt and pungency, like a blue or washed rind, will go well with a floral or spicy Pinot Gris or a Riesling, or a dessert wine like port.

### At a loss? Go with Champagne!

If you're ever stumped for what to serve with a diverse group of cheeses, choose bubbles. Champagne or sparkling wines help cleanse your palate of the mouth-coating butterfat from the cheese and won't conflict with most cheese flavors. Not into bubbles? Try a fruitier white or lighter red wine, such as Beaujolais.

## A quick primer on wine and a few pairings to win you over

When starting to learn about wine, you need to consider two major things: the variety of the grape (also called the *varietal*) and how and where the grape is grown (the *terroir*, which we explain in Chapter 2). Most red grapes become red wines, although there are exceptions to this (Pinot Noir, for example, when used for Champagne). The wine's color comes from the grape juice's contact with the red skins, so white grapes can also be added to juice that will be made into red wine.

Wines grown in hotter climates often have a higher sugar content and generally possess fruitier flavors and a higher alcohol content (due to the increase in sugar). Both sugar and alcohol content require consideration when pairing wine with cheese.

Other important tasting factors for pairing cheese and other foods are the origin and age of the oak barrels used for aging wine, as well as the length of time a wine is aged. The use of new oak in winemaking imparts stronger flavors to the wine, often of vanilla, coconut, and toast. When older barrels are used, the oak influence is more subtle. Barrels' interiors are also *toasted* to different degrees (light, medium, dark, and so on), imparting a range of flavors from caramel to chocolate or charcoal. All of these factors are important to consider when pairing wine.

In "New World" countries (The Americas, South Africa, New Zealand, and Australia), the focus is generally on varietals rather than regions when discussing wine. "Old World" countries (Europe, the Mediterranean, and so on) mainly designate by regions, which have been growing and making wines from specific grapes for hundreds of years, so the two have become synonymous.

For our purposes in this section, we focus on varietals. There are literally thousands of types of red and white wine grapes; here, we touch on a few of the more frequently encountered varieties.

### Ravishing reds

One of the most full-bodied and tannic red wine grapes is Cabernet Sauvignon, a main component in the wines of Bordeaux and California (particularly Napa Valley). Other big red varietals are Merlot, Zinfandel, Syrah (known as Shiraz, in Australia), Cabernet Franc, and Nebbiolo. If a wine is made with one or more of these grapes and is less than 5 years old, you'll likely need a bolder, sharper cheese such as cheddar or aged pecorino to stand up to it.

Softer and generally more cheese/food-friendly are the more docile red wine grapes. Pinot Noir, Gamay, Grenache, Sangiovese, and Tempranillo, for example, tend to be less tannic and more subtly flavored.

Try these with Brie, camembert, or semi-firm to hard natural-rind varieties such as Tomme Crayeuse or Ossau-Iraty (see Chapter 4), or some of the milder truffle-infused cheeses.

### White nights

Like softer red wine varietals or blends, white wines are typically more compatible with cheese and other foods. Factors that dominate white wines and become the focus for pairings are fruit, acidity, oak, and malolactic fermentation (refer to the earlier section "Aiming for similarities or contrasts" for info about type of fermentation). The main white varietals are Chardonnay, Sauvignon Blanc, Riesling, Pinot Grigio (Pinot Gris), Viognier, and Gewurztraminer.

Fruit-driven wines (Riesling, Sauvignon Blanc, Pinot Gris, and Gewurztraminer) are often aged in stainless tanks so there's no oak to take into account when pairing. Versatile and easy to drink, these wines go well with some of the cheeses that clash with reds, notably blue cheeses and surface-ripened goat cheeses. Chardonnay tends to be aged in oak and can go through malolactic fermentation, which imparts a buttery, toasty aroma and rich texture.

These wines are classic pairings with buttery, nutty cheeses, like triple crèmes and aged Goudas. Unoaked and lightly oaked Chardonnay is becoming more popular: French Chablis is a wonderful example. It's leaner and has less oak influence, so a cheese that is normally paired with an oaked Chardonnay won't fit the same way. Try a classic Alpine cheese like Comté, instead.

### A rosé is a rosé is a rosé

Rosé is a cheese-friendly choice and is made from most red wine varietals. The majority of rosé is produced by crushing red wine grapes and running the juice off in a matter of hours so that little to no skin contact occurs. This process minimizes the influence of tannins in the final product and leaves a crisp, bright, blush-colored wine.

Rosé wines often possess some of the complexity of red wines, but with the delicate nuances of whites. Some are juicy and fruit-driven; others are bone-dry and lean. For that reason, the same rule that applies to red and white wine pairings works here: Think about the dominant flavors and features of the wine when you pair it with cheese and other foods.

Typically a good pairing bet is a gentle, semi-firm sheep or goat milk cheese like Abbaye de Belloc or Garrotxa, but if you want to get a little racy, try rosé with a washed-rind or blue cheese.

### Tiny bubbles

Every sparkling wine has bubbles, which are merely carbon dioxide. One of the best known "bubblies" is Champagne, which comes from a small region in France of the same name. (To be a true Champagne, the grapes must come from the Champagne region itself and follow the strict rules for production.)

The world has plenty of other sparkling wines, however, produced from grapes of many varieties, and they all have different flavors and nuances, which means some cheeses make better pairings than others, depending upon what you're drinking.

Like beer, those little bubbles make sparkling wines a great choice for cheese. Focus on the flavor components to find the right cheese match; some sparklers are dry (*brut*) and have zingy acid; others are toasty and yeasty, or sweet and fruity (*sec*). Follow the general rule of thumb of matching intensities and let the predominant flavor of the wine be your guide.

### Sweet dreams

Sweet wines make fantastic partners with cheese, in general, and when we say "sweet," we mean those luscious dessert-styles like port, Madeira, Vin Dolce, sweet sherries, Sauternes, and ice wine (*eiswein*).

The term *dessert wine* is a broad generalization, but the main point is that these are sweet and often fruit-laden — the very characteristics that make them ideal to sip while nibbling cheese. Cheese *loves* fruity and sweet, which is why you often see these flavors as accompaniments on a cheese plate.

In general, you're safe serving a dessert wine with cheese: the only thing to take into account is intensity. This is the time to create studies in contrasts (serving a salty, strong-flavored blue cheese with Madeira, for example) or matching intensities (if you're offering an ice wine, serve honey; if you're pouring port, pair it with a heavier fruit paste like fig jam or raspberry preserves). Your guests will thank you.

## Bad relationships

The best way to understand pairing is to have a bad pairing. Yes, we said it: Sometimes bad relationships are a good thing. After you experience a pairing that doesn't work, you'll understand that there is a reason to care about what wine you serve with a specific cheese. Here are a couple of experiments you can try to educate your palate:

- Take red wine with lots of tannins and plenty of oak and try it with a mold-ripened goat milk cheese, like a bucheron. You'll find that the rind tastes bitter and the wine increases the goaty flavor . . . and neither is the better for it.
- Try an oaked, buttery Chardonnay alongside a truffle-infused cheese. Both are strong flavors but not exactly compatible or pleasing when put together.

## A quick list of time-tested pairings

Who doesn't love saving time (it allows you to do other things, like eat more cheese). Table 16-1 gives you a cheat sheet to take the guesswork out of wine and cheese pairings.

| Table 16-1 | Time-Tested Wine and Cheese Pairings |
|---|---|
| *This Wine* | *Goes Well with This Cheese* |
| Sparkling wine | Fresh cow or goat milk cheese, triple-crème cheeses, or Parmigiano Reggiano |
| Crisp white wines like Sauvignon Blanc | Mold-ripened goat milk cheeses (Chapter 3) |
| Buttery Chardonnays | Buttery, creamy cheeses; try a triple-crème cow milk or an aged Gouda (Chapter 3) |
| Sweet or crisp Riesling | Washed-rind cow milk cheeses (Chapter 3) |
| Lighter red wines, such as Pinot Noir and Sangiovese | Semi-firm sheep or goat milk cheeses; try Ossau-Iraty, Manchego, or younger Gouda (Chapter 4) |
| Syrah | Comté (Chapter 4) |
| Big red wines, like Cabernet Sauvignon, Bordeaux blend, full-bodied Zinfandels | Aged cheddar or another cheese with some bite and heft, such as an aged pecorino, Parmigiano Reggiano, or Grana Padano (Chapter 4) |
| Dessert wines (port, Sauternes, or Late Harvest Riesling) | Blue cheeses and triple-crème cow milk cheeses (Chapter 3) |

# *Hop to It: Pairings for Beer Nuts*

In some ways, beer is easier to pair with cheese than wine is. Although all start as raw agricultural products (beer from grain, wine from grapes, and cheese from milk), beer and cheese have more in common. Consider these points:

- ✔ Beer is usually made from barley, a cereal grain that's a species of grass, and milk, in a cheese-making context, is produced by a dairy animal consuming grass.

- ✔ Beer generally lacks the acidity and more astringent qualities that make cheese matches with wine so tricky.

- ✔ Beer and cheese share similar aromas and flavor profiles (nutty, toasty, yeasty) that make for easier pairings.

As with wine, the key when pairing beer and cheese is to look for matching intensities and complementary flavors or suitable contrasts to bring out the best in each. Remember, you don't want to overpower either the food or the beverage.

# Sorting through styles of beer

Most styles of beer fall under one of two umbrella categories: lager and ale. Here's what you need to know:

- ✔ Lagers use yeast that ferments at the bottom of the liquid and prefers cooler fermentation temperatures. They usually display crisper flavors and sharper aromas.

- ✔ Ales use yeast that ferments beer at the top of the liquid and prefers warmer fermentation temperatures, resulting in beer that is typically fruity.

Beyond that, beer can be (and has been for thousands of years) spiked with herbs, spices, and fruit, resulting in all manner of flavor profiles — some more intriguing than others. Lemongrass, pine tips, juniper berries, coriander, chili, coffee, cherries, blueberries, peaches . . . pumpkin. These unusual additions can transform a generic cold one into a specialty brew, which explains why this is one of the fastest growing sectors of the craft beer industry.

# Finding a perfect pairing

In the following sections, we outline the different styles of beer and offer suggestions on what kinds of cheeses make the best pairings. You're sure to find several combinations — complete with serving suggestions — to love.

- ✔ **Lager/Pilsner:** Pilsner is a pale lager. These golden hued lighter brews make up a larger percentage of the more familiar beer varieties on U.S. shelves.

  This is the most versatile, easy-drinking beer style and a go-to when pairing with cheese. Because lager lacks the deeper malt flavors and bitter hops, the more delicate cheeses won't be overpowered (rule number one to avoid in pairing). Try matching a cold one with burrata, chèvre, a pepper Jack, or a habanero cheddar — a refreshing Pils will soothe the palate and ease the heat.

- ✔ **Pale Ale:** Pale ales come in many colors and flavors. Amber ale, Red ale, and the hoppier American Pale Ale styles all fall under this category.

  Because of the flavor profile, try these ales alongside less aggressive, more buttery cheeses like Havarti, Muenster, or very young Gouda.

- ✔ **India Pale Ale:** India Pale Ale (IPA) is strongly hopped, which makes for a beer with more bitter flavors. Bitter, however, doesn't mean higher in alcohol.

Tart and refreshing, IPAs are fun partners with bold, stinky, washed-rind cheeses like Livarot and Taleggio, but a good, sharp cheddar is always appropriate.

✔ **Barleywine:** Darker in color, this is an earthy, fruity, deeply-flavored ale that can reach the higher alcohol percentages of wine (8 to 12 percent).

Varying dramatically in depth and flavor from one producer to the next makes it difficult to make a blanket statement about cheese pairings. Generally, a good Stilton or clothbound cheddar (see Chapter 4) are a good fit, because the salt and earthiness match the same characteristics of the beer. Some barleywines work well with sweeter, richer cheeses like Comté and Gruyère.

✔ **Lambic/Sour ales:** These beers are literally sour, with a strong aroma. . . just like some cheeses. They're aged in wooden barrels and are often blends, as well as flavored.

Dry, cidery, and winey, these sour beers beg for a pairing with something that's aromatic and slightly acidic, such as surface-ripened goat milk cheeses. Like barleywine, lambics vary greatly between producers, but cheeses like Coupole (Vermont Butter & Cheese Creamery) and Humboldt Fog (Cypress Grove Chevre) are ideal.

✔ **Wheat beer:** Wheat beer (also known as *wiessbier, witbier,* or *hefeweizen*) is generally lower in alcohol and unfiltered.

Light and refreshing, wheat beers are great partners with surface-ripened goat and cow milk cheeses. Try robiola, which can be made with one, two, or three blended milks.

✔ **Stout/Porter:** These beers have deeply roasted flavors that echo those of coffee or chocolate. Imperial stout is higher in alcohol.

With the deeper, richer, maltier flavors in these brews, go for nutty alpine cheeses like Gruyère and Beaufort, or rich, butterscotchy aged Goudas, like Beemster XO or Old Amsterdam.

✔ **Trappist/Belgian-style Ale:** To be authentic, these beers must be brewed or overseen in production by Trappist monks, although plenty of other brewers make this style of ale. Belgian styles are relatively strong in flavor and higher in alcohol.

The robust style and strength of these ales need stronger cheeses to stand up to them. Go for washed-rind cheeses like the ones suggested for IPAs or salty blue cheeses like Gorgonzola, Rogue Creamery's Crater Lake Blue, or Original Blue (Pt. Reyes Cheese). Chimay, one of the best-known Belgian Trappist producers, makes a cow milk cheese washed in their own ale, making things easy for you!

✔ **Saison:** The recipes for this light and uplifting, usually golden-hued and cloudy beer vary, and the resulting beers run the gamut from spicy and bracing to gentle and aromatic.

Slightly funky yet relatively light, these farmhouse-style brews are ideal with an earthy, nutty cheese. Look to alpine styles or some of the less pungent washed-rind cheeses such as Dèlice du Jura or Pont l'Évêque.

✔ **Fruit/vegetable beer:** Made using real fruit or fruit extract, these beers can be flavored with anything from blueberries to banana, pumpkin, sour cherries, apples, herbs, or spices. Some of the results are subtle, others brazen.

The intensity of the beer is really what dictates the pairing. Fruity beers (including pumpkin, even though it's botanically a vegetable) go well with blue cheeses ranging from creamy, delicate Monbriac to the more assertive, sheepy Roquefort or salty Valdeon.

✔ **Beers with high IBUs:** Beers with extra-high IBU scores (International Bitterness Units) are quite bitter and very popular, although they can make for a tricky, less standard cheese or food pairing option.

For one of these hoppy brews, reach for that chunk of aged cheddar or an aged, caramel-colored Gouda (such as a 5-year). Add some slices of apple or pear and invite that special someone over (or enjoy it all by yourself!).

ASK THE EXPERT

# Eight great craft beer and cheese pairings

We asked Joshua M. Bernstein, *culture* magazine contributor and our resident craft beer consultant; freelance food, drink, and travel writer; and author of *Brewed Awakening: Behind the Beers and Brewers Leading the World's Craft Brewing Revolution* (Sterling Epicure) for his favorite beer and cheese combos. So raise a pint to these matches made in heaven:

✔ Crisp, briskly herbal Prima Pils cuts through the luscious richness of Brie or camembert.

✔ Russian River's super-hoppy Pliny the Elder is a terrific match for a sharp, well-aged cheddar.

✔ North Coast Brewing Co.'s smooth, chocolaty Old No. 38 Stout goes nicely with nutty-sweet Dubliner, a hard Irish cheese.

✔ A strong, dark Belgian ale such as Chimay Grande Reserve (a Trappist beer) gets cozy with earthy washed rinds.

✔ Anchor Steam's strong, belly-warming Old Foghorn Barleywine Style Ale is burly enough to stand up to the assertiveness of Stilton.

✔ A fresh chèvre is an ace mate for the cloudy, gently spiced Allagash White — quite possibly one of America's best *witbiers*.

✔ Few things beat a slice of freshly-made mozzarella coupled with a terrific hefeweizen such as Germany's hazy, clove-kissed Weihenstephaner Hefeweissbier.

# *If the Spirit Moves You*

A premium gin, tequila, or rum is designed to be enjoyed straight up or on the rocks, just as you would a fine Scotch, brandy, or port. Add some good cheese, and you've got a truly sophisticated pairing. We turned to Bryan Dayton, award-winning beverage professional (and cheese lover), and co-owner of OAK at Fourteenth in Boulder, Colorado, for expert advice on serving cheese with spirits. In the following sections we share some of our favorite pairings.

## *White spirits*

This category, which includes vodka, gin, un-aged tequila, and some aperitifs, is self-explanatory: If it's clear, it's a white spirit. In general, think lighter, fresh cheese with these selections.

### *Aperitifs*

Aperitifs run the gamut from bitter and herbal to floral and fruity. Following are different aperitifs and the spirits that go well with them:

- **Lillet Blanc,** an aperitif blending wine with citrus liqueur, or a rich, high-quality vermouth possess both acidity and botanical elements, which play off the creamy texture and earthy flavors inherent to blue cheese or buttery alpine styles.

- **Aquavit,** a high-alcohol Scandinavian aperitif, also works well with cheese, due in part to its sinus-clearing qualities. Aquavit is often flavored with spices or other botanicals such as coriander, caraway, dill, berries, or citrus. Traditionally consumed ice-cold in *drinking snaps* (essentially, as a shot), aquavit cleanses the palate when paired with light, tangy, soft goat milk cheeses.

- **Grappa** is a traditional Italian aperitif made from grape *pomace* (the seeds, stems, and stalks that are a by-product of winemaking). A craft-distilled grappa is smooth, viscous, and contains subtle hints of fruit or other flavors, such as herbs or honey, that may have been infused into it. Pairing it with cheese makes sense when you think about the flavors inherent to summer milk. Try it, or other grappas, with a rich, buttery cow milk cheese such as a young Gouda or Montasio.

Eau-de-vie are colorless dry brandies, most commonly made with apricot, cherry, or pear. Served with a fresh or mold-ripened goat milk cheese or a sweet, unassertive blue, the fruit flavors shine and complement the tangy or earthy nature of the cheese.

### Vodka

Because it's odorless and lacking a distinct color or flavor, think of vodka as a neutral canvas to be paired with any type of cheese, depending upon what it's flavored or mixed with. There are also plenty of infused vodkas made in a variety of flavors, including citrus, pomegranate, and green tea. Focus on the infused flavoring when pairing, rather than the type of alcohol.

When it comes to cheese, few things can beat a vodka martini paired with a strong blue. In fact, many people enjoy their martinis with blue cheese-stuffed olives.

### Gin

There are many styles of gin: Dutch Genever, Plymouth, and London Dry are just a few. Each category has its own characteristics, such as a pronounced juniper flavor, augmentation with spices and/or citrus, or a more feminine, subtle, floral quality.

Where cheese is concerned, juniper brings a little something to the party. Its piney earthiness makes it a good fit with milder sheep milk cheeses, like a young Pecorino or Berkswell, a natural-rind version from the U.K. Fresh and mold-ripened goat milk cheeses also make for a good match. A more lemony gin also marries well with a strong blue, and the citrus cuts through rich, buttery, slightly pungent washed rinds such as Dèlice du Jura or Pont l'Évêque.

### Tequila

No, we're not talking about Spring Break poppers. Drinking tequilas are surprisingly smooth and complex. Un-aged tequilas (*blanco* or *plata*) can be simple, clean, and glorious with cheese, adding a sweet note that comes from the tequila itself.

White tequila goes well with rich, milky cheeses such as Queso Oaxaca and burrata. It's also compatible with most fresh and aged styles of Mexican cheese, which are traditionally used for cooking. In these cases, the food is usually spicy, aromatic, and complex. A white tequila won't compete with those flavors and will refresh the palate.

*Reposado* and *añejo* tequilas are considered brown spirits because they're aged in French or American oak or used bourbon, whiskey, Cognac, or wine barrels: these tequilas are sweet and nutty or fruity. Try them with a caramelly aged Gouda, or, for a contrast, sip them with drier, more salty cheese like Manchego or Roncal, which counterbalances the sweetness.

# Brown spirits

You can probably guess what falls into this category: rum, bourbon, and bourbon's cousins, Scotch, brandy, and some aperitifs and digestifs. (We categorized tequila under white spirits but the aged "brown" varieties are mentioned there, too.) Brown spirits tend to be higher in sugar (and thus alcohol content). You'll be pleasantly surprised at how compatible this category is with dairy, especially if it's aged or blue.

## Rum

A great sipping rum is a beautiful thing, bursting with flavors of coconut, vanilla, butterscotch, or spices. The flavor profiles are the same as bourbon, but because rum is made from sugarcane, it's more viscous in the glass and in the mouth, making it comparable to dessert wines when it comes to cheese pairings.

Rum calls for a cheese that's not too fatty or rich, to provide contrast and avoid overkill. Try an aged Gruyère, Comté, or Pleasant Ridge Reserve, an alpine-style cheese from Wisconsin's Uplands Cheese Company (see Chapter 21). These cheeses complement the sugar but remain light on the palate. For a darker (and thus sweeter) rum, a chunk of aged, crystallized Gouda is a memorable — if unorthodox — dessert (we'll take it over a cupcake, any day).

## Bourbon and rye whiskey

The flavor profiles within this group vary, depending upon proof, age, and what type of barrels they're aged in. To break this complex category down to its bare essentials, remember these key factors:

- ✔ **Bourbon:** Most bourbon is made in Kentucky. It must be made from at least 51 percent corn and aged for a minimum of 2 years in new, charred oak barrels. The dominant flavors are vanilla, butterscotch, caramel, spice, honey, toffee, or chocolate, and it has a lingering presence on the palate. Try bourbon with sharper blues and clothbound cheddars, which counterbalance and heighten the attributes of the bourbon.

- ✔ **Rye whiskey:** Rye has the same production as bourbon, but must be made from at least 51 percent rye; its flavor is more potent and less sweet. It's drier, with more spiciness and toasted grain flavor. With rye whiskey, go for buttery alpine cheeses, which coat the palate and adds texture.

### Scotch

As its name implies, true Scotch whisky (the "e" is used in American product) is produced in Scotland. It can be made from malted barley or blended with other grains or cereals, but it must be aged for at least 3 years in oak. Five different types of Scotch are produced, ranging from Single Malt to Blended, and the flavor profiles range from smoky, peaty, citrusy, nutty, floral, and honeyed.

Because its flavors are so varied, Scotch is a great companion for many styles of cheese. Blue cheeses are often an excellent match, and a yeasty, meaty, washed-rind cheese can be heavenly with malty blends or single malt — think Munster (from France, not to be confused with American Muenster) or Livarot.

### Brandy

Brandy is made from distilled wine grapes specific to a region (such as Cognac, in France), but a diverse variety of brandies abound. Cognac, which must be aged for a minimum of 2 years in French oak, has rounder, softer, more fruity flavors, which agree with aged goat milk cheeses like Garrotxa and the drier Majorero Pimenton.

Armagnac is a brandy produced in the French wine region of the same name. It's also aged in oak and is considerably more expensive than regular brandy because it's produced in vintages, just like wine.

In France, the locals drink Armagnac alongside the rustic farmers' cheeses produced in the same region. As a replacement, try mild cow milk cheeses such as a young Jack or Gouda (Beemster's Graskaas, for example).

## The Teetotaling Table

You needn't be a wine, beer, or spirits drinker (nor an adult) to enjoy cheese with a beverage. Juices, specialty sodas, teas, or even coffee can make a great match with cheese. Just avoid anything too sweet and cloying, which will overload your palate.

Following are some suggestions for pairing cheese with non-alcoholic beverages:

 ✔ **Juices:** Fruit is often paired with cheese, so experiment with interesting fruit juices (many of which are available in sparkling versions): Pair white grape, pear, or cherry juice, or a fresh-pressed, soft apple cider with chèvre, or other fresh or surface-ripened cheeses.

✔ **Sodas:** *Dry* (not sweet) sodas bring out the best in washed-rind, surface-ripened, or semi-firm cheeses with a rich, buttery texture. Experiment with brands that make fruit and herbal or spice blends, such as the brand DRY, or try the refreshing fruit flavors offered by Izze.

✔ **Tea:** Tea can be successfully paired with cheese, too. The rules are essentially the same as for pairing wine: Match intensity and attributes. Here are some duos we like:

- Bright, herbaceous green teas match soft, creamy cheeses like chèvre or triple crèmes. Sweet or floral teas such as jasmine also complement these cheeses.

- Complex or spicy, fruity, or smoky teas like Earl Grey and Lapsang Souchong go well with blue cheeses.

- Slightly tannic, fruity, or spiced teas, like Darjeeling, do right by nutty alpine cheeses, cheddars, and Goudas.

✔ **Coffee:** Coffee can be great with top-quality fresh cheeses such as ricotta, mascarpone, crème fraiche, or fromage blanc. These can be a component of a dessert, such as cannoli, cheesecake, coffee cake, or pound cake, or served with biscotti or other cookies. Note that good coffee can vary in flavor profile from bright, citrusy, and tannic to chocolaty, so it can be tricky to pair with cheese.

# Mixing Things Up: DIY Cocktails

We love to watch a good mixologist in action. But sometimes, it's fun to be the star of your own show. At your next cocktail or dinner party, try shaking or stirring up one of the following cheese-friendly drinks.

# The Widow's Kiss

**Prep time:** 5 min • **Yield:** 1 drink

Bryan Dayton of Boulder's OAK at Fourteenth recommends serving this fall-inspired cocktail with a soft blue cheese like Cambozola, which mellows the combination of Chartreuse and Benedictine.

| Ingredients | Directions |
|---|---|
| 1½ ounces Calvados | **1** Combine the Calvados, Chartreuse, Benedictine, and bitters in a mixing glass. Stir for 30 seconds. Serve up in a cocktail glass, garnished with a cherry. |
| ¾ ounce yellow Chartreuse | |
| ¾ ounce Benedictine | |
| 2 dashes orange bitters | |
| Cherry garnish | |

*Per serving: Calories 258 (From Fat 0); Fat 0g (Saturated 0g); Cholesterol 0mg; Sodium 1mg; Carbohydrate 1g (Dietary Fiber 0g); Protein 0g.*

**Tip:** For the cherry garnish, we recommend brandied Maraschinos, available at specialty food stores or from www.deandeluca.com.

*Source: Bryan Dayton, proprietor, OAK at Fourteenth (**culture:** the word on cheese, Fall 2010)*

# The SweetWater

***Prep time:*** 5 min • ***Yield:*** 1 drink

From the rooftop garden bar at The Surrey hotel in New York City comes this hearty, cold-weather cocktail. Pair it with Caerphilly cheese, such as the one from Tonejes Farm Dairy (New York), or a caramelly, aged Gouda.

| *Ingredients* | *Directions* |
|---|---|
| **3 dashes of Fee Brothers Whiskey Barrel-Aged Aromatic Bitters** | *1* Add bitters and honey to a sturdy rocks glass; then add bourbon and stir with a bar spoon. Add ice cubes and seltzer. Stir again. Garnish with apple slice. |
| **1 tablespoon of honey (local, unfiltered is preferable for the best flavor)** | |
| **2 ounces Tuthilltown Spirits Hudson Baby Bourbon** | |
| **2 ice cubes** | |
| **2 ounces Vermont Sweetwater Maple Seltzer** | |
| **1 slice apple** | |

*Per serving: Calories 238 (From Fat 1) Fat 0g (Saturated 0g); Cholesterol 0mg; Sodium 2mg; Carbohydrate 25g (Dietary Fiber 0g); Protein 0g.*

***Tip:*** Maple seltzer is a light, not-too-sweet beverage made of carbonated maple sap. It's available at www.vtsweetwater.com. You can substitute regular seltzer for the maple seltzer, but the end result will be missing a little somethin' somethin'. Another option is to add a drop of pure maple extract or a few drops of pure maple syrup — not imitation — in with the honey. The extract carries more real maple flavor than the syrup does, but either works beautifully in a pinch.

*Source: The Surrey Hotel (**culture:** the word on cheese, Fall 2010)*

# Blueberry Cobbler

*Prep time:* 15 min • *Yield:* 1 drink

A delicious and refreshing summer cocktail based on a classic dessert recipe. This recipe was created by Seattle's TASTE Restaurant bartender Tiffany Friday. We love this summer sparkler with fresh chèvre or a young, surface-ripened goat cheese such as Leonora. Omit the vodka and add more soda for a non-alcoholic version.

## Ingredients

8 (or so) fresh blueberries, plus one for garnish

Crushed ice

1 ounce Thyme Simple Syrup (see the following recipe)

¾ ounce fresh squeezed lemon juice

1½ ounces Dry Fly Craft-Distilled Vodka

2 to 3 ounces soda water

Sprig of fresh organic or unsprayed thyme, for garnish

## Directions

1 In the bottom of a Collins glass (or other tall glass), muddle the blueberries (crush them lightly). Fill the glass with crushed ice. Add the thyme simple syrup, lemon juice, and vodka, and stir with a bar spoon. Top off with soda water and garnish with blueberry and a sprig of thyme.

## Thyme simple syrup

2 cups sugar

2 cups water

4 sprigs fresh organic or unsprayed thyme, rinsed

1 Combine 2 cups of sugar and 2 cups of water in a small saucepan and bring to a boil. Remove the mixture from the stove and promptly add 1 bunch of rinsed thyme. Stir well and let the mixture steep for 2½ to 3 hours. Run the syrup through a fine-mesh strainer. Store in a clean, tightly sealed glass jar in refrigerator for up to 1 month.

*Per serving: Calories 158 (From Fat 0); Fat 0g (Saturated 0g); Cholesterol 0mg; Sodium 1mg; Carbohydrate 16g (Dietary Fiber 0g); Protein 0g.*

*Tip:* You can use the simple syrup to flavor iced tea (use in place of sugar), lemon sparkling water, or drizzle it atop a pound, angel food, or almond cake (serve with unsweetened whipped cream on the side).

*Source: Bartender Tiffany Friday, TASTE Restaurant, Seattle (**culture:** the word on cheese, Summer 2010)*

# Chapter 17

# Cooking with Cheese, Pt. 1: Appetizers, Salads, and Sides

**Recipes in This Chapter**

▶ Comté Wafers

▶ Crispy Cheese Croquettes

▶ Queso Fundido con Pollo

▶ Gougères

▶ Nectarine, Prosciutto, and Arugula Salad with Crescenza Toasts

▶ Salad Greens with Roasted Pears, Cornbread Croutons, and Camembert Dressing

▶ Bistro Salad with Poached Egg and Parmigiano Reggiano

▶ Fennel, Tangerine, and Hazelnut Salad with Crottin

▶ Sopa de Quinoa

▶ Grilled Asparagus with Chèvre and Orange Zest

▶ Israeli Couscous with Preserved Lemon, Sugar Snap Peas, Feta, and Mint

▶ Haricot Verts and Miniature Tomatoes with Bocconcini

▶ Wood-Roasted New Potatoes with Délice du Jura and Black Truffle Oil

▶ Pan-Roasted Wild Mushrooms over Cheddar Polenta with Pumpkinseed Oil

## In This Chapter

▶ Learning tips for cooking with cheese

▶ Exploring cheese recipes suitable for every meal

Cheese is one of the most beloved ingredients in the kitchen, even by those who don't particularly enjoy cooking. Grating cheese is one — if not *the* first — kitchen skill learned by many children, and who doesn't love grilled cheese sandwiches?

In this chapter, we tell you what you need to know when you're cooking with cheese, share a few cheese-specific tips, and offer a collection of cheesy recipes for beginning and intermediate cooks. Even if you're an old hand at the stove, give them a look. Sometimes, the simplest of recipes is the most impressive — especially when cheese plays a starring role.

Even if you're not an experienced cook, don't let this section intimidate you. We've designed almost all of these recipes with the novice in mind, and our philosophy is, the better your ingredients (note that "better" doesn't necessarily translate to "the most expensive"), the less you have to do to make a successful final dish. Throw some cheese in the mix, and you've just upped the ante.

# Cheese in the Kitchen

In general, cheese is a low maintenance ingredient. Toss it in, and it melts or otherwise enriches a dish. But there are some general rules to follow. Remove rinds, which can be bitter and don't incorporate well. Some cheeses, like cheddar and aged Gouda, don't melt due to their chemical composition. Goat cheese and blues get stronger in flavor and aroma when heated, so use sparingly and/or opt for a more mild variety. These nitpicks aside, cheese is perhaps the easiest, most versatile ingredient you can add to enhance a dish, and cooking or baking is an ideal way to use up the odds and ends in your cheese drawer.

## Measure by measure: Cheese conversion chart

When you're cooking with cheese, remember that not all measurements are equal. While some recipes call for cheese by the ounce, others call for cheese by the cup; some — the particularly helpful kind — give both measurements, as in "1 cup (about ¼ pound) cheese." When you're stumped, turn to Table 17-1, which is a handy conversion chart.

| Table 17-1 | Cheese Conversion Chart* | |
|---|---|---|
| *Ounces* | *Pounds* | *Cups* |
| 16 ounces | 1 pound | 4 cups grated |
| 8 ounces | ½ pound | 2 cups grated |
| 4 ounces | ¼ pound | 1 cup grated |
| 2 ounces | ⅛ pound | ½ cup grated |

*\* **Note:** Measurements are approximate.*

When you use this table, keep these points in mind:

✔ **If you're using a hard cheese with a thick rind, you need slightly more than the ounces or pounds specified to get an accurate cup measurement**. Because you don't grate the rind, you need more than the ½ pound specified, for example. Grate as far down as you can to the rind.

Don't throw out your Parmigiano Reggiano rinds! They're traditionally used to enrich broths, soups, or stews; most cheese shops save their Parmigiano rinds, so ask if you don't have any at home. Keep them stored in an airtight container in the freezer and toss what's left in your soup pot.

✔ **Take volume into account:** Softer cheeses are lighter because they have less solid matter and more water. Thus, with these varieties, you can get more for your money if you're purchasing in large quantity or are on a budget. A pound of hard Piave versus a pound of Brie makes a big difference in terms of quantity and price.

# Which cheese do I choose?

Often, recipes specify a particular type of cheese, removing the guesswork for you. Sometimes, though, you may want to experiment with something different, or perhaps you're unable to find the specific cheese a recipe calls for. In these cases, you need to know how to choose an alternative. Here are some considerations that can put you on the right path:

✔ **Decide what you're trying to achieve in the end result.** Do you want something melty and gooey? Then try mozzarella, young Monterey Jack, or an alpine style such as Emmentaler, but skip clothbound cheddars or aged Goudas, which lack the protein composition to melt properly.

If you want a cheese that will disperse well in a pasta, grain, or salad dish, focus on a brined cheese like feta or fresh cheeses such as ricotta or chèvre (but choose a drier chèvre or add it to hot dishes at the last minute so that it doesn't melt everywhere and overpower the dish). Or think hard or aged grating cheeses, such as Grana Padano, Pecorino Romano, or Dry Jack.

✔ **Take the rind into account.** Will you use the rind in the dish? Will the rind enhance the dish? Unless you're making a cheese plate or serving cheese on the side (refer to Chapter 15 for details on that), the answer is probably not. For that reason, avoid using bloomy-rind cheeses, which are largely about the rind (and can overpower a dish), because you won't really get your money's worth if you're throwing that part out.

✔ **Think about flavor.** Goat or sheep milk cheeses can get more pungent when they're heated (as many recipes using cheese are), so take that under consideration. On the other hand, some stinkier washed rinds, such as Pont l'Eveque, or surface-ripened cheeses like St. Marcellin, are glorious when heated up.

Ultimately, you should choose what you like. But bear in mind that, when cooking for others, sometimes it's best to err on the side of caution (in other words, don't assume your guests share your penchant for cheeses that smell like a sweaty armpit!). Now, go forth and cook!

# How Appetizing! Cheesy Starters Your Guests Will Love

Cheese is one of the most popular ingredients for appetizers, partly because of its melting capabilities, but also because the combination of protein and fat found in cheese is satiating, without being too heavy or appetite-dulling. In this section, we offer a few delicious appetizers in which cheese plays a key role.

Cheese is also an ideal companion to beer and wine (hop to Chapter 16 for more on pairing cheese with drinks) but has enough substance to absorb some of the alcohol. Whatever you're drinking, cheese always helps set a festive mood.

## A few famous cheese dishes

Certain dishes from around the world are synonymous with cheese. Here, some of our favorites:

✔ **Raclette:** Hailing from the Swiss Alps, this is the name of both a cheese and a regional dish. Traditionally, a half wheel of this firm, buttery cheese would be propped up in front of the fireplace; once its surface had begun to blister, a *racler* (scraper) was used scoop the cheese into bowls filled with boiled potatoes.

✔ **Fondue:** Fondue was promoted as the Swiss National Dish during a 1930's PR campaign, but variations are also found in the French Alps. A classic cheese fondue is usually enhanced with kirsch (a clear cherry brandy) and a cut clove of garlic, heated over an open flame in a *caquelon,* and served with cubes of bread for dipping.

✔ **Welsh rarebit:** Also know as "Welsh Rabbit," this beloved English dish is nothing more than a thick slice of bread spread with a savory sauce enhanced with various ingredients such as mustard powder, ale, or Worcestershire, and melted cheese — usually an aged cheddar. Pop under a broiler, serve, and instant happiness is achieved.

✔ **Aligot:** From the Midi-Pyrenees region of France comes this decadent dish made with Laguiole, Cantal, or other regional cheeses. Hot mashed potatoes are whipped with butter (and sometimes crème fraiche), and seasoned with garlic, salt, and pepper into a thick, elasticky fondue.

# Comté Wafers

***Prep time:*** 10 min • ***Cook time:*** 12 min • ***Yield:*** 16 wafers

From *culture* magazine comes these lacy discs of crispy cheese. Like the Friulian (Italy) cheese wafer called *frico,* these can be served as a snack with a glass of wine, as a garnish for salad, or an accompaniment to a bowl of soup.

| Ingredients | Directions |
|---|---|
| **1 cup lightly packed, coarsely shredded Comté cheese** | *1* Preheat oven to 350 degrees. Line baking sheets with nonstick liners or parchment paper. |
| | *2* Use a rounded tablespoon to measure out mounds of shredded cheese on the prepared baking sheets, positioning them about 1 inch apart. Using your fingertips, spread the cheese into a mounded oval about 1 inch wide and 2 inches long. |
| | *3* Bake the cheese for 12 minutes, or until golden and bubbly. Remove the baking sheet from the oven. Using a paper towel, carefully blot the oil around the edges of the cheese. Let the wafers stand about 20 minutes, or until firm. |
| | *4* Lay a double layer of paper towels on a tray and transfer each wafer with a thin spatula to the paper towels to blot excess oil. Transfer the wafers to a dish and serve. They will keep stored in an airtight container for several days. |

*Per serving: Calories 28 (From Fat 20); Fat 2g (Saturated 1g); Cholesterol 7mg; Sodium 23mg; Carbohydrate 0g (Dietary Fiber 0g); Protein 2g.*

*Source:* **culture:** the word on cheese *(Fall 2009)*

# Crispy Cheese Croquettes

**Prep time:** 20 min • **Cook time:** 15 min • **Yield:** Serves 8-10 as hors d'oeuvres

Like your favorite bar snacks, only better, this recipe from *culture* magazine lends itself well to all manner of cheeses, not just cheddar (although Beehive Cheese Co.'s Promontory Cheddar is a great one for this recipe!). You can also try it with Gouda or an alpine cheese such as Gruyère. If you serve it as an hors d'oeuvre with other nibbles, plan on around two or three per person).

| *Ingredients* | *Directions* |
|---|---|
| **2 pounds of dense, flavorful cheddar**<br><br>**2 large eggs**<br><br>**2 tablespoons cold water**<br><br>**2 cups panko breadcrumbs, plus more if needed**<br><br>**1½ cups semolina flour or Asian rice flour**<br><br>**2 quarts canola oil, blended olive oil, or peanut oil, for frying** | **1** Slice the cheese into bricks about 3 inches long, 1½ inches wide, and ½ inch thick. Set aside. In a medium bowl, whisk together the eggs and cold water. Place the egg mixture, the panko, and the flour in three separate, shallow bowls for dipping and dredging.<br><br>**2** Working in batches of two, dip the cheese pieces very briefly into the flour, then into the egg mixture, and finally into the panko to make a crust. Be sure to firmly press the breadcrumbs onto all sides of the cheese. Lay the finished pieces on a baking sheet lined with parchment paper and refrigerate for 30 to 60 minutes.<br><br>**3** Heat the oil in a large, heavy-bottomed pot to 350 degrees. Fry the croquettes in the oil until golden brown and crisp on the outside (the key is to get the cheese soft but not liquefied). To test for doneness, remove a croquette and pat dry with a paper towel; then press lightly. The crust should be firm and crisp, with a bit of give on the inside.<br><br>**4** Transfer the croquettes to a baking sheet lined with paper towels before placing on a serving platter. Serve the croquettes as is or with a side salad of greens drizzled with tarragon vinegar and olive oil. |

*Per serving: Calories 700 (From Fat 416); Fat 46g (Saturated 25g); Cholesterol 172mg; Sodium 743mg; Carbohydrate 35g (Dietary Fiber 2g); Protein 35g.*

*Source:* **culture:** the word on cheese *(Spring 2010)*

*Tip:* Panko are Japanese breadcrumbs that possess a lighter, crisper texture — ideal for an otherwise rich, heavy dish like croquettes. If you do make your own breadcrumbs, use a day-old baguette or other rustic bread. Cube and toast until golden, and whirl in a food processor until the crumbs have achieved the desired size and texture.

# Queso Fundido con Pollo

**Prep time:** 30 min • **Cook time:** 35-40 min • **Yield:** Eight ¼ cup servings

From chef/owners Thomas Schnetz and Dona Savitsky of Oakland, California's Doña Tomás comes this insanely rich dish. Serve it as a party dip, fondue, or casserole.

| Ingredients | Directions |
|---|---|
| 1½ cups heavy whipping cream | **1** To prepare the sauce, combine the cream, allspice, and salt in a small saucepan over medium-high heat, stirring constantly, and bring to a simmer. Reduce the heat to medium and cook for 10 to 15 minutes, until the sauce is reduced by one-third. Pass the sauce through a fine mesh sieve to remove any film and set aside to cool. |
| ½ teaspoon ground allspice | |
| Kosher salt, to taste | |
| 2 poblano chiles, roasted, peeled, stemmed, and seeded | |
| 3 tablespoons canola oil | **2** To prepare the filling, cut the chiles into ½-by-2-inch strips. In a large sauté pan, heat the oil over high heat. Add the onion and sauté for 3 to 5 minutes, until the onions are translucent (lower the heat if necessary). Add the chile strips and the chicken, and gently stir until evenly mixed. Season to taste with salt and remove from heat. |
| 1 white onion, cut into ½-inch slices | |
| ¾ pound shredded cooked chicken | |
| ½ pound Queso Oaxaca, shredded | |
| ¼ bunch cilantro, stemmed and chopped (about ½ cup), for garnish | **3** Preheat the broiler. In a 9-x-12-inch casserole, spread the chicken mixture in an even layer. Add the cream sauce on top. Cover with cheese. Place the casserole under the broiler for 10 to 15 minutes, or until all the ingredients have melted together and the top is lightly browned. Remove the casserole from the broiler and sprinkle with cilantro. Serve immediately with the warm tortillas. |
| 8 fresh corn tortillas, warmed, or tortilla chips | |

*Per ¼ cup serving: Calories 388 (From Fat 252); Fat 28g (Saturated 13g); Cholesterol 18mg; Sodium 166mg; Carbohydrate 18g (Dietary Fiber 3g); Protein 17g.*

**Tip:** Try homemade tortilla chips with this recipe. They're easy to make and add to the "Wow!" factor: Simply cut good-quality corn tortillas into wedges, sprinkle them with salt, and bake at 350 degrees until crisp.

*Source: Chefs Thomas Schnetz and Dona Savitsky, Doña Tomás, Oakland, California (**culture:** the word on cheese, Spring 2009)*

# *Gougères*

***Prep time:*** 5 min • ***Cook time:*** 30 min • ***Yield:*** 8–10 gougères

A French classic, these airy, cheesy puffs are seriously addictive, so make a double batch!

| *Ingredients* | *Directions* |
|---|---|
| 1 cup water | **1** Preheat oven to 450 degrees. Line two baking sheets with parchment paper. |
| 7 tablespoons unsalted butter | |
| 1 tablespoon kosher salt or more, to taste | **2** In a medium saucepan, combine water, butter, salt, and sugar and bring to a boil. Add all the flour at once, reduce the heat to medium, and stir for 2 minutes or until the mixture forms a ball and the excess moisture has evaporated. |
| 1 pinch sugar | |
| 1⅓ cups flour | |
| 4 large eggs, plus an extra if needed | **3** Transfer the mixture to a mixing bowl. Using the paddle attachment, beat at medium speed for about 30 seconds to cool slightly. |
| 1⅓ cups grated alpine-style cheese, young Gouda, or other semi-firm, buttery, meltable cheese | **4** Add 4 of the eggs all at once and continue to mix until completely combined and the batter has a smooth, silky texture. Stop the machine and check the consistency of the batter: It should form a peak with a soft tip that falls over. If it's too stiff, beat in the white of the remaining egg. Check again and, if necessary, add the yolk. |
| Freshly ground white pepper, to taste | |
| Pinch cayenne pepper | |
| | **5** Mix in ¾ cup of the cheese and adjust the seasoning with salt and white pepper. Incorporate the cayenne. |
| | **6** Using a pastry bag fitted with a ⅜-inch round pastry tip, pipe the batter into tablespoon-size mounds about 2 inches apart on the baking sheets. Sprinkle the top of each with about ½ teaspoon of the remaining grated cheeses. Bake for 8 to 9 minutes, or until they puff and hold their shape. |

**7** Reduce the heat to 350 degrees and bake for an additional 15 to 20 minutes. When done, the outside of the gougères will be a light golden brown, and the inside will be hollow and slightly moist. Remove the pans from the oven and serve immediately.

*Per serving: Calories 269 (From Fat 161); Fat 18g (Saturated 10g); Cholesterol 155mg; Sodium 608mg; Carbohydrate 17g (Dietary Fiber 1g); Protein 10g.*

**Tip:** A great cheese for this recipe is Pleasant Ridge Reserve, from Uplands Cheese Company (Wisconsin).

*Source:* **culture:** the word on cheese *(Winter 2008)*

# *Soup, Salad, and Side Days*

We love crunchy iceberg drenched in blue cheese dressing as much as the next guy, but salads are really where cheese lets your creativity shine. Our suggestion: Focus on local, seasonal ingredients and keep things simple. Be sure to provide a balance of flavors: tart, sweet, nutty, salty. Not the inventive type? The following recipes are easy and delicious but still adapt well to a seasonal switch of an ingredient or two.

For salad recipes, allow for 1 ounce of cheese per person if you're going to crumble or slice it. If you're just shaving a few pieces as a garnish, you don't need as much.

In this section, we also offer a variety of side dishes. Whether it's potatoes, rice or other grains, pasta, or vegetables, cheese can literally make a side dish or first course. It can be as simple as crumbled chèvre scattered over grilled vegetables or a buttery hard cheese shaved into a brothy soup: however you use it, cheese elevates the simple to sublime.

# Nectarine, Prosciutto, and Arugula Salad with Crescenza Toasts

*Prep time:* 20 min • *Cook time:* 10 min • *Yield:* Serves 4

Full of lush flavors — the intense creaminess and tang of the cheese (also konwn as Stracchino di Crescenza), syrupy-sweet nectarines, and salty ham — this salad is a celebration of summer. It's equally delicious if you grill the fruit first or substitute a blue cheese for the crescenza.

| Ingredients | Directions |
|---|---|
| Vinaigrette dressing (see the following recipe) | *1* Prepare the Vinaigrette dressing. |
| ½ baguette <br><br> 4 ounces Stracchino di Crescenza (such as Bellwether Farms and BelGioioso) <br><br> 5 cups arugula | *2* Preheat the oven to 450 degrees. Cut eight slices from the baguette ¼-inch thick on the diagonal and brush lightly with extra virgin olive oil. (Reserve the rest of the uncut loaf for another use.) Place bread slices on a baking sheet and toast until crisp but not browned. Set aside. |
| 2 to 3 medium nectarines, ripe but not mushy <br><br> 4 ounces (about 8 slices, total) prosciutto or other high-quality, very thinly sliced ham, | *3* To prepare the ingredients for assembly, pat the Stracchino di Crescenza dry to remove any excess liquid, slice the nectarines into ¼-inch slices, and tear each prosciutto slice into halves or thirds. |
| Freshly ground black pepper, to taste | *4* In a large bowl, gently toss the arugula with just enough vinaigrette to lightly coat the leaves (don't feel you need to use all of it). Season to taste with salt and pepper. Add the nectarine slices and gently toss one more time to coat the nectarines without bruising them. |
|  | *5* To serve, arrange a mound of arugula on each of four salad plates, adding several nectarine segments tucked into the sides. Gently crumple the prosciutto slices and add them to the salad. Spread each toast slice with 1 ounce of Stracchino di Crescenza and place two on each plate. Season with a twist of fresh pepper and serve immediately. |

## Vinaigrette Dressing

**2 teaspoons finely minced shallot**

**2 tablespoons white Balsamic vinegar or Champagne vinegar**

**Pinch of salt**

**⅓ cup extra virgin olive oil, or to taste**

**1** Place the shallot, vinegar, and salt together in a small bowl and let macerate for at least 10 minutes and up to 1 hour to mellow the flavor of the shallot.

**2** Add the olive oil in slow stream, whisking to combine. Add more vinegar or oil, if necessary, and adjust seasoning to taste. If you're not using it immediately, rewhisk before dressing the greens.

*Per serving: Calories 272 (From Fat 172); Fat 19g (Saturated 6g); Cholesterol 46mg; Sodium 630mg; Carbohydrate 13g (Dietary Fiber 2g); Protein 14g.*

***Vary it:*** Substitute fresh or grilled peaches or plums for the nectarines and try chèvre or a mellow blue cheese.

***Vary it:*** Rather than toast the baguette slices, you can grill them.

*Source: Laurel Miller, The Sustainable Kitchen*

Forget about smell when it comes to choosing stone fruit such as nectarines or peaches. Depending upon the variety, look for bright yellow or gold on the "shoulders" of the fruit. The deeper the color, the higher the sugar content. Note that commercially grown fruit is picked while unripe to prevent it from bruising: a shame, because while they'll continue to soften, stone fruit don't get any sweeter after having been picked. Buy local, sustainable produce, preferably from the nearest farmers' market.

# Salad Greens with Roasted Pears, Cornbread Croutons, and Camembert Dressing

***Prep time:*** 20 min • ***Cook time:*** 15 min • ***Yield:*** Serves 8

At Blackberry Farm, a sheep dairy/luxury retreat in Walland, Tennessee, chef Josh Feathers likes to use red-skinned Bartlett pears for this late summer/fall recipe. The slightly firmer texture of these pears adds contrast to the other components. If Bartletts are unavailable, any crisp variety will do (see note at end of recipe). Be sure they're ripe; otherwise, they'll taste too astringent and fail to caramelize properly. ***Note:*** You will need to purchase 1 wheel of camembert, total, for this recipe.

| *Ingredients* | *Directions* |
|---|---|
| 6 ripe (but not mushy) pears | ***1*** Prepare Camembert Dressing. (***Note:*** You can make this up to a day ahead.) |
| Kosher salt and cracked black pepper, to taste | |
| ¼ cup grapeseed oil | ***2*** Preheat a cast-iron skillet or heavy baking sheet in a 475 degree oven. Peel, core, and slice the pears into 8 wedges; then toss them with the salt, pepper, and one-third of the oil. |
| Camembert Dressing (see the following recipe) | |
| 10 cups mixed greens, such as frisée, red leap, Bibb, arugula, and radicchio | ***3*** Working in batches, add a tablespoon or two of oil to the pan. Lay enough pear wedges, flat side down, to cover the surface of the pan. Roast for 2 minutes; then flip the pears over and roast 1 minute longer, or until soft and slightly caramelized. Remove from the oven and set aside. Repeat until all the pears are prepared. |
| 2 cups cornbread croutons | |
| 8 slices camembert, for garnish | |
| | ***4*** To serve, toss the greens in a large bowl with just enough dressing to lightly coat the leaves. (You will have some dressing left over; store it in the refrigerator.) Divide the greens and croutons among 8 plates and top each with six roasted pear wedges and a slice of cheese. |

## Camembert Dressing

3 to 4 ounces camembert, cut into chunks, with rind

4 tablespoons good quality, pectin-free plain yogurt

3 tablespoons Banyuls vinegar or Champagne vinegar

1 tablespoon Dijon mustard

2 cups grapeseed oil

¼ cup water

Kosher salt, to taste

*1* Place the cheese, yogurt, vinegar, and mustard in a blender; puree until smooth. Slowly drizzle in the grapeseed oil, blending until well-mixed. Adjust the consistency with the water as needed and add salt to taste.

*Per serving: Calories 438 (From Fat 365); Fat 41g (Saturated 6g); Cholesterol 14mg; Sodium 376mg; Carbohydrate 16g (Dietary Fiber 3g); Protein 7g.*

**Tip:** Homemade croutons are best (make them a day ahead and store them in an airtight container), but good-quality store-bought cornbread (or one made from a mix) will also work; cube day-old pieces and toast until golden. You can also substitute good-quality sourdough bread.

**Shortcut:** The dressing can be made several days in advance and stored in the refrigerator. Let it sit at room temperature before serving.

*Source: Chef Josh Feathers, Blackberry Farm, Walland, Tennessee (**culture:** the word on cheese, Winter 2009)*

There are two categories of pear: Asian and European. Asian pears, also known as apple pears, are round, with crisp, white, perfumed flesh. The European varieties are what you're probably most familiar with, although they're diverse in flavor and texture. If you prefer firmer varieties — best for use on cheese plates and in salads — look for the aforementioned Bartlett or Anjou (also known as D'Anjou), Seckel, or French Butter pears. Softer varieties such as Bosc and Comice are delicate and bruise easily, but are good for poaching or baking.

# Bistro Salad with Poached Egg and Parmigiano Reggiano

**Prep time:** 20 min • **Cook time:** 30 min • **Yield:** Serves 4

This salad is **culture** magazine's take on a bistro classic. Serve it with a hearty soup and crusty loaf of bread for a satisfying winter lunch or dinner.

| Ingredients | Directions |
|---|---|
| **Vinaigrette Dressing (see the following recipe)** | *1* Prepare the Vinaigrette Dressing and set aside. |
| **8 slices (½-inch thick) crusty baguette or bread**<br><br>**2 tablespoons plus 3 tablespoons olive oil**<br><br>**¼ cup grated plus 2 ounces shaved Parmigiano Reggiano**<br><br>**Freshly ground black pepper** | *2* Preheat the broiler. Arrange bread slices on a cookie sheet or tray. Using 2 tablespoons of the oil, brush the tops of the slices and broil for 1 minute, or until the bread just begins to turn golden brown. Remove and flip slices over. Sprinkle the grated cheese over each and broil 1 to 2 minutes more, or until cheese is completely melted. Remove from the oven and sprinkle with black pepper; cover and leave at room temperature until needed. |
| **1 cup shelled pistachios or walnut halves** | *3* Heat a small skillet over medium heat. Add the nuts and cook, stirring once or twice, for 4 to 5 minutes, or until they are fragrant and just beginning to brown. Remove from the heat, coarsely chop, and set aside. |
| **12 scallions, green ends trimmed, to leave 5- to 6-inch lengths**<br><br>**4 very thin slices prosciutto, cut into strips**<br><br>**½ pound frisée and/or other bitter greens, torn, washed, and thoroughly dried** | *4* Meanwhile, in another large skillet, heat the remaining 3 tablespoons of oil over medium heat. Add the scallions and cook for about 5 minutes, tossing them once or twice until tender and just beginning to brown. Remove them from the heat and add the prosciutto strips to the skillet (you want them to just warm up from the residual heat). |
| **4 large eggs**<br><br>**Salt, to taste** | *5* Fill a large skillet with water and bring it to a boil. Carefully crack each egg into a bowl, keeping the yolk intact. Gently add the eggs, one at a time, to the boiling water. Reduce the heat to medium-high so that the water is at a low simmer and cook for 3 minutes for a runny yolk and longer for a firmer yolk. Remove the eggs with a slotted spoon and place in bowl. Set aside. |

*6* On a large serving platter, arrange the greens; top
with the scallions and scatter the prosciutto over the
salad. Spoon half the Vinaigrette Dressing on top of
the greens and scallions. Add the eggs to center of
the salad and season them with salt and freshly
ground black pepper. Scatter the top of salad with
the walnuts and cheese shavings. Tuck the cheese
toasts around edges of salad. Serve with the remaining Vinaigrette Dressing and cheese on side.

## Vinaigrette Dressing

1½ teaspoons Dijon mustard

Salt and freshly ground
black pepper, to taste

¼ cup good-quality white or
red wine vinegar

½ cup plus 1 tablespoon
extra virgin olive oil

*1* In a small bowl, mix the mustard with salt and pepper
to taste. Add the vinegar and stir. Slowly add the oil,
whisking to create a smooth, thickened vinaigrette.

*Per serving: Calories 994 (From Fat 694); Fat 77g (Saturated 15g); Cholesterol 240mg; Sodium 1,661mg;
Carbohydrate 48g (Dietary Fiber 8g); Protein 32g.*

*Vary it:* Substitute sautéed wild mushrooms, or grilled or sauteed asparagus, leeks, spring
onions, or green garlic for scallions.

*Source:* **culture:** the word on cheese *(Winter 2010)*

# Fennel, Tangerine, and Hazelnut Salad with Crottin

**Prep time:** 30 min • **Yield:** Serves 4

Winter means all manner of citrus fruit becomes available; you can easily substitute blood oranges or grapefruit for the tangerines and a blue cheese for the crottin. Refreshing and full of clean flavors, this salad makes a nice start to a rich, heavier meal such as braised short ribs or pot roast.

| Ingredients | Directions |
|---|---|
| **Vinaigrette Dressing (see the following recipe)** | **1** Prepare the Vinaigrette Dressing and set aside. |
| **5 to 6 cups frisée, mache, or mixed salad greens** | **2** To prepare the ingredients for the salad, half and then thinly slice the fennel bulb. Remove the pith (the bitter white layer) from the peeled tangerines and separate the tangerine into segments. Toast the hazelnuts; then remove the skin and chop them. Cut the crottin into 8 thin horizontal slices. **Note:** if you can't get them thin enough, just make 4 slices and use one per plate. |
| **1 medium fennel bulb** | |
| **2 tangerines, peeled** | |
| **¼ cup hazelnuts** | |
| **1 crottin (goat cheese "button"), any age** | **3** Place the salad greens, fennel, and tangerine segments in a large bowl. Toss the greens with just enough Vinaigrette Dressing to lightly coat the leaves (don't feel you need to use all of it). Season to taste with salt and pepper. |
| **Kosher salt and freshly ground black pepper, to taste** | |
| | **4** On each of four salad plates, place a small mound of greens, making sure the fennel and tangerines are evenly distributed. Place two slices of crottin on top of each salad (if you're only using one slice of crottin and it's too heavy for the greens, prop it up against them instead). Garnish with hazelnuts. |

## *Vinaigrette Dressing*

2 teaspoons finely minced
shallot

2 tablespoons good-quality
Champagne vinegar

Pinch of salt

⅓ cup extra virgin olive oil, or
to taste

*1* Place the shallot, vinegar, and salt together in a small
bowl and let macerate for at least 10 minutes and up to
1 hour to mellow the flavor of the shallot. Add the olive
oil in slow stream, whisking to combine. Add more vinegar or oil, if necessary, and adjust seasoning to taste.
If you're not using the dressing immediately, rewhisk it
before dressing the greens.

*Per serving: Calories 217 (From Fat 156); Fat 17g (Saturated 4g); Cholesterol 11mg; Sodium 395mg; Carbohydrate
14g (Dietary Fiber 4g); Protein 6g.*

**Tip:** To remove the skin from a hazelnut, rub the hot nuts in a dish towel to whisk the papery
skins off. To remove the pith (the white membrane) from the tangerine segments, gently scrape
them with a very sharp paring knife.

*Source: Laurel Miller, The Sustainable Kitchen*

Toasting nuts heightens their flavor and aroma to its full potential. You can
either place them in a frying pan over medium heat and shake every few seconds to prevent the nuts from scorching, or you can place them on a baking
sheet and put them in a 350 degree oven until they're golden. Be sure to shake
the pan every couple of minutes to prevent them from burning.

# Sopa de Quinoa

***Prep time:*** 15 min • ***Cook time:*** 90 min • ***Yield:*** Serves 4

Laurel got this simple recipe while visiting a cheesemaker at Hacienda Zuleta in Ecuador for a ***culture*** magazine story. From the grandmother of longtime Zuleta chef Jose Maria Pumisacho, this traditional, brothy Andean soup (loaded with protein-rich quinoa, one of the world's oldest grains) shines due to the quality of its dairy ingredients. Use the best you can find and afford.

| *Ingredients* | *Directions* |
|---|---|
| **2 cups quinoa** <br><br> **6 cups water** <br><br> **1 tablespoon unsalted butter** | *1* Bring a stockpot of water to a boil. Add the quinoa, lower the heat to a simmer, and cook, covered, for approximately 20 minutes, stirring occasionally, until the grains are soft. |
| **2 scallions, white part only, sliced** <br><br> **½ cup milk** <br><br> **2 large eggs, yolks only** <br><br> **⅓ cup heavy cream** <br><br> **½ cup of grated alpine cheese or similar nutty, firm cheese that melts well** <br><br> **Kosher salt and freshly ground black pepper, to taste** | *2* While the quinoa is cooking, heat the butter in an 8-inch frying pan over medium heat. When the butter is melted, add the scallions and cook until they're transparent. When the quinoa is ready, add the cooked scallions and half of the milk to the quinoa and bring the mixture to a boil. Reduce the heat to medium-low and let the mixture simmer until the quinoa is cooked through (it will still be firm but shouldn't taste chalky; the color will be a translucent yellow). *Note:* Quinoa cooks fairly quickly; allow the same amount of time you would for white rice. |
| | *3* While the quinoa mixture is simmering, puree the egg yolks, the remaining milk, the cream, and the cheese in a blender for 1 minute. Stir this mixture into the soup immediately before serving and season to taste with salt and pepper. |

*Per serving: Calories 490 (From Fat 190); Fat 21g (Saturated 10g); Cholesterol 150mg; Sodium 165mg; Carbohydrate 60g (Dietary Fiber 5g); Protein 17g.*

***Do-ahead:*** Cook the quinoa up to a day ahead, reserving the cooking liquid separately. When preparing the final dish, heat and incorporate the quinoa cooking liquid in small amounts with the rest of the ingredients that go into the blender.

*Source: Chef Jose Maria Pumisacho, Hacienda Zuleta, Zuleta, Ecuador (**culture:** the word on cheese, Spring 2009)*

# Grilled Asparagus with Chèvre and Orange Zest

***Prep time:*** 10 min  •  ***Cook time:*** 10-12 min  •  ***Yield:*** Serves 4

Too tired to prepare an elaborate recipe? Have last minute guests or produce that needs to be used up? Consider this your template for all manner of seasonal vegetables.

| *Ingredients* | *Directions* |
|---|---|
| **1 pound asparagus, preferably pencil-thin spears, washed and trimmed**<br><br>**Extra virgin olive oil (about 1 tablespoon)**<br><br>**Kosher salt and freshly ground black pepper, to taste**<br><br>**4 ounces of fresh chèvre, crumbled**<br><br>**Zest of 1 orange** | *1* Preheat the grill until the coals are white-hot. As your grill warms up, on a baking sheet, toss the asparagus with just enough olive oil to lightly coat the spears; then add salt and pepper to taste.<br><br>*2* When the coals are ready, place the spears at a diagonal (so they don't fall through grate), leaving a bit of space between them so they can cook fully. Watch them carefully and turn them with tongs so that they cook evenly and achieve a wilted, slightly crispy appearance at the tips.<br><br>*3* Remove the asparagus from the grill and place them on a decorative platter. Test one spear to make sure the seasoning is adequate, and add more salt and pepper as necessary. Garnish the spears with orange zest and the chèvre and serve immediately. |

*Per serving: Calories 121 (From Fat 86); Fat 10g (Saturated 5g); Cholesterol 13mg; Sodium 181mg; Carbohydrate 3g (Dietary Fiber 1g); Protein 7g.*

***Tip:*** If you don't have a grill, roast the asparagus or other vegetables (toss them in olive oil, salt, and pepper first) on a rimmed baking sheet in the oven.

***Vary it!*** Utterly adaptable, this recipe tastes just as delicious with baby artichokes, Japanese eggplant, or summer squash. You can also forgo the grill and roast new potatoes or beets, or toss the chèvre and zest with blanched and sautéed fava beans or fresh peas.

*Source: Laurel Miller, The Sustainable Kitchen*

# Israeli Couscous with Preserved Lemon, Sugar Snap Peas, Feta, and Mint

***Prep time:*** 30 min • ***Cook time:*** about 15 min • ***Yield:*** Serves 4

This refreshing spring dish from chef MJ Adams of Rapid City, South Dakota's The Corn Exchange is easily adapted to other seasonal ingredients. Using a drier feta will make for a cleaner-looking salad, while a more creamy variety (you can also use fresh chèvre) will add a lush note to the final dish.

| Ingredients | Directions |
|---|---|
| **3 cups Israeli couscous, uncooked** | *1* In a large pot, bring 10 cups of water to a boil and add 1 tablespoon of extra virgin olive oil and a pinch of salt. Add the couscous and stir. Lower the heat to medium and cook until the couscous is al dente, about 3 to 6 minutes. Drain, reserving one tablespoon of the water. |
| **Good-quality extra virgin olive oil** | |
| **½ cup fresh mint** | |
| **1 whole preserved lemon, quartered** | *2* Return the couscous to the pot and drizzle with 3 to 4 tablespoons of the extra virgin olive oil and the reserved tablespoon of water. Mix well with a rubber spatula and pour the mixture out onto a rimmed baking sheet. Cool, stirring the couscous every 5 minutes to prevent clumping. |
| **1 cup sugar snap peas** | |
| **1 or 2 lemons (you may not need the second one)** | |
| **¾ to 1 cup crumbled feta** | *3* To prepare the ingredients for the salad, cut the fresh mint into a chiffonade by stacking similar-sized leaves on top of one another, rolling them up, and slicing them thinly crosswise. (***Note:*** *Chiffonade* means "rags.") Also blanch the sugar snap peas and julienne them into sixths, making sure the pieces are large enough to retain some crunch. |
| **Kosher salt, to taste** | |
| **Freshly ground black pepper, to taste** | |
| **2 tablespoons chopped Italian parsley** | |
| | *4* In a bowl, add the cooled couscous, mint, sugar snap peas, preserved lemons, two tablespoons of the extra virgin olive oil, and the juice of one whole lemon. Toss gently with a spatula to avoid bruising the mint. Season to taste with salt and pepper (be aware that the feta will increase the salt content, so go easy). |

**5** Gently fold the feta into the salad (you don't want the cheese to fall apart). Adjust the seasoning and add more lemon juice, if needed. Serve in a large, decorative bowl, garnished with chopped Italian parsley. If you make this salad ahead of time, remove it from the refrigerator 15 minutes before serving.

*Per serving: Calories 566 (From Fat 95); Fat 11g (Saturated 5g); Cholesterol 25mg; Sodium 744mg; Carbohydrate 97g (Dietary Fiber 2g); Protein 19g.*

*Tip:* You can find preserved lemons at specialty food stores or Mediterranean markets. If the preserved lemon is too hard to find, just leave it out; the recipe is fine without it.

*Source: Chef MJ Adams, The Corn Exchange, Rapid City, South Dakota (**culture:** the word on cheese, Summer 2011)*

Couscous is nothing more than tiny pellets of semolina flour — the same stuff used to make various types of pasta. This staple food of Morocco, Tunisia, and Algeria is most commonly served beneath stewed or roasted vegetables or meat.

---

# Thick or thin?

What's better: thick or thin spears of asparagus? The answer is personal preference, although what you plan to do with your asparagus should also affect your decision. For grilling or roasting, thin spears cook more quickly and evenly; they can also be shaved, raw, on a mandoline for use in salads. Fat spears are ideal for battering and frying or just plain dipping into melted butter or sauces. The important thing is to check the bottoms of the stalks: If they're dry and woody, the asparagus isn't fresh, so give it a pass.

---

# Haricot Verts and Miniature Tomatoes with Bocconcini

*Prep time:* 45 min  •  *Cook time:* 7–8 min  •  *Yield:* Serves 4

This lively-looking salad is ideal for picnics and other al fresco meals. Make this when tomatoes are in season; for the best flavor, opt for ones that are grown locally. ***Note:*** *Haricot verts* are French green beans, similar to the green beans you're used to but thinner and longer. If you can't find haricot verts, substitute fresh green beans (make sure they're young and thin), string beans, or sugar snap peas.

| *Ingredients* | *Directions* |
|---|---|
| 1½ pounds haricot verts<br><br>1 pint assorted ripe miniature or cherry tomatoes, halved<br><br>¼ cup extra virgin olive oil | *1* After removing the stems from the haricot verts, blanch and thoroughly drain them. Halve the tomatoes. Place the haricot verts and tomatoes in a large bowl. Set aside. |
| 1 medium shallot, finely minced<br><br>2 cloves garlic, finely minced<br><br>One 8-ounce container of bocconcini, drained | *2* In a small frying pan, heat the olive oil over medium-high heat. Add the shallots and garlic and lower heat so that they just barely sizzle. Cook for about 2 to 3 minutes, or until they become fragrant and soft but not browned. Remove the mixture from the heat and allow to cool for 5 minutes. |
| 1 to 2 tablespoons Champagne vinegar<br><br>Kosher salt and freshly ground black pepper, to taste<br><br>10 large fresh basil leaves, julienned | *3* Using your hands (to avoid bruising the tomatoes), toss together the shallot mixture, the beans and tomatoes, and the bocconcini. Add the Champagne vinegar, using more if necessary, and season to taste with salt and pepper. Let sit at room temperature for half an hour so that the flavors can develop. Just before serving, add the basil and toss again to combine the ingredients. |

*Per serving: Calories 362 (From Fat 256); Fat 28g (Saturated 10g); Cholesterol 41mg; Sodium 113mg; Carbohydrate 18g (Dietary Fiber 6g); Protein 14g.*

***Tip:*** Bocconcini are tiny (2 ounce) fresh mozzarella balls. If you can't find bocconcini, you can substitute 4 ounces of fresh mozzarella. Simply drain it and cut it into bite-sized cubes.

***Vary it:*** This recipes works equally well with feta, chèvre, or ricotta salata.

*Source: Laurel Miller, The Sustainable Kitchen*

# Wood-Roasted New Potatoes with Délice du Jura and Black Truffle Oil

**Prep time:** 5 min • **Cook time:** 30 min • **Yield:** Serves 4

Executive chef Joseph Lenn of Blackberry Farm, a farm/luxury retreat in Walland, Tennessee, serves this simple but nuanced dish as a course on tasting menus, an accompaniment to entrées, or as a family-style side dish. He uses Princess LaRatte, Pontiac, or Kennebec potatoes grown on the farm, but any fingerling variety or red bliss potato will work. If you prefer an aged cheese, Lenn suggests using a microplane to grate Parmigiano Reggiano over the final dish.

| Ingredients | Directions |
|---|---|
| **12 new potatoes, approximately golf-ball size**<br><br>**1 ounce grapeseed oil**<br><br>**1½ teaspoons kosher salt**<br><br>**¼ teaspoon freshly ground black pepper**<br><br>**4 ounces Délice du Jura or crème fraiche**<br><br>**2 tablespoons finely minced chives**<br><br>**2 to 3 tablespoons black truffle, walnut, or hazelnut oil, or to taste** | **1** Heat a wood, charcoal, or gas grill until the coals are glowing. Gently scrub the potatoes to remove the dirt. In a mixing bowl, combine the potatoes, grapeseed oil, and salt, and toss to coat.<br><br>**2** Place the potatoes on the grill and cook until tender, 30 to 45 minutes. Remove them from the grill and place on a serving platter. Smash each potato with the back of a spoon, and then season with pepper to taste. Place the sliced Reblochon over the top of the potatoes, allowing the cheese to melt slightly. Garnish with chives and a drizzle of the truffle oil. Serve immediately. |

*Per serving: Calories 603 (From Fat 231); Fat 26g (Saturated 9g); Cholesterol 41mg; Sodium 463mg; Carbohydrate 82g (Dietary Fiber 8g); Protein 11g.*

**Vary it:** If you don't have a grill, roast the potatoes at 375 degrees until tender and slightly browned.

*Source: Executive chef Joseph Lenn, Blackberry Farm, Walland, Tennesseee (**culture:** the word on cheese, Winter 2008)*

# Pan-Roasted Wild Mushrooms over Cheddar Polenta with Pumpkinseed Oil

**Prep time:** 15 min  •  **Cook time:** 20–30 min  •  **Yield:** Serves 6 as a first course or 4 as an entree

From chef Matthew Jennings of La Laiterie at Farmstead in Providence, Rhode Island, comes a dish bursting with the flavors of fall. This combination of humble ingredients — polenta, mushrooms, and cheddar — turns into a stunning vegetarian entrée or first course when dressed with rich, emerald-colored pumpkinseed oil.

| Ingredients | Directions |
|---|---|
| 3 to 4 cups chicken or vegetable broth | |
| 3 cups non-instant polenta (stone ground, if available) | |
| 1 cup whole milk | |
| ¾ cup grated cheddar | |
| ¼ stick unsalted butter, cubed and chilled | |
| 1 tablespoon chopped fresh thyme | |
| ¼ cup olive oil | |
| ½ cup finely diced red onion | |
| 4 cups wild mushrooms, cleaned well and roughly chopped | |
| 1 tablespoon minced garlic | |
| 1 tablespoon minced shallots | |
| Kosher salt and cracked black pepper to taste | |
| ¼ cup toasted pumpkin seed oil, for garnish | |
| Fresh herbs or baby greens, for garnish | |

**1** To prepare the polenta, in a medium-size saucepot, bring 3 cups chicken broth to a rolling boil over high heat. Reduce the heat to medium and pour in the polenta, whisking constantly. Reduce the heat to low and let the mixture simmer until the polenta thickens (be careful, it might splatter if it's too hot). Add the milk and continue cooking until the mixture begins to thicken, about 8 minutes. Add the cheese, butter, and thyme to the mixture and stir well.

**2** The polenta should have the consistency of porridge. If the mixture is too thick, add some broth to thin it out to the desired consistency. If it's too thin, whisk in more polenta and cook longer. Remove the saucepan from heat and cover to keep warm.

**3** In a large sauté pan, heat the olive oil over medium heat. Add the diced onion and sauté gently. Turn the heat to low. When the onion is translucent, add the wild mushrooms, stirring constantly. Note that, after several minutes, the mushrooms will begin to release moisture; should the pan become dry before you add the garlic and shallots, use another tablespoon of olive oil to prevent them from burning. Incorporate the garlic and shallots, and cook gently for several minutes, allowing the flavors to merge (be careful not to burn the garlic or shallots). Season with salt and pepper to taste. Remove from heat.

*4* To serve, spoon the polenta onto the warm plates and top with the mushroom mixture. Drizzle about one teaspoon of the pumpkinseed oil over each plate. Garnish with herbs or baby greens.

*Per serving: Calories 626 (From Fat 257); Fat 29g (Saturated 8g); Cholesterol 31mg; Sodium 658mg; Carbohydrate 80g (Dietary Fiber 9g); Protein 16g.*

***Tip:*** When chef Matthew Jennings prepares this recipe, he uses Grafton Clothbound Cheddar from Vermont.

***Tip:*** You can find toasted pumpkin seed oil at specialty food or natural food stores.

*Source: Chef Matthew Jennings, La Laiterie at Farmstead, Providence, Rhode Island (***culture:*** the word on cheese, Winter 2008)*

# Q & A with Master sommelier Bobby Stuckey

Bobby Stuckey is a busy man. In addition to being one of just 118 Master Sommeliers in the U.S., he's co-owner of Scarpetta Wines and co-owner and wine director of one of the nation's most acclaimed restaurants, Frasca Food and Wine, in Boulder, Colorado (home to *five* Master Sommeliers!).

His partner at Frasca Food and Wine is award-winning chef Lachlan Mackinnon-Patterson, who creates soulful renditions of the rustic cuisine of Friuli-Venezia Giulia, a little-known region of northeastern Italy. Both men are experts in their respective fields on Italian wine and food. The duo also own Pizzeria Locale, adjacent to Frasca Food and Wine, and il caffe, a pastry, panini, and espresso bar.

When not playing gracious host or conducting wine seminars nationwide, Stuckey, a former competitive cyclist, runs marathons for fun and always, always rides his bike to work, sun or snow, wearing his trademark suit. *Whew*.

We stopped Stuckey in his tracks to ask him a few questions about pairing wine with cheese:

**Cheese For Dummies**: If a wine is from a specific region, can we assume that it pairs with any cheese from that region, as well?

**Bobby Stuckey:** No, not always. For example, a rich *mozzarella di bufala* doesn't go well with the local Aglianico, a full-bodied red wine from Basiliacata and Campania.

**CFD**: Since you recently opened a pizzeria (January of 2011), what wine pairings would you recommend? Is there any cheese other than the classic — mozzarella — that you particularly love to use that's wine-compatible?

**BS:** Pizza and wine is the one left turn in the Italian food and wine pairing book. In most regions of Italy, the wines fit like a glove with the local cuisine: Piedmonte Barolo and truffles; Tocai Friulano and prosciutto in Friuli. In Campania, the delicate flavors of pizza usually need tender red wines or soft, round, non-wooded whites — or, in many cases, beer. I also love frothy *lambrusco*, a sparkling red wine from several regions in the north, with pizza. Smoked provolone can also be a great asset with pizza.

**CFD**: What's your favorite Italian cheese and wine pairing?

**BS:** I love a piece of great hard cheese with a mature, world-class red. For example, an aged Montasio cheese from Friuli with a glass of Brunello (from Tuscany).

**CFD**: What is *frico*, and why is it so emblematic of Frasca? What kind of wine should we drink with it?

**BS:** *Frico* is one of the building blocks of Friuliano cuisine — it's essentially a cheese crisp. It's based on Montasio cheese, which is from the Carnic Alps, a range that extends from the Tyrol into Friuli. There are a couple of ways to make *frico*, although it always calls for shredded cheese. One is hot, made with potatoes and lightly cooked onions; the other is the classic *frico croccante*, which is a crunchy version. The *croccante* is based on *vecchio* (aged) Montasio, which allows the cook to make it into a crispy basket or disk. Its salty crunchiness is best with a glass of Friuliano Bianco.

**CFD**: Are there any other notable cheeses from Friuli?

**BS:** Smoked ricotta from the Carnic Alps, but Montasio is truly a great DOC raw cow milk cheese. It was originally made by monks in the 13th century. As it ages, it grows more rich and nutty in flavor. It's just so representative of the region.

# Chapter 18

# Cooking with Cheese, Pt. 2: Main Dishes and Desserts

## Recipes in This Chapter

▶ Sheep Milk Ricotta Gnocchi with Fresh Peas, Spring Onions, and Bacon

▶ Chicken Cacciatore with Ricotta Salata

▶ Farmstead's Cheesemonger Mac 'n' Cheese

▶ Grilled Sausages with Grapes, Wilted Greens, and Pecorino Romano

▶ Broiled Gruyère Sandwiches with Maple-Caramelized Apples

▶ Peppered Pear and Goat Cheese Scones

▶ Stinky Cheese Omelet with Herb Topping

▶ Blue Cheese and Potato Tartlets

▶ New Classic Cheese Souffle

▶ Grilled Peaches with Mascarpone, Pistachios, and Raspberries

▶ Aged Gouda and Walnut Biscotti

▶ Rhubarb-Brown Sugar Cake with Strawberry-Rhubarb Compote and Crème Fraiche

▶ Dried Apricot-Goat Cheese Tart

▶ Ginger-Poached Pears with Roquefort-Honey Ice Cream

## In This Chapter

▶ Tips for cooking with cheese

▶ Exploring cheese recipes suitable for every meal

In this chapter, we focus on integrating cheese into main courses and desserts. Not surprisingly, it's just as compatible as when used in appetizers, soups, and salads. In addition to useful tips on technique, sourcing other ingredients, and cooking with cheese, we've compiled a selection of cheese-centric, seasonally-focused recipes suitable for beginning and novice cooks. Even if you're an experienced home cook, these recipes are sure to impress, because they're designed to let the key ingredients — including cheese — shine.

## The Main Event

If you love cheese, it makes sense to showcase it in a main course. Even if the actual amount called for is negligible, the right cheese can make a dish memorable.

# Sheep Milk Ricotta Gnocchi with Fresh Peas, Spring Onions, and Bacon

**Prep time:** 60–90 min  •  **Cook time:** 30 min  •  **Yield:** Serves 4

Gnocchi are small Italian dumplings that are most often made using potato, ricotta, or semolina flour to give them a light, airy consistency. This gnocchi recipe comes from Picholine in New York. We've added to it a simple sauté of spring vegetables and bacon, which won't obscure the sweet, delicate nature of the sheep milk. In summer, you can try serving the gnocchi with pesto (homemade yields the best flavor).

| *Ingredients* | *Directions* |
|---|---|
| **1 cup sheep or cow milk ricotta** | **1** Put the ricotta in a cheesecloth-lined colander and use a rubber spatula to push as much liquid as possible out of the cheese. Then gather up the ends of the cloth and turn them over and over again (as though wringing a towel), tightening its hold on the cheese and squeezing out any remaining liquid. |
| **2 tablespoons finely grated Parmigiano Reggiano** | |
| **½ cup plus 3 tablespoons all-purpose flour, plus more for dusting** | |
| **1 large egg yolk** | **2** Put the ricotta, Parmigiano Reggiano, flour, egg yolk, ½ teaspoon of salt, and cayenne pepper in the bowl of a food processor fitted with a steel blade, and process until the mixture comes together into a smooth ball of dough, taking care not to overmix. (Alternatively, mix the ingredients in a bowl, using a wooden spoon, until no lumps remain.) If the dough feels sticky, work in some more flour. Transfer the dough to a bowl, cover with plastic wrap, and refrigerate for 30 minutes. |
| **Kosher salt** | |
| **Pinch of cayenne pepper** | |
| **6 quarts of water** | |
| **2 slices of bacon, diced** | |
| **1 bunch of spring onion, thinly sliced** | **3** Remove the gnocchi from the refrigerator. Dust a rimmed baking sheet or cookie sheet lightly with flour. Lightly flour a work surface and turn the dough out onto it. Divide the dough into 4 equal portions. Roll out one portion at a time into a rope-like cylinder, ¾-inch in diameter. With a serrated knife, cut the cylinder into 1-inch pieces. Gently make an indentation with your thumb in one side of each piece and arrange the pieces in a single layer on the baking sheet. Repeat with remaining cylinders, adding more flour to the surface as needed. (Figure 18-1 shows how to shape gnocchi.) Cover the gnocchi with plastic wrap and refrigerate for 1 hour to firm them up and help them hold their shape when cooked. |
| **½ to 1 cup chicken stock** | |
| **½ pound fresh peas, shelled** | |
| **Salt and freshly ground black pepper, to taste** | |

**4** While the gnocchi are resting, add the bacon to a large sauté pan and cook over medium heat until crispy. Remove the bacon pieces with a slotted spoon and drain on the paper towel. Add the onion and sauté it in bacon fat until soft, about 3 minutes (if you don't have enough bacon fat, add some olive oil). Add the chicken stock to the pan and cook with the onions until the stock is slightly reduced. Season to taste with salt and pepper, and set aside.

**5** Pour 6 quarts of the water into an 8-quart stockpot and add 1 tablespoon of salt. Bring the water to a boil over high heat. Fill a large bowl halfway with ice water. Add the gnocchi to the boiling water and cook them until they float to the surface, approximately 2 to 3 minutes. Use a slotted spoon to transfer the gnocchi to the ice water and then to a clean, dry bowl.

**6** As you wait for the gnocchi water to boil, reheat the onions and stock mixture. Add the peas to the sauté pan and a little more stock if the mixture is too dry. (***Remember:*** You don't want the stock soupy or saucy, which will make the gnocchi soggy; you want it just moist enough to coat gnocchi.)

**7** Add the cooked gnocchi and bacon to the pan to brown the gnocchi a bit and let the flavors meld, about 1 to 2 minutes; add a bit of the reserved cooking water to moisten and enrich the mixture, if needed. Plate and serve immediately.

*Per serving: Calories 247 (From Fat 101); Fat 11g (Saturated 6g); Cholesterol 37mg; Sodium 495mg; Carbohydrate 24g (Dietary Fiber 2g); Protein 13g.*

***Tip:*** You can prepare the gnocchi ahead of time. Just toss with 1½ tablespoons of olive oil, cover, and set aside for up to 1 hour, or refrigerate for up to 24 hours. To serve, simply reheat in boiling water until they rise to the surface; set aside one cup of cooking water for use in final dish, if needed. After you've made the gnocchi dough, avoid overhandling it, because that results in a tough end product, as well.

***Tip:*** You can substitute green onions, green garlic, or 2 leeks (white and light green parts only) for the spring onion.

***Note:*** The key to this recipe is using a high-quality ricotta. We suggest making this dish in the spring or summer months, when fresh (as in newly made) ricotta is available in cheese shops. Some larger dairies freeze their milk or ricotta so they have product to make and sell during the winter months, but the quality may suffer; if nothing else, the ricotta will have a higher water content, which will result in leaden gnocchi.

*Source: Laurel Miller, The Sustainable Kitchen (***culture:*** the word on cheese, Fall 2009)*

## All(ium) in the family: Shallots, scallions, and green onions

While all are members of the allium family, a *shallot* resembles a small red onion in flavor and taste, while green onions have sharp-flavored white bulbs and edible, dark green stalks. And a *scallion* is just a term for young green onions. Shallots and green onions (young or old) aren't interchangeable, per se: You wouldn't want to sub green onions for shallots in a vinaigrette, for example.

In our opinion, green onions are best when sautéed in butter or olive oil, which tempers their strong flavor and aroma; try them in stir fries, quesadillas, or macaroni and cheese. The milder shallot is more versatile and adds a little somethin' somethin' to sauces, ground hamburger, and vegetable dishes or braised beef when roasted whole and added to the dish.

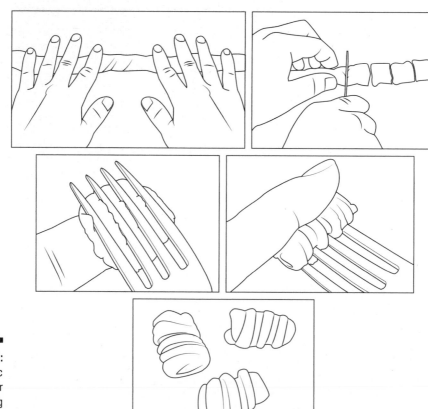

**Figure 18-1:** The basic steps for shaping gnocchi.

# Chicken Cacciatore with Ricotta Salata

**Prep time:** 30 min • **Cook time:** 35 min • **Yield:** Serves 4

The addition of crumbled ricotta salata on this beloved classic gives it a salty, zesty kick. Serve with crusty bread to soak up the juice and a glass of hearty Zinfandel.

| *Ingredients* | *Directions* |
|---|---|
| ¼ cup all-purpose flour | **1** In a medium bowl, combine the flour, salt, and pepper. Add the chicken and toss to coat. In a large nonstick pan, heat the olive oil over medium heat. Working in two batches, brown the chicken, turning once, about 3 minutes per side. Set aside. |
| ½ teaspoon kosher salt | |
| ¼ teaspoon freshly ground black pepper | |
| 8 boneless, skinless chicken thighs (about 1½ pounds) | **2** Add a little more oil to the skillet if necessary and sauté the onion, stirring often, until softened, about 4 minutes. Add the peppers and sauté another 2 minutes. Add the garlic and sauté another 1 minute. Add the mushrooms and sauté for another 2 minutes. Then add the tomatoes (with their juices) and the oregano. Bring to a boil. |
| 2 tablespoons olive oil | |
| 1 medium yellow onion, sliced | |
| 2 Anaheim or banana peppers, thinly sliced | |
| 2 garlic cloves, minced | **3** Return the chicken plus any juices to the skillet and reduce the heat to low. Simmer, covered, until the chicken is cooked through, about 15 minutes. Remove the skillet from the heat. Top with the olives and ricotta salata and serve. |
| 8 ounces cremini mushrooms, sliced | |
| One 14 ½-ounce can of fire-roasted crushed tomatoes | |
| ½ teaspoon dried oregano | |
| ½ cup pitted Kalamata olives | |
| ⅔ cup crumbled ricotta salata | |

*Per serving: Calories 454 (From Fat 242); Fat 27g (Saturated 8g); Cholesterol 121mg; Sodium 906mg; Carbohydrate 18g (Dietary Fiber 3g); Protein 35g.*

*Source:* **culture:** the word on cheese *(Spring 2011)*

# Farmstead's Cheesemonger Mac 'n' Cheese

***Prep time:*** 20 min • ***Cook time:*** 20 min • ***Yield:*** Serves 6

This signature dish is from chef Matthew Jennings of La Laiterie at Farmstead in Providence, Rhode Island. It has the requisite oozy, gooey, cheesy characteristics, but it's made a bit more grown-up because it uses a great sharp cheddar, earthy Gruyère, and ripe Brie. Bake with breadcrumbs and, says Jennings, "Heaven awaits."

| *Ingredients* | *Directions* |
|---|---|
| 1½ cups coarsely grated Gruyère cheese | *1* Heat oven to 375 degrees. Mix all of the cheeses in a large bowl and set aside. Reserve 1 cup for topping the casserole. |
| 1½ cups coarsely grated very sharp cheddar cheese | |
| 1½ cups diced rindless ripe Brie (cut from 1-pound wedge) | *2* To make the breadcrumbs, melt the remaining tablespoon of butter in large, heavy skillet over medium-high heat. Add the breadcrumbs and toss. Stir and pan-toast the crumbs until golden, about 2 minutes. Set aside. |
| 5 tablespoons butter, divided | |
| ¼ cup all-purpose flour | |
| 2 teaspoons chopped fresh thyme leaves | *3* Cook the pasta in boiling salted water until almost al dente (this ensures a little firmness after baking). Drain. Transfer the drained pasta to a large bowl. |
| ¾ teaspoon (scant) nutmeg | |
| 1 quart whole milk | *4* While the pasta is cooking, make the cheese sauce: In a large saucepan, melt 4 tablespoons of the butter over medium heat. Add the flour and stir until the mixture turns golden brown, about 4 minutes. Add the thyme and nutmeg. Gradually whisk in the milk. Simmer over low heat until thickened and smooth, stirring often, for about 4 minutes. Add the cheeses to the saucepan and stir until melted and smooth. Pour the cheese sauce over the pasta and mix well. |
| 1¾ cups fresh breadcrumbs made from crustless French bread | |
| 1 pound penne pasta | |
| | *5* Place the pasta and cheese mixture in a 9-x-11 casserole dish (alternatively divide the mixture among six custard cups or ramekins large enough to hold about 2 cups each). Sprinkle the mixture with the reserved grated cheese. |

*6* Sprinkle the breadcrumbs over the pasta and cheese. Then bake until the mixture begins to bubble and the tops are golden, about 20 minutes. (If you're using custard cups, place them on a rimmed baking sheet for baking.)

*Per serving: Calories 860 (From Fat 402); Fat 45g (Saturated 27g); Cholesterol 143mg; Sodium 648mg; Carbohydrate 75g (Dietary Fiber 3g); Protein 40g.*

*Tip:* To save time, prepare the recipe up to a day ahead. Follow Steps 1 through 5. Then cover the ramekins with foil and chill, and store the breadcrumbs in an airtight container. When you're ready to cook the pasta, reheat it by moistening each with a teaspoon of cream, covering it with foil, and warming it in a 350-degree oven for 15 minutes. Then bake as specified in Step 6.

*Source: Chef Matthew Jennings, La Laiterie at Farmstead, Providence, Rhode Island (**culture:** the word on cheese, Winter 2008)*

---

# Good cheeses for cheeseburgers

Few cheeses don't make for a love match when paired with a burger. Some specific cheeses, however, can elevate a good hamburger to greatness. Next time, try one of the following:

- Pleasant Ridge Reserve (Uplands Cheese Company, WI)
- Caveman Blue (Rogue Creamery, OR)
- Montgomery's Cheddar (Neal's Yard Dairy, U.K.)

- Boursin (France)
- Taleggio (Italy)
- Midnight Moon (Cypress Grove, Holland)
- Gruyère (Switzerland)

*Tip:* Bloomy-rind varieties would be one category we'd shy away from, in part because the rinds are often bitter, and removing them is a waste of money.

# Grilled Sausages with Grapes, Wilted Greens, and Pecorino Romano

**Prep time:** 15 min • **Cook time:** 7–8 min • **Yield:** Serves 4

Rustic and satisfying, this dish is ideal for blustery fall or winter nights. Serve it with some extra cheese and crusty bread on the side, and a sturdy red wine or a robust dark lager.

| Ingredients | Directions |
|---|---|
| 8 pork sausages, such as sweet or hot Italian lamb<br><br>2 cups seedless purple grapes, washed and stemmed<br><br>Kosher salt and freshly ground black pepper, to taste<br><br>2 to 3 tablespoons of extra virgin olive oil<br><br>2 sprigs of thyme<br><br>1 medium shallot, finely minced<br><br>⅛ to ¼ cup red wine<br><br>4 handfuls baby arugula (about 5 cups)<br><br>¼ pound Pecorino Romano, shaved with a vegetable peeler | *1* Preheat the grill until the coals are white hot and the oven to 375 degrees. On a baking sheet (don't use non-stick), toss the grapes with just enough olive oil to lightly coat them. Add the salt, pepper, and thyme, and toss once again to distribute the seasoning. Bake for 15 minutes, checking every 5 minutes and using a spatula to move them around, until the grapes are slightly golden, a bit shriveled, and have released some of their juices, and the juice has carmelized a bit in places.<br><br>*2* Remove the pan of grapes from the oven. Pour the red wine onto the hot baking sheet; with a spatula, scrape up the caramelized bits (be careful not to squash the grapes). Allow the residual heat from the pan to evaporate most of the wine so that you're left with a thin glaze. Scrape the contents into a small frying pan and set aside. |

*3*  While the grapes are roasting, add the sausages to the grill, taking care not to overcrowd them. Cook until they're done (they'll be firm with tight skins and juice should spurt out when pierced with a fork). Place the sausages on a plate and cover with foil to keep warm.

*4*  Reheat the grapes and glaze in the frying pan over medium-high heat, adding a bit more wine and seasoning if necessary. Remove from the heat.

*5*  Divide the arugula among four dinner plates, making a mound in the center of each. Add two sausages to each plate and top with the grape/glaze mixture. Garnish the top of each with Pecorino Romano shavings. Serve immediately.

*Per serving: Calories 678 (From Fat 453); Fat 50g (Saturated 19g); Cholesterol 133mg; Sodium 1,815mg; Carbohydrate 18g (Dietary Fiber 1g); Protein 40g.*

*Source: Laurel Miller, The Sustainable Kitchen*

# Cheese for Breakfast and Brunch

In continental Europe, cheese is always a part of breakfast — usually buttery, semi-soft or semi-firm varieties such as Havarti or Tilsiter. In this section, we incorporate cheese into breakfast and brunch recipes, but we won't tell if you serve some extra cheese straight-up on the side!

# Broiled Gruyère Sandwiches with Maple-Caramelized Apples

***Prep time:*** 5 min • ***Cook time:*** 10 min • ***Yield:*** Serves 2

Served open-face or in the more traditional manner, this sophisticated sandwich from ***culture*** magazine's archives works equally well with pears. It's also adaptable to many different varieties of cheeses (aged Gouda and clothbound cheddar being the exceptions because they don't melt well).

| *Ingredients* | *Directions* |
|---|---|
| **1 teaspoon butter** | *1* In a medium skillet, heat the butter and oil over medium heat. When the butter begins to sizzle, add the apple slices and cook, gently stirring once or twice, for 3 minutes. Drizzle the maple syrup over the apples and increase the heat to medium-high. Cook another 2 minutes, or until the apples are caramelized and just tender but not mushy. Remove from heat. |
| **1 teaspoon olive oil** | |
| **1 tart apple, peeled, cored, and thinly sliced** | |
| **1½ tablespoons maple syrup** | |
| **2 pieces (4 inches long) baguette or crusty bread** | *2* Preheat the broiler to high. Place the bread on a small broiler sheet. Divide the caramelized apples and their syrup between the two pieces of bread. Place the cheese on top of the apples and place the bread under the broiler (the distance from the heat doesn't really matter, but closer is better if you can manage it). Broil for 2 to 3 minutes (keep the oven light on and peek in after one minute, because broiler temperatures vary) or until the cheese is bubbling and melted. |
| **2½ ounces very thinly sliced Gruyère** | |

*Per serving: Calories 461 (From Fat 196); Fat 22g (Saturated 9g); Cholesterol 44mg; Sodium 459mg; Carbohydrate 52g (Dietary Fiber 5g); Protein 16g.*

*Source:* **culture:** the word on cheese *(Winter 2010)*

# Peppered Pear and Goat Cheese Scones

**Prep time:** 15 min • **Cook time:** 35 min • **Yield:** 6 large scones

These savory-sweet scones have a wonderful balance of flavors: tangy chèvre, floral pear, spicy black peppercorns. The addition of yogurt makes for a tender, moist texture similar to that of a muffin.

| Ingredients | Directions |
|---|---|
| 2 cups all-purpose flour | **1** Heat the oven to 375 degrees and line a baking sheet with parchment paper or a nonstick baking mat. In a medium bowl, combine the flour, baking powder, sugar, salt, and pepper. Add the butter and break into pea-size pieces with your fingertips. Sprinkle the pear pieces and goat cheese over the flour mixture and gently toss together, being careful not to break the cheese into smaller pieces. *Note:* It's important to cut the butter in fully. If it's too lumpy the dough has a hard time coming together, which leads to overmixing and a tough crust. |
| 1½ teaspoons baking powder | |
| 2 tablespoons sugar | |
| 1¼ teaspoons salt | |
| 1¼ teaspoons freshly cracked black pepper | |
| ½ cup cold, unsalted butter, cut into ½-inch cubes | |
| 1 medium pear, peeled, cored, and roughly chopped | **2** Whisk the milk into the yogurt to soften it. Then pour the yogurt mixture over the flour mixture and gently blend them together with a spatula, being careful not to break up the cheese. (The dough may look slightly dry and crumbly, but it will produce a very moist scone.) Divide the dough into six mounds on the baking sheet, leaving about 1 inch between them. |
| 4 ounces chèvre, broken into walnut-size pieces | |
| ½ cup whole or low-fat plain yogurt | |
| 2 tablespoons whole milk, plus more for brushing | **3** Brush the tops of each scone with a little milk and place the baking sheet in the center of the oven. Bake until lightly brown, about 35 minutes. Remove the sheet to a cooling rack. Serve warm or at room temperature. |

*Per serving: Calories 377 (From Fat 180); Fat 20g (Saturated 13g); Cholesterol 52mg; Sodium 669mg; Carbohydrate 40g (Dietary Fiber 2g); Protein 9g.*

**Tip:** When making scones, be careful not to overmix or overhandle the dough or batter. Doing so results in a tough, dry final product that more closely resembles a hockey puck!

**Vary It!** If you like smaller scones, divide the dough into 8 pieces and bake for about 30 minutes.

*Source:* **culture:** the word on cheese *(Winter 2009)*

# Stinky Cheese Omelet with Herb Topping

***Prep time:*** 10 min • ***Cook time:*** 20 min • ***Yield:*** 2 single-egg omelets

Jonathon Sawyer, the 30-year-old chef/owner of downtown Cleveland's Greenhouse Tavern, frequently changes the cheese in this menu staple, but he's especially besotted with Epoisses. Alternatives include Petit Munster, Dèlice du Jura, or a domestic washed-rind such as Meadow Creek Dairy's Grayson.

| Ingredients | Directions |
|---|---|
| **Herb Topping (see the following recipe)** | **1**   Prepare the Herb Topping. Set aside. |
| **2 large eggs, room temperature** | **2**   Crack 1 egg into a small bowl. Season to taste with the kosher salt and beat with a fork. |
| **Kosher salt, to taste** | |
| **1 tablespoon salted butter** | **3**   Heat an 8-inch nonstick skillet over medium heat. When the pan is hot, add half of the butter. After the butter stops foaming, pour the beaten egg into the center of the pan and stir vigorously with a spatula. As soon as the egg begins to lift from the pan, use the spatula to loosen the edges and shape the omelet. Remove from heat and let the omelet rest for about 3 minutes and then top with half of the Epoisses and 1 to 2 tablespoons of the herb topping (to taste). While the first omelet rests, prepare the second egg for the next omelet. |
| **2 tablespoons Epoisses** | |
| | **4**   After the omelet has rested, shake the pan to loosen it and then fold the omelet into thirds (lift up and fold one side toward the center; repeat with the other side). Slide the omelet onto one of the prepared plates. |
| | **5**   Wipe out the pan with a paper towel, add the remaining butter, and prepare the second. |

## Herb Topping

1 tablespoon extra virgin olive oil

Juice and zest of 1 lemon

Kosher salt, to taste

Freshly ground black pepper, to taste

½ cup chopped fresh soft herbs such as tarragon, chervil, Italian parsley, mint, or chives

*1* In a small bowl, whisk together the olive oil, lemon juice and zest, salt, and pepper. Adjust seasonings as necessary. Add the herbs and toss gently to coat.

*Per serving: Calories 248 (From Fat 195); Fat 22g (Saturated 9g); Cholesterol 243mg; Sodium 517mg; Carbohydrate 4g (Dietary Fiber 1g); Protein 10g.*

*Source: Chef Jonathon Sawyer, The Greenhouse Tavern, Cleveland, Ohio (**culture:** the word on cheese, Spring 2011)*

Herbs aren't just for omelets; toss them into pasta, rice, or other grains; add them to scrambled eggs, or include them in a meat marinade. Use them within a day or so; you can keep them fresh by placing them in a small airtight container, covering them with a damp (not wet) paper towel, and sealing the lid.

If an omelet seems too daunting, rest assured that cheese adores eggs, no matter how they're prepared. We love to add a dollop (or three) of ricotta to scrambled eggs, but crème fraiche is also nice. Baked (shirred) eggs can always benefit from a dusting of grated cheese before going into the oven, and what would a fried egg sandwich be without a blanket of melted cheese (lonely, that's what)?

# Blue Cheese and Potato Tartlets

***Prep time:*** 90 min • ***Cook time:*** 40–50 min • ***Yield:*** Six 4-inch pastries or one 9-inch tart

From chef MJ Adams of Rapid City, South Dakota's The Corn Exchange comes this rustic, satisfying tart. Earthy baby potatoes are a summertime treat where Adams lives, due to the short growing season. She suggests serving the tart at room temperature, paired with mizuna or arugula dressed with extra virgin olive oil and a squeeze of lemon juice, alongside a glass of chilled Sauvignon Blanc.

| *Ingredients* | *Directions* |
|---|---|
| ¾ **pound small fingerling or new potatoes, cut into ¼-inch slices** | *1* Prepare the pastry dough. After the dough chills or, if you prepared the dough the night before, when you're ready to make the tartlets, start the potatoes in cold water in a medium saucepan, bring to a boil, and lower heat to a simmer until they're al dente. (After about 4 to 5 minutes, pierce one with the tip of a paring knife; there should still be a little resistance.) Drain the water and allow the potatoes to cool. |
| ¾ **cup heavy cream** | |
| **1 large egg yolk** | |
| ¾ **cup of a rich, creamy blue cheese such as Montbriac, Cambozola, or Caveman Blue** | |
| ½ **tablespoon finely chopped rosemary or thyme (optional)** | *2* Preheat the oven to 350 degrees. When the pastry shells are chilled and the potatoes are cool, you're ready to assemble the tarts: In each shell, arrange 4 to 5 overlapping potato slices. Crumble 2 tablespoons of the cheese over the potatoes. Whisk the egg yolk into the cream and divide the mixture between the shells, being careful not to overfill (each shell should be about one-eighth full; leaving room keeps the mixture from bubbling over during baking). Sprinkle each tartlet with the chopped rosemary or thyme (optional). |
| **Fleur de sel or other large-grained sea salt, for garnish** | |
| **Pastry Dough (see the following recipe)** | |
| | *3* Bake the tartlets on the parchment-lined baking sheet for 40 to 50 minutes, or until they're golden brown and bubbly. Remove the tartlets from oven, sprinkle each tartlet with Fleur de sel, remove them from the baking sheet, and allow them to cool on a baking rack. If you're using removable tart pans, gently push up the bottoms a little while they're still warm to help release the crust. If you're using tart rings, lift them up when the tartlets have cooled, in case any cooked cream has stuck to the ring. |

## Pastry Dough

1½ cups all-purpose flour

⅛ teaspoon kosher salt

½ cup cold, unsalted butter or duck fat

3 to 4 tablespoons of cold tap water or sparkling water

*1* Line a baking sheet with parchment and set aside. Blend together the flour and salt. Using a small knife, cut the cold butter (or duck fat) into pieces and drop it into the flour mixture. Using your fingertips or a pastry cutter, gently work the flour into the butter, retaining some rough, pea-size pieces.

*2* Drizzle water, one tablespoon at a time, evenly over the flour mixture. Work each addition of water into the dough, being sure to add only as much water as you need to form the dough into a ball (how much water you need depends upon the air temperature and the humidity). Being careful not to overwork the dough, pat it into a disk, wrap it in plastic wrap or parchment paper, and let it rest for 30 minutes in refrigerator.

*3* Remove the dough from the refrigerator and cut it into 6 even portions. Roll each piece into a 5-inch circle, using a floured rolling pin. Gently press the pieces of dough into the tartlet pans or rings and trim away any excess. Chill the pastry shells on a parchment-covered baking sheet for 30 minutes.

*Per serving: Calories 446 (From Fat 282); Fat 31g (Saturated 19g); Cholesterol 130mg; Sodium 230mg; Carbohydrate 33g (Dietary Fiber 2g); Protein 9g.*

**Tip:** Go for the richest butter you can find. Chef Adams recommends a Plugra or European Valley.

**Tip:** To save time, make the dough the night before. Simply follow the instructions as written, expect cover the baking sheet with plastic wrap before placing it in the refrigerator in Step 2.

**Tip:** The key to a flaky crust is to keep the fat (here, the butter) cold while you work it into the flour, and to not overwork the dough. If your kitchen is warm and the butter begins to melt while you prepare this recipe, place the mixture in the refrigerator for a minute. Alternatively, prepare this tart in early morning, before temperatures rise.

**Vary it:** Substitute fresh chèvre for the blue cheese. You can also cook the potatoes whole for a more attractive presentation.

*Source: Chef MJ Adams, The Corn Exchange, Rapid City, South Dakota (**culture:** the word on cheese, Summer 2011)*

# New Classic Cheese Souffle

***Prep time:*** 20 min • ***Cook time:*** 60 min • ***Yield:*** Serves 4

**culture** magazine puts a spin on this most traditional of recipes. The mix of sheep milk cheeses elevates the soufflé to a new level, giving it a zesty edge. Serve with a simple green salad and a glass of crisp white wine for an impressive brunch or light dinner.

| *Ingredients* | *Directions* |
|---|---|
| 1 tablespoon unsalted butter, softened | **1** Position a rack on the bottom third of your oven and preheat the oven to 400 degrees. |
| 2 tablespoons finely grated pecorino cheese | |
| 2 cups heavy cream | **2** Generously butter the sides and bottom of a 1½-quart soufflé dish. Add the pecorino to the dish and shake to coat the dish evenly. Set aside. |
| 4 large egg yolks, at room temperature | |
| ¼ teaspoon sea salt | **3** In a 2-quart heavy-bottomed saucepan, bring the cream to a boil over medium heat. Reduce the heat to maintain a brisk simmer. Continue simmering, stirring constantly with a heatproof spatula to prevent sticking, until the cream has reduced by nearly half and thickened to the consistency of a sauce, about 25 minutes. Remove from the heat. (***Note:*** Watch the cream carefully, because it tends to boil over. If it bubbles too high in the pan, whisk it to reduce the foaming.) |
| Pinch of cayenne pepper | |
| Pinch of nutmeg | |
| Pinch of white pepper | |
| 3 ounces of a buttery sheep milk cheese, coarsely grated or shredded to make ¾ to 1 cup | |
| 5 large egg whites, at room temperature | **4** Place the egg yolks in a small bowl, whisking gently; very slowly stir in a small amount of the sauce (your goal is to warm the yolks so that you can add them to the cream without causing them to scramble). Stir the tempered egg yolks into the cream. Add the salt, cayenne, nutmeg, and white pepper. Add the sheep milk cheese and stir until smooth. Cover the pan and set aside. (***Note:*** The sauce can be prepared up to 2 hours in advance.) |
| 1 ounce (⅓ cup) Zamorano sheep milk cheese, coarsely grated or shredded | |

**5** Beat the egg whites just until stiff peaks form. Fold about one-fourth of the whites into the cheese sauce; then fold in one-third of the Zamorano. Continue folding in equal quantities of egg white and Zamorano until all have been added. Transfer the result to the prepared soufflé dish (The batter will not fill the dish).

**6** Place the soufflé dish on the oven rack and immediately reduce the oven temperature to 375 degrees. Bake until the top of the soufflé has puffed up and turned golden brown, about 25 minutes (***Note:*** The center should move only slightly when the dish is jiggled). Serve immediately, scooping from top to bottom with two spoons. Include some of the creamy center with each serving.

*Per serving: Calories 636 (From Fat 554); Fat 62g (Saturated 37g); Cholesterol 412mg; Sodium 470mg; Carbohydrate 5g (Dietary Fiber 0g); Protein 18g.*

***Tip:*** If you can't find the Zamorano, substitute Manchego or Iberico. Another good buttery sheep milk cheese is Marisa (Carr Valley Cheese Company).

***Note:*** The trick to a successful soufflé (besides following the directions to the letter) is to not overmix, because that deflates the egg whites. You must use a rubber spatula for folding, as well.

*Source:* **culture:** the word on cheese *(Fall 2010)*

Souffles have a tendency to intimidate even professional cooks or chefs. While it's true they're delicate due to the fragile structural composition of the beaten egg whites, soufflés really aren't difficult to make (unless you live at high altitude, in which case you may need to play around a bit with the recipe). The trick is to not overfold the ingredients; doing so causes the egg whites to deflate, resulting in a flat or soggy soufflé. At worst, if your soufflé does fail to rise or collapses before you have a chance to serve it (note that this will occur, so you want to bring it from oven to table as quickly as possible), do as the professionals do: pass it off as a "custard" or "molten cake"!

# The Sweet Hereafter

Even if you're not serving a cheese plate for dessert, there's still a surprisingly diverse variety of cheeses that take well to sweet applications. Blues; many fresh cheeses; buttery, semi-soft types such as Havarti or Carmody — all can work with fruit, whether it's fresh, dried, or incorporated into baked goods. Cheese also lends itself well to baked sweets, and as we show you in a later recipe, even ice cream.

You'll notice that most of the following recipes call for fruit. We're big on seasonal fruit because, well, it's seasonal. There's something really special about waiting for the first peaches of the season or savoring the last of the fall pear crop.

Although we live in an era when getting "seasonal" ingredients year-round is possible, that doesn't mean the product you're getting is good, or even safe. The older produce is, the more it degrades, losing vital nutrients and flavor. Produce imported from developing countries may also be sprayed with pesticides that are banned in the U.S. (not only is this practice bad for you, but it's also detrimental to the health of farm workers and their families and communities). In addition, "organic" produce imported from these countries may not be; there isn't an international watchdog agency to oversee farming methods.

We prefer to support local growers by purchasing sustainably grown or raised foods (note that this doesn't mean they need to be certified organic — a process that is costly and time-consuming and beyond the economic means of many small farmers; see the sidebar "Why 'small and local' beats 'organic'" for details). We believe this strategy is the best way to increase food security and keep family farms in business.

Better yet, why not buy extra seasonal produce and can or freeze it so that you can enjoy it year-round — sustainably!

---

# Why "small and local" beats "organic"

*Organic* is a misleading term, now that the federal government oversees certification: A 1,000-acre organic broccoli farm is still contributing to soil erosion and nutrient depletion, and it's hard on farm workers, who must perform the same repetitive movements throughout the day. Also, many small farms can't afford to become certified organic, or they may object to government interjection.

We're not saying organic is bad — and certainly it's better than conventional (that is, grown with the aid of chemical fertilizers, pesticides, and herbicides) — it's just better in general if you can purchase organic produce from a small-scale farmer or be open to purchasing non-organic certified product.

Get to know your local farmers and let your tastebuds be your guide. For us, buying something local, delicious, and conventionally grown is better than buying something organic, less tasty, and grown 3,000 miles away, but ultimately, the choice is yours.

One last thing: Don't suffer from food guilt. The world won't end if you don't buy that organic apple or purchase an out-of-season apricot. Our goal is simply to encourage you to relearn the joys of seasonal eating, because it heightens the pleasures of the table so much.

# Grilled Peaches with Mascarpone, Pistachios, and Raspberries

***Prep time:*** 5 min • ***Cook time:*** 10–15 min • ***Yield:*** Serves 4

It doesn't get any easier than this. The key is great fruit, so resist the temptation to use something out of season or unripe. This recipe also works well with apricots, nectarines, or plums; you can also poach or bake the fruit in a simple syrup of sugar and water.

Regarding the raspberries (you may also substitute blackberries, Marionberries, and so on): Don't wash these delicate fruits because they absorb water like a sponge, even if given a quick rinse. (This is why we recommend buying organic or unsprayed domestic product.)

| *Ingredients* | *Directions* |
|---|---|
| **4 ripe (but not squishy) local peaches, halved, pit discarded** | *1* Preheat the grill until the coals are white hot. Lightly brush the cut halves of the peaches with olive oil. |
| **1 teaspoon extra virgin olive oil** | *2* When the coals are white hot, place the peaches, cut side-down, on the grill. Do not move them for several minutes, or they'll stick and tear and won't caramelize properly. Ideally, you want the fruit to soften and shrivel slightly and for the cut surface to get brown and sticky — not burned. If necessary, however, use tongs to relocate the peaches to a cooler location on the grill if they're burning. |
| **1 container (about 8 ounces) of mascarpone, room temperature** | |
| **¼ cup toasted pistachios, coarsely chopped** | |
| **1 pint raspberries (do not wash)** | *3* Remove the peaches from grill and place the two halves, one propped up against the other, on each of four dessert plate. Add a large dollop of marscarpone on top of the peaches and garnish with the chopped pistachios. Scatter a small amount of raspberries around the peaches. Serve immediately. |

*Per serving: Calories 379 (From Fat 284); Fat 32g (Saturated 15g); Cholesterol 73mg; Sodium 65mg; Carbohydrate 22g (Dietary Fiber 7g); Protein 7g.*

***Tip:*** The peaches (or other fruit) fare best when they're not directly over the heat source but close enough to benefit from its warmth. If you're using a gas grill, don't place them directly over the burners. Better to go slow and long than high and hot, which will result in scorched, rather than caramelized, fruit.

*Source: Laurel Miller, The Sustainable Kitchen*

# Aged Gouda and Walnut Biscotti

***Prep time:*** 2½ hrs • ***Cook time:*** 1 hr 15 min • ***Yield:*** 4 dozen biscotti

From chef Terrance Brennan, the successful restaurateur behind a number of eateries including New York's Artisanal Fromagerie, Bistro, and Wine Bar, comes this creative take on traditional biscotti. Serve with a sweet dessert wine or ice cream (but they're also delicious alongside soup or salad).

| *Ingredients* | *Directions* |
|---|---|
| 2¼ teaspoons (1 envelope) active-dry yeast | **1** In a medium-size bowl, combine the yeast and the ½ cup lukewarm water, stirring to dissolve the yeast. Set aside for 5 minutes until creamy. (If the yeast fails to foam, it means the water was too cool to activate it; too warm, and it will kill the yeast.) |
| ½ cup warm water | |
| 2¾ cups unbleached all-purpose flour, divided, plus more for kneading | |
| 1 tablespoon sugar | **2** Add ¾ cup of the flour to the yeast mixture to make a rough, wet dough. Cover with plastic wrap and let rise in a warm, draft-free place for 1 hour to create a sponge (starter). |
| ½ teaspoon salt | |
| ⅓ cup plus 1 tablespoon warm water | |
| 1¾ cups shredded aged Gouda | **3** Combine the remaining 2 cups of flour, the sugar, and the salt in a large bowl. Make a well in the center and add the sponge. Add the ⅓ cup plus 1 tablespoon warm water and the Gouda, butter, and walnuts. Mix to form a rough dough. Transfer the dough to a lightly floured surface and knead for 3 minutes, adding as little flour as possible to keep the dough from sticking; in fact, for this recipe, you may not need to add any flour at all (adding too much will make the biscotti tough). Invert the mixing bowl over the dough and let it rest for 15 minutes. |
| 6 tablespoons unsalted butter, softened at room temperature | |
| ½ cup walnuts, finely chopped | |
| | **4** After the dough has rested, sprinkle it with a little flour if it's too sticky to work with, and then divide the dough into 2 equal pieces. Shape each piece into a 12-inch-long loaf. |
| | **5** Arrange the loaves on a large baking sheet lined with parchment paper, leaving at least a 2-inch space between the loaves so that they can expand. Cover with a clean, damp kitchen towel and set aside in a warm place to rise for 45 minutes. |

**6** Heat the oven to 350 degrees. Uncover the loaves and set them aside for 15 minutes. Bake the loaves for 15 minutes, rotate the baking sheet to evenly brown the loaves, and bake 15 minutes longer. Remove the loaves from the oven and let cool for 20 minutes. Reduce the oven temperature to 200 degrees.

**7** Place the loaves on a cutting board. With a serrated knife, cut the loaves diagonally into ½-inch-thick slices. Arrange the slices, cut side up, on a parchment-lined sheet pan (you can reuse the previous liners, as long as they're not burned) and bake until toasted, about 45 minutes. Transfer to a wire rack to cool. Store in an airtight container.

*Per serving: Calories 63 (From Fat 31); Fat 3g (Saturated 2g); Cholesterol 9mg; Sodium 59mg; Carbohydrate 6g (Dietary Fiber 0g); Protein 2g.*

***Tip:*** 100–110 degrees Fahrenheit is typically a good temp to activate yeast without killing it.

*Source: Chef Terrance Brennan, Artisanal, New York (****culture:*** the word on cheese, *Fall 2009)*

# Move over, Lorraine: Other cheesy ideas for quiche and tarts

Eggs, pastry crust, and cheese: the holy trinity of saturated fats (everything in moderation, including moderation)! This trio — or just a tart shell minus the egg filling — is so versatile and adaptable, we'd be hard-pressed to list all the possible combinations here. For inspiration, here are some ideas, based around the seasons:

✔ **Spring:** Asparagus and Gruyère quiche; spring onion, chèvre, and chicken-apple sausage tart

✔ **Summer:** Ricotta and fresh herb quiche; tomato, pecorino, and dry-cured olive tart

✔ **Fall:** Cheddar and smoked ham quiche; pear and blue cheese tart

✔ **Winter:** Chard and Beaufort quiche; caramelized onion, bacon, and blue cheese tart

# Rhubarb-Brown Sugar Cake with Strawberry-Rhubarb Compote and Crème Fraiche

**Prep time:** 60 min • **Cook time:** 55 min • **Yield:** Serves 8

Chef MJ Adams of The Corn Exchange in Rapid City, South Dakota, loves this homey dessert. Rhubarb has a late and short-but-sweet season in South Dakota — May through June — and Adams celebrates its brief appearance in the market with this cake. Garnished with sparkling sugar and served with sides of crème fraiche and compote, it transforms into the ideal brunch dish. For this recipe, Adams uses Plugra or European Valley Brand, both of which are richer than common store-brand butter.

| *Ingredients* | *Directions* |
|---|---|
| 1 stick (4 ounces) plus 2 tablespoons softened, unsalted butter | *1* Preheat the oven to 350 degrees. Grease a 9-inch cake pan; then line it with a parchment circle and grease that. Dust the parchment with flour. Set aside. |
| 1½ cups light brown sugar, such as muscovado, plus 1 tablespoon for dusting | *2* By hand, cream the butter and the brown sugar; then add the eggs one at a time until combined. Add the buttermilk to the butter mixture and lightly stir. Sift the flour, baking soda, and baking power together, and add salt. Add the dry ingredients and the rhubarb to the butter mixture and mix everything together, using same technique as for making muffins: fold until the ingredients just come together. Don't overmix: If you still have a few specks of dry ingredients, that's okay. |
| 2 large eggs | |
| 1 teaspoon baking soda | |
| 1 teaspoon baking powder | |
| 1 cup buttermilk | |
| 2 cups all-purpose flour (Adams prefers King Arthur brand) | |
| 1½ cups fresh rhubarb, sliced into nickel-sized pieces | *3* Place the batter in the greased and floured cake pan. Sprinkle the top of the cake with the almonds (optional) and the remaining tablespoon of the light brown sugar, and the sparkling sugar. |
| Pinch of kosher salt | |
| 1 tablespoon sparkling sugar, for dusting | |
| ½ cup almond slices, plus 1 tablespoon for garnish (optional) | *4* Bake for 55 minutes or until a toothpick comes out clean when inserted into the cake's center. Remove the cake from the oven and allow it to cool completely before removing it from the pan. To remove the cake from the pan, run a thin knife around cake pan; then place a plate on top of cake pan and flip both plate and cake over to release. Flip cake back over onto a cake plate or cake stand. |
| Compote (see the following recipe) | |
| Crème fraiche, for passing | |

*5* Place slices of cake on a small plate and pass dishes of crème fraiche and compote.

## Compote

2 tablespoons unsalted butter

½ cup raw or white sugar

Juice from half of a lemon

4 ounces sweet wine, such as Gewurtztraminer or Moscato

3 cups of rhubarb cut into slightly larger pieces than for cake

16 ounces (2 cups) of hulled ripe strawberries, quartered (or halved if small)

*1* In a large sauté pan, melt the butter. Add the rhubarb, sugar, the juice of the lemon, and the wine. Bring the mixture to a simmer and cook for about 10 minutes or until the rhubarb is a bit al dente. (Adams suggests leaving the rhubarb a little firm, to give the compote some texture and contrast.)

*2* Add the strawberries and simmer 5 minutes, or until the strawberries are soft but not mushy. Cool to room temperature before serving.

*Per serving: Calories 495 (From Fat 175); Fat 20g (Saturated 10g); Cholesterol 93mg; Sodium 719mg; Carbohydrate 75g (Dietary Fiber 4g); Protein 8.*

*Tip:* You can find sparkling sugar at baking supply stores or online at www.indiatree.com, but it's not a necessary addition to the recipe.

*Vary it:* Substitute 12 ounces of fresh blueberries for the rhubarb.

*Source: Chef MJ Adams, The Corn Exchange, Rapid City, South Dakota (**culture:** the word on cheese, Summer 2011)*

A *compote* refers to fresh or dried fruit stewed in a sugar syrup. The liquid is usually water-based and may contain aromatics such as herbs or spices. We love compotes because they're so versatile and seasonally adaptable. In winter, for example, try a citrus compote with a ginger-cinnamon (or star anise, cardamom, and so on) syrup. A wedge of blue or mold-ripened or fresh goat cheese alongside makes for a light, refreshing finale after a heavy, cold-weather meal.

# Dried Apricot-Goat Cheese Tart

*Prep time:* 40 min, plus resting time • *Cook time:* 1 hr • *Yield:* One 9-inch tart

Something magical happens when apricots and goat cheese get together. Their respective tangy, creamy, and sweet, floral qualities meld into a harmonious duo that is especially lovely in tart form. **Note:** You need a springform pan for this recipe.

| *Ingredients* | *Directions* |
|---|---|
| Tart crust (see the following recipe) | *1* Prepare the Tart Crust. When the crust is finished baking, remove it from the oven and reduce the oven temperature to 350 degrees. |
| 10 ounces fresh chèvre, room temperature | |
| 8 ounces Neufchâtel-style cream cheese, room temperature | *2* For the filling, in the large bowl of an electric mixer, beat together the goat cheese, cream cheese, and the ¾ cup sugar until well-mixed. Beat in the eggs one at a time until blended. Scrape down the sides of the bowl, add the cream, and beat until very smooth. |
| ¾ cup sugar | |
| 2 large eggs | |
| ¼ cup heavy cream | *3* Pour the filling into the cooked tart crust and bake 35 to 40 minutes, or until the filling is set in the center and tiny cracks appear at the edges. Cool the tart in the pan for 15 minutes. Remove the sides of the springform pan and cool the tart completely. Refrigerate at least 4 hours or overnight. |
| 2 cups dried apricots | |
| 1 cup water | |
| ½ cup sugar, plus a little for sprinkling | |
| Reserved almonds from crust (see the following recipe) | *4* To make the apricot topping, divide each apricot in half along its seam. Combine the apricots, water, and the ½ cup sugar in a saucepan. Stir and simmer until the apricots are soft and the liquid is reduced by half. Set aside. |
| | *5* When you're ready to serve, arrange the apricot topping to cover the filling. If desired, sprinkle the top with a little sugar and place the tart under the broiler to brown the fruit slightly. Brush the side of the tart with some of the leftover apricot syrup, press the reserved ground almonds (from the preparation of the crust) into the sides to cover, and serve. |

## Tart Crust

²⁄₃ cup toasted almond slices

1 cup all-purpose flour

½ cup sugar

½ teaspoon salt

1 stick (4 ounces) cold, unsalted butter, cut into small cubes

1 large egg

¼ teaspoon almond extract

*1* Heat the oven to 375 degrees. In a food processor fitted with a chopping blade, coarsely grind the almonds. Set aside 3 tablespoons of the ground almonds for later.

*2* Add the flour, sugar, and salt to the almonds remaining in the processor. Pulse to mix and finely grind the almonds. Add the butter and pulse briefly, just until the butter is in fine pebbles and distributed throughout.

*3* In a small bowl, whisk together the egg and almond extract. With the processor running, add the egg mixture and mix briefly, until a soft dough forms.

*4* Press the dough evenly into the bottom of a 9-inch springform pan and bake 22 to 24 minutes, or until golden.

*Per serving: Calories 675 (From Fat 311); Fat 35g (Saturated 19g); Cholesterol 159mg; Sodium 421mg; Carbohydrate 79g (Dietary Fiber 4g); Protein 16g.*

***Tip:*** Pour the filling over a store bought (or homemade) graham cracker crust, and use a good-quality apricot jam as the topping as a time-saver.

***Vary it:*** Poach fresh, in-season apricots in simple syrup instead of using dried fruit, and serve them alongside the tart.

*Source:* **culture:** the word on cheese *(Winter 2008)*

# Ginger-Poached Pears with Roquefort-Honey Ice Cream

***Prep time:*** 1 hr • ***Cook time:*** 20 min • ***Yield:*** Six ½-cup servings (about 3 cups of ice cream)

Adapted from an ice cream recipe in **culture** magazine, this fall or winter dessert combines gently spiced poached pears with an intense, nearly savory ice cream. If you want to add a hint more sweetness, drizzle the ice cream with a bit of honey before serving; you can also serve it alongside a seasonal fruit tart.

| *Ingredients* | *Directions* |
|---|---|
| **4 Bosc pears, peeled and blossom end dug out**<br><br>**3 cups sugar**<br><br>**8 cups water**<br><br>**Six ¼-inch-thick peeled slices of ginger, bashed with the flat edge of a knife to release juices**<br><br>**Two cinnamon sticks**<br><br>**5 star anise pods**<br><br>**8 tablespoons premium honey**<br><br>**4 ounces Roquefort or other pungent blue cheese**<br><br>**1 cup whole milk**<br><br>**4 large egg yolks**<br><br>**1 cup heavy cream (not ultrapasteurized)**<br><br>**Chopped, toasted walnuts or pecans, for garnish (optional)**<br><br>**Edible flowers, for garnish (optional)** | *1* Warm the honey in a small saucepan; then set aside. Crumble the cheese into a large bowl and set aside.<br><br>*2* Warm the milk in a medium saucepan. In a medium bowl, whisk together the egg yolks. When the milk is warm (about 100 degrees), slowly pour it into the egg yolks, whisking constantly; then scrape the warmed egg yolk-milk mixture back into the pan. Stir the mixture constantly over medium heat, scraping the bottom as you stir, until the mixture thickens and coats the back of a spoon. Basically, you're making a custard.<br><br>*3* Add the crumbled cheese to the hot custard and stir until most of the cheese is melted; some small bits are fine and add texture to the finished ice cream. Add the cream and honey to the custard-cheese mixture and stir over an ice bath until the mixture is cool. Chill thoroughly, about 20 minutes, in the refrigerator.<br><br>*4* When the ice-cream mixture is completely chilled, process it in an ice cream maker according to the manufacturer's instructions. |

**5** To poach the pears, bring the water, sugar, ginger, cinnamon, and star anise to a boil; then lower the heat to a gentle simmer and add the pears. Poach the pears until they're tender when pierced with the tip of a paring knife. Using a slotted spoon, remove the pears from the poaching liquid and set upright on a plate to cool. Turn off heat and reserve poaching liquid.

**6** A few minutes before serving, spoon a bit of the reserved poaching liquid over each pear to moisten it slightly (do this on the holding plate, not on your serving plate). Place a pear in the middle of each serving plate (cut a thin slice off the bottom of each pear so it doesn't fall over), and place a scoop of ice cream next to it. Garnish the ice cream with chopped nuts and place 2 to 3 edible flowers on the plate (optional). Serve immediately.

*Per serving: Calories 450 (From Fat 228); Fat 25g (Saturated 15g); Cholesterol 219mg; Sodium 386mg; Carbohydrate 52g (Dietary Fiber 3g); Protein 9g.*

*Tip:* An easy way to peel ginger is to scrape it with the edge of a spoon.

*Source:* **culture:** the word on cheese *(Summer 2009); Pear recipe: Laurel Miller, The Sustainable Kitchen*

# Chapter 19

# Making Cheese at Home

## In This Chapter

▶ Knowing what equipment you need for home cheesemaking

▶ The how and where of sourcing milk

▶ Beginning cheesemaker recipes

**Recipes in This Chapter**

▶ Ricotta

▶ Crème fraiche

▶ Chèvre

▶ Mozzarella

*G*iven the increasing availability of great cheeses in supermarkets, specialty shops, and farmers' markets, why on earth would you bother to make your own? We're not afraid to admit we're lazy cooks, but there's something magical about homemade cheese. For one, making your own cheese is surprisingly easy and inexpensive. Plus turning milk into curd is incredibly gratifying, for adults as well as kids. Many people find home cheesemaking a relaxing pastime, and it's also a great way to get friends and family involved in your next dinner party.

If nothing else, few things taste as good as fresh cheese, still warm from the stockpot. Spread on toast, eaten with berries or grilled vegetables, or just drizzled with extra virgin olive oil and a pinch of sea salt, homemade cheese hits all the right notes.

One caveat before you get all inspired and start cranking out vats of cheese: No matter how delicious, ***selling your creations is against federal law*** unless you have the proper certifications. Despite your best intentions, homemade cheese can be a potential source of foodborne illness. If you genuinely want to explore making cheese on a retail level, the best thing to do is enroll in food-safety *and* cheesemaking courses: See whether your state has an artisan cheese guild, which can offer educational resources for guidance. Also, many higher education institutions including culinary schools are adding cheesemaking to their curriculums. *The Joy of Cheesemaking* (see the later sidebar "Taking your cheesemaking to the next level") has a list of U.S. resources.

# Sourcing Your Equipment and Supplies

While some styles of fresh cheese require little more in the way of equipment than a stockpot, ladle, and thermometer, other varieties call for considerably more equipment and other supplies, such as rennet and cultures. Fortunately, all of these items are readily available at hardware and cooking stores and through online cheesemaking suppliers. Our best advice is to start simple, with ricotta and work your way up from other fresh styles to bloomy-rind varieties such as camembert.

## Equip yourself

It's true that cheesemaking (aside from ricotta) does require investment in a few key items, but odds are, you already own a stockpot and a slotted spoon. The remaining equipment, which you'll need for anything more complicated than ricotta, can be purchased directly or ordered online from a cheesemaking supply company (you can find a few suppliers in the sidebar "Sources for cheesemaking supplies").

Here's a list of basic cheesemaking equipment and supplies necessary for producing most fresh styles of cheese (check out Figure 19-1 for a look at some of these supplies):

- **Sanitizer or iodine:** Sanitation, above all else, is paramount in cheesemaking. Dirty equipment, work surfaces, or milk won't just result in a bad-tasting cheese: it can have dire effects upon human health. Keep your equipment and hands clean, and your cheese will remain free of unwanted hitchhikers (bad bacteria).

- **Thermometer:** A thermometer is crucial for cheesemaking. Look for high-end, dial-equipped versions for the greatest accuracy.

- **Ladle:** You need a perforated flat ladle to transfer curds to forms or to a ripening mat for draining. No need to buy one from a cheese supply: any decent kitchen store will have one.

- **Whisk:** Whisks are useful for stirring and cutting curd. Look for a good-sized, stainless steel balloon whisk (its more bulbous shape aerates liquid ingredients such as egg whites or, in this case, curd).

- **10-inch flat-blade knife:** This knife is necessary for releasing whey from newly formed curd.

✔ **Cheesecloth:** You use the cheesecloth to drain curds and line forms; you can purchase these at most grocery, drug, or fabric stores.

✔ **Draining bag:** You can use cheesecloth, but this special bag makes removing the whey from the curd much easier. Draining bags are reuseable, and they stand up to the abuse (like squeezing and wringing) necessary for removing whey.

✔ **Ripening mat:** A ripening mat is a clean, ventilated surface on which new cheeses are ripened (aged). You can also use them to drain cheeses that don't go in a form or for drying tools.

✔ **Ripening pan:** Aging and ripening cheese is one of the most technical aspects of cheesemaking. This deep, see-through plastic tub allows you to keep cheese clean and in a controlled environment, but enables you to view its progress. Think of it as a portable, mini cheese cave.

✔ **Forms (molds):** Usually made of plastic and perforated, forms come in a variety of shapes and sizes: cylindrical, pyramid, and round. You most commonly use forms when making fresh, surface-ripened, or washed-rind cheeses. (***Note:*** Forms are more commonly known as *molds,* but we prefer to use the term *form* to avoid confusion with the organisms used in cheesemaking.)

## Sources for cheesemaking supplies

If you don't have a cheesemaking supplier in your area, check out the following suppliers:

✔ **The Beverage People:** Cheese cultures, kits, and forms (as well as wine and beer making supplies); 800-544-1867, www.thebeveragepeople.com.

✔ **Dairy Connection:** Equipment and cultures specifically for home use; 608-242-9030, www.dairyconnection.com.

✔ **Hoegger Supply Company:** Equipment, kits, churns, and more; 800-221-4628, www.hoeggergoatsupply.com.

✔ **New England Cheesemaking Supply Company:** Everything you could ever need, plus workshops; 413-397-2012, www.cheesemaking.com.

✔ **The Cheesemaker:** Equipment, kits, cultures, and workshops; 414-745-5483, www.thecheesemaker.com.

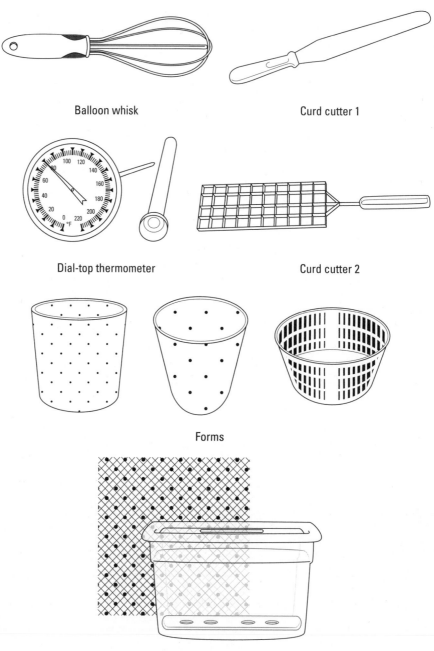

Balloon whisk

Curd cutter 1

Dial-top thermometer

Curd cutter 2

Forms

Ripening mat & pan

**Figure 19-1:**
Cheese-
making
equipment.

# *Getting the (rest of the) goods for cheesemaking*

After you have your equipment lined up, you'll require some of the following "additives" in order to coagulate the milk and aid in the development of specific cheese styles. All are readily available from online cheesemaking supplies:

- ✔ **Calcium chloride:** Calcium chloride assists in coagulation. When called for in a recipe, it's usually added with the rennet to create a firmer curd.

- ✔ **Rennet:** A necessity for most cheesemaking, rennet is a coagulating agent that's made either from an enzyme obtained from the stomach of baby ruminants (cud-chewing mammals) such as calves, goat kids, or lambs, or in a microbial form (also known as vegetarian rennet). It takes only a few drops of rennet to coagulate a vat of milk, so you won't need to purchase it often. Rennet is available in liquid, powder, or tablet form.

- ✔ **Cultures:** These are beneficial bacteria added during cheese production to aid in the development of a specific style of cheese (such as, say, a bloomy rind or a cheddar). The culture has a strong impact upon the rind, aroma, texture, smell, and flavor of the final product.

## *Where to get your milk*

The most important thing about making cheese at home — besides being vigilant about sanitation — is to use great milk. Locally-produced milk — raw or pasteurized — is usually the freshest and will make the largest volume of curd. Look for it at your local farmers' market, food co-op, grocery, or natural foods store.

Your cheese is only as good as its primary ingredient, so seeking out a local farmer who will sell you raw milk is worth it, if selling raw milk is legal in your state or county. That said, a dairy farmer and cheesemaker we know once gave us this advice: Never purchase raw milk from a dairy farm you haven't visited. You want to be able to see for yourself the sanitation practices; a reputable farmer shouldn't object to this request (an outright refusal, according to our source, is a red flag). Note that, by law, visitors aren't allowed into creameries without taking special sanitation precautions, so you may not be able to examine things up close, but you can get a good sense of how clean an operation is just by touring the property.

If you use pasteurized milk, you have to add calcium chloride (available online through a cheesemaking supply) to get a good yield. But don't use ultrapasteurized milk, which can only be used for making yogurt.

## Udderly wonderful: Cow share agreements

The sale of raw, fluid milk is illegal in many parts of the United States due to health concerns over diseases that may be transmitted if the milk is contaminated (see Chapter 2 for the details on potential public health issues related to unpasteurized milk).

To circumvent these restrictions, consumers and dairy farmers in some states have come up with a legal way to exchange raw milk. With a *cow* (or *herd) share agreement,* consumers pay the farmer a fee for boarding their cow, or a share of a cow (or goat), and in return the consumer gets a share of the milk. Some states prohibit cow shares, so be sure to check the laws of your state before entering into such an agreement.

If you'd like information on whether raw milk is legal in your state or county, or how to find a cow or goat share in your area, contact the Farm-to-Consumer Legal Defense Fund at www.farmtoconsumer.org or go to www.realmilk.com/cowfarmshare.html.

# A Quick Review of the Basic Cheesemaking Steps

Believe it or not, making cheese isn't a particularly complicated endeavor, although crafting *good* — or great — cheese is. But there's no reason why you shouldn't try your hand at cheesemaking at home. We explain the process in detail in Chapter 2, but here's a quick review of the basic steps:

1. **Be sure all of your equipment and work surfaces are clean and sanitized.**

2. **Bring the milk "up to temperature" and add the starter culture.**

   Warming the milk to the right temperature simulates the animal's body temperature and activates the starter culture. The job of the starter culture is to acidify the milk in order to increase the population of beneficial bacteria. When the pH is low enough (about 4.7 or so), the milk begins to coagulate.

   The starter culture is beneficial bacteria that aids in the development of a specific style of cheese (say, a surface-ripened or a cheddar).

3. **Add a coagulant, such as rennet.**

   The proteins in milk coagulate (clump together) to form curds, which are a combination of the butterfat and casein (a main protein in milk).

4. **Place the curd in a form, if necessary, and drain the whey.**

   Whey is the liquid that remains after cheese production.

5. **Salt the cheese or wash it with brine.**

   Brine is a saltwater solution used to wash a ripening cheese in order to encourage the rind to develop.

   *Note:* The cheese recipes in this chapter don't call for brine; this step is included to provide the full scope of the cheesemaking process.

6. **Allow the cheese to ripen (age).**

   *Note:* The cheese recipes in this chapter are all fresh, and require no to very little aging.

# Four Cheeses to Make on Your Own

All of the following recipes are easy enough for beginners or children assisted by adults. It may take a few tries to yield the ideal results because there are always variables with regard to quality of milk, temperature, and technique. All of these cheeses have a short shelf life, but that shouldn't be a problem because few people can resist just-made cheese, warm from the stockpot!

## Taking your cheesemaking to the next level

The recipes in this section are all very basic, beginning recipes for fresh cheeses. If you find yourself smitten with cheesemaking, you can move on to more advanced techniques and styles, and from there, you can experiment on your own. Here are some books that can help you practice and develop your cheesemaking skills:

✔ *Home Cheese Making: Recipes for 75 Delicious Cheeses*, by Ricki Carroll (Storey Publishing, LLC): Unofficially dubbed the "home cheesemaker's bible," this is excellent for beginners. Recipes include soft, hard, and mold-ripened varieties.

✔ *Artisan Cheese Making at Home: Techniques and Recipes for Mastering World-Class Cheeses*, by Mary Karlin (Ten Speed Press): A wonderful, recent (2011) release from a popular cooking instructor and food writer who specializes in cheesemaking classes.

✔ *Making Artisan Cheese: 50 Fine Cheeses That You Can Make in Your Own Kitchen*, by Tim Smith (Quarry Books): For the intermediate home cheesemaker, the recipes in this book include blues and cheddar, as well as tips on assembling cheese plates and wine and beer pairings.

✔ *The Joy of Cheesemaking*, by Jody M. Farnham and Marc Druart (Skyhorse Publishing): This book provides more technical advice, including resources for those interested in taking their cheesemaking to a more professional level. The authors are the Administrative Director of the Vermont Institute of Artisan Cheese (VIAC) and VIAC's Master Cheesemaker, respectively.

# Ricotta

**Prep time:** 20 min, plus overnight  •  **Cook time:** 5–10 min  •  **Yield:** about 1¼ cups (10 ounces)

Unless you're fortunate enough to live near a specialty food or cheese shop that sells fresh ricotta, your best bet is to make your own. It's fast and easy, and the sweet, milky flavor and fluffy texture surpass that of commercially made ricottas.

| Equipment | Directions |
|---|---|
| **Nonreactive saucepan** **Dial-top thermometer** **Ladle** **Cheesecloth** **Strainer** **Bowl** *Ingredients* ½ **cup heavy cream** **4 cups whole milk (not ultrapasteurized)** **2 tablespoons freshly squeezed lemon juice** **Pinch of kosher salt** | **1** In a nonreactive saucepan, combine the cream, milk, and lemon juice. Cook over medium-low heat, stirring constantly to prevent scorching, until the mixture reaches 205 degrees. (Remember, cheesemaking is a science, and temperature is crucial.) <br><br> **2** Remove the saucepan from the heat and let the mixture rest for about 15 minutes. During this time, the curds and whey will separate. <br><br> **3** Line a strainer with cheesecloth and set the strainer over a bowl. Ladle the curds into the strainer to drain the whey. Cover the strainer and bowl tightly with plastic wrap. Then refrigerate overnight to let the whey drain. <br><br> **4** Discard the whey and wipe the bowl dry. Transfer the ricotta to the bowl. Stir in the salt, cover the cheese tightly, and refrigerate until needed. Alternatively, you may transfer the ricotta to an airtight container. Refrigerated, this cheese will keep for up to 3 days. |

*Per ¼ cup serving: Calories 204 (From Fat 138); Fat 15g (Saturated 10g); Cholesterol 59g; Sodium 161mg; Carbohydrate 10g (Dietary Fiber 0g); Protein 7g.*

**Vary It!** Before serving, add chopped fresh herbs or orange (or lemon) zest and a bit of honey to the ricotta; then stir to combine.

**Tip:** If you have difficulty finding non-ultrapasteurized milk, look at Whole Foods or similar grocery chains, in the organic section of larger grocery stores, or in independent natural food stores.

*Source:* The Paley's Place Cookbook: Recipes and Stories from the Pacific Northwest *(Ten Speed Press, 2008), by Vitaly and Kimberly Paley.*

# Crème Fraiche

*Prep time:* 12 hrs • *Cook time:* 10 min • *Yield:* 1 pint

While not a true cheese, crème fraiche — which is like a more luxurious sour cream — is a cultured dairy product. It's usually sold in the cheese department and is wonderful used as a thickener or garnish for soups, dolloped on baked potatoes or grilled or roasted vegetables, or served in place of whipped cream for a twist on tradition. This recipe came to us from The Beverage People, a cheesemaking supply in Northern California.

Note that some crème fraiche recipes call for buttermilk and live-culture yogurt rather than a mesophilic culture. While easier, using buttermilk and live-culture can produce mixed results, depending upon how the buttermilk has been processed.

| *Equipment* | *Directions* |
|---|---|
| **2-quart saucepan** | *1* Pour the cream into the sanitized jar, place the jar in the pot, and add warm water to the pot up to the level of the cream. |
| **1-quart Mason jar, sterilized, (you can do this by dunking into boiling water)** | |
| **Stainless steel iced-tea spoon (or other long, narrow stainless steel spoon)** | *2* Heat the pot gently, raising the cream temperature to 86 degrees. Stir the cream with the iced-tea spoon as you are warming it. |
| **Dial-top thermometer (a second thermometer is helpful, for monitoring the water bath)** | *3* Add the Aroma B starter solution and stir gently and thoroughly. |
| *Ingredients* | *4* Check the water bath temperature and adjust the water temperature to 86–88 degrees (add ice cubes or hot water, as needed). |
| **1 pint heavy whipping cream (not ultrapasteurized)** | |
| **¼ teaspoon mesophilic Aroma B culture, dissolved in ¼ cup water** | *5* Place the lid loosely on the jar. Place the jar and pot in a warm place. An empty picnic cooler provides good insulation and will keep them warm enough. Let stand for 12 hours. |
| | *6* Gently stir your new crème fraiche; it will be about the thickness of creamy yogurt. You can use it right away, or you can chill it for a few hours for a thicker, spreadable consistency and tangier flavor. Keep it in the Mason jar in the refrigerator for up to 2 weeks. |

*Per 2-ounce serving: Calories 205 (From Fat 198); Fat 22g (Saturated 14g); Cholesterol 82mg; Sodium 23mg; Carbohydrate 2g (Dietary Fiber 0g); Protein 1g.*

*Source: The Beverage People, Santa Rosa, California*

# Chèvre

**Prep time:** 36 hrs • **Cook time:** about 10 min • **Yield:** Four small rounds.

Creamy, tangy, and slightly crumbly, this fresh goat cheese takes well to pre-serving additions such as chopped herbs, orange or lemon zest, or chile flakes.

| Equipment | Directions |
|---|---|
| **3-quart stainless steel pot with lid** | *1* Add the milk to a 3-quart stainless steel pot and slowly bring it to 86 degrees. Remove the warmed milk from heat. |
| **Perforated ladle or slotted spoon** | |
| **Dial-top thermometer** | *2* Sprinkle in the culture, wait 5 minutes, and then stir with 20 gentle strokes. |
| **4 plastic perforated flared forms (about 4 inches tall; 2-inch diameter at the bottom, 3-inch diameter at the top)** | *3* Add the calcium chloride–water mixture and stir gently. |
| **Cheese ripening pan** | *4* Add the rennet mixture, stir, and cover. Let the mixture stand at about 72 degrees for at least 12 hours. (In the summer, let it rest in a cool, lower kitchen cupboard; in the winter, in a warm cupboard above the refrigerator or in a closet with a light on to create more heat.) Do not agitate or stir the mixture while the curd sets. |
| **Cheese ripening drain tray** | |
| **Ingredients** | |
| **½ gallon pasteurized or raw goat milk (not ultrapasteurized)** | *5* Place a draining rack inside the drain pan and place the forms onto the draining rack. Ladle the curd — which should look like thickened yogurt — into the forms, leaving the whey. Allow the curd to drain for 24 hours at room temperature, pouring off the whey from the drain pan as needed to keep the cheeses above the liquid. |
| **⅛ teaspoon MA4001 or similar freeze-dried, direct-set mesophilic culture** | |
| **¼ teaspoon liquid calcium choloride mixed with 1 tablespoon water** | |
| **⅛ teaspoon liquid rennet, mixed with 1 tablespoon water** | |
| **Flaked or kosher salt** | |
| **1 teaspoon dried herbs or spices, or more to taste (optional)** | |

**6** Remove the cheeses from the forms and place them directly on the draining rack. Sprinkle all sides of each cheese lightly with salt. Let the cheeses dry for another 24 hours, at room temperature or refrigerated if it's very warm in your kitchen, turning once or twice. You may lightly cover them with cheesecloth if desired, to keep them clean, but it's essential that air is able to circulate around them.

**7** If desired, roll the cheeses in herbs before wrapping. Wrap each cheese in wax paper; then wrap it in plastic wrap or specialty cheese paper. Refrigerate for up to several weeks.

*Per 1-ounce serving (about ⅛ of the round): Calories 42 (From Fat 23); Fat 3g (Saturated 2g); Cholesterol 7mg; Sodium 66mg; Carbohydrate 3g (Dietary Fiber 0g); Protein 2g.*

***Tip:*** You can purchase starter cultures and rennet from a cheesemaking supply shop.

***Tip:*** Good herbs or spices for this cheese include dill, herbes de Provence, or crushed black peppercorns. Purchase only as much as you think you'll need from a bulk container like those found at Whole Foods or natural foods stores. By doing so, you ensure they'll be fresh and thus more potent.

*Source: The Beverage People, Santa Rosa, California*

# Mozzarella

*Prep time:* 25 min  •  *Cook time:* 30-40 min  •  *Yield:* 2 pounds

Although it seems complicated, making mozzarella is actually very easy — and a lot of fun — once you get the hang of it. Fresh, milky, and delicious, mozzarella is a treat when served with sliced, ripe tomatoes, a drizzle of good extra virgin olive oil, and a sprinkle of sea salt, or as a topping for pizza. This recipe came to us courtesy of The Beverage People, who also sell cheesemaking supplies (see "Sources for cheesemaking supplies" sidebar) online and from their retail store in Santa Rosa, California.

| *Equipment* | *Directions* |
|---|---|
| **Large stainless steel double boiler** | **1** Using the double-boiler, warm the milk to 55 degrees. Gently stir in the dissolved citric acid. Then stir in the dissolved lipase. |
| **Dial-top thermometer** | |
| **Slotted spoon or perforated ladle** | **2** Slowly heat the milk to 88 degrees over low to medium heat. The milk will begin to curdle. |
| **Strainer** | |
| **2-quart (or larger) bowl** | **3** Stir in the rennet as you raise the temperature of the milk to 100 to 105 degrees. Within a few minutes, you'll begin to see more curds forming. After you reach the appropriate temperature, turn off the heat and remove the pan from the stove. When the whey is relatively clear, the curds are ready. |
| **Neoprene or coated latex gloves** | |
| *Ingredients* | |
| **2 gallons whole raw or pasteurized (not ultrapasteurized) milk** | **4** Remove the curds from the whey by either pouring them out through a strainer or ladling the curds into a bowl. Whichever method you choose, reserve the whey in a separate stock pot. |
| **1 tablespoon citric acid, dissolved in ¼ cup water** | |
| **½ teaspoon liquid rennet, mixed in ¼ cup water** | **5** Now you need to begin the kneading process that will make the mozzarella nice and elastic. To do so, heat the reserved whey to 170–180 degrees. Wearing the gloves, shape the curd into a ball, set the ball on the ladle, and submerge the ladle into the whey, dipping it as needed (you want the curd to be smooth and elastic in texture). Knead the curd again and resubmerge into the hot whey. Continue kneading and redipping the curd until it reaches 145 degrees, the temperature at which the curd will stretch. |
| **½ teaspoon lipase powder, dissolved in ¼ cup water, and set aside for 10-20 minutes** | |
| **Kosher salt** | |

**6** When the curd is the right temperature (145 degrees), it's ready to be stretched: Sprinkle a small amount of Kosher salt on the cheese (as you would seasoning food to flavor it) and then fold the salt into the cheese. Continue to knead and pull the cheese until it's smooth and elastic. When the cheese pulls with the consistency of taffy, it's done.

**7** Shape the mozzarella into small or large balls. You can eat it while it's still warm, or you can place the balls in ice water for about 5 minutes to quickly bring the inside temperature of the cheese down. Hot or cold, the cheese is best served fresh. For storage, place the balls in a freezer bag with a few tablespoons of milk and keep refrigerated. Eat within a few days.

*Per 4-ounce serving: Calories 600 (From Fat 293); Fat 33g (Saturated 20g); Cholesterol 133mg; Sodium 618mg; Carbohydrate 46g (Dietary Fiber 0g); Protein 32g.*

***Note:*** If you're cow milk intolerant, you can substitute raw goat milk in this recipe. Look for it at your local farmers' market or store (if it's legal; not all states or counties allow the sale of raw milk). If you have a local goat cheesemaker who doesn't sell raw milk, ask whether you can purchase some, if doing so is legal.

*Source: The Beverage People, Santa Rosa, California*

# Part V
# The Part of Tens

"Do you want the cheese on your sandwich melted or not? Hurry up—the iron's hot."

## In this part . . .

Whether you're looking for trivia, history, or what cheese festivals are worth checking out, this part has it. Want to know what effect cheese mites have on a wheel of cheese? How to go about milking a moose? Or who produces the best blue in the United States? You'll find the answers here.

# Chapter 20

# Ten of the World's Most Bizarre Cheeses

. . . . . . . . . . . . . . . . . . . . . . . . . . . . . . . . . . . . . . . . . . . . . . . . . . . .

### In This Chapter

▶ Cheeses made from uncommon milks

▶ Cheeses containing strange (to us) things

▶ And one cheese that comes in a can

. . . . . . . . . . . . . . . . . . . . . . . . . . . . . . . . . . . . . . . . . . . . . . . . . . . .

*I*f you think about it, cheese is a pretty weird food concept all on its own. But we take it for granted that most cheese comes from cows, and we accept that some cheeses smell a bit funky. Beyond that, we probably don't give the provenance, odor, or what might be living in our cheese much thought. In this chapter, we take a look at some of the world's strangest cheeses. If they sound scary, just remember that in other parts of the world, "cheese" in a spray can may be the stuff of nightmares.

## Casu Marzu

This Sardinian sheep milk cheese has achieved global fame for its gross-out factor. Whole pecorino cheeses are left outside, with a piece removed, so that the female cheese fly (*Piophila casei*) can lay her eggs in its interior. After the eggs hatch, the larvae — maggots — feed upon the cheese, and the acids from their digestive system ferment the cheese and break down the fat, resulting in a very soft, soupy texture.

Because the larvae are capable of leaping distances up to six inches, eating casu marzu requires a special technique: It's traditionally spread on Sardinian flatbread (*pane carasu*), and diners eat it while covering the flatbread with their hands to thwart escapees. Those wishing to savor their cheese maggot-free place a slice in a sealed bag to suffocate the maggots, who leap about trying to get oxygen (keep in mind, though, that the cheese is only considered safe to eat if the maggots are alive). Any way you slice it, casu marzu requires an adventurous palate.

The European Union, which had formerly banned the cheese, now permits its production as a traditional food, because it's been made for thousands of years.

# Airaq

A horse is a horse, as the saying goes, but to the peoples of Central Asia, mare milk is more than just liquid refreshment. Despite the fact that they raise a variety of dairy-producing livestock including goats, sheep, cattle, and camels, airaq is the national beverage. The fermented and thus slightly alcoholic milk of female horses, airaq is only available during the mares' brief lactation period, usually June through early October.

Known as *kumis* by the Turks, Kyrgyz, Uzbeks, and other nomadic steppe cultures of the region, airaq is traditionally produced by placing fresh milk into a horse or goatskin bag, attaching it to the saddle, and allowing the agitation from the animal's movement to churn the liquid into a kefir-like substance. The bag may also be stored on top of a *yurt* (a portable dwelling structure the nomadic people of this region use) and turned by hand, although airaq is now more commonly produced in barrels and churned with a paddle. Commercial production of kumis uses the more readily available cow milk, but mare milk is extremely high in lactose, which is what enables the natural sugars to convert so readily to alcohol. Ironically, most Inner Mongolians are lactose intolerant; the fermentation process breaks down the lactose, making airaq not just a cheap buzz, but an essential source of nutrients. No matter what you call it, don't turn down a cup if it's offered to you; airaq is the most revered form of hospitality a shepherd of the steppe can bestow.

# Pule

Pule cheese, made from the milk of a herd of 100 domesticated Balkan donkeys from the Zasavica Special Nature Reserve in Serbia, costs over $1,000 a pound, which makes it the world's most expensive cheese. The smoked cheese, named after the Serbian word for "foal," is extremely low in solids, which is why it takes 25 liters (6.6 gallons) of milk to produce just one kilo (2.2 pounds) of pule.

Donkey milk was consumed by the ancient Egyptians, Greeks, and Romans, and studies show it offers substantial nutritional and antimicrobial properties. The Masai people of Kenya drink it to ward off disease, while southern Italian women feed it to children allergic to cow milk. China, Pakistan, and Ethiopia are all large producers of donkey milk, which is also used in beauty products such as shampoo and face cream.

Despite its apparent popularity in certain parts of the world, donkey milk is hardly a mass-market item. The demand for pule cheese is great, due to its luxury item status, and it's only available by advance order. Unfortunately, we couldn't find any information on how to obtain it. We highly doubt that it's coming soon to a grocer near you.

# Chhurpi

Made from cow, yak, or *chauri* (a cow-yak hybrid) milk, chhurpi varies slightly depending upon its country of origin: the Indian Himalayas, Nepal, Tibet, or Bhutan. It can be a fresh, slightly sour, cottage cheese-like product, often eaten with rice; or dried, cubed, and smoked over a fire until rock hard and brown in color. In this form, it resembles a pair of dice and is sucked or chewed, sometimes for hours, as a source of sustenance.

When made in the home (dairies may also produce it), chhurpi is extracted from buttermilk called *sergem,* which is boiled. The resulting curd is wrapped in cloth or a jute bag and pressed to remove the whey. It may then be eaten fresh or dried.

In India, chhurpi soup is a traditional food of the Sikkim (a landlocked state in Northern India bordered by Nepal, Tibet, and Bhutan). Chhurpi is also eaten as a snack or used in the popular condiment, *chhurip ka achar*, which is a type of pickle. While other types of cheese are made throughout Northern Asia, chhurpi is fairly ubiquitous, although it may have different names in different countries or regions. The Sherpas call it *sherkam*, for example, and the Bhutanese refer to it as *durukowa* or *durukho*.

Imported yak cheese has been available in the United States in recent years, but apparently the novelty wasn't worth the red tape. There are, however, a number of yak ranchers in the U.S., mostly in Colorado, where a sizeable Nepalese population lives (that mountain thing). One farmer we know occasionally makes cheese for his own use from his yak milk, but he hasn't had enough requests to warrant trying to sell it commercially. Still, if you're interested in trying yak milk — which is described as exceptionally rich and sweet — or cheese, talk to your cheesemonger. Demand creates supply!

# Moose Cheese

Who knew? Commercial moose dairies are a thing in Russia, in part because of the milk's purported nutritional and medicinal value. It's thought to help digestive problems, as well as other chronic ailments. Moose milk has 10 to 12 percent butterfat, as compared to the 4.9 percent in Jersey cow milk (considered the highest among major dairy breeds). Holy cholesterol! But that very butterfat is what convinced one Swedish couple, Christer and Ulla Johansson, to start the only moose dairy in Europe and begin producing the world's only moose cheese.

At their *Älgens Hus* (Elk House; moose are sometimes referred to as elk in that part of the world although they're different species), the Johanssons milk their moose and make three different cheeses: a fresh, feta-style, a blue cheese, and a bloomy rind similar to camembert.

Moose only lactate from May to September, and milking a single animal takes two hours (in silence — a stressed moose cow will dry up) for approximately a half-gallon of milk. No wonder moose cheese costs upward of $500 per pound! Should you still desire a taste, pay a visit to the Älgens Hus' restaurant, where you'll find it served in both sweet and savory preparations.

## Leipäjuusto

North Americans — especially those in the Midwest or Quebec — are no strangers to cheese curds or "squeaky" cheese made from cow milk. If you live near the Arctic Circle, you can have squeaky cheese, too; just expect it to be made from reindeer milk. Known as leipäjuusto, the cheese is sometimes made from goat milk or cow *beestings* (colostrum-rich milk full of antibodies from an animal that has recently calved) if it's an artisanal product; commercially, regular cow milk is used.

Also known as *jusstoleipä* (cheese bread), leipäjuusto is a fresh, mild cheese made from curdled milk that is then formed into a disk. Traditionally, it was dried and stored for up to several years as sustenance through the long, dark winters. To soften it enough to make it edible, the cheese was heated on a fire. Today, leipäjuusto is baked or grilled to give it a delectable caramelized crust or grill marks (hence the bread nickname).

You can serve leipäjuusto warm or cold as a snack; cubed and put into a cup with hot coffee poured over it; pan-fried and served with cloudberry jam; soaked in cream and sprinkled with cinnamon and sugar before grilling, or used in salads. We like.

## Caravane ("Camelbert")

While fresh cheeses made from camel milk can be found in Jordan, they're usually made from more accessible (and easier to milk) goats and sheep. Camel milk also lacks an enzyme that enables it to curdle; for that reason, cheesemaking isn't a very practical endeavor to the nomadic peoples of the Middle East and North and West Africa.

But Nancy Abeiderrahmane, an English engineer, decided not to let a little thing like an enzyme stand in her way. When she visited the West African country of Mauritania, she noticed the locals all drank imported milk (despite the fact that livestock outnumber people and poverty is rampant). In 1989, Tiviski, her Mauritanian camel dairy, was born. In addition to selling camel milk, Abeiderrahmane started producing Caravane, a camembert-style camel milk cheese she makes by adding calcium phosphate and vegetarian rennet to the milk.

Due to cost and customs regulations, Caravane isn't available in the U.S. but Tiviski is still thriving in Mauritania and surrounding areas, so hopefully we can look forward to more dromedary dairy on our shores in the future.

# Milbenkäse (Spinnenkäse)

The Sardinians aren't the only ones who prefer their cheese fermented by crawly creatures. *Milbenkäse* ("mite" cheese, also erroneously known as *spinnenkäse,* or spider cheese) comes from the German village of Würchwitz, in the state of Saxony-Anhalt. In this case, cheese mites (*Tyroglyphus casei*) do the same work performed by cheese fly larvae in casu marzu, which we discuss earlier.

The recipe dates back to the Middle Ages (which may explain why ingesting critters was no big thing). Quark, a fresh cow milk cheese, is flavored with salt and caraway, shaped into small balls, cylinders, or wheels, and dried. The cheese is then placed in a wooden box of rye flour and cheese mites (the flour provides an alternate food source so the mites don't devour the entire cheese. . . *that* would be a bad thing). For the next three or more months, the digestive juices of the mites break down the fats in the exterior of the cheese and cause it to ferment. After several months, the rind takes on a reddish-brown color, although some producers prefer to age the cheese for up to a year, at which point it turns black (we know, we know).

Milbenkäse has a strong, sour flavor, with a piquant aftertaste and bitter notes that increase with age. Any mites unlucky enough to find themselves attached to the rind are consumed, as well. It's said that milbenkäse is also beneficial for digestion. Frankly, we prefer Rolaids.

# Stinking Bishop

Charles Martell of Dymock, Gloucestershire, in the southwest of England has been making what has been dubbed Britain's "smelliest cheese" since 1972. Stinking Bishop, a leathery, yellowish washed-rind cow milk cheese, gets its powerful aroma from regular immersions in perry, a fermented beverage made from a local variety of pear also known as Stinking Bishop. Combined with the traditional *B. linens* bacteria used to make washed rinds, the two forces form a lethal olfactory weapon.

Stinking Bishop the cheese is more mild than one would guess; it has small eyes (holes), the result of air bubbles, an oozy to soupy interior, and a full, rich, creamy flavor.

The recipe is based upon one used by the Cisterian monks of the region, which is what inspired Martell to revive the tradition, but the name isn't a diss on the local clergy. The pear was named after a man called Bishop, who was famously short of temper and lacking in character. He developed the pear variety in the 19th century, and posthumously, it was given the unfortunate moniker that also belongs to the cheese. Cheers!

# Cougar Gold

Cheese in a can? *Real* cheese? Say it ain't so. In the 1940s, researchers at Washington State University combined forces with the American Can Company to develop potential ways to pack nutrient-rich cheese into cans. Why? Just because. Cramming cheese into a can is harder than you'd expect, however. The gases emitted by the microorganisms in the cheese (it's a living thing, remember) caused test cans to explode.

WSU finally came up with a cheese recipe that worked, and Cougar Gold, a surprisingly palatable, sharp, crumbly white cheddar, was born. There was still a hitch, though: Canned cheese requires refrigeration (at which point it will last indefinitely), so don't expect to see it as an MRE anytime soon. But *you* can enjoy Cougar Gold. It — and seven flavored versions — are available at WSU's Creamery store (it's made by WSU students) or online (`http://cougarcheese.wsu.edu/`). One more note of trivia: Cougar Gold received a gold medal at the 2006 World Cheese Awards. They had *that* one in the can.

# Chapter 21

# Ten of America's Most Influential Artisanal Cheesemakers

*In This Chapter*

▶ Award-winning U.S. cheesemakers

▶ Breaking the mold for American cheeses

▶ Broadening U.S. markets and palates

*T*he road has been a long one for American cheese artisans during these last 25 years. The modern domestic cheese revolution began in the early 1980s, and in time, the consumer palate created a demand for more, more, more! Today, the United States has nearly 1,000 artisan cheesemakers, with more starting up each year. In this chapter, we celebrate ten visionaries who helped put cheese on the map in America. Many more U.S. cheese industry leaders exist, but space is limited. Check out ***culture:*** *the word on cheese* for cheese luminaries, makers, and mentors in every issue.

## Alison Hooper and Bob Reese, Vermont Butter & Cheese Creamery

In 1984, Alison Hooper and Bob Reese joined forces to form a cheesemaking partnership focused on crafting European-style dairy products, including butter, crème fraiche, mascarpone, and cheese. At that time, Bob was the marketing director for the Vermont Department of Agriculture, and Alison was a state dairy lab technician who had spent time after college making cheese in rural France. When a French chef needed chèvre for a state dinner that Bob was in charge of, Bob turned to Alison. Her cheeses stole the show that night, and an entrepreneurship was born.

Since that time, the company has grown into a much-loved, viable business that supports more than 20 local dairies and serves as a mentor for many cheesemakers. In 2006, the partners expanded into a 4,000-square-foot facility and now employ over 30 people. Their products are available nationwide and online (www.vermontcreamery.com).

# Tom and Nancy Clark, Old Chatham Sheepherding Company

When he was 10, Tom Clark won a blue ribbon at an upstate New York county fair for his Hampshire sheep. When interviewed by a local paper, Clark said he wanted to raise sheep when he grew up. It was a long time before he circled back to fulfill his dream.

In 1993, Tom Clark and wife Nancy moved onto 600 acres in New York's lush Hudson Valley; a year later, they started a150- sheep dairy. It was successful beyond their imagining; they now produce farmstead cheese (including a popular camembert-style and a blue cheese) and yogurt year-round, and are the largest sheep dairy in the country. Their distinctive black sheep logo with its Kelly green background is ubiquitous in cheese shops and grocery chains throughout the U.S.; products are also available online (www.blacksheepcheese.com).

# Mary Keehn, Cypress Grove Chevre

Mary Keehn started raising goats in the 1970s and became a championship breeder. She began experimenting with cheesemaking in her home kitchen and soon realized she had a knack for that as well; in 1983, she founded Cypress Grove Chevre. At a time when nearly all goat cheese in America was imported from France, Mary began taking her cheeses around to restaurants and stores. Acceptance was slow but steady, as the American palate began to accept the smooth, creamy, more mellow taste of domestic goat cheeses after years of strong-flavored French imports.

Cypress Grove became one of the premier producers of goat cheese in the country. Humboldt Fog and Purple Haze — the company's most popular offerings — are known nationwide. Mary also commissioned cheesemakers in the Netherlands to make both a goat milk Gouda (Midnight Moon) and a sheep milk Gouda (Lambchopper) for the American market. In 2010, Cypress Grove Chevre was acquired by Emmi Roth USA, a leading provider of specialty and artisan cheeses. Mary, however, and the core team at Cypress Grove are still at the production helm. You can find Cypress Grove products in most grocery stores and online (www.cypressgrovechevre.com).

# Judy Schad, Capriole Farmstead Goat Cheeses

In 1976, Judy Schad and her husband Larry moved with their three young children from the suburbs to 80 acres in southern Indiana, seeking a more sustainable lifestyle. Although Judy grew up spending summers at her grandmother's farm in the same region, the couple really had no idea what they were getting into when they established themselves on an abandoned farmstead (after running the title, they discovered the property had once belonged to Larry's great, great grandfather in the 1870s!). Whether seredipity or fate, the couple began putting the place back together, abandoned their plan to buy a milk cow, and instead bought their first goat in 1977. It was love at first sight, and soon Judy was experimenting with making goat cheese in her kitchen.

Today, Judy is one of the nation's premier producers of artisan goat cheese. She and her team manage a herd of 500 goats and produce both pasteurized fresh and surface-ripened cheeses and raw milk aged goat cheeses, including Old Kentucky Tomme and herb-encrusted Juliana. Like others of her generation, Judy has paved the way for artisanal cheesemakers in the U.S., and she continues to be heavily involved in cheese and food-related organizations. Her cheeses are available nationwide at grocery stores, cheese shops, and select farmers' markets, as well as online (www.capriolegoatcheese.com).

# Cary Bryant and David Gremmels, Rogue Creamery

Rogue Creamery was founded in southern Oregon during World War II by Italian immigrant Gaetano "Tom" Vella. In 1935, Vella was a successful cheese producer in Sonoma, California, when his brother wrote from Italy and told him that war was imminent. Vella predicted that the milk used in his creamery would be needed by military bases and that large quantities of cheese would be called for to provide a source of nutrition to Allied troops. Vella proved to be quite the visionary. After talks with J.L. Kraft (yes, *that* Kraft), Vella was given the funds to purchase an abandoned cheese plant, which he named Rogue Creamery. He bought milk from local farmers and was soon in businesss. Vella ended up producing a total of five million pounds of cheese a year during the war.

During that time, Vella's son, Ignazio ("Ig"), worked by his side. In time, Ig went on to take over both Vella Cheese Company, his family's business in Sonoma, and Rogue Creamery. In 1956, he spent three months in Roquefort, France, and returned to produce the first Oregon Blue Vein to much acclaim.

Ig became "the godfather of the American artisan cheese movement," according to current Rogue Creamery president and cheesemaker David Gremmels, and is most famous for his award-winning Dry Jack (produced in Sonoma). Vella, who passed away in June 2011, sold the creamery to David and Rogue CEO/cheesemaker Cary Bryant in 2002, with a handshake deal and a promise from them to carry on the tradition of artisan cheesemaking. The two men have never looked back.

By 2003, David and Cary were producing award-winning cheeses and received a World Cheese Award for best blue in 2003. Today, some of their best sellers include Rogue River Blue (Best of Show, American Cheese Society, 2009 and 2011), Caveman Blue, and Oregonzola. The men are recognized throughout the industry as mentors and leaders in protecting and promoting the craft of artisan cheesemaking, and their products are available at cheese shops nationwide, as well as at their local farmers' markets, at the creamery store, and online (www.roguecreamery.com).

# Cindy and Liam Callahan, Bellwether Farms

Cindy Callahan and her husband Ed relocated their family (including son Liam, who is Bellwether's cheesemaker today) from San Francisco to rural Valley Ford, California. The couple had vague notions of raising beef cattle, but were persuaded to try sheep instead after a livestock adviser informed them that raising the animals for wool and meat would be more profitable. Their foray into dairying and cheesemaking was inspired by a visit from a Syrian friend, who described the delicious sheep milk yogurt of his homeland. The Callahans started out making fromage blanc in 1992. Finding an enthusiastic reception, Cindy and Ed traveled to Italy in 1994 to visit sheep dairies, and that's how Bellwether Farms, California's first sheep dairy, was born.

While Liam was finishing a degree at U.C. Berkeley (Political Economy), Cindy suggested he go into business with her. Without hesitation, he agreed. In the beginning, Cindy and Liam milked each ewe by hand, an incredibly laborious, time-consuming task. But their rich, buttery cheeses — including the award-winning San Andreas, Pepato, and sheep milk ricotta — were garnering them major recognition from chefs, cheesemongers, and a food-loving public newly exposed to sheep milk cheese. After building a state-of-the-art creamery, Bellwether's line continued to expand to include more cheeses, including a few made from cow milk (which comes from a neighboring Jersey dairy), in addition to sheep milk yogurt. You can find Bellwether products in major grocery stores nationwide and online (www.bellwetherfarms.com).

# Jennifer Bice, Redwood Hill Farm

Jennifer Bice, the eldest of 10 children, got her first goats when she was 10, after her family relocated to Sonoma County from Los Angeles. The family started a dairy and sold goat milk to Bay Area natural food stores. In college in the 1970s, she met her future husband, the late Steven Schack, who also had a herd of goats. In 1978, the couple combined their herds and founded Redwood Hill Farm in Sebastopol, a sleepy, bohemian town located near the Sonoma County coast. They sold goat milk for several years and then began selling yogurt, as well. Bice now offers a lactose-free cow milk line of products called Green Valley Organics.

In the early 1980s, as consumer interest in goat cheese began to grow, the couple started experimenting with cheesemaking and traveled to France to tour dairies and cheese plants. Soon after, they rented a production space in which to produce mozzarella and ricotta. In 1993, they began construction on their own creamery and, in the interim, began making chèvre at nearby Bellwether Farms. Once in their new facility, Bice and Schack expanded their line to include award-winning surface-ripened cheeses, including their best-selling Camellia, a camembert-style, and a crottin. Today, Redwood Hill is a certified humane, 100 percent solar-powered dairy, and thriving business enterprise. Their cheeses (which also include goat milk feta and cheddars), kefir, fluid milk, and yogurt are available at major grocery chains nationwide and online (www.redwoodhill.com).

# Mike and Carol Gingrich, Uplands Cheese Company

Uplands is the unlikely result of two neighboring dairy farming families in southwest Wisconsin deciding to join together. After years of owning adjacent land, Mike and Carol Gingrich co-purchased a farm with Dan and Jeanne Patenaude in order to join their small herds and expand their seasonal, pasture-based rotational grazing system. The move turned out to be fortuitous. In 2000, the resulting spectacular milk was used to make Pleasant Ridge Reserve, a nutty, grassy raw milk cheese inspired by the hard, aged cheeses the foursome saw in the French and Swiss Alps. Since then, Pleasant Ridge has won Best of Show from the American Cheese Society three times. In 2003, the cheese also won Best in Show in the World Cheese Championships, making it the only cheese to hold both awards.

In 2007, cheesemaker Andy Hatch joined the Uplands team. In late 2010, Uplands debuted its second cheese, Rush Creek Reserve, which is made only from the rich, hay-based fall milk. Inspired by French Vacherin Mont d'Or, Rush Creek is a delectably creamy, satiny, raw milk washed-rind cheese wrapped in spruce bark. It's a custardy, sweet, smokey cheese, with a distinct "hammy" undertone. Getting your hands on Rush Creek cheese is no easy feat because it tends to sell out before it even hits the store. Do yourself a favor next winter: Ask your cheesemonger to place an order for you or get it yourself online (www.uplandscheese.com).

# Sue Conley and Peggy Smith, Cowgirl Creamery

Made with organic cow milk from nearby Straus Family Creamery, Northern California's Cowgirl Creamery cheeses have been at the forefront of the U.S. artisan cheese movement since 1997. Not only is Cowgirl one of the best-loved artisanal cheesemakers in the country, but its founders Sue Conley and Peggy Smith are also supporters and mentors for cheesemakers, cheesemongers, restaurateurs, and others in the cheese industry.

With the help of longtime cheesemaker Maureen Cunnie, the Cowgirls now produce over 3,000 pounds of cheese and other dairy products a week (including one of the most delicious cottage cheeses available). They also operate three stores (two in Northern California and one in Washington, D.C., Conley's hometown) and a thriving wholesale distribution business. Their comprehensive website provides descriptions of their products and other cheeses. Their cheeses are widely available nationwide, as well as online (www.cowgirlcreamery.com).

# Mateo and Andy Kehler, Jasper Hill Farm

With the milk of their own Ayrshire cows and the aid of their family and growing staff, brothers Mateo and Andy Kehler produce several award-winning cheeses, including Winnimere, Bayley Hazen Blue, and Constant Bliss in their rural Vermont dairy and creamery. More recently, they built an elaborate underground cave system — 22,000 square feet — to age and care for a select group of their fellow New England cheesemakers' cheeses.

The Cellars at Jasper Hill now consult for, age, and distribute an expanding number of local cheeses. This European model is groundbreaking in the United States, where most cheesemakers are on their own, every step of the way. The Kehlers are at the forefront of artisan cheesemaking and are dedicated to their mission of reestablishing the depleted numbers of viable family farms in their area. Jasper Hill products are available at cheese shops nationwide. For more information go to www.jasperhillfarm.com and www.cellarsatjasperhill.com.

# Chapter 22

# Ten Cheese Festivals You Shouldn't Miss

*In This Chapter*

▶ U.S, Canadian, and European cheese festivals

▶ Family-friendly festivals

▶ Festivals for cheese novices and experts

*O*ne of the most endearing qualities about artisan cheesemakers is their desire to watch you taste their handcrafted products so that they can see your eyes light up. Festivals (and frequently, farmers' markets) are the best way to make this connection between producer and consumer.

Cheese festivals are held all over the world, many of them centered around competitions ranging from cheesemaking to cheesemongering. The best thing about these events is that, no matter where you are, you're guaranteed to get a taste of the local terroir. In this chapter, we give you our picks of the best cheese festivals open to the public. Visit www.culturecheesemag.com/events to find a listing of cheesy gatherings worldwide.

## The Festival of Cheese, American Cheese Society

The big wheel of U.S. cheese festivals, the ACS Annual Conference boasts educational seminars for cheesemakers and aficionados alike. You can choose tasting or pairing seminars, or spend an afternoon making cheese with an expert. Throughout is a rigorous competition featuring over 1,500 cheese entries in more than 100 categories. The truly staggering Festival of Cheese (featuring all the entries) takes place the final evening and is open to the public for a fee. The competition winners are announced, and then you can dive in and sample: Every single entry is portioned and plated, making for a stunning display of dairy decadence. This festival takes place in August, and its location changes annually. For more information, go to www.cheese society.org.

# California Artisan Cheese Festival

What better place for a domestic cheese festival than wine country? The California Artisan Cheese Festival (CACF) is held every March in Petaluma (located in Sonoma County, about 40 minutes north of San Francisco) and pulls in over 2,000 attendees sampling cheeses from the West Coast, Pacific Northwest, and Rockies. Sign up early to get in on local creamery tours, cheese-centric dinners, and educational seminars. For more information, go to www.artisancheesefestival.com.

# Cheese School of San Francisco

Founded in 2006 by Sara Vivenzio, the Cheese School of San Francisco is a stand-alone institution focused solely on classes and tasting events that bolster cheese-loving students' knowledge and appreciation of dairy.

With an ongoing curriculum of classes ranging from Cheese 101 to a truly inspiring three-day intensive cheese education program, this is a great place to familiarize yourself with what cheese is, delve deeper into your favorite hobby, or take your professional knowledge to the next level.

The instructors are cheese professionals from the Bay Area and beyond, and the intimate classes (maximum 32 students) allow plenty of time for questions and mingling with those who work in the industry. You may even get lucky enough to take a class from our very own Lassa Skinner. Check it out! For more information, go to www.cheeseschoolsf.com

# Vermont Cheesemaker's Festival

Vermont is America's top cheesemaking state per capita (over 40 in all), which makes this festival the ideal place for caseophiles to mingle with the cheesemakers. Held each July at historic Shelburne Farms, a 1,400-acre working farm and education center on the shores of Lake Champlain, festival highlights include regional food and wine tastings, cooking demonstrations, educational seminars, and a whole lot of cheese. Think of this as the cheesemaker's cheese festival. For more information, go to www.vtcheesefest.com.

# Oregon Cheese Festival

Hosted by the Oregon Cheese Guild and Rogue Creamery in Central Point, Oregon, this fun, much-loved local festival features dozens of cheese-, beer-, and winemakers. General admission is minimal, the sampling is free, and the makers sell their products at great prices. The festival is held at Rogue Creamery in Southern Oregon and takes on the vibe of a farmers' market, with all of the vendors gathered beneath a giant tent. Events include a "Meet the Cheesemakers" dinner (held the night before), seminars, and tastings, including chocolate and cider. For more information, go to www. roguecreamery.com.

# Great British Cheese Festival

The United Kingdom loves its cheese, as "Britain's Biggest Cheese Market" can attest. Over 400 cheeses made from cow, goat, sheep, and water buffalo milk are accompanied by artisan wine, beer, cider, and perry (a fermented beverage made from pears), and the people who produce them. Judges conduct a blind cheese tasting and award gold, silver, and bronze medals. Other events include cheese rolling, market stalls, seminars, and demonstrations. There's even a festival pub. You get to meet regional cheesemaking stars and taste the best Britain has to offer. The event is held in late September, and locations vary. For more information, go to www.greatbritishcheese festival.co.uk.

# Bra Cheese Festival

The most nostalgic and romantic of cheese festivals, the biennial Bra Cheese Festival, attracts cheese lovers and professionals from all over the world. Held every other September outside of Turin in Piedmont, Italy, the events and temporary venues include a Cheese Market; the Great Hall of Cheese; an *enoteca* (wine bar) featuring DIY cheese plates; a pizza piazza; tasting booths of regional Italian food; street food and beer pairings; and workshops, special dinners, and tastings. The Cheese Market is a showcase for herders, small-scale cheesemakers, and affineurs to display their (mostly raw milk) products. With a massive array of artisanal cheeses, including ones rarely found outside of their villages of origin and 700 wines, this is a truly special event worth the plane ticket. For more information, go to http://cheese.slowfood.it/ welcome_en.lasso.

# Great Wisconsin Cheese Festival

We wouldn't expect less from the great cheese state of Wisconsin than one heck of a cheese festival. Every first weekend of June since 1988, cheese fans have descended upon the town of Little Chute to celebrate the state's dairy industry and salute local cheese producers. This family-friendly event offers three days of music, a Big Cheese Parade, tastings, a cheese carving demonstration, cheesecake contest, cheese curd-eating contest, and rowdy carnival. (Tip: stay off the rides if you've been competing for the cheese curd-eating title.) For more information, go to www.littlechutewi.org/index.aspx?nid=226.

# The Great Canadian Cheese Festival

Canada has quietly been producing phenomenal artisan cheeses for decades, and now the country has a festival calling attention to this fact. First held in 2010, this June celebration is held in Prince Edward County, Ontario, an up-and-coming culinary destination and Canada's newest VQA (Vintners Quality Alliance) wine region. Events include cheese tasting seminars, cheese tours (sign up early; they sell out weeks ahead), a judging competition known as the Canadian Cheese Grand Prix; a Cheese Fair where you can buy what you try, and a celebrity chef Cooks & Curds Cheese Gala, featuring pairings with Ontario wine and craft beer. Sounds like fun, eh? For more information, go to http://cheesefestival.ca.

# Seattle Cheese Festival

Every May, Seattle's famous Pike Place Market becomes a Pacific Northwest and imported cheese fest, with stalls set up along the cobbled streets. The event is free and draws cheese-loving crowds ready to sample and purchase their favorites. The festival also conducts ongoing seminars (advanced sign-up required) and chef demonstrations. Though outdoors, the event is held rain or shine . . . and this being Seattle, be prepared for the former. Don't worry; the views of Elliot Bay and Puget Sound just steps away are still stunning when wet. For more information, go to www.seattlecheesefestival.com.

# Amish Country Cheese Festival

At 40 years and counting, this authentic, early fall country festival provides more than just a taste of cheese. Expect traditional Amish foods and handicrafts, a farm shop, music, a parade, a tractor pull, the National Cheese Eating Championships, and the International Cheese Curling Championships (as in the Olympic event, only using a four-pound cheese "stone"), with family and kids divisions. Because the family that throws cheese together. . . . For more information, go to www.arthurcheesefestival.com.

# Chapter 23

# Ten Cheeses We'd Like You to Try

## In This Chapter

▶ Classic cheeses

▶ Regional favorites

▶ Cheeses that are just too good to pass up

*W*ith hundreds of varieties of cheese worldwide, how on earth did we distill a list down to just ten? It wasn't easy. Without further ado, here are our picks for the ten cheeses you really must try. We include a broad spectrum to please most palates.

## Banon (Surface-ripened, Goat Milk)

Banon is a PDO raw goat or sheep milk cheese produced in southern France. Its appearance is distinct because the little rounds, after being aged for 5 to 10 days, are wrapped in chestnut leaves held in place with raffia. The cheese is then aged at least another 14 days. The leaves keep the cheese soft and pliable and impart a slightly earthy flavor. When ready to eat, the leaves are unwrapped. Banon is a rindless, goaty, yeasty, white cheese that becomes softer and more intensely flavored as it ages.

Some producers of Banon garnish their cheeses with pepper, savory, thyme, or bay leaves. If you're lucky enough to try Banon in its place of origin, you'll find it sold at outdoor markets in the cities and throughout the countryside.

## Barely Buzzed (Coated-Rind, Cow Milk)

Utah's Beehive Cheese Co. is one of the newer domestic cheesemakers (established in 2005), but it produces spectacular — and highly original — cow milk cheeses. Barely Buzzed starts with the company's flagship cheese, Promontory, a zesty, aged Irish-style cheddar. Coffee beans and lavender buds are finely ground together and mixed with oil before being hand-rubbed on the rind. The resulting cheese is distinct but delicious, with obvious flavors of coffee and floral qualities as well as prolonged sweet notes and a full-bodied, rich, savory finish.

The same cheesemakers also produce TeaHive (rubbed with black tea and bergamot oil), SeaHive (with local wildflower honey and salt), and Promontory (smoked over walnut shells and slices of red apple).

# Stracchino di Crescenza (Fresh, Cow Milk)

Known as *stracchino* or just *crescenza,* this incredibly creamy, gooey cheese is a direct reflection of the milk it's made from. Produced from the fall and winter milk of cows coming down from the summer mountain pastures of Lombardy, Piedmont, and Veneto, stracchino di crescenza is so rich because the physical exertion creates milk that is extra-high in butterfat. Aged for just 1 week, the result is a lactic, faintly tangy, rindless cheese that's smooth and spreadable.

Domestically-produced stracchino di crescenza is made year-round from pasteurized milk. We highly recommend the versions made by California's Bellwether Farms (see Chapter 21) and Wisconsin's Belgioioso Cheese.

Serve stracchino di crescenza straight up with fresh fruit or try it in a simple recipe like our Nectarine, Prosciutto, and Arugula Salad with Crescenza Toasts (see Chapter 17).

# Epoisses (Washed-Rind, Cow Milk)

One of the most-loved stinky cheeses, Epoisses has been produced since the late 1700s near the town of the same name in Burgundy, France. The cheese was granted PDO status in 1991. Handmade slowly and gently, the curd remains uncooked and is allowed to drain naturally so that as much moisture as possible remains in the finished cheeses. Aging lasts for a minimum of four weeks. During this period, the cheeses are washed repeatedly in brine and then with wine or *marc* (brandy), which encourages the growth of the *B. linens,* giving the cheese its signature deep, rust-colored rind, sticky exterior, and seriously stinky aroma (which, admittedly, is much stronger than the interior flavor).

When ripe, the texture of Epoisses is satiny and unctuous, with complex, meaty flavors that include waves of sweet, salt, butter, and clean milk. You eat Epoisses by cutting a "lid" from the top of the cheese and spooning up the oozy interior.

Epoisses was very popular through the beginning of the 20th century, but production declined and then ceased entirely during World War II. M. Berthaut, of the village of Epoisses, revived production in 1956, and although other excellent versions are available, Berthaut's Epoisses is still one of the best, sold in a round wooden box, as is traditional.

Enjoy Epoisses with a freshly sliced baguette, some dried fruit, and a chilled Sauternes wine — and you've got a little wheel of heaven.

# Clisson (Washed-Rind, Goat Milk)

Washed-rind goat milk cheeses aren't common, but this lovely and unusual version (also known as Tome d'Aquitaine) is produced in 12-pound wheels at the Union Laiterie de la Venise Verte, in the Loire region of France (famed for its goat cheese). The young wheels are then transported to Bordeaux, where they're aged in the caves of *affineur* Jean d'Alos. As they age, the cheeses are washed regularly with a brine solution that contains Muscadet (a French white wine), in addition to receiving applications of Sauternes, the regal dessert wine of Bordeaux.

The result — aided by the growth of *B. linens* bacteria — is a cheese with complex flavors and a pungent aroma. Clisson's texture is silky, slightly moist, and supple, with the pure white color that is the hallmark of goat (and sheep) milk. The flavor is sweet and aromatic, with delicate notes of fruit and Sauternes; this is a cheese born to be served with fresh fruit and a glass of Sauternes, of course!

# Pleasant Ridge Reserve (Firm, Cow Milk)

Talk about a winner! Produced by Wisconsin's Uplands Cheese Company, this cheese is the only three-time Best in Show winner from the American Cheese Society. It's also won the 2003 Best in Show at the World Cheese Championships. (It's the only cheese to hold both awards.)

What's the appeal? Summer milk from cows fed only on lush pasture. The result is a nutty, grassy, slightly crunchy raw milk cheese based upon Beaufort, a classic alpine cheese. Pleasant Ridge is produced only from May to October, and the longer it ages, the more crystallization it presents and caramelly it becomes. Younger wheels tend to be more overtly grassy and fragrant.

Pleasant Ridge Reserve is a wonderful all-purpose cheese; we recommend it for cheese plates, sandwiches, and melting. (A small number of wheels are aged for over a year; these "Extra-Aged" versions are released only in fall and winter.)

# Pondhopper (Firm, Goat Milk)

If you think you don't like goat cheese, this delicious, farmstead Gouda-style number will likely change your mind. Produced by Tumalo Farms in Bend, Oregon, Pondhopper is washed with a local microbrew, Mirror Pond Ale, before being coated in yellow wax. The resulting cheese is firm, dense, and supple, and the interior is a creamy ivory. The flavor reflects a hint of yeasty hops, which balances its sharpness. There's no marked goaty flavor, although hints may creep through on older wheels (cheeses are aged 2 to 3 months). We find the younger wheels have a more creamy texture that's irresistible with sliced apples and perhaps a cold glass of Pacific Northwest IPA.

# Comté (Firm, Cow Milk)

Made in the Jura Mountain region of France from raw cow milk, Comté has been produced for over eight centuries and is consumed by at least 40 percent of the French population on a regular basis. To keep up with this demand, approximately 350 cooperatives, known as *fruitieres,* produce this PDO cheese in substantial quantities from the milk of small, local herds. (It takes 140 gallons of milk — the daily output of 30 cows — to make one 80–90 pound wheel of Comté!)

Smooth and dense, with occasional holes in the paste, the cheese itself is a straw-colored yellow that varies from pale to darker, depending on the animals' diet and thus the color of the milk at the time of production. Comté's flavors are rich and famously complex (including hints of butter, chocolate, toast, hazelnuts, and even leather) and vary according to the fruitiere.

Comté is one of the most versatile cheeses, great for melting, layering on a sandwich, or snacking. We can't get enough.

# Rogue River Blue (Blue, Cow Milk)

Aged between 8 to 12 months, Rogue River Blue is produced by Southern Oregon's Rogue Creamery (Chapter 21) and has won, in addition to numerous other awards, the ACS's Best in Show award in both 2009 and 2011. This luscious blue is cloaked in grape leaves (from nearby Carpenter Hills Vineyard) that are themselves soaked in Clear Creek Distillery's pear brandy — a combination that lends a distinct alcohol note to the cheese and makes it an aesthetic stunner on a cheese plate. Rogue River Blue is earthy and winey, with a syrupy, fruity aroma. Crystallized amino acids lend a slight crunch to the otherwise creamy texture; the flavor is a complex blend of port, spice, caramel, and savory, earthy notes.

We love Rogue River Blue with fresh or dried fruit. It's also good with a spicy salami or slightly sweet ham, accompanied by dark, hearty pumpernickel or walnut bread, and a glass of fruit-driven, dry red wine.

# Abbaye de Belloc (Semi-Firm, Sheep Milk)

Made by the Benedictine monks at the Abbaye de Notre-Dame de Belloc in France's western Pyrenees, Abbaye de Belloc is made from raw sheep milk sourced from the Manech breed.

The recipe is based on another classic cheese of the area, Ossau Iraty, which is also produced from sheep milk. However, the origination of Abbaye de Belloc is relatively recent, having been developed by the monks in the 1960s, and production is strictly seasonal, with cheesemaking taking place mainly between December and the end of July. The cheese are then aged from 4 to 10 months.

Velvety and smooth, Abbaye de Belloc's interior is sweet and rich, with brown-butter flavors and hints of nuts and caramel. This is a cheese that goes with just about anything — and there are very few who don't fall for it. When it doubt, try it with a glass of Pinot Blanc or Noir, or a dry rosé.

# Metric Conversion Guide

· · · · · · · · · · · · · · · · · · · · · · · · · · · · · · · · · · · · · · · · · · · · · · · · · · · · · ·

*N*ote: The recipes in this book weren't developed or tested using metric measurements. There may be some variation in quality when converting to metric units.

## Common Abbreviations

| Abbreviation(s) | What It Stands For |
| --- | --- |
| cm | Centimetre |
| C., c. | Cup |
| G, g | Gram |
| kg | Kilogram |
| L, l | Litre |
| lb. | Pound |
| mL, ml | Millilitre |
| oz. | Ounce |
| pt. | Pint |
| t., tsp. | Teaspoon |
| T., Tb., Tbsp. | Tablespoon |

## Volume

| U.S. Units | Canadian Metric | Australian Metric |
|---|---|---|
| ¼ teaspoon | 1 millilitre | 1 millilitre |
| ½ teaspoon | 2 millilitres | 2 millilitres |
| 1 teaspoon | 5 millilitres | 5 millilitres |
| 1 tablespoon | 15 millilitres | 20 millilitres |
| ¼ cup | 50 millilitres | 60 millilitres |
| ⅓ cup | 75 millilitres | 80 millilitres |
| ½ cup | 125 millilitres | 125 millilitres |
| ⅔ cup | 150 millilitres | 170 millilitres |
| ¾ cup | 175 millilitres | 190 millilitres |
| 1 cup | 250 millilitres | 250 millilitres |
| 1 quart | 1 litre | 1 litre |
| 1½ quarts | 1.5 litres | 1.5 litres |
| 2 quarts | 2 litres | 2 litres |
| 2½ quarts | 2.5 litres | 2.5 litres |
| 3 quarts | 3 litres | 3 litres |
| 4 quarts (1 gallon) | 4 litres | 4 litres |

## Weight

| U.S. Units | Canadian Metric | Australian Metric |
|---|---|---|
| 1 ounce | 30 grams | 30 grams |
| 2 ounces | 55 grams | 60 grams |
| 3 ounces | 85 grams | 90 grams |
| 4 ounces (¼ pound) | 115 grams | 125 grams |
| 8 ounces (½ pound) | 225 grams | 225 grams |
| 16 ounces (1 pound) | 455 grams | 500 grams (½ kilogram) |

## Length

| Inches | Centimetres |
|--------|-------------|
| 0.5 | 1.5 |
| 1 | 2.5 |
| 2 | 5.0 |
| 3 | 7.5 |
| 4 | 10.0 |
| 5 | 12.5 |
| 6 | 15.0 |
| 7 | 17.5 |
| 8 | 20.5 |
| 9 | 23.0 |
| 10 | 25.5 |
| 11 | 28.0 |
| 12 | 30.5 |

## Temperature (Degrees)

| Fahrenheit | Celsius |
|------------|---------|
| 32 | 0 |
| 212 | 100 |
| 250 | 120 |
| 275 | 140 |
| 300 | 150 |
| 325 | 160 |
| 350 | 180 |
| 375 | 190 |
| 400 | 200 |
| 425 | 220 |
| 450 | 230 |
| 475 | 240 |
| 500 | 260 |

# Index

## • A •

Abbaye de Belloc, 157
Abbaye Saint Benoît du Lac, 130
Abeiderrahmane, Nancy, 337
about this book, 1–5
accessories, 95–97
ackawi, 228
affinage. *See also* aging
  about, 10
  art of, 31
  French fromageries best known for, 162
affineurs, 31
Aged Gouda and Walnut Biscotti, 308–309
aging. *See also* ripening
  hard cheese, 60
  Loire Valley goat cheeses, 155
  Manchego cheese, 187
airaq, 334
Alberta, 128
alcohol. *See* beer; spirits; wine
ales, 252–253
Aligot, 158, 266
Allgäu cheeses, 205–207
alpine cheeses
  characteristics of, 197–198
  Italian, 167
  from Switzerland, 198–203
Alsace-Lorraine cheeses, 163–164
American Cheese Society, 13, 83, 345–346
American cheeses. *See* North American
  cheeses
American Livestock Breed Conservancy, 20
Amish Country Cheese Festival, 349
ammoniated aroma, 41, 48, 61, 152
Androuët, 90
AOC (Appellation d'originee contrôlle), 36
aperitifs, 255
appearance of cheese, 77

Appenseller cheese, 200
appetizers
  Comté wafers, 267
  Crispy Cheese Croquettes, 268
  famous, 266
  Gougères, 270–271
  Queso Fundido con Pollo, 269
apple pectin powder, 243
apricots, 312–313
Arding, Kate, 37, 139
Argentine cheesemaking, 133
Armenian cheeses, 211
*Artisan Cheese Making at Home* (Karlin),
  323
artisan cheeses. *See also* artisanal
  cheesemakers
  Alberta and Ontario, 128
  books on, 323
  British Columbian, 128
  California's, 113–115
  costs of, 37
  found in Rockies, 120
  Idaho's, 118
  Irish, 146
  New York, 125
  New Zealand's emerging, 222–223
  Oregon, 116
  Quebec and Maritimes, 129–130
  Southern U.S., 122–123
  U.S. production of, 112
  Vermont, 124
  Washington State's, 117–118
Artisanal, 31, 88
artisanal cheesemakers
  Alison Hooper, 339
  Bob Reese, 339
  British, 141, 142
  Cary Bryant, 341–342
  Cindy and Liam Callahan, 342

artisanal cheesemakers *(continued)*
  David Gremmels, 341–342
  Jennifer Bice, 342–343
  Judy Schad, 340–341
  Mary Keehn, 340
  Mateo and Andy Kehler, 344
  Midwestern, 120–122
  Mike and Carol Gingrich, 343
  Peggy Smith, 344
  Sue Conley, 344
  Tom and Nancy Clark, 340
  touring, 123
Arzúa Ulloa cheese, 182
Aschekäse cheese, 204–205
Asiago cheese, 52, 171
asparagus, 281, 283
Asturias, Spain, 182–183
Australia
  cheese and wine trails of, 218
  cheesemaking in, 213–214, 216
  culture of, 216
  goat cheeses in, 217
  King Island Dairy, 219
  map of, 215
  other regions of, 220
  South Australia, 218–220
  Tasmania, 219–220
  Victoria, 215–217
Auvergne cheeses, 158–159
Avalanche Cheese Company, 120
Azeitão cheese, 191
Azores, 189, 191

• *B* •

Back Forty Artisan Cheese, 129
bacteria. *See also specific types*
  beneficial species of, 32
  found in Emmentaler, 200
  killing with pasteurization, 30
  preventing bad, 318
  ripening of cheese and, 12, 31–32
Ballard Family Dairy and Cheese, 118

Barbour, Lucy, 219
Basque Country cheeses, 184–185
Bavarian and Allgäu cheeses, 205–207
Beaufort, 67, 160
Beechers Handmade Cheese, 88, 117
Beehive Cheese Co., 120
Beeler, Rolf, 31
Beemster cheesemakers, 210
beer
  about, 251
  pairing with cheese, 252–254
  styles of beer, 252
beestings, 336
Bellwether Farms, 114, 342
Berger, Ueli, 219
Berner Oberland cheeses, 199–200
Bernstein, Joshua M., 254
Berthaut, 162
Bethmale, 157
Beyaz Peynir, 193
bGH (bovine growth hormone), 21
Bice, Jennifer, 342–343
Bistro Salad with Poached Egg and
    Parmigiano Reggiano, 276–277
Black Sheep Creamery, 118
Blackberry Farm, 122
Bleu Mont Dairy, 121
bloomy-rind cheese
  defined, 33, 41
  signs of ripeness, 45–46
blue cheeses
  Bleu d'Auvergne, 56, 159
  Bleu de Basque, 157
  Bleu de Gex cheese, 164
  Blu del Moncenisio, 167
  Blue Castello, 55
  Blue Cheese and Potato Tartlets, 302–303
  Cashel Blue, 146
  Caveman Blue, 56
  Danish Blue, 210
  Gorgonzola, 168–169
  Maytag Blue, 122
  Original Blue, 56
  preserving freshness of, 106

Shropshire Blue, 142
Stilton, 142
styles of, 55–57
Blueberry Cobbler, 262
bocconcini, 284
Boeren-Goudse Oplegkass cheese, 209
Boeren-Leidse met sleutels, 209
Boerenkaas cheese, 209
Bonne Bouche, 50
books on cheesemaking, 323
Bosnian cheeses, 211
bourbon, 257
box grater, 96
Bra Cheese Festival, 168, 347
brandy, 258
Brazilian cheesemaking, 133
breakfast recipes. *See* main courses
*Brevibacterium linens*, 32, 48
*Brewed Awakening* (Bernstein), 254
Brie cheese
  about, 46
  camembert versus, 49
  *Penicillium candidum* mold on, 32
  from Île-de-France, 150–152
Brillat-Savarin, 153–154
British Columbia cheeses, 127–128
British Isles cheeses
  characteristics of, 136–138
  history of, 137
  Ireland, 144–146
  Midlands, 141–142
  North of England and the Borders,
    142–143
  regions of, 136
  Scotland and Wales, 143–144
  size of, 138
  Southeast and East, 140–141
  Southwest and West, 139–140
  terrior of, 137–138
  tradition of, 135–136
Brocciu, 161
Broiled Gruyère Sandwiches with Maple-
  Caramelized Apples, 298
Brown, Bonnie, 237

brown spirits, 257–258
brunch recipes. *See* main courses
Bruny Island Cheese Company, 220
Bryant, Cary, 341–342
bST (bovine growth hormone), 21
buffalo milk. *See* water buffalo milk
Bulgarian cheeses, 211–212
Burgandy cheeses, 161–162
burrata, 43–44, 177
Buster, Michele, 187
butterfat averages, 18, 21, 185
Buttermilk-Oat Crackers, 241

• *C* •

Cabrales cheese
  about, 28, 57
  making of, 182–183
  mixed milks for, 22
Caciocavallo Podolico, 177
calcium chloride, 321
California Artisan Cheese Festival, 346
California regional cheeses, 113–115
Callahan, Cindy and Liam, 342
Cambozola cheese, 55, 207
camel milk, 228
camembert cheese
  about, 46
  Brie versus, 49
  Camembert de Normandie, 153
  Camembert Dressing recipe, 275
Campania cheeses, 175–176
Caña de Cabra, 187
Canadian cheeses
  about, 125–127
  Alberta and Ontario, 128
  British Columbia, 127–128
  cheesemaking regions in, 127
  islands known for, 129
  Quebec and Maritimes provinces,
    129–130
Canadienne cows, 126
Canary Islands cheeses, 187–188

canning, 242
Cantabria, Spain, 183
Cantal cheese, 64, 159
Canterbury Cheesemongers, 90
Capriole Farmstead Goat Cheeses, 121, 340–341
Caravane, 336–337
cardoon, 190
Carephilly cheese, 144
Caramelized Shallots in Port Wine, 244
Carmody, 63
Carpenter, Jeanne, 83
Carr Valley Cheese, 121
Carroll, Ricki, 323
casein, 18
caseophile, 80
Cashel Blue, 146
Castellan, Martin, 181
Castelmagno, 167
Castelo Branco cheese, 190
Castile-Leon cheeses, 185–186
casu marzu, 333–334
Catalonian cheeses, 184
Cato Corner Farm, 125
Caveman Blue, 56
Cellars at Jasper Hill, 31, 124
Celsius, 353
Central and South American cheeses, 132–133
Central Asia
  cheese styles of, 225
  map of, 224
  yak milk in, 226
Central Italy cheeses, 172–175
Certification Exam for Cheese Professionals, 11
Chabichou, 155
chaeshappech, 202
chal, 225
Champagne cheeses, 162–163
Champagne wine, 247, 249–250
Chaource, 163
cheddar
  about, 62
  clothbound, 70–71

Pan-Roasted Wild Mushrooms over Cheddar Polenta with Pumpkinseed Oil, 286–287
salting, 28
cheddaring, 70, 126
cheese. See also cheesemaking; terrior; and specific styles and types
  ammonia smell of, 48, 61, 152
  armchair travel via, 16, 34–36, 107
  artisan, 37
  benefits of, 15
  best beers for, 251–254
  Brie versus camembert, 49
  burgers with, 295
  characteristics of, 12–13
  cheesemakers and cheesemongers, 10–12
  consumption of, 11
  conversion charts, 264, 351–353
  curds in, 18, 27
  cutting, 99–101, 102
  enjoying, 14, 16, 34–36, 107
  evaluating, 77–78
  farmstead, 23
  fresh, 40–44
  judging competitions, 83
  lactose intolerance to, 26, 329
  live culture of, 12
  making, 10, 23–24, 322–323
  matching wine intensity, 246–247, 250
  milk for, 17–22
  moisture content in, 28
  names of British, 140
  origins of, 9–10, 25
  pronouncing names of, 14, 150
  qualities of, 76–77
  quiz on selecting, 81–82
  raw milk, 30
  reasons to eat, 14, 15
  rinds of, 32–34
  salt in, 28–29
  sensory components of, 75
  smoking, 84
  spirits with, 255–258
  starter cultures, 25–26
  styles of, 31–34

terminology of, 13–14
time-tested wines with, 250–251
traditions reflecting terroir in, 28
unusual, 333–338
cheese and wine trails of South Australia, 218
cheese cleaver, 96, 97
cheese fly larvae, 333–334
Cheese Library, 147
*Cheese* (Michelson), 147
cheese mites, 337
cheese plane, 96, 97
*Cheese Primer* (Jenkins), 125, 147
cheese regions. *See* maps of cheese regions
cheese retailers, 85–89
Cheese School of San Francisco, 346
cheeseburgers, 295
cheesecloth, 319
cheesemakers. *See also* artisanal cheesemakers
  alternate fuels used by, 22
  best French fromageries, 162
  buying cheese from, 89
  cheesemongers and, 10–12
  influential artisanal, 339–344
  producing farmstead cheese, 23
  touring regional, 123
  using mixed milks, 22
  working with affineurs, 31
cheesemaking. *See also* home cheesemaking
  affineurs' role in, 31
  applying salt in, 28–29
  basics of, 23–24
  coagulation in, 26–27
  costs of, 37
  federal laws on home, 317
  forming and draining whey, 27–28
  making from mixed milk, 22
  needling blue cheeses, 55
  producing farmstead cheese, 23
  Spanish traditions of, 179–181
  spicing rinds during, 69
  starter cultures for, 25–26

cheesemongers
  about, 10–12
  asking for samples, 80
  buying cheese without, 13
  knowledge of, 86
  talking with, 87, 93, 232, 234
  visiting local, 80
Chenel, Laura, 114
Cherry Preserves, 242–243
Cheshire, 142
chèvre. *See* goat cheese
chhurpi, 225, 335
Chicken Cacciatore with Ricotta Salata, 293
Chile-Citrus Olives, 240
Chimay cheese, 54
CLA (conjugated linoleic acid), 15
Clark, Tom and Nancy, 340
cleaning cutting boards, 97
clothbound rinds, 34, 70–71
clotted cream, 137, 137–138, 138
Coach Farm, 125
coated-rind cheeses
  about coated rinds, 34
  nutty flavors of, 69–70
  sharp to earthy flavored, 70–71
  sweet, 71
Cockman, Alan, 217
cocktail recipes
  Blueberry Cobbler, 262
  SweetWater, The, 261
  Widow's Kiss, The, 260
coffee, 259
Colby cheese, 62
competitions, 83
compote, 311
Comté cheese, 65, 164
Comté wafers, 267
condiment recipes
  Buttermilk-Oat Crackers, 241
  Caramelized Shallots in Port Wine, 244
  Cherry Preserves, 242–243
  Chile-Citrus Olives, 240
Conley, Sue, 344
Connecticut regional cheeses, 125

cooking with cheese
  about, 264
  appetizers, 266–271
  common recipe abbreviations, 351
  conversion chart, 264, 351–353
  desserts, 305–315
  main courses, 289–305
  quiche and tart cheeses, 309
  selecting cheese, 265
  shaping gnocchi, 292
  soufflés, 305
  stone fruit selections when, 273
  toasting nuts, 279
  types of pears, 275
  using herbs, 301
Corsican cheeses, 160–161
costs
  artisan cheese, 37
  volume and, 265
cotija, 51
cottage cheese, 42
Cougar Gold, 338
Cowgirl Creamery, 88, 114, 344
cows
  Canadienne, 126
  characteristics of milk, 18–19
  cow share agreements, 322
  heritage breeds of, 20
  sustainable dairy farming for, 22
Crave Brothers, 121
cream cheese, 42
crème fraiche
  about, 42
  adding to eggs, 301
  recipe for, 325
  Rhubarb-Brown Sugar Cake with
    Strawberry-Rhubarb Compote and
    Crème Fraiche, 310–311
  Wood-Roasted New Potatoes with Délice
    du Jura and Black Truffle Oil, 285
Crispy Cheese Croquettes, 268
Croatian cheeses, 212
crottin
  defined, 155
  Fennel, Tangerine, and Hazelnut Salad
    with, 278–279

Crottin de Chavignol, 155
croutons, 275
Cuixart, Josep, 184
culture, 13, 321
*culture* magazine website, 13, 86
Cunnie, Maureen, 344
curds
  about, 18, 27
  coagulation of, 26
  cooked, 198
  forming and draining whey from, 27–28
  freezing, 92
cutting boards, 97–98
Cypress Grove Chevre, 115, 340
Cyprus, 195–196
Czech Republic cheeses, 212

d'Alos, Jean, 162
Danbo cheese, 210
Danish Blue cheese, 210
Danish Fontina cheese, 210
Deichkäse cheese, 205
Delannes, Cécile, 151
Délice de Bourgogne, 162
Délice du Jura, 285
designation, 34, 35–36
designing cheese plates
  arranging on plates, 102–103, 234
  choosing garnishes and sides, 234–235
  compatible foods for plates, 233
  planning serving amounts, 231–232
  recipes for condiments, 239–244
  savory offerings, 235
  selecting cheese, 232–233
  serving sweet plates, 235, 237
  tips for, 101–105, 238–239
dessert wines, 250
desserts
  Aged Gouda and Walnut Biscotti, 308–309
  Dried Apricot-Goat Cheese Tart, 312–313
  Ginger-Poached Pears with Roquefort-
    Honey Ice Cream, 314–315

Grilled Peaches with Mascarpone, Pistachios, and Raspberries, 307
Rhubarb-Brown Sugar Cake with Strawberry-Rhubarb Compote and Crème Fraiche, 310–311
using seasonal fruits in, 306
Di Bruno Bros, 88
Dilliscus, 146
DOC (Denominazione di origine contrallata), 36
donkey milk, 334–335
DOP (Denominación de origen protegida), 36
Dorling Kindersley, 147
double-crème soft cheese, 47
Double Gloucester, 140
draining bag, 319
dressings
　Camembert, 274–275
　Vinaigrette, 273, 277, 279
Dried Apricot-Goat Cheese Tart, 312–313
Druart, Marc, 323
Drunken Goat cheese, 187

**• E •**

E. Braingdorge, 162
East British cheeses, 140–141
Eastern and Central European cheeses, 211–212
Eastern France, 161–164
eating
　Epoisses, 162
　soft cheese, 41
Ecuador's cheesemaking, 132
Edam cheeses, 209–210
eezgii, 225
eggs
　Bistro Salad with Poached Egg and Parmigiano Reggiano, 276–277
　Blue Cheese and Potato Tartlets, 302–303
　Ginger-Poached Pears with Roquefort-Honey Ice Cream, 314–315

New Classic Cheese Soufflé, 304–305
Sheep Milk Ricotta Gnocchi with Fresh Peas, Spring Onions, and Bacon, 290–291, 292
Sopa de Quinoa, 280
Stinky Cheese Omlet with Herb Topping, 300–301
Emilia-Romagna cheeses, 172–173
Emmental cheeses, 199–200
Emmentaler cheese, 69–70, 200
Epoisses cheese, 48, 161, 161–162
Esrom cheese, 210
European Union cheeses, 179–188
　British Isles, 135–146
　Cyprus, 195–196
　Czech Republic, 212
　Eastern and Central Europe, 211–212
　France, 147–164
　Germany, 203–207
　Greece, 194–195
　Italy, 165–178
　Netherlands, 207–210
　Nordic cheeses, 210–211
　Portugal, 188–192
　protected designations within, 35–36
　Spain, 179–188, 190
　Turkey, 192–194
Everona Dairy, 122
Evora cheese, 192

**• F •**

Fahrenheit, 353
Farm House Natural Cheeses, 128
farmstead cheese
　British, 138
　Farmstead's Cheesemonger Mac 'n' Cheese, 294–295
　producing, 23
　Pt. Reyes Farmstead Cheese, 114
Farnham, Jody M., 323
feel of cheese, 78

Fennel, Tangerine, and Hazelnut Salad with Crottin, 278–279
Ferguson, Giana and Tom, 146
Fermier, 90
festivals
  American Cheese Society Annual Conference, 345–346
  Amish Country Cheese Festival, 349
  Bra Cheese Festival, 168, 347
  California Artisan Cheese Festival, 346
  Cheese School of San Francisco, 346
  German Cheese Market, 205
  Great British Cheese Festival, 347
  Great Canadian Cheese Festival, The, 348
  Great Wisconsin Cheese Festival, 348
  Oregon Cheese Festival, 347
  Seattle Cheese Festival, 348
  Vermont Cheesemaker's Festival, 346
feta
  about, 51
  Israeli Couscous with Preserved Lemon, Sugar Snap Peas, Feta, and Mint, 282–283
  origins of, 195
Fior di Latte, 176
Fiore Sardo, 177
Fiscalini Farms, 115
flat-blade knife, 318
flavors
  combining on savory platters, 235, 238
  defined, 78–79
  discovering favorite, 76
  milk's seasonal, 91
  pairing cheese and wine, 247
  pesticide-free, 239
  selecting, 265
  sides for sweet cheese plates, 235, 237
  umami, 78
  when tasting cheese, 78
Fleur du Maquis, 161
fondue, 200–201, 266
Fontina val d'Aosta, 67, 167
Formaggio Kitchen, 31, 89
Formatgeria La Seu, 180

forms, 319, 319–320, 320
Fourme d'Ambert, 159
France
  Alsace-Lorraine, 163–164
  Auvergne, 158–159
  best fromageries of, 162
  Burgandy, 161–162
  Champagne, 162–163
  Corsica, 160–161
  Franche-Comté, 164
  Île-de-France, 150–152
  Loire Valley, 155–156
  map of, 149
  Midi-Pyrenees, 158
  Normandy, 153–154
  Pays Basque, 156–157
  purchasing in U.S., 148–150
  regional varieties in, 148
  Rhône-Alpes and Haute-Savoie, 159–160
  role in life, 147
  South and Southeast, 157–158
  thistle rennet in, 190
Franche-Comté cheeses, 164
freezing
  milk or curd, 92
  seasonal produce, 306
*French Cheeses* (Dorling Kindersley), 147
fresh cheese
  defined, 40
  pasta filata, 43–44
  perishability of, 41
  preserving freshness of, 106
  types of, 42
  whey cheese, 43, 194–195
Fribourg-Vaud fondue cheeses, 200–201
frico, 171, 288
Friuli-Venezia Giulia and Veneto cheeses, 169, 171–172
Fromage de Brebis, 156
Fromage de Meaux, 151
Fromagerie du Presbytère, 130
Fromagerie L'Amuse, 31, 82, 90
Fromagerie Le Détour, 130
Fromagerie Rouzaire, 162

Fromagination, 89
fruit
  bloomy-rind cheeses with, 46
  Broiled Gruyère Sandwiches with Maple-
    Caramelized Apples, 298
  Dried Apricot-Goat Cheese Tart, 312–313
  enjoying fresh cheese with, 42
  Fennel, Tangerine, and Hazelnut Salad
    with Crottin, 278–279
  Ginger-Poached Pears with Roquefort-
    Honey Ice Cream, 314–315
  Grilled Peaches with Mascarpone,
    Pistachios, and Raspberries, 307
  Nectarine, Prosciutto, and Arugula Salad
    with Crescenza Toasts, 272–273
  oxidization of, 237
  pairing fresh cheese with, 42
  Peppered Pear and Goat Cheese Scones,
    299
  Rhubarb-Brown Sugar Cake with
    Strawberry-Rhubarb Compote and
    Crème Fraiche, 310–311
  Salad Greens with Roasted Pears,
    Cornbread Croutons, and Camembert
    Dressing, 274–275
  selecting stone, 273
  Strawberry-Rhubarb compote, 311
  types of pears, 275
  using seasonal, 306
  washed-rind cheeses with, 48
Fryar, Natalie, 246
further reading
  books on home cheesemaking, 323
  cheese websites, 13, 180

• G •

Gabietou, 157
Galicia region of Spain, 182
Garrotxa cheese, 64, 184
Georgia cheeses, 212
*Geotricum candidum* mold, 32, 41, 44

Germany
  Bavarian and Allgäu, 205–207
  cheesemaking in, 203
  map of, 204
  northern cheeses of, 203–205
  serving Handkäse and quark, 205
gin, 256
Ginger-Poached Pears with Roquefort-
    Honey Ice Cream, 314–315
Gingrich, Mike and Carol, 343
girolles, 95
Gjetost cheese, 210
Glengarry Fine Cheese, 128
goat cheese (chèvre)
  about, 42
  Australian, 217
  Dried Apricot-Goat Cheese Tart, 312–313
  French varieties of, 156
  Grilled Asparagus with Chèvre and
    Orange Zest, 281
  home recipe for, 326–327
  Peppered Pear and Goat Cheese Scones,
    299
  pungent smell of, 101
  substituting for cow milk, 329
  U.S. introduction of, 114
goat milk. *See also* goat cheese
  butterfat averages of, 18
  characteristics of, 20
Golden Cross, 141
Gorgonzola Dolce, 55, 168–169
Gorgonzola Piccante, 57, 169
Gorwydd Caerphilly cheese, 53
Gouda cheeses
  about, 71, 207–209
  Aged Gouda and Walnut Biscotti, 308–309
Gougères, 270–271
Graindorge, Thierry, 151
Grana Padano, 66, 173
Grandvewe Cheeses, 220
Graskaas cheeses, 210
Great British Cheese Festival, 347
Great Canadian Cheese Festival, The, 348
Great Wisconsin Cheese Festival, 348

Greek cheeses, 194–195
green onions, 292
Gremmels, David, 341–342
Greve cheese, 211
Grilled Asparagus with Chèvre and Orange
   Zest, 281
Grilled Peaches with Mascarpone,
   Pistachios, and Raspberries, 307
Grilled Sausages with Grapes, Wilted
   Greens, and Pecorino Romano,
   296–297
Grotenstein, David, 83
Gruyère cheese, 35, 67, 200–201
Gubbeen, 146

### • *H* •

Halloumi cheese, 52, 195
Handkäse cheese, 205
hard cheese
   aging of, 60
   classifying, 60
   coated-rind and clothbound, 68–71
   natural-rind, 63–66
   rindless, 61–63
   soft versus, 61
   washed-rind, 66–68
Haricot Verts and Miniature Tomatoes
   with Bocconcini, 284
Hatch, Andy, 343
Haute-Savoie cheeses, 159–160
Havarti cheese, 62, 211
Haystack Mountain Goat Dairy, 120
Healey, Jon, 219
herbs, 301
heritage breeds of livestock, 20
Herzegovina cheeses, 211
Hobelkaese cheese, 200
Holziner, Anton and Luise, 207
*Home Cheese Making* (Carroll), 323
home cheesemaking
   additives for, 321
   books on, 323

equipment for, 318–320
federal laws on, 317
finding supplies for, 319
milk for, 321
steps for, 322–323
Hook's Cheese Company, 121
Hooper, Alison, 339
Hostettler, Caroline, 31
HTST (high temperature short time), 30
Hungary cheeses, 212

### • *I* •

ice cream, 314–315
icons in book, 5
Idaho regional cheeses, 118
Idiazabal cheeses, 184–185
importing raw milk cheeses, 30
international specialty shops, 90
"Invalid's Story, The" (Twain), 54
iodine, 318
Irish cheeses, 144–146
islands
   Azores, 189, 191
   Canary Islands, 187–188
   known for Canadian cheeses, 129
   Madeira Islands, 189
Isle of Mull cheese, 144
Israeli Couscous with Preserved Lemon,
   Sugar Snap Peas, Feta, and Mint,
   282–283
Italy
   best pecorinos of, 170–171, 178
   Campania, 175–176
   Central, 172–175
   cheesemaking tradition in, 165
   Emilia-Romagna, 172–173
   Friuli-Venezia Giulia and Veneto,
      169, 171–172
   Lombardy, 168–169
   map of, 166
   Northern, 166–169, 171
   Parmigiano Reggiano, 15, 64, 66, 173

Puglia/Sardinia and Sicily, 176–178
salumi of, 74, 174
Southern, 175–178
styles of alpine cheeses in, 167
Tuscany, 174–175
Valle d'Aosta, 167–168
Île-de-France cheeses, 150–152

● *J* ●

James Ranch, 120
Jarlsberg cheese, 69–70, 211
Jasper Hill Farm, 124, 344
Jenkins, Steven, 125, 147
Johansson, Christer and Ulla, 336
*Joy of Cheesemaking, The* (Farnham and
    Druart), 323
juices, 258
juju dhau, 225
Jura Mountain specialties, 201–202
jusstoleipä, 336

● *K* ●

Kamin, Charlotte, 104
Kapiti, 223
Karlin, Mary, 323
Käsespätzle, 206
Kaşkaval cheese, 193
Kasseri cheese, 195
Keen's Cheddar, 140
Kefalotyri cheese, 194–195
Kehler, Mateo and Andy, 344
Kelle Peynir, 193
Kervella, Gabrielle, 217
King Island Dairy, 219
KISS (Keep It Simple, Stupid), 234
knives
    flat-blade, 318
    soft-cheese, 96, 97
Kootenay Alpine Cheese Company, 128
Kryddost cheese, 211
kumis, 334

● *L* ●

La Chivita cheese, 183
La Fromagerie, 31, 90
La Tur, 49
labneh, 228
lactase, 61
lactation periods
    cows, 19
    goats, 29
    sheep, 21
    timing of, 91
lactose intolerance, 26, 329
ladle, 318
lagers, 252
Laguiole, 158
Lambert, Paula, 119
Lancashire, 143
Langres, 163
Lappi cheese, 211
Lark's Meadow Farms, 118
Le Meunier, Rodolphe, 162
leipäjuusto cheese, 211, 336
length conversion chart, 353
Leonora cheese, 186
L'Etivaz cheese, 201
Limburger cheese, 54, 206–207
Lincet, 162
Lincolnshire Poacher, 142
Livarot, 153
livestock
    heritage breeds of, 10
    milk production by, 19
    ruminant, 26
    sustainable dairy farming for, 22
    synthetic hormones used for, 21
local farmers, 306
Loire valley cheeses, 155–156
Lombardy cheeses, 168–169
Los Beyos cheese, 182
Luigi Guffanti 1876, 31

## • M •

Madeira Islands, 189
Mahon cheese, 188
main courses
  Blue Cheese and Potato Tartlets, 302–303
  Broiled Gruyère Sandwiches with Maple-Caramelized Apples, 298
  Chicken Cacciatore with Ricotta Salata, 293
  Farmstead's Cheesemonger Mac 'n' Cheese, 294–295
  Grilled Sausages with Grapes, Wilted Greens, and Pecorino Romano, 296–297
  New Classic Cheese Soufflé, 304–305
  Peppered Pear and Goat Cheese Scones, 299
  Sheep Milk Ricotta Gnocchi with Fresh Peas, Spring Onions, and Bacon, 290–291, 292
  Stinky Cheese Omlet with Herb Topping, 300–301
Majorero, 28
Majorero cheeses, 188
*Making Artisan Cheese* (Smith), 323
Manchego cheese, 69, 186–187
Manouri cheese, 194
maps of cheese regions
  Australia, 215
  Canadian regions, 127
  Central Asia, 224
  France, 149
  Germany, 204
  Ireland, 145
  Italy, 166
  Middle Eastern, 227
  Netherlands, 208
  New Zealand, 221
  Portugal, 189
  Spain, 180
  Switzerland, 199
  United Kingdom, 136
  United States, 112
Mariposa Dairy, 128
Martell, Charles, 338
mascarpone
  about, 42
  Grilled Peaches with Mascarpone, Pistachios, and Raspberries, 307
Massachusetts regional cheeses, 125
mastitis, 21
Maytag Dairy Farms, 56, 122
Meadow Creek Dairy, 123
Mediterranean cheeses
  Cypriot, 195–196
  Greek, 194–195
  Turkish, 192–194
membrillo, 187, 188
Meredith Dairy, 217
metric conversion guide, 351–353
Mexican cheeses, 130–131
Michelson, Patricia, 147
Middle Eastern cheeses, 226–228
Midi-Pyrenees cheeses, 158
Midlands cheeses, 141–142
Midwest cheesemaking, 120–122
Mihaliç Peynir, 193
Milawa Cheese Company, 217
milbenkäse, 337
milk. *See also* goat milk; sheep milk; water buffalo milk
  about, 17
  camel, 228, 336–337
  composition of, 18
  discovering favorite kinds of, 76
  donkey, 334
  freezing, 92
  mixing for cheese, 22
  pasteurized versus raw, 30
  preserving with cheese making, 25
  purchasing for home cheesemaking, 321
  raw, 30, 149, 222, 322
  rBST in, 21
  ripening, 12, 25–26

seasonal flavors of, 91
types of animal, 18, 19
yak, 21, 226, 335
Miller, Laurel, 236
Mimolette, 66, 154
mixed-milk cheeses, 22
mold-ripened soft cheese,
    33, 40, 40–41, 49–50
molds
  beneficial, 32
  classifying cheese on, 45
  ripening of cheese and, 31–32
  types of, 32, 44
Mongolia, 224
Mons Fromager Affineur, 90
Mons, Herve, 90, 162
Montasio, 171
Monte Enebro cheese, 186
Monterey Jack, 62
Montgomery's Cheddar, 140
moose cheese, 335–336
Morbier cheese, 68, 164
mozzarella
  about, 43
  Italian, 175–176
  making home-made, 328–329
Mozzarella Company, 119
Mt. Tam cheese, 46
Mt. Townsend Creamery, 117
Munster cheese, 48, 163–164, 164
Murcian cheeses, 187
Murray's Cheese Shop, 31, 89
Myzithra cheese, 195

• *N* •

nabulsi, 228
names
  British cheese, 140
  Italian cheese, 165
  pronouncing cheese, 14, 150

natural-rind hard cheese
  about natural rinds, 33
  buttery, 63
  earthy, 64
  nutty, 65
  sharp, 65–66
Neal's Yard Dairy, 90, 136, 139
Nectarine, Prosciutto, and Arugula Salad
    with Crescenza Toasts, 272–273
needling, 55
Netherlands
  Boerenkaas, 209
  Edam cheeses, 209–210
  Gouda cheese of, 207–209
  Graskaas, 210
  location of, 207, 208
Nevat cheese, 184
New Classic Cheese Soufflé, 304–305
New South Wales, Australia, 220
New York regional cheeses, 124–125
New Zealand
  cheesemaking in, 214, 220–221
  emerging industry in, 222–223
  map of, 221
Nisa cheese, 191–192
non-alcoholic beverages, 258–259
Noord-Hollandse Oplegkaas cheese, 208
Nordic cheeses, 210–211
Nordost-Schweiz regional cheeses, 202–203
Normandy regional cheese, 153–154
North American cheeses. *See also*
    Canadian cheeses
  Canadian, 125–130
  maps, 112, 127
  Mexican, 130–131
  Midwest, 120–122
  Northeast and New England, 123–125
  Pacific Northwest, 115–118
  regions of, 112
  Rockies, 119–120
  Southern, 122–123
  Southwest, 119

North American cheeses *(continued)*
  U.S. cheeses, 109–110
  West Coast, 113–115
North of England and the Borders, 142–143
Northeast and New England regional
    cheeses, 123–125
Northern Italian cheeses, 166–169, 171
Neufchatel, 154
nuts, 279
nutty flavors
  natural-rind hard cheese, 65
  washed-rind hard cheese with, 65

Obaztda, 206
Old Chatham Sheepherding Company,
    125, 340
Ontario, 128
Oregon Cheese Festival, 347
Oregon cheeses, 115
organic, 306
organoleptic, 75
Original Blue, 56
origins of cheese, 9–10, 25
Örme Peynir, 193
Ossau-Iraty cheese, 63, 157

Pacific Northwest regional cheeses,
    115–118
pairing wine and cheese
  bad combinations in, 250
  best wines with Munster, 164
  Champagne in, 247, 249–250
  choosing red wines, 248
  dessert wines, 250
  finding similarities or contrasts, 247
  intensities when, 246–247, 250
  matching Champagne cheeses and
    wines, 163
  partnering flavors, 245–250
  recommended, 250–251
  rosés, 249
  sparkling wines, 249–250
  tips for white wines, 248–249
palate fatigue, 232
Pan-Roasted Wild Mushrooms over
    Cheddar Polenta with Pumpkinseed
    Oil, 286–287
paneer, 52
panko, 268
Parmesan, 64
Parmigiano Reggiano
  about, 66, 173
  Bistro Salad with Poached Egg and,
    276–277
  cooking with rinds, 264
  low-sodium variety of, 15
  Parmesan versus, 64
  Sheep Milk Ricotta Gnocchi, 290–291,
    290–292, 292
pasta filata, 43–44
pastas
  Farmstead's Cheesemonger Mac 'n'
    Cheese, 294–295
  shaping gnocchi, 292
  Sheep Milk Ricotta Gnocchi, 290–291, 292
paste, 32, 101
pasteurized milk, 30
Pastoral Artisan Cheese, Bread & Wine, 89
pastoralists, 226
pastry
  Blue Cheese and Potato Tartlets, 302–303
  cheeses for seasonal, 309
  Dried Apricot-Goat Cheese Tart, 312–313
Patenaude, Dan and Jeanne, 343
Pays Basque cheeses, 156–157
PDO (Protected Designation of Origin),
    35–36
peaches, 307
pears
  Ginger-Poached Pears with Roquefort-
    Honey Ice Cream, 314–315
  Peppered Pear and Goat Cheese
    Scones, 299

Salad Greens with Roasted Pears,
    Cornbread Croutons, and Camembert
    Dressing, 274–275
Stinking Bishop, 338
pecorinos
  best Italian, 170–171, 178
  defined, 165
  Grilled Sausages with Grapes, Wilted
    Greens, and Pecorino Romano,
    296–297
  pecorino fresco, 52
  Pecorino Pienza Gran Reserva, 175
  Pecorino Romano, 178
  Pecorino Toscano, 65, 174–175
*Penicillum candidum* mold, 32, 44
*Penicillum roqueforti* mold, 32, 55, 158
perishability
  ammonia smell and, 48, 61, 152
  fresh cheese, 41
  signs of bloomy-rind ripeness, 45–46
  soft cheese, 41
  traveling with cheese and, 107
peynir, 193
Pfunds Molkerei, 90
pH, 25
Pholia Farms, 116
Piave, 65, 171
Picón cheese, 183
pilsners, 252
platters, 98, 103
Polish cheeses, 212
Poncelet cheese bar, 90, 180
Pont l'Évêque cheese, 54, 153
Portugal
  cheesemaking in, 188–189
  cheeses from Azores, 189, 191
  cheeses of north and central, 190
  map of, 189
  southern, 191–192
  thistle rennet in cheeses of, 190
pronouncing cheese names, 14, 150
*Proprionibacterium freudenreichii*, 32
Provolone, 172
Pt. Reyes Farmstead Cheese, 114
P'tit Basque, 157

Puck, Wolfgang, 114
Puglia/Sardinia cheeses, 176–178
Puhoi Valley Cheese, 223
pule, 334, 335
purchasing cheese
  buying French cheese in U.S., 148–150
  direct from producer, 89
  finding freshest sources, 85, 86
  how buyers select cheese, 107–108
  judging ripeness before, 94
  online, 87–89
  Spanish shops for, 180
  talking with cheesemongers, 93
  visiting cheese shops, 85–87
  when to buy, 91–92
Pyengana Cheese Factory, 219

### • Q •

quark cheese, 205
Quebec and Maritimes provinces, 129–130
Queensland, Australia, 220
queso blanco, 52
Queso de Cantabria Nata cheese, 183
Queso de Murcia, 187
Queso Fundido con Pollo, 269
quiches, 309
quiz on cheese selection, 81–82
qurut, 225

### • R •

raclers, 95, 201
Raclette, 68, 201, 266
raspberries, 307
raw milk
  Australian laws on, 214
  cow share agreements for, 322
  exporting cheeses of, 149
  legality of raw milk cheese, 30
  New Zealand laws for cheeses of, 222
  purchasing, 321

rBST (recombinant bovine somatotropin), 21
Reblochon cheese, 54, 160
recipes. *See also specific types of recipes*
  appetizers, 267–271
  chèvre, 326–327
  cocktails, 259–262
  common abbreviations in, 351
  condiments, 239–244
  home-made mozzarella, 328–329
  home-made ricotta, 324
  main courses, 289–305
  making crème fraiche, 325
  side dishes, 280–287
  soup and salad, 271–280
red wines, 248
Redwood Hill Farm, 115, 342–343
Reese, Bob, 339
regional cheeses
  Alberta and Ontario, 128
  Alsace-Lorraine, 163–164
  Asturias, 182–183
  Auvergne, 158–159
  Basque Country, 184–185
  Bavarian and Allgäu, 205–207
  Berner Oberland and Emmental cheeses, 199–200
  Boerenkaas, 209
  British Columbia, 128
  Californian, 114–115
  Campania, 175–176
  Canadian islands, 129
  Canary Islands, 187–188
  Cantabria, Spain, 183
  Castile-Leon, 185–186
  Central Asian, 223–226
  Champagne, 162–163
  Corsican, 161
  Cypriot, 195
  Eastern and Central European, 211–212
  Edam cheeses, 209–210
  Emilia-Romagna, 172–173
  Fribourg-Vaud fondue cheeses, 200–201

Friuli-Venezia Giulia and Veneto, 169, 171–172
Galicia region of Spain, 182
Gouda, 207–209
Graskaas, 210
Idaho, 118
Irish, 146
Île-de-France, 150–152
Jura Mountain specialties, 201–202
Loire Valley, 155–156
Lombardy, 168–169
Mexican, 131
Middle Eastern cheeses, 226–228
Midlands, 141–142
Midwest, 121
Murcian, 187
Netherlands, 207–210
New Zealand, 220–223
Nordost-Schweiz, 202–203
North of England and Border regions, 142–143
Northeast and New England, 123–125
northern Germany, 203–205
Oregon's, 116–117
Pays Basque, 156–157
popular Nordic cheeses, 210–211
Portugal, 190–192
Puglia/Sardinia, 176–178
Quebec and Maritimes provinces, 130
Rhône-Alpes and Haute-Savoie, 159–160
Rockies, 120
Southeast and East British, 140–141
Southern, 122–123
Southwest, 119
Southwest and West British, 140
Switzerland, 198–203
Tasmanian, 219–220
Turkish, 192–194
Tuscany, 174–175
U.S. mixed-milk, 22
Valais, 201
Valle d'Aosta, 167–168
Victoria, Australia, 215–217
Washington State, 117–118

rennet
  about, 10, 26, 321
  thistle, 190
  vegetarian, 26
Rhône-Alpes cheeses, 159–160
Rhubarb-Brown Sugar Cake with
    Strawberry-Rhubarb Compote and
    Crème Fraiche, 310–311
ricotta
  adding to eggs, 301
  classic Italian, 169
  making, 324
  recipe for, 290–291, 324
  ricotta salata versus, 178
  serving suggestions for, 43
ricotta salata
  Chicken Cacciatore with, 293
  defined, 51, 178
rind
  bloomy, 33, 40, 45–46
  choosing to eat or not, 101
  clothbound, waxed, or coated, 34
  considering when cooking, 265
  defined, 13, 32
  discovering favorite kinds of, 76
  Garrotxa cheese, 64, 184
  natural, 33
  saving Parmigiano Reggiano, 264
  spicing during cheesemaking, 69
  surface-ripened, 33
  washed, 41, 47–49, 48–49
rindless cheeses
  hard, 61–63
  semi-soft, 52–53
ripening
  agents added for, 31
  aging of hard cheese, 60
  ammoniated aroma of, 48, 61, 152
  continuing process of, 12, 26
  defined, 29
  judging ripeness, 94
  process of, 29, 31
  signs of bloomy-rind, 45–46
  starter cultures and, 25–26

temperatures accelerating, 106
  traveling with cheese, 107
ripening mat and pan, 319, 320
River's Edge Chèvre, 116
Robiola Lombardia, 169
Rockhill Creamery, 120
Rockies regional cheeses, 119–120
Rogue Creamery, 116, 341–342
Rollingstone Chevre, 118
Romadur cheese, 206
Romanian cheeses, 212
Roncal cheese, 185
Roquefort
  about true, 57
  beneficial molds in, 32
  example of PDO cheese, 36
  Ginger-Poached Pears with Roquefort-
    Honey Ice Cream, 314–315
  from Midi-Pyrenees, 158
rosé wines, 249, 259
rum, 257
ruminants, 10
rye whiskey, 257

• S •

Saint-Nectaire, 159
Sainte-Maure de Touraine, 155
Salad Greens with Roasted Pears, Cornbread
    Croutons, and Camembert Dressing,
    274–275
Salers, 159
salt
  about, 15
  applying or adding, 28–29
  brined and dry-salted cheeses, 50–51
salumi, 74, 174
San Simon cheese, 182
sandwiches
  Broiled Gruyère Sandwiches with Maple-
    Caramelized Apples, 298
  cheeseburgers, 295
sanitizer, 318

savory cheese plates, 235, 238
savory semi-soft cheeses, 53
Sbrinz cheese, 200
scallions, 292
Scamorza, 176
Schad, Judy, 340–341
Scotch, 258
Scotland cheeses, 143–144
seasonal purchases
  cheeses, 92, 160
  fruits, 306
  seasonal milk flavors, 91
Seattle Cheese Festival, 348
selecting cheeses
  browsing grocery stores, 81
  quiz on, 81–82
  shopping locally, 80
Selles-Sur-Cher, 155
semi-hard cheese, 106
semi-soft cheese
  about, 50
  defined, 39
  non-melting, 51–52
  preserving freshness of, 106
  pressed, brined, and dry-salted, 50–51
  rindless, 52–53
  savory, 53
  testing ripeness of, 94
  texture of, 50
  washed-rind, 53–54
sensory qualities of cheese
  about, 75
  discovering favorite, 76–77
  evaluating using, 77–78
  technical terms describing flavors, 78–79
Serpa cheese, 192
Serra da Estrela cheese, 190
serving tips. *See also* pairing wine and
   cheese
  about, 95
  adding decorative elements, 103
  arranging plates, 234
  beer and cheese pairings, 251–254
  bloomy-rind cheeses, 46

blue cheeses, 56, 57
boards and platters for, 97–98
burrata and mozzarella, 44
cheese course, 104, 147
coated-rind cheeses, 70, 71
compatible foods with cheese, 233
cutting cheese, 99–101, 102
designing cheese plate, 101–105, 238–239
eating Epoisses, 162
fresh cheese with fruit, 42
frico, 171
Handkäse and quark, 205
leipäjuusto, 336
Majorero, 188
Manchego, 187
mold-ripened soft cheese, 50
natural-rind hard cheese, 63, 64, 65
non-alcoholic beverages, 258–259
non-melting semi-soft cheese, 51–52, 52
planning serving size, 231–232
Raclette and Morbier, 68
ricotta, 43
rindless hard cheese, 62, 63
rindless semi-soft cheese, 53
selecting for occasions, 102, 232–233
semi-soft cheese, 51
sharp natural-rind cheese, 66
sheep milk cheeses, 185
with spirits, 255–258
temperatures for, 101
washed-rind cheese, 48, 54, 67, 68
wrinkly soft cheese, 50
shallots, 292
Shaw River Buffalo Cheese, 217
sheep milk. *See also* pecorinos
  butterfat averages in, 18, 185
  characteristics of, 21
  Italian cheesemaking with, 165
  Manchego cheese from, 186–187
  New Classic Cheese Soufflé, 304–305
  Sheep Milk Ricotta Gnocchi, 290–291, 292
shosha, 225
Shropshire Blue, 142
Sicily cheeses, 176–178

side dishes
  Grilled Asparagus with Chèvre and
    Orange Zest, 281
  Haricot Verts and Miniature Tomatoes
    with Bocconcini, 284
  Israeli Couscous with Preserved Lemon,
    Sugar Snap Peas, Feta, and Mint,
    282–283
  Pan-Roasted Wild Mushrooms over
    Cheddar Polenta with Pumpkinseed
    Oil, 286–287
  Wood-Roasted New Potatoes with Délice
    du Jura and Black Truffle Oil, 285
sides, 234–235, 238
Single Gloucester, 140
Skinner, Thalassa, 237, 346
Skyr cheese, 211
smell
  ammonia, 48, 61, 152
  evaluating cheese by, 77–78
  of warm goat cheeses, 101
  washed-rind cheese, 47–48
Smith, Peggy, 344
Smith, Tim, 323
smoked cheese, 84
sodas, 259
soft cheese
  about, 39
  bloomy-rind, 45–46
  blue cheeses, 55–57
  Brie versus camembert, 49
  double- or triple-crème, 47
  fresh cheeses, 41–44
  hard versus, 61
  moisture content and, 28
  mold-ripened soft cheese, 40, 40–41,
    49–50
  semi-soft cheeses, 50–54
  testing ripeness of, 94
  types of, 40–41
  washed-rind, 41, 47–49
  when to eat, 41
soft-cheese knife, 96, 97

soft cheeses
  Stinking Bishop, 338
  surface-ripened cheese, 44–50
sommeliers, 288
Sopa de Quinoa, 280
Sottocenere, 172
soufflés, 304–305
Souffront, Carlos, 49
soup and salad recipes
  Bistro Salad with Poached Egg and
    Parmigiano-Reggiano, 276–277
  Fennel, Tangerine, and Hazelnut Salad
    with Crottin, 278–279
  Nectarine, Prosciutto, and Arugula Salad
    with Crescenza Toasts, 272–273
  Salad Greens with Roasted Pears,
    Cornbread Croutons, and Camembert
    Dressing, 274–275
  serving quantities in, 271
  Sopa de Quinoa, 280
Southeast British Isles cheeses, 140–141
Southern and Southeastern France
  cheeses, 157–158
Southern Italy, 175–178
Southern U.S. cheeses, 122–123
Southwest British Isles cheeses, 139–140
Southwest regional cheeses, 119
Spain
  Asturias, 182–183
  Basque Country cheeses, 184–185
  Canary Islands cheeses, 187–188
  Cantabria, 183
  Castile-Leon, 185–186
  Catalonian cheeses, 184
  central and southern regions of, 185–187
  cheesemaking in, 179–181
  cheeses of Galicia, 182
  map of, 180
  Murcia, 187
  thistle rennet in cheeses of, 190
sparkling wines, 249–250
Special Select Dry Jack, 71
specialty shops, 85–87, 90
Spicherhalder Alpkäse cheese, 206

spirits
  aperitifs, 255
  bourbon and rye whiskey, 257
  brandy, 258
  brown, 257–258
  gin, 256
  rum, 257
  Scotch, 258
  tequila, 256
  vodka, 256
  white, 255–256
spreader, 96, 97
St. Agur, 56
St. Marcellin, 50
St. Tola Original, 146
starter cultures, 25–26
Stilton cheese, 56, 142
Stinking Bishop, 338
Stinky Cheese Omlet with Herb Topping,
    300–301
stinky cheeses. *See* washed-rind cheese
stone fruits, 273
storing cheese, 105–106
Stracchino, 169
Strange, Cathy, 107–108
string cheese, 44, 193–194
Stuckey, Bobby, 288
suppliers, 319
surface-ripened cheese
  about, 44–45
  bloomy rind, 45–46
  preserving freshness of, 106
  rinds for, 33
  types of, 40–41
sustainability, 22, 306
Sutton Grange Organic Farm, 216
sweet cheese plates, 235, 237
Sweet Grass Dairy, 123
sweet wines, 250
SweetWater, The, 261
Switzerland
  Berner Oberland and Emmental cheeses,
    199–200
  cheeses from, 198–199
  Fribourg-Vaud fondue cheeses, 200–201
  Jura Mountain specialties, 201–202
  map of, 199
  Nordost-Schweiz, 202–203
  Valais regional cheeses, 201
Sylvan Star Cheese, 128

### • T •

Taleggio cheese, 54, 168
Tarago River Cheese Company, 217
tarts
  Blue Cheese and Potato Tartlets, 302–303
  Dried Apricot-Goat Cheese, 312–313
  seasonal selections for, 209
Tasmania, Australia, 219–220
tasting cheeses
  flavors when, 78
  judging ripeness by, 94
tea, 259
temperatures
  accelerating ripening, 106
  conversion chart for, 353
  ranges for serving washed-rind cheeses,
    101
tequila, 256
terrior
  British Isles cheeses, 137–138
  considering wine's, 247
  designations identifying, 35–36
  importance of, 34–35
  traditions adding, 28
Tête de Moine cheese, 202
Tetilla cheese, 182
texture
  defined, 76
  semi-soft cheese, 50
That Dutchman's Farm, 130
thermalization, 30
thermometer, 318, 320
Ticklemore, 140
Tilsiter cheese, 203, 204

toma
  about, 168
  Toma Piemontese, 167–168
tome
  about, 160
  Tomme de Savoie, 53, 160
Tongola Goat Products, 220
Tower, Jeremiah, 114
transhumance, 181
traveling with cheese, 107
triple-crème soft cheese, 47
Tumalo, 116
Tunworth, 141
Turkish cheeses, 192–194
turophile, 80
Tuscany cheeses, 174–175
Twain, Mark, 54

• U •

Ubriaco, 172
umami, 78
United States
  cheese region map of, 112
  legality of raw milk cheese, 30
  Midwest cheeses, 120–122
  Pacific Northwest cheeses, 115–118
  purchasing French cheese in, 148–150
  Rockies cheeses, 119–120
  Southern cheeses, 122–123
  Southwest cheeses, 119
  tradition of cheeses in, 109–110
  unprotected cheese names in, 35
  West Coast cheeses, 113–115
Uplands Cheese Company, 121, 343
urum, 225

• V •

Vacherin cheese
  about, 48
  Vacherin Fribourgeois cheese, 201
  Vacherin Mont d'Or cheese, 164, 202

Valais regional cheeses, 201
Valdeon cheese, 28, 186
Valençay cheese, 155
varietals, 247
vat pasturization, 30
vegetarian rennet, 26
Vella Cheese Company, 115
Vella, Gaetano "Tom", 341
Veneto cheeses, 169, 171–172
Vermont
  regional cheeses of, 124
  Vermont Butter & Cheese Creamery,
    124, 339
  Vermont Cheesemaker's Festival, 124, 346
  Vermont Institute of Artisan Cheese, 124
  Vermont Sheperd, 124
Victoria, Australia cheeses, 215–217
Vinaigrette Dressing recipes, 273, 277, 279
Vinvenzio, Sara, 346
vodka, 256
volume
  about costs and, 265
  conversion chart for, 352

• W •

washed-rind cheese, 41, 48–49
  defined, 33
  hard, 66–68
  preserving freshness of, 106
  soft, 41, 47–49
  temperatures for serving, 101
  testing ripeness of, 94
  types of semi-soft, 53–54
Washington regional cheeses, 116–117
water buffalo milk
  Australian cheeses of, 217
  butterfat averages of, 18, 21
  characteristics of, 21, 176
  history of use, 176
  mozzarella di bufala, 43, 175–176
Waters, Alice, 114
waxed rinds, 34

websites
  resources on cheese, 13
  Spanish cheese, 180
weight conversion chart, 264, 352
Weisslacker cheese, 206
Welsh cheeses, 143–144
Welsh rarebit, 266
Wensleydale, 143
West British Isles cheeses, 139–140
West Coast cheeses, 113–115
West France cheeses, 154–157
Western Australia, 220
Westfield Farm, 125
whey
  draining, 27–28
  uses for, 29
  whey cheeses, 43, 194–195
whisk, 318, 320
white spirits, 255–256
white wines, 248–249
Whole Foods Market, 107–108
Widow's Kiss, The, 260
Wigmore, 141
Willapa Hills Cheese, 118
wine. *See also* pairing wine and cheese
  Alsace-Lorraine cheeses and, 164
  bad pairings with cheese, 250
  Champagnes, 247, 249–250
  matching cheese intensity, 246–247, 250

partnering with cheese, 163, 245–250
reds, 248
rosés, 249, 259
sommeliers, 288
South Australia's self-tours of cheese and,
    218
sparkling wines, 249–250
sweet, 250
time-tested pairings of, 250–251
tips for white, 248–249
varietals, 247
white, 248–249
Wood-Roasted New Potatoes with Délice
    du Jura and Black Truffle Oil, 285
wooden boards, 97, 98

yak milk and cheese, 21, 226, 335
Yarra Valley Dairy, 216

## • Z •

Zamorano cheese, 185–186
zesters, 96
Zingerman's, 89

## EDUCATION, HISTORY, & REFERENCE

978-0-7645-2498-1    978-0-470-46244-7

**Also available:**
- ○ Algebra For Dummies
  978-0-7645-5325-7
- ○ Art History For Dummies
  978-0-470-09910-0
- ○ Chemistry For Dummies
  978-0-7645-5430-8

- ○ English Grammar For Dummies
  978-0-470-54664-2
- ○ French For Dummies
  978-0-7645-5193-2
- ○ Statistics For Dummies
  978-0-7645-5423-0
- ○ World History For Dummies
  978-0-470-44654-6

## FOOD, HOME, & MUSIC

978-0-7645-9904-0    978-0-470-67895-4

**Also available:**
- ○ 30-Minute Meals For Dummies
  978-0-7645-2589-6
- ○ Bartending For Dummies
  978-0-470-05056-9
- ○ Brain Games For Dummies
  978-0-470-37378-1

- ○ Gluten-Free Cooking For Dummies
  978-0-470-17810-2
- ○ Home Improvement All-in-One Desk
  Reference For Dummies
  978-0-7645-5680-7
- ○ Wine For Dummies
  978-0-470-04579-4

## GARDENING

978-0-470-58161-2    978-0-470-57705-9

**Also available:**
- ○ Gardening Basics For Dummies
  978-0-470-03749-2
- ○ Organic Gardening For Dummies
  978-0-470-43067-5

- ○ Sustainable Landscaping For
  Dummies 978-0-470-41149-0
- ○ Vegetable Gardening For Dummies
  978-0-470-49870-5

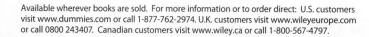

## GREEN/SUSTAINABLE

978-0-470-84098-6    978-0-470-59678-4

**Also available:**
- ○ Alternative Energy For Dummies 978-0-470-43062-0
- ○ Energy Efficient Homes For Dummies 978-0-470-37602-7

- ○ Green Building & Remodelling For Dummies 978-0-470-17559-0
- ○ Green Cleaning For Dummies 978-0-470-39106-8
- ○ Green Your Home All-in-One For Dummies 978-0-470-59678-4

## HEALTH & SELF-HELP

 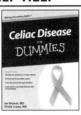

978-0-471-77383-2    978-0-470-16036-7

**Also available:**
- ○ Borderline Personality Disorder For Dummies 978-0-470-46653-7
- ○ Breast Cancer For Dummies 978-0-7645-2482-0
- ○ Cognitive Behavioural Therapy For Dummies 978-0-470-01838-5

- ○ Emotional Intelligence For Dummies 978-0-470-15732-9
- ○ Healthy Aging For Dummies 978-0-470-14975-1
- ○ Neuro-linguistic Programming For Dummies 978-0-7645-7028-5
- ○ Understanding Autism For Dummies 978-0-7645-2547-6

## HOBBIES & CRAFTS

978-0-470-28747-7    978-0-470-29112-2

**Also available:**
- ○ Crochet Patterns For Dummies 97-0-470-04555-8
- ○ Digital Scrapbooking For Dummies 978-0-7645-8419-0
- ○ Knitting Patterns For Dummies 978-0-470-04556-5

- ○ Oil Painting For Dummies 978-0-470-18230-7
- ○ Quilting For Dummies 978-0-7645-9799-2
- ○ Sewing For Dummies 978-0-7645-6847-3
- ○ Word Searches For Dummies 978-0-470-45366-7

## HOME & BUSINESS COMPUTER BASICS

978-0-470-49743-2    978-0-470-48953-6

**Also available:**
- ○ Office 2010 All-in-One Desk Reference For Dummies 978-0-470-49748-7
- ○ Pay Per Click Search Engine Marketing For Dummies 978-0-471-75494-7

- ○ Search Engine Marketing For Dummies 978-0-471-97998-2
- ○ Web Analytics For Dummies 978-0-470-09824-0
- ○ Word 2010 For Dummies 978-0-470-48772-3

## INTERNET & DIGITAL MEDIA

978-0-470-44417-7    978-0-470-39062-7

**Also available:**
- ○ Blogging For Dummies
  978-0-471-77084-8
- ○ MySpace For Dummies
  978-0-470-09529-4

- ○ The Internet For Dummies
  978-0-470-12174-0
- ○ Twitter For Dummies
  978-0-470-47991-9
- ○ YouTube For Dummies
  978-0-470-14925-6

## MACINTOSH

978-0-470-27817-8    978-0-470-58027-1

**Also available:**
- ○ iMac For Dummies
  978-0-470-13386-6
- ○ iPod Touch For Dummies
  978-0-470-50530-4

- ○ iPod & iTunes For Dummies
  978-0-470-39062-7
- ○ MacBook For Dummies
  978-0-470-27816-1
- ○ Macs For Seniors For Dummies
  978-0-470-43779-7

## PETS

978-0-470-60029-0    978-0-7645-5267-0

**Also available:**
- ○ Cats For Dummies
  978-0-7645-5275-5
- ○ Ferrets For Dummies
  978-0-470-13943-1
- ○ Horses For Dummies
  978-0-7645-9797-8

- ○ Kittens For Dummies
  978-0-7645-4150-6
- ○ Puppies For Dummies
  978-1-118-11755-2

## SPORTS & FITNESS

 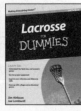

978-0-471-76871-5    978-0-470-73855-9

**Also available:**
- ○ Exercise Balls For Dummies
  978-0-7645-5623-4
- ○ Coaching Volleyball For Dummies
  978-0-470-46469-4
- ○ Curling For Dummies
  978-0-470-83828-0
- ○ Fitness For Dummies
  978-0-7645-7851-9

- ○ Mixed Martial Arts For Dummies
  978-0-470-39071-9
- ○ Sports Psychology For Dummies
  978-0-470-67659-2
- ○ Ten Minute Tone-Ups For Dummies
  978-0-7645-7207-4
- ○ Wilderness Survival For Dummies
  978-0-470-45306-3
- ○ Yoga with Weights For Dummies
  978-0-471-74937-0